Pandas Cookbook

Recipes for Scientific Computing, Time Series Analysis and
Data Visualization using Python

Theodore Petrou

BIRMINGHAM - MUMBAI

Pandas Cookbook

First published: October 2017

Production reference: 1181017

Published by Packt Publishing Ltd.
Livery Place
35 Livery Street
Birmingham
B3 2PB, UK.
ISBN 978-1-78439-387-8

www.packtpub.com

Credits

Author
Theodore Petrou

Reviewers
Sonali Dayal
Kuntal Ganguly
Shilpi Saxena

Commissioning Editor
Veena Pagare

Acquisition Editor
Tushar Gupta

Content Development Editor
Snehal Kolte

Technical Editor
Sayli Nikalje

Copy Editor
Tasneem Fatehi

Project Coordinator
Manthan Patel

Proofreader
Safis Editing

Indexer
Tejal Daruwale Soni

Graphics
Tania Dutta

Production Coordinator
Deepika Naik

About the Author

Theodore Petrou is a data scientist and the founder of Dunder Data, a professional educational company focusing on exploratory data analysis. He is also the head of Houston Data Science, a meetup group with more than 2,000 members that has the primary goal of getting local data enthusiasts together in the same room to practice data science. Before founding Dunder Data, Ted was a data scientist at Schlumberger, a large oil services company, where he spent the vast majority of his time exploring data.

Some of his projects included using targeted sentiment analysis to discover the root cause of part failure from engineer text, developing customized client/server dashboarding applications, and real-time web services to avoid the mispricing of sales items. Ted received his masters degree in statistics from Rice University, and used his analytical skills to play poker professionally and teach math before becoming a data scientist. Ted is a strong supporter of learning through practice and can often be found answering questions about pandas on Stack Overflow.

Acknowledgement

I would first like to thank my wife, Eleni, and two young children, Penelope, and Niko, who endured extended periods of time without me as I wrote.

I'd also like to thank Sonali Dayal, whose constant feedback helped immensely in structuring the content of the book to improve its effectiveness. Thank you to Roy Keyes, who is the most exceptional data scientist I know and whose collaboration made Houston Data Science possible. Thank you to Scott Boston, an extremely skilled pandas user for developing ideas for recipes. Thank you very much to Kim Williams, Randolph Adami, Kevin Higgins, and Vishwanath Avasarala, who took a chance on me during my professional career when I had little to no experience. Thanks to my fellow coworker at Schlumberger, Micah Miller, for his critical, honest, and instructive feedback on anything that we developed together and his constant pursuit to move toward Python.

Thank you to Phu Ngo, who critically challenges and sharpens my thinking more than anyone. Thank you to my brother, Dean Petrou, for being right by my side as we developed our analytical skills through poker and again through business. Thank you to my sister, Stephanie Burton, for always knowing what I'm thinking and making sure that I'm aware of it. Thank you to my mother, Sofia Petrou, for her ceaseless love, support, and endless math puzzles that challenged me as a child. And thank you to my father, Steve Petrou, who, although no longer here, remains close to my heart and continues to encourage me every day.

About the Reviewers

Sonali Dayal is a masters candidate in biostatistics at the University of California, Berkeley. Previously, she has worked as a freelance software and data science engineer for early stage start-ups, where she built supervised and unsupervised machine learning models as well as data pipelines and interactive data analytics dashboards. She received her bachelor of science (B.S.) in biochemistry from Virginia Tech in 2011.

Kuntal Ganguly is a big data machine learning engineer focused on building large-scale data-driven systems using big data frameworks and machine learning. He has around 7 years of experience building several big data and machine learning applications.

Kuntal provides solutions to AWS customers in building real-time analytics systems using managed cloud services and open source Hadoop ecosystem technologies such as Spark, Kafka, Storm, Solr, and so on, along with machine learning and deep learning frameworks such as scikit-learn, TensorFlow, Keras, and BigDL. He enjoys hands-on software development, and has single-handedly conceived, architected, developed, and deployed several large scale distributed applications. He is a machine learning and deep learning practitioner and very passionate about building intelligent applications.

Kuntal is the author of the books: *Learning Generative Adversarial Network* and *R Data Analysis Cookbook - Second Edition*, Packt Publishing.

Shilpi Saxena is a seasoned professional who leads in management with an edge of being a technology evangelist--she is an engineer who has exposure to a variety of domains (machine-to-machine space, healthcare, telecom, hiring, and manufacturing). She has experience in all aspects of the conception and execution of enterprise solutions. She has been architecturing, managing, and delivering solutions in the big data space for the last 3 years, handling high performance geographically distributed teams of elite engineers. Shilpi has around 12+ years (3 years in the big data space) experience in the development and execution of various facets of enterprise solutions, both in the product/services dimensions of the software industry. An engineer by degree and profession who has worn various hats--developer, technical leader, product owner, tech manager--and has seen all the flavors that the industry has to offer. She has architected and worked through some of the pioneer production implementation in big data on Storm and Impala with auto scaling in AWS. LinkedIn: http://in.linkedin.com/pub/shilpi-saxena/4/552/a30

www.PacktPub.com

For support files and downloads related to your book, please visit `www.PacktPub.com`. Did you know that Packt offers eBook versions of every book published, with PDF and ePub files available? You can upgrade to the eBook version at `www.PacktPub.com` and as a print book customer, you are entitled to a discount on the eBook copy. Get in touch with us at `service@packtpub.com` for more details. At `www.PacktPub.com`, you can also read a collection of free technical articles, sign up for a range of free newsletters and receive exclusive discounts and offers on Packt books and eBooks.

`https://www.packtpub.com/mapt` Get the most in-demand software skills with Mapt. Mapt gives you full access to all Packt books and video courses, as well as industry-leading tools to help you plan your personal development and advance your career.

Why subscribe?

- Fully searchable across every book published by Packt
- Copy and paste, print, and bookmark content
- On demand and accessible via a web browser

Customer Feedback

Thanks for purchasing this Packt book. At Packt, quality is at the heart of our editorial process. To help us improve, please leave us an honest review on this book's Amazon page at https://www.amazon.com/dp/1784393878. If you'd like to join our team of regular reviewers, you can email us at customerreviews@packtpub.com. We award our regular reviewers with free eBooks and videos in exchange for their valuable feedback. Help us be relentless in improving our products!

Table of Contents

Preface

The popularity of data science has skyrocketed since it was called *The Sexiest Job of the 21st Century* by the Harvard Review in 2012. It was ranked as the number one job by Glassdoor in both 2016 and 2017. Fueling this skyrocketing popularity for data science is the demand from industry. Several applications have made big splashes in the news, such as Netflix making better movie recommendations, IBM Watson defeating humans at Jeopardy, Tesla building self-driving cars, Major League Baseball teams finding undervalued prospects, and Google learning to identify cats on the internet.

Nearly every industry is finding ways to use data science to build new technology or provide deeper insights. Due to such noteworthy successes, an ever-present aura of hype seems to encapsulate data science. Most of the scientific progress backing this hype stems from the field of machine learning, which produces the algorithms that make the predictions responsible for artificial intelligence.

The fundamental building block for all machine learning algorithms is, of course, data. As companies have realized this, there is no shortage of it. The business intelligence company, Domo, estimates that 90% of the world's data has been created in just the last two years. Although machine learning gets all the attention, it is completely reliant on the quality of the data that it is fed. Before data ever reaches the input layers of a machine learning algorithm, it must be prepared, and for data to be prepared properly, it needs to be explored thoroughly for basic understanding and to identify inaccuracies. Before data can be explored, it needs to be captured.

To summarize, we can cast the data science pipeline into three stages--data capturing, data exploration, and machine learning. There are a vast array of tools available to complete each stage of the pipeline. Pandas is the dominant tool in the scientific Python ecosystem for data exploration and analysis. It is tremendously capable of inspecting, cleaning, tidying, filtering, transforming, aggregating, and even visualizing (with some help) all types of data. It is not a tool for initially capturing the data, nor is it a tool to build machine learning models.

For many data analysts and scientists who use Python, the vast majority of their work will be done using pandas. This is likely because the initial data exploration and preparation tend to take the most time. Some entire projects consist only of data exploration and have no machine learning component. Data scientists spend so much time on this stage that a timeless lore has arisen--*Data scientists spend 80% of their time cleaning the data and the other 20% complaining about cleaning the data.*

Although there is an abundance of open source and free programming languages available to do data exploration, the field is currently dominated by just two players, Python and R. The two languages have vastly different syntax but are both very capable of doing data analysis and machine learning. One measure of popularity is the number of questions asked on the popular Q&A site, Stack Overflow (`https://insights.stackoverflow.com/trends`):

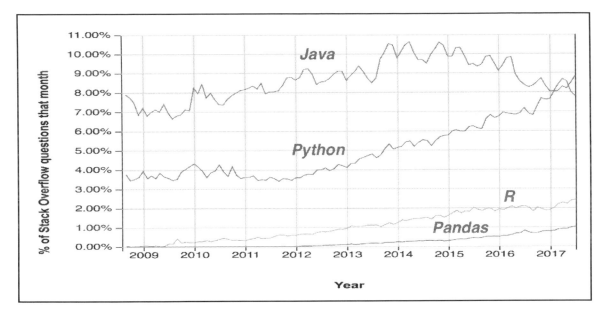

While this is not a true measure of usage, it is clear that both Python and R have become increasingly popular, likely due to their data science capabilities. It is interesting to note that the percentage of Python questions remained constant until the year 2012, when data science took off. What is probably most astonishing about this graph is that pandas questions now make up a whopping one percent of all the newest questions on Stack Overflow.

One of the reasons why Python has become a language of choice for data science is that it is a fairly easy language to learn and develop, and so it has a low barrier to entry. It is also free and open source, able to run on a variety of hardware and software, and a breeze to get up and running. It has a very large and active community with a substantial amount of free resources online. In my opinion, Python is one of the most fun languages to develop programs with. The syntax is so clear, concise, and intuitive but like all languages, takes quite a long time to master.

As Python was not built for data analysis like R, the syntax may not come as naturally as it does for some other Python libraries. This actually might be part of the reason why there are so many Stack Overflow questions on it. Despite its tremendous capabilities, pandas code can often be poorly written. One of the main aims of this book is to show performant and idiomatic pandas code.

For all its greatness, Stack Overflow, unfortunately perpetuates misinformation and is a source for lots of poorly written pandas. This is actually not the fault of Stack Overflow or its community. Pandas is an open source project and has had numerous major changes, even recently, as it approaches its tenth year of existence in 2018. The upside of open source, though, is that new features get added to it all the time.

The recipes in this book were formulated through my experience working as a data scientist, building and hosting several week-long data exploration bootcamps, answering several hundred questions on Stack Overflow, and building tutorials for my local meetup group. The recipes not only offer idiomatic solutions to common data problems, but also take you on journeys through many real-world datasets, where surprising insights are often discovered. These recipes will also help you master the pandas library, which will give you a gigantic boost in productivity. There is a huge difference between those who have only cursory knowledge of pandas and those who have it mastered. There are so many interesting and fun tricks to solve your data problems that only become apparent if you truly know the library inside and out. Personally, I find pandas to be a delightful and fun tool to analyze data with, and I hope you enjoy your journey along with me. If you have questions, please feel free to reach out to me on Twitter: `@TedPetrou`.

What this book covers

Chapter 1, *Pandas Foundations*, covers the anatomy and vocabulary used to identify the components of the two main pandas data structures, the Series and the DataFrame. Each column must have exactly one type of data, and each of these data types is covered. You will learn how to unleash the power of the Series and the DataFrame by calling and chaining together their methods.

Chapter 2, *Essential DataFrame Operations*, focuses on the most crucial and common operations that you will perform during data analysis.

Chapter 3, *Beginning Data Analysis*, helps you develop a routine to get started after reading in your data. Other interesting discoveries will be made.

`Chapter 4`, *Selecting Subsets of Data*, covers the many varied and potentially confusing ways of selecting different subsets of data.

`Chapter 5`, *Boolean Indexing*, covers the process of querying your data to select subsets of it based on Boolean conditions.

`Chapter 6`, *Index Alignment*, targets the very important and often misunderstood `index` object. Misuse of the Index is responsible for lots of erroneous results, and these recipes show you how to use it correctly to deliver powerful results.

`Chapter 7`, *Grouping for Aggregation, Filtration, and Transformation*, covers the powerful grouping capabilities that are almost always necessary during a data analysis. You will build customized functions to apply to your groups.

`Chapter 8`, *Restructuring Data into Tidy Form*, explains what tidy data is and why it's so important, and then it shows you how to transform many different forms of messy datasets into tidy ones.

`Chapter 9`, *Combining Pandas Objects*, covers the many available methods to combine DataFrames and Series vertically or horizontally. We will also do some web-scraping to compare President Trump's and Obama's approval rating and connect to an SQL relational database.

`Chapter 10`, *Time Series Analysis*, covers advanced and powerful time series capabilities to dissect by any dimension of time possible.

`Chapter 11`, *Visualization with Matplotlib, Pandas, and Seaborn*, introduces the matplotlib library, which is responsible for all of the plotting in pandas. We will then shift focus to the pandas `plot` method and, finally, to the `seaborn` library, which is capable of producing aesthetically pleasing visualizations not directly available in pandas.

What you need for this book

Pandas is a third-party package for the Python programming language and, as of the printing of this book, is on version 0.20. Currently, Python has two major supported releases, versions 2.7 and 3.6. Python 3 is the future, and it is now highly recommended that all scientific computing users of Python use it, as Python 2 will no longer be supported in 2020. All examples in this book have been run and tested with pandas 0.20 on Python 3.6.

In addition to pandas, you will need to have the matplotlib version 2.0 and seaborn version 0.8 visualization libraries installed. A major dependence for pandas is the NumPy library, which forms the basis of most of the popular Python scientific computing libraries.

There are a wide variety of ways in which you can install pandas and the rest of the libraries mentioned on your computer, but by far the simplest method is to install the Anaconda distribution. Created by Continuum Analytics, it packages together all the popular libraries for scientific computing in a single downloadable file available on Windows, Mac OSX, and Linux. Visit the download page to get the Anaconda distribution (`https://www.anaconda.com/download`).

In addition to all the scientific computing libraries, the Anaconda distribution comes with Jupyter Notebook, which is a browser-based program for developing in Python, among many other languages. All of the recipes for this book were developed inside of a Jupyter Notebook and all of the individual notebooks for each chapter will be available for you to use.

It is possible to install all the necessary libraries for this book without the use of the Anaconda distribution. For those that are interested, visit the pandas *Installation* page (`http://pandas.pydata.org/pandas-docs/stable/install.html`).

Running a Jupyter Notebook

The suggested method to work through the content of this book is to have a Jupyter Notebook up and running so that you can run the code while reading through the recipes. This allows you to go exploring on your own and gain a deeper understanding than by just reading the book alone.

Assuming that you have installed the Anaconda distribution on your machine, you have two options available to start the Jupyter Notebook:

- Use the program Anaconda Navigator
- Run the `jupyter notebook` command from the Terminal/Command Prompt

The Anaconda Navigator is a GUI-based tool that allows you to find all the different software provided by Anaconda with ease. Running the program will give you a screen like this:

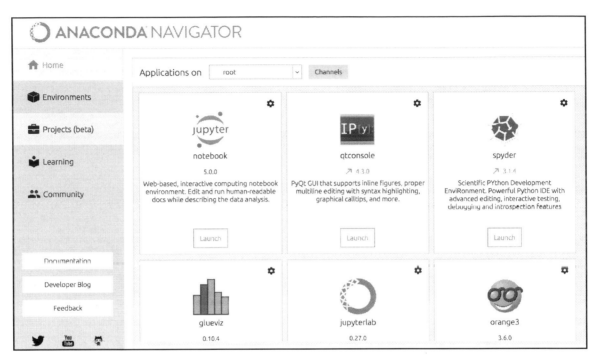

As you can see, there are many programs available to you. Click *Launch* to open the Jupyter Notebook. A new tab will open in your browser, showing you a list of folders and files in your home directory:

Instead of using the Anaconda Navigator, you can launch Jupyter Notebook by opening up your Terminal/Command Prompt and running the `jupyter notebook` command like this:

```
2. bash
Theodores-MacBook-Pro:~ Ted$ jupyter notebook
```

It is not necessary to run this command from your home directory. You can run it from any location, and the contents in the browser will reflect that location.

Although we have now started the Jupyter Notebook program, we haven't actually launched a single individual notebook where we can start developing in Python. To do so, you can click on the **New** button on the right-hand side of the page, which will drop down a list of all the possible kernels available for you to use. If you just downloaded Anaconda, then you will only have a single kernel available to you (Python 3). After selecting the **Python 3** kernel, a new tab will open in the browser, where you can start writing Python code:

You can, of course, open previously created notebooks instead of beginning a new one. To do so, simply navigate through the filesystem provided in the Jupyter Notebook browser home page and select the notebook you want to open. All Jupyter Notebook files end in `.ipynb`. For instance, when you navigate to the location of the notebook files for this book, you will see all of them like this:

Who this book is for

This book contains nearly 100 recipes, ranging from very simple to advanced. All recipes strive to be written in clear, concise, and modern idiomatic pandas code. The *How it works...* sections contain extremely detailed descriptions of the intricacies of each step of the recipe. Often, in the *There's more...* section, you will get what may seem like an entirely new recipe. This book is densely packed with an extraordinary amount of pandas code.

As a generalization, the recipes in the first six chapters tend to be simpler and more focused on the fundamental and essential operations of pandas than the last five chapters, which focus on more advanced operations and are more project-driven. Due to the wide range of complexity, this book can be useful to both the novice and everyday user alike. It has been my experience that even those who use pandas regularly will not master it without being exposed to idiomatic pandas code. This is somewhat fostered by the breadth that pandas offers. There are almost always multiple ways of completing the same operation, which can have users get the result they want but in a very inefficient manner. It is not uncommon to see an order of magnitude or more performance difference between two sets of pandas solutions to the same problem.

The only real prerequisite for this book is fundamental knowledge of Python. It is assumed that the reader is familiar with all the common built-in data containers in Python, such as lists, sets, dictionaries, and tuples.

How to get the most out of this book

There are a couple of things you can do to get the most out of this book. First, and most importantly, you should download all the code, which will be stored in Jupyter Notebooks. While reading through each recipe, run each step of code in the notebook. Make sure you explore on your own as you run through the code. Second, have the pandas official documentation open (http://pandas.pydata.org/pandas-docs/stable/) in one of your browser tabs. The pandas documentation is an excellent resource containing over 1,000 pages of material. There are examples for most of the pandas operations in the documentation, and they will often be directly linked from the *See also* section. While it covers the basics of most operations, it does so with trivial examples and fake data that don't reflect situations that you are likely to encounter when analyzing datasets from the real world.

Conventions

In this book, you will find a few text styles that distinguish between different kinds of information. Most commonly you will see blocks of code during each recipe that will look like this:

```
>>> employee = pd.read_csv('data/employee')
>>> max_dept_salary = employee.groupby('DEPARTMENT')['BASE_SALARY'].max()
```

The pandas Series and DataFrames are stylized differently when output in the notebook. The pandas Series have no special formatting and are just raw text. They will appear directly preceding the line of code that creates them in the code block itself, like this:

```
>>> max_dept_salary.head()
DEPARTMENT
Admn. & Regulatory Affairs      140416.0
City Controller's Office         64251.0
City Council                    100000.0
Convention and Entertainment     38397.0
Dept of Neighborhoods (DON)      89221.0
Name: BASE_SALARY, dtype: float64
```

DataFrames, on the other hand, are nicely stylized in the notebooks and appear as images outside of the code box, like this:

```
>>> employee.pivot_table(index='DEPARTMENT',
                         columns='GENDER',
                         values='BASE_SALARY').round(0).head()
```

GENDER	Female	Male
DEPARTMENT		
Admn. & Regulatory Affairs	48758.0	57592.0
City Controller's Office	58980.0	42640.0
City Council	59260.0	58492.0
Convention and Entertainment	38397.0	NaN
Dept of Neighborhoods (DON)	50578.0	43995.0

Code words in text, database table names, folder names, filenames, file extensions, pathnames, dummy URLs, user input, and Twitter handles are shown as follows: In order to find the average BASE_SALARY by GENDER, you can use the pivot_table method.

New terms and **important words** are shown in bold. Words that you see on the screen, for example, in menus or dialog boxes, appear in the text like this: "In a Jupyter notebook, when holding down *Shift* + *Tab* + *Tab* with the cursor placed somewhere in the object, a window of the docsstrings will pop out making the method far easier to use."

Tips and tricks appear like this.

Warnings or important notes appear in a box like this.

Assumptions for every recipe

It should be assumed that at the beginning of each recipe, pandas, NumPy, and matplotlib are imported into the namespace. For plots to be embedded directly within the notebook, you must also run the magic command %matplotlib inline. Also, all data is stored in the data directory and is most commonly stored as a CSV file, which can be read directly with the read_csv function.

```
>>> import pandas as pd
>>> import numpy as np
>>> import matplotlib.pyplot as plt
>>> %matplotlib inline

>>> my_dataframe = pd.read_csv('data/dataset_name.csv')
```

Dataset Descriptions

There are about two dozen datasets that are used throughout this book. It can be very helpful to have background information on each dataset as you complete the steps in the recipes. A detailed description of each dataset may be found in the dataset_descriptions Jupyter Notebook found at https://github.com/PacktPublishing/Pandas-Cookbook. For each dataset, there will be a list of the columns, information about each column and notes on how the data was procured.

Sections

In this book, you will find several headings that appear frequently (Getting ready, How to do it..., How it works..., There's more..., and See also).

To give clear instructions on how to complete a recipe, we use these sections as follows:

Getting ready

This section tells you what to expect in the recipe, and describes how to set up any software or any preliminary settings required for the recipe.

How to do it...

This section contains the steps required to follow the recipe.

How it works...

This section usually consists of a detailed explanation of what happened in the previous section.

There's more...

This section consists of additional information about the recipe in order to make the reader more knowledgeable about the recipe.

See also

This section provides helpful links to other useful information for the recipe.

Reader feedback

Feedback from our readers is always welcome. Let us know what you think about this book-what you liked or disliked. Reader feedback is important to us as it helps us develop titles that you will really get the most out of.

To send us general feedback, simply email `feedback@packtpub.com`, and mention the book's title in the subject of your message.

If there is a topic that you have expertise in and you are interested in either writing or contributing to a book, see our author guide at `www.packtpub.com/authors`.

Customer support

Now that you are the proud owner of a Packt book, we have a number of things to help you to get the most from your purchase.

Downloading the example code

You can download the example code files for this book from your account at `http://www.packtpub.com`. If you purchased this book elsewhere, you can visit `http://www.packtpub.com/support` and register to have the files e-mailed directly to you.

You can download the code files by following these steps:

1. Log in or register to our website using your e-mail address and password.
2. Hover the mouse pointer on the **SUPPORT** tab at the top.
3. Click on **Code Downloads & Errata**.
4. Enter the name of the book in the **Search** box.
5. Select the book for which you're looking to download the code files.
6. Choose from the drop-down menu where you purchased this book from.
7. Click on **Code Download**.

You can also download the code files by clicking on the **Code Files** button on the book's webpage at the Packt Publishing website. This page can be accessed by entering the book's name in the search box. Please note that you need to be logged in to your Packt account.

Once the file is downloaded, please make sure that you unzip or extract the folder using the latest version of:

* WinRAR / 7-Zip for Windows
* Zipeg / iZip / UnRarX for Mac
* 7-Zip / PeaZip for Linux

The code bundle for the book is also hosted on GitHub at `https://github.com/PacktPublishing/Pandas-Cookbook`. We also have other code bundles from our rich catalog of books and videos available at `https://github.com/PacktPublishing/`. Check them out!

Downloading the color images of this book

We also provide you with a PDF file that has color images of the screenshots/diagrams used in this book. The color images will help you better understand the changes in the output. You can download this file from `https://www.packtpub.com/sites/default/files/downloads/PandasCookbook_ColorImages.pdf`.

Errata

Although we have taken every care to ensure the accuracy of our content, mistakes do happen. If you find a mistake in one of our books--maybe a mistake in the text or the code-- we would be grateful if you could report this to us. By doing so, you can save other readers from frustration and help us improve subsequent versions of this book. If you find any errata, please report them by visiting `http://www.packtpub.com/submit-errata`, selecting your book, clicking on the **Errata Submission Form** link, and entering the details of your errata. Once your errata are verified, your submission will be accepted and the errata will be uploaded to our website or added to any list of existing errata under the Errata section of that title.

To view the previously submitted errata, go to `https://www.packtpub.com/books/content/support` and enter the name of the book in the search field. The required information will appear under the **Errata** section.

Piracy

Piracy of copyrighted material on the internet is an ongoing problem across all media. At Packt, we take the protection of our copyright and licenses very seriously. If you come across any illegal copies of our works in any form on the Internet, please provide us with the location address or website name immediately so that we can pursue a remedy.

Please contact us at `copyright@packtpub.com` with a link to the suspected pirated material.

We appreciate your help in protecting our authors and our ability to bring you valuable content.

Questions

If you have a problem with any aspect of this book, you can contact us at `questions@packtpub.com`, and we will do our best to address the problem.

1
Pandas Foundations

In this chapter, we will cover the following:

- Dissecting the anatomy of a DataFrame
- Accessing the main DataFrame components
- Understanding data types
- Selecting a single column of data as a Series
- Calling Series methods
- Working with operators on a Series
- Chaining Series methods together
- Making the index meaningful
- Renaming row and column names
- Creating and deleting columns

Introduction

The goal of this chapter is to introduce a foundation of pandas by thoroughly inspecting the Series and DataFrame data structures. It is vital for pandas users to know each component of the Series and the DataFrame, and to understand that each column of data in pandas holds precisely one data type.

In this chapter, you will learn how to select a single column of data from a DataFrame, which is returned as a Series. Working with this one-dimensional object makes it easy to show how different methods and operators work. Many Series methods return another Series as output. This leads to the possibility of calling further methods in succession, which is known as **method chaining**.

The Index component of the Series and DataFrame is what separates pandas from most other data analysis libraries and is the key to understanding how many operations work. We will get a glimpse of this powerful object when we use it as a meaningful label for Series values. The final two recipes contain simple tasks that frequently occur during a data analysis.

Dissecting the anatomy of a DataFrame

Before diving deep into pandas, it is worth knowing the components of the DataFrame. Visually, the outputted display of a pandas DataFrame (in a Jupyter Notebook) appears to be nothing more than an ordinary table of data consisting of rows and columns. Hiding beneath the surface are the three components--the **index**, **columns**, and **data** (also known as **values**) that you must be aware of in order to maximize the DataFrame's full potential.

Getting ready

This recipe reads in the movie dataset into a pandas DataFrame and provides a labeled diagram of all its major components.

How to do it...

1. Use the `read_csv` function to read in the movie dataset, and display the first five rows with the `head` method:

```
>>> movie = pd.read_csv('data/movie.csv')
>>> movie.head()
```

2. Analyze the labeled anatomy of the DataFrame:

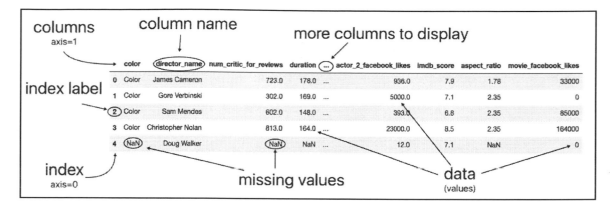

How it works...

Pandas first reads the data from disk into memory and into a DataFrame using the excellent and versatile `read_csv` function. The output for both the columns and the index is in bold font, which makes them easy to identify. By convention, the terms **index label** and **column name** refer to the individual members of the index and columns, respectively. The term *index* refers to all the index labels as a whole just as the term *columns* refers to all the column names as a whole.

The columns and the index serve a particular purpose, and that is to provide labels for the columns and rows of the DataFrame. These labels allow for direct and easy access to different subsets of data. When multiple Series or DataFrames are combined, the indexes align first before any calculation occurs. Collectively, the columns and the index are known as the **axes**.

 A DataFrame has two axes--a vertical axis (the index) and a horizontal axis(the columns). Pandas borrows convention from `NumPy` and uses the integers 0/1 as another way of referring to the vertical/horizontal axis.

DataFrame data (values) is always in regular font and is an entirely separate component from the columns or index. Pandas uses **NaN (not a number)** to represent missing values. Notice that even though the `color` column has only string values, it uses NaN to represent a missing value.

The three consecutive dots in the middle of the columns indicate that there is at least one column that exists but is not displayed due to the number of columns exceeding the predefined display limits.

 The Python standard library contains the csv module, which can be used to parse and read in data. The pandas read_csv function offers a powerful increase in performance and functionality over this module.

There's more...

The head method accepts a single parameter, n, which controls the number of rows displayed. Similarly, the tail method returns the last n rows.

See also

- Pandas official documentation of the read_csv function (http://bit.ly/2vtJQ9A)

Accessing the main DataFrame components

Each of the three DataFrame components--the index, columns, and data--may be accessed directly from a DataFrame. Each of these components is itself a Python object with its own unique attributes and methods. It will often be the case that you would like to perform operations on the individual components and not on the DataFrame as a whole.

Getting ready

This recipe extracts the index, columns, and the data of the DataFrame into separate variables, and then shows how the columns and index are inherited from the same object.

How to do it...

1. Use the DataFrame attributes `index`, `columns`, and `values` to assign the index, columns, and data to their own variables:

```
>>> movie = pd.read_csv('data/movie.csv')
>>> index = movie.index
>>> columns = movie.columns
>>> data = movie.values
```

2. Display each component's values:

```
>>> index
RangeIndex(start=0, stop=5043, step=1)

>>> columns
Index(['color', 'director_name', 'num_critic_for_reviews',
       ...
       'imdb_score', 'aspect_ratio', 'movie_facebook_likes'],
      dtype='object')

>>> data
array([['Color', 'James Cameron', 723.0, ..., 7.9, 1.78, 33000],
       ...,
       ['Color', 'Jon Gunn', 43.0, ..., 6.6, 1.85, 456]],
      dtype=object)
```

3. Output the type of each DataFrame component. The name of the type is the word following the last dot of the output:

```
>>> type(index)
pandas.core.indexes.range.RangeIndex

>>> type(columns)
pandas.core.indexes.base.Index

>>> type(data)
numpy.ndarray
```

4. Interestingly, both the types for both the index and the columns appear to be closely related. The built-in `issubclass` method checks whether `RangeIndex` is indeed a subclass of `Index`:

```
>>> issubclass(pd.RangeIndex, pd.Index)
True
```

How it works...

You may access the three main components of a DataFrame with the `index`, `columns`, and `values` attributes. The output of the `columns` attribute appears to be just a sequence of the column names. This sequence of column names is technically an `Index` object. The output of the function `type` is the **fully qualified class name** of the object.

The fully qualified class name of the object for the variable `columns` is `pandas.core.indexes.base.Index`. It begins with the package name, which is followed by a path of modules and ends with the name of the type. A common way of referring to objects is to include the package name followed by the name of the object type. In this instance, we would refer to the columns as a pandas `Index` object.

The built-in `subclass` function checks whether the first argument inherits from the second. The `Index` and `RangeIndex` objects are very similar, and in fact, pandas has a number of similar objects reserved specifically for either the index or the columns. The index and the columns must both be some kind of `Index` object. Essentially, the index and the columns represent the same thing, but along different axes. They're occasionally referred to as the **row index** and **column index**.

In this context, the `Index` objects refer to all the possible objects that can be used for the index or columns. They are all subclasses of `pd.Index`. Here is the complete list of the `Index` objects: `CategoricalIndex`, `MultiIndex`, `IntervalIndex`, `Int64Index`, `UInt64Index`, `Float64Index`, `RangeIndex`, `TimedeltaIndex`, `DatetimeIndex`, `PeriodIndex`.

A `RangeIndex` is a special type of `Index` object that is analogous to Python's `range` object. Its entire sequence of values is not loaded into memory until it is necessary to do so, thereby saving memory. It is completely defined by its start, stop, and step values.

There's more...

When possible, Index objects are implemented using hash tables that allow for very fast selection and data alignment. They are similar to Python sets in that they support operations such as intersection and union, but are dissimilar because they are ordered with duplicates allowed.

 Python dictionaries and sets are also implemented with hash tables that allow for membership checking to happen very fast in constant time, regardless of the size of the object.

Notice how the values DataFrame attribute returned a NumPy n-dimensional array, or ndarray. Most of pandas relies heavily on the ndarray. Beneath the index, columns, and data are NumPy ndarrays. They could be considered the base object for pandas that many other objects are built upon. To see this, we can look at the values of the index and columns:

```
>>> index.values
array([   0,    1,    2, ..., 4913, 4914, 4915])

>>> columns.values
array(['color', 'director_name', 'num_critic_for_reviews',
 ...
 'imdb_score', 'aspect_ratio', 'movie_facebook_likes'],
 dtype=object)
```

See also

- Pandas official documentation *of Indexing and Selecting data* (http://bit.ly/2vm8f12)
- *A look inside pandas design and development* slide deck from pandas author, Wes McKinney (http://bit.ly/2u4YVLi)

Understanding data types

In very broad terms, data may be classified as either continuous or categorical. Continuous data is always numeric and represents some kind of measurement, such as height, wage, or salary. Continuous data can take on an infinite number of possibilities. Categorical data, on the other hand, represents discrete, finite amounts of values such as car color, type of poker hand, or brand of cereal.

Pandas does not broadly classify data as either continuous or categorical. Instead, it has precise technical definitions for many distinct data types. The following table contains all pandas data types, with their string equivalents, and some notes on each type:

Common data type name	NumPy/pandas object	Pandas string name	Notes
Boolean	`np.bool`	*bool*	Stored as a single byte.
Integer	`np.int`	*int*	Defaulted to 64 bits. Unsigned ints are also available - `np.uint`.
Float	`np.float`	*float*	Defaulted to 64 bits.
Complex	`np.complex`	*complex*	Rarely seen in data analysis.
Object	`np.object`	*O, object*	Typically strings but is a catch-all for columns with multiple different types or other Python objects (tuples, lists, dicts, and so on).
Datetime	`np.datetime64,` `pd.Timestamp`	*datetime64*	Specific moment in time with nanosecond precision.
Timedelta	`np.timedelta64,` `pd.Timedelta`	*timedelta64*	An amount of time, from days to nanoseconds.
Categorical	`pd.Categorical`	*category*	Specific only to pandas. Useful for object columns with relatively few unique values.

Getting ready

In this recipe, we display the data type of each column in a DataFrame. It is crucial to know the type of data held in each column as it fundamentally changes the kind of operations that are possible with it.

How to do it...

1. Use the `dtypes` attribute to display each column along with its data type:

```
>>> movie = pd.read_csv('data/movie.csv')
>>> movie.dtypes
color                        object
director_name                object
num_critic_for_reviews       float64
duration                     float64
director_facebook_likes      float64
                             ...
title_year                   float64
actor_2_facebook_likes       float64
imdb_score                   float64
aspect_ratio                 float64
movie_facebook_likes         int64
Length: 28, dtype: object
```

2. Use the `get_dtype_counts` method to return the counts of each data type:

```
>>> movie.get_dtype_counts()
float64    13
int64       3
object     12
```

How it works...

Each DataFrame column must be exactly one type. For instance, every value in the column `aspect_ratio` is a 64-bit float, and every value in `movie_facebook_likes` is a 64-bit integer. Pandas defaults its core numeric types, integers, and floats to 64 bits regardless of the size necessary for all data to fit in memory. Even if a column consists entirely of the integer value 0, the data type will still be `int64`. `get_dtype_counts` is a convenience method for directly returning the count of all the data types in the DataFrame.

Homogeneous data is another term for referring to columns that all have the same type. DataFrames as a whole may contain **heterogeneous data** of different data types for different columns.

The object data type is the one data type that is unlike the others. A column that is of object data type may contain values that are of any valid Python object. Typically, when a column is of the object data type, it signals that the entire column is strings. This isn't necessarily the case as it is possible for these columns to contain a mixture of integers, booleans, strings, or other, even more complex Python objects such as lists or dictionaries. The object data type is a catch-all for columns that pandas doesn't recognize as any other specific type.

There's more...

Almost all of pandas data types are built directly from NumPy. This tight integration makes it easier for users to integrate pandas and NumPy operations. As pandas grew larger and more popular, the object data type proved to be too generic for all columns with string values. Pandas created its own categorical data type to handle columns of strings (or numbers) with a fixed number of possible values.

See also

- Pandas official documentation for *dtypes* (http://bit.ly/2vxe8ZI)
- NumPy official documentation for *Data types* (http://bit.ly/2wq0qEH)

Selecting a single column of data as a Series

A Series is a single column of data from a DataFrame. It is a single dimension of data, composed of just an index and the data.

Getting ready

This recipe examines two different syntaxes to select a Series, one with the indexing operator and the other using dot notation.

How to do it...

1. Pass a column name as a string to the indexing operator to select a Series of data:

```
>>> movie = pd.read_csv('data/movie.csv')
>>> movie['director_name']
```

2. Alternatively, you may use the dot notation to accomplish the same task:

```
>>> movie.director_name
```

3. Inspect the Series anatomy:

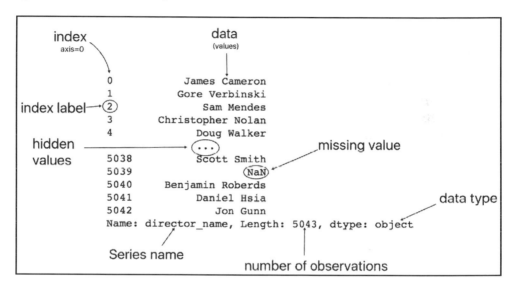

4. Verify that the output is a Series:

```
>>> type(movie['director_name'])
pandas.core.series.Series
```

How it works...

Python has several built-in objects for containing data, such as lists, tuples, and dictionaries. All three of these objects use the indexing operator to select their data. DataFrames are more powerful and complex containers of data, but they too use the indexing operator as the primary means to select data. Passing a single string to the DataFrame indexing operator returns a Series.

The visual output of the Series is less stylized than the DataFrame. It represents a single column of data. Along with the index and values, the output displays the name, length, and data type of the Series.

Alternatively, while not recommended and subject to error, a column of data may be accessed using the dot notation with the column name as an attribute. Although it works with this particular example, it is not best practice and is prone to error and misuse. Column names with spaces or special characters cannot be accessed in this manner. This operation would have failed if the column name was `director name`. Column names that collide with DataFrame methods, such as `count`, also fail to be selected correctly using the dot notation. Assigning new values or deleting columns with the dot notation might give unexpected results. Because of this, using the dot notation to access columns should be avoided with production code.

There's more...

Why would anyone ever use the dot notation syntax if it causes trouble? Programmers are lazy, and there are fewer characters to type. But mainly, it is extremely handy when you want to have the autocomplete intelligence available. For this reason, column selection by dot notation will sometimes be used in this book. The autocomplete intelligence is fantastic for helping you become aware of all the possible attributes and methods available to an object.

The intelligence will fail to work when attempting to chain an operation after use of the indexing operator from step 1 but will continue to work with the dot notation from step 2. The following screenshot shows the pop-up window that appears after the selection of the `director_name` with the dot notation. All the possible attributes and methods will appear in a list after pressing **Tab** following the dot:

```
movie.director_name.|
movie.director_name.abs
movie.director_name.add
movie.director_name.add_prefix
movie.director_name.add_suffix
movie.director_name.agg
movie.director_name.aggregate
movie.director_name.align
movie.director_name.all
movie.director_name.any
movie.director_name.append
```

In a Jupyter notebook, when holding down *Shift + Tab + Tab* with the cursor placed somewhere in the object, a window of the docsstrings will pop out making the method far easier to use. This intelligence again disappears if you try to chain an operation after selecting a column with the indexing operator.

Yet another reason to be aware of the dot notation is the proliferation of its use online at the popular question and answer site Stack Overflow. Also, notice that the old column name is now the `name` of the Series and has actually become an attribute:

```
>>> director = movie['director_name']
>>> director.name
'director_name'
```

It is possible to turn this Series into a one-column DataFrame with the `to_frame` method. This method will use the Series name as the new column name:

```
>>> director.to_frame()
```

See also

- To understand how Python objects gain the capability to use the indexing operator, see the Python documentation on the __getitem__ special method (http://bit.ly/2u5ISN6)
- Refer to the *Selecting multiple DataFrame columns* recipe from Chapter 2, *Essential DataFrame operations*

Calling Series methods

Utilizing the single-dimensional Series is an integral part of all data analysis with pandas. A typical workflow will have you going back and forth between executing statements on Series and DataFrames. Calling Series methods is the primary way to use the abilities that the Series offers.

Getting ready

Both Series and DataFrames have a tremendous amount of power. We can use the `dir` function to uncover all the attributes and methods of a Series. Additionally, we can find the number of attributes and methods common to both Series and DataFrames. Both of these objects share the vast majority of attribute and method names:

```
>>> s_attr_methods = set(dir(pd.Series))
>>> len(s_attr_methods)
442

>>> df_attr_methods = set(dir(pd.DataFrame))
>>> len(df_attr_methods)
445

>>> len(s_attr_methods & df_attr_methods)
376
```

This recipe covers the most common and powerful Series methods. Many of the methods are nearly equivalent for DataFrames.

How to do it...

1. After reading in the movies dataset, let's select two Series with different data types. The `director_name` column contains strings, formally an object data type, and the column `actor_1_facebook_likes` contains numerical data, formally `float64`:

```
>>> movie - pd.read_csv('data/movie.csv')
>>> director = movie['director_name']
>>> actor_1_fb_likes = movie['actor_1_facebook_likes']
```

2. Inspect the head of each Series:

```
>>> director.head()
0        James Cameron
1       Gore Verbinski
2           Sam Mendes
3    Christopher Nolan
4          Doug Walker
Name: director_name, dtype: object

>>> actor_1_fb_likes.head()
0     1000.0
```

```
1      40000.0
2      11000.0
3      27000.0
4        131.0
Name: actor_1_facebook_likes, dtype: float64
```

3. The data type of the Series usually determines which of the methods will be the most useful. For instance, one of the most useful methods for the object data type Series is `value_counts`, which counts all the occurrences of each unique value:

```
>>> director.value_counts()
Steven Spielberg        26
Woody Allen             22
Martin Scorsese         20
Clint Eastwood          20
                        ..
Fatih Akin               1
Analeine Cal y Mayor     1
Andrew Douglas           1
Scott Speer              1
Name: director_name, Length: 2397, dtype: int64
```

4. The `value_counts` method is typically more useful for Series with object data types but can occasionally provide insight into numeric Series as well. Used with `actor_1_fb_likes`, it appears that higher numbers have been rounded to the nearest thousand as it is unlikely that so many movies received exactly 1,000 likes:

```
>>> actor_1_fb_likes.value_counts()
1000.0      436
11000.0     206
2000.0      189
3000.0      150
            ...
216.0         1
859.0         1
225.0         1
334.0         1
Name: actor_1_facebook_likes, Length: 877, dtype: int64
```

5. Counting the number of elements in the Series may be done with the `size` or `shape` parameter or the `len` function:

```
>>> director.size
4916
>>> director.shape
```

```
(4916,)
>>> len(director)
4916
```

6. Additionally, there is the useful but confusing `count` method that returns the number of non-missing values:

```
>>> director.count()
4814
>>> actor_1_fb_likes.count()
4909
```

7. Basic summary statistics may be yielded with the `min`, `max`, `mean`, `median`, `std`, and `sum` methods:

```
>>> actor_1_fb_likes.min(), actor_1_fb_likes.max(), \
    actor_1_fb_likes.mean(), actor_1_fb_likes.median(), \
    actor_1_fb_likes.std(), actor_1_fb_likes.sum()
(0.0, 640000.0, 6494.488490527602, 982.0, 15106.98, 31881444.0)
```

8. To simplify step 7, you may use the `describe` method to return both the summary statistics and a few of the quantiles at once. When `describe` is used with an object data type column, a completely different output is returned:

```
>>> actor_1_fb_likes.describe()
count       4909.000000
mean        6494.488491
std        15106.986884
min            0.000000
25%          607.000000
50%          982.000000
75%        11000.000000
max       640000.000000
Name: actor_1_facebook_likes, dtype: float64

>>> director.describe()
count                   4814
unique                  2397
top         Steven Spielberg
freq                      26
Name: director_name, dtype: object
```

9. The `quantile` method exists to calculate an exact quantile of numeric data:

```
>>> actor_1_fb_likes.quantile(.2)
510
```

```
>>> actor_1_fb_likes.quantile([.1, .2, .3, .4, .5,
                                .6, .7, .8, .9])
0.1        240.0
0.2        510.0
0.3        694.0
0.4        854.0
           . . .
0.6       1000.0
0.7       8000.0
0.8      13000.0
0.9      18000.0
Name: actor_1_facebook_likes, Length: 9, dtype: float64
```

10. Since the `count` method in step 6 returned a value less than the total number of Series elements found in step 5, we know that there are missing values in each Series. The `isnull` method may be used to determine whether each individual value is missing or not. The result will be a Series of booleans the same length as the original Series:

```
>>> director.isnull()
0          False
1          False
2          False
3          False
           . . .
4912        True
4913       False
4914       False
4915       False
Name: director_name, Length: 4916, dtype: bool
```

11. It is possible to replace all missing values within a Series with the `fillna` method:

```
>>> actor_1_fb_likes_filled = actor_1_fb_likes.fillna(0)
>>> actor_1_fb_likes_filled.count()
4916
```

12. To remove the Series elements with missing values, use `dropna`:

```
>>> actor_1_fb_likes_dropped = actor_1_fb_likes.dropna()
>>> actor_1_fb_likes_dropped.size
4909
```

How it works...

Passing a string to the indexing operator of a DataFrame selects a single column as a Series. The methods used in this recipe were chosen because of how frequently they are used in data analysis.

The steps in this recipe should be straightforward with easily interpretable output. Even though the output is easy to read, you might lose track of the returned object. Is it a scalar value, a tuple, another Series, or some other Python object? Take a moment, and look at the output returned after each step. Can you name the returned object?

The result from the `head` method in step 1 is another Series. The `value_counts` method also produces a Series but has the unique values from the original Series as the index and the count as its values. In step 5, `size` and `count` return scalar values, but `shape` returns a one-item tuple.

 It seems odd that the `shape` attribute returns a one-item tuple, but this is convention borrowed from NumPy, which allows for arrays of any number of dimensions.

In step 7, each individual method returns a scalar value, and is outputted as a tuple. This is because Python treats an expression composed of only comma-separated values without parentheses as a tuple.

In step 8, `describe` returns a Series with all the summary statistic names as the index and the actual statistic as the values.

In step 9, `quantile` is flexible and returns a scalar value when passed a single value but returns a Series when given a list.

From steps 10, 11, and 12, `isnull`, `fillna`, and `dropna` all return a Series.

There's more...

The value_counts method is one of the most informative Series methods during exploratory analysis, especially with categorical columns. It defaul_ counts, but by setting the normalize parameter to True, the relative frequencies are returned instead, which provides another view of the distribution:

```
>>> director.value_counts(normalize=True)
Steven Spielberg        0.005401
Woody Allen             0.004570
Martin Scorsese         0.004155
Clint Eastwood          0.004155
                          . . .
Fatih Akin              0.000208
Analeine Cal y Mayor    0.000208
Andrew Douglas          0.000208
Scott Speer             0.000208
Name: director_name, Length: 2397, dtype: float64
```

In this recipe, we determined that there were missing values in the Series by observing that the result from the count method did not match the size attribute. A more direct approach is to use the hasnans attribute:

```
>>> director.hasnans
True
```

There exists a complement of isnull: the notnull method, which returns True for all the non-missing values:

```
>>> director.notnull()
0          True
1          True
2          Truc
3          True
         . . .
4912      False
4913       True
4914       True
4915       True
Name: director_name, Length: 4916, dtype: bool
```

See also

- To call many Series methods in succession, refer to the *Chaining Series methods together* recipe in this chapter

Working with operators on a Series

There exist a vast number of operators in Python for manipulating objects. Operators are not objects themselves, but rather syntactical structures and keywords that force an operation to occur on an object. For instance, when the plus operator is placed between two integers, Python will add them together. See more examples of operators in the following code:

```
>>> 5 + 9    # plus operator example adds 5 and 9
14

>>> 4 ** 2  # exponentiation operator raises 4 to the second power
16

>>> a = 10   # assignment operator assigns 10 to a

>>> 5 <= 9   # less than or equal to operator returns a boolean
True
```

Operators can work for any type of object, not just numerical data. These examples show different objects being operated on:

```
>>> 'abcde' + 'fg'
'abcdefg'

>>> not (5 <= 9)
False

>>> 7 in [1, 2, 6]
False

>>> set([1,2,3]) & set([2,3,4])
set([2,3])
```

Visit tutorials point (http://bit.ly/2u5g5Io) to see a table of all the basic Python operators. Not all operators are implemented for every object. These examples all produce errors when using an operator:

```
>>> [1, 2, 3] - 3
TypeError: unsupported operand type(s) for -: 'list' and 'int'

>>> a = set([1,2,3])
>>> a[0]
TypeError: 'set' object does not support indexing
```

Series and DataFrame objects work with most of the Python operators.

Getting ready

In this recipe, a variety of operators will be applied to different Series objects to produce a new Series with completely different values.

How to do it...

1. Select the imdb_score column as a Series:

    ```
    >>> movie = pd.read_csv('data/movie.csv')
    >>> imdb_score = movie['imdb_score']
    >>> imdb_score
    0       7.9
    1       7.1
    2       6.8
            . . .
    4913    6.3
    4914    6.3
    4915    6.6
    Name: imdb_score, Length: 4916, dtype: float64
    ```

2. Use the plus operator to add one to each Series element:

    ```
    >>> imdb_score + 1
    0       8.9
    1       8.1
    2       7.8
            . . .
    4913    7.3
    4914    7.3
    ```

```
4915      7.6
Name: imdb_score, Length: 4916, dtype: float64
```

3. The other basic arithmetic operators minus (−), multiplication (*), division (/), and exponentiation (**) work similarly with scalar values. In this step, we will multiply the series by 2.5:

```
>>> imdb_score * 2.5
0          19.75
1          17.75
2          17.00
        . . .
4913       15.75
4914       15.75
4915       16.50
Name: imdb_score, Length: 4916, dtype: float64
```

4. Python uses two consecutive division operators (//) for floor division and the percent sign (%) for the modulus operator, which returns the remainder after a division. Series use these the same way:

```
>>> imdb_score // 7
0          1.0
1          1.0
2          0.0
        . . .
4913       0.0
4914       0.0
4915       0.0
Name: imdb_score, Length: 4916, dtype: float64
```

5. There exist six comparison operators, greater than (>), less than (<), greater than or equal to (>=), less than or equal to (<=), equal to (==), and not equal to (!=). Each comparison operator turns each value in the Series to `True` or `False` based on the outcome of the condition:

```
>>> imdb_score > 7
0          True
1          True
2          False
        . . .
4913       False
4914       False
4915       False
Name: imdb_score, Length: 4916, dtype: bool
```

```
>>> director = movie['director_name']
>>> director == 'James Cameron'
0         True
1         False
2         False
          ...
4913      False
4914      False
4915      False
Name: director_name, Length: 4916, dtype: bool
```

How it works...

All the operators used in this recipe apply the same operation to each element in the Series. In native Python, this would require a for-loop to iterate through each of the items in the sequence before applying the operation. Pandas relies heavily on the NumPy library, which allows for vectorized computations, or the ability to operate on entire sequences of data without the explicit writing of for loops. Each operation returns a Series with the same index, but with values that have been modified by the operator.

There's more...

All of the operators used in this recipe have method equivalents that produce the exact same result. For instance, in step 1, imdb_score + 1 may be reproduced with the add method. Check the following code to see the method version of each step in the recipe:

```
>>> imdb_score.add(1)                 # imdb_score + 1
>>> imdb_score.mul(2.5)               # imdb_score * 2.5
>>> imdb_score.floordiv(7)            # imdb_score // 7
>>> imdb_score.gt(7)                  # imdb_score > 7
>>> director.eq('James Cameron')      # director == 'James Cameron'
```

Why does pandas offer a method equivalent to these operators? By its nature, an operator only operates in exactly one manner. Methods, on the other hand, can have parameters that allow you to alter their default functionality:

Operator Group	Operator	Series method name
Arithmetic	+, −, *, /, //, %, **	add, sub, mul, div, floordiv, mod, pow
Comparison	<, >, <=, >=, ==, !=	lt, gt, le, ge, eq, ne

You may be curious as to how a Python Series object, or any object for that matter, knows what to do when it encounters an operator. For example, how does the expression `imdb_score * 2.5` know to multiply each element in the Series by `2.5`? Python has a built-in, standardized way for objects to communicate with operators using **special methods**.

Special methods are what objects call internally whenever they encounter an operator. Special methods are defined in the Python data model, a very important part of the official documentation, and are the same for every object throughout the language. Special methods always begin and end with two underscores. For instance, the special method `__mul__` is called whenever the multiplication operator is used. Python interprets the `imdb_score * 2.5` expression as `imdb_score.__mul__(2.5)`.

There is no difference between using the special method and using an operator as they are doing the exact same thing. The operator is just syntactic sugar for the special method.

See also

- Python official documentation on operators (`http://bit.ly/2wpOId8`)
- Python official documentation on the data model (`http://bit.ly/2v0LrDd`)

Chaining Series methods together

In Python, every variable is an object, and all objects have attributes and methods that refer to or return more objects. The sequential invocation of methods using the dot notation is referred to as **method chaining**. Pandas is a library that lends itself well to method chaining, as many Series and DataFrame methods return more Series and DataFrames, upon which more methods can be called.

Getting ready

To motivate method chaining, let's take a simple English sentence and translate the chain of events into a chain of methods. Consider the sentence, *A person drives to the store to buy food, then drives home and prepares, cooks, serves, and eats the food before cleaning the dishes.*

A Python version of this sentence might take the following form:

```
>>> person.drive('store')\
        .buy('food')\
        .drive('home')\
        .prepare('food')\
        .cook('food')\
        .serve('food')\
        .eat('food')\
        .cleanup('dishes')
```

In the preceding code, the `person` is the object calling each of the methods, just as the person is performing all of the actions in the original sentence. The parameter passed to each of the methods specifies how the method operates.

Although it is possible to write the entire method chain in a single unbroken line, it is far more palatable to write a single method per line. Since Python does not normally allow a single expression to be written on multiple lines, you need to use the backslash line continuation character. Alternatively, you may wrap the whole expression in parentheses. To improve readability even more, place each method directly under the dot above it. This recipe shows similar method chaining with pandas Series.

How to do it...

1. Load in the movie dataset, and select two columns as a distinct Series:

```
>>> movie = pd.read_csv('data/movie.csv')
>>> actor_1_fb_likes = movie['actor_1_facebook_likes']
>>> director = movie['director_name']
```

2. One of the most common methods to append to the chain is the `head` method. This suppresses long output. For shorter chains, there isn't as great a need to place each method on a different line:

```
>>> director.value_counts().head(3)
Steven Spielberg    26
Woody Allen         22
Clint Eastwood      20
Name: director_name, dtype: int64
```

3. A common way to count the number of missing values is to chain the `sum` method after `isnull`:

```
>>> actor_1_fb_likes.isnull().sum()
7
```

4. All the non-missing values of `actor_1_fb_likes` should be integers as it is impossible to have a partial Facebook like. Any numeric columns with missing values must have their data type as `float`. If we fill missing values from `actor_1_fb_likes` with zeros, we can then convert it to an integer with the `astype` method:

```
>>> actor_1_fb_likes.dtype
dtype('float64')

>>> actor_1_fb_likes.fillna(0)\
                     .astype(int)\
                     .head()
0     1000
1    40000
2    11000
3    27000
4      131
Name: actor_1_facebook_likes, dtype: int64
```

How it works...

Method chaining is possible with all Python objects since each object method must return another object that itself will have more methods. It is not necessary for the method to return the same type of object.

Step 2 first uses `value_counts` to return a Series and then chains the `head` method to select the first three elements. The final returned object is a Series, which could also have had more methods chained on it.

In step 3, the `isnull` method creates a boolean Series. Pandas numerically evaluates `False`/`True` as 0/1, so the `sum` method returns the number of missing values.

Each of the three chained methods in step 4 returns a Series. It may not seem intuitive, but the `astype` method returns an entirely new Series with a different data type

There's more...

Instead of summing up the booleans in step 3 to find the total number of missing values, we can take the mean of the Series to get the percentage of values that are missing:

```
>>> actor_1_fb_likes.isnull().mean()
0.0014
```

As was mentioned at the beginning of the recipe, it is possible to use parentheses instead of the backslash for multi-line code. Step 4 may be rewritten this way:

```
>>> (actor_1_fb_likes.fillna(0)
                      .astype(int)
                      .head())
```

Not all programmers like the use of method chaining, as there are some downsides. One such downside is that debugging becomes difficult. None of the intermediate objects produced during the chain are stored in a variable, so if there is an unexpected result, it will be difficult to trace the exact location in the chain where it occurred.

The example at the start of the recipe may be rewritten so that the result of each method gets preserved as/in a unique variable. This makes tracking bugs much easier, as you can inspect the object at each step:

```
>>> person1 = person.drive('store')
>>> person2 = person1.buy('food')
>>> person3 = person2.drive('home')
>>> person4 = person3.prepare('food')
>>> person5 = person4.cook('food')
>>> person6 = person5.serve('food')
>>> person7 = person6.eat('food')
>>> person8 = person7.cleanup('dishes')
```

Making the index meaningful

The index of a DataFrame provides a label for each of the rows. If no index is explicitly provided upon DataFrame creation, then by default, a `RangeIndex` is created with labels as integers from 0 to n-1, where n is the number of rows.

Getting ready

This recipe replaces the meaningless default row index of the movie dataset with the movie title, which is much more meaningful.

How to do it...

1. Read in the movie dataset, and use the `set_index` method to set the title of each movie as the new index:

```
>>> movie = pd.read_csv('data/movie.csv')
>>> movie2 = movie.set_index('movie_title')
>>> movie2
```

2. Alternatively, it is possible to choose a column as the index upon initial read with the `index_col` parameter of the `read_csv` function:

```
>>> movie = pd.read_csv('data/movie.csv', index_col='movie_title')
```

movie_title	color	director_name	num_critic_for_reviews	duration	...	actor_2_facebook_likes	imdb_score	aspect_ratio	movie_facebook_likes
Avatar	Color	James Cameron	723.0	178.0	...	936.0	7.9	1.78	33000
Pirates of the Caribbean: At World's End	Color	Gore Verbinski	302.0	169.0	...	5000.0	7.1	2.35	0
Spectre	Color	Sam Mendes	602.0	148.0	...	393.0	6.8	2.35	85000
The Dark Knight Rises	Color	Christopher Nolan	813.0	164.0	...	23000.0	8.5	2.35	164000
Star Wars: Episode VII - The Force Awakens	NaN	Doug Walker	NaN	NaN	...	12.0	7.1	NaN	0

How it works...

A meaningful index is one that clearly identifies each row. The default RangeIndex is not very helpful. Since each row identifies data for exactly one movie, it makes sense to use the movie title as the label. If you know ahead of time which column will make a good index, you can specify this upon import with the `index_col` parameter of the `read_csv` function.

By default, both `set_index` and `read_csv` drop the column used as the index from the DataFrame. With `set_index`, it is possible to keep the column in the DataFrame by setting the `drop` parameter to `False`.

There's more...

Conversely, it is possible to turn the index into a column with the `reset_index` method. This will make `movie_title` a column again and revert the index back to a `RangeIndex`. `reset_index` always puts the column as the very first one in the DataFrame, so the columns may not be in their original order:

```
>>> movie2.reset_index()
```

See also

- Pandas official documentation on `RangeIndex` (http://bit.ly/2hs6DNL)

Renaming row and column names

One of the most basic and common operations on a DataFrame is to rename the row or column names. Good column names are descriptive, brief, and follow a common convention with respect to capitalization, spaces, underscores, and other features.

Getting ready

In this recipe, both the row and column names are renamed.

How to do it...

1. Read in the movie dataset, and make the index meaningful by setting it as the movie title:

```
>>> movie = pd.read_csv('data/movie.csv', index_col='movie_title')
```

2. The `rename` DataFrame method accepts dictionaries that map the old value to the new value. Let's create one for the rows and another for the columns:

```
>>> idx_rename = {'Avatar':'Ratava', 'Spectre': 'Ertceps'}
>>> col_rename = {'director_name':'Director Name',
                  'num_critic_for_reviews': 'Critical Reviews'}
```

3. Pass the dictionaries to the `rename` method, and assign the result to a new variable:

```
>>> movie_renamed = movie.rename(index=idx_rename,
                                 columns=col_rename)
>>> movie_renamed.head()
```

movie_title	color	Director Name	Critical Reviews	duration	...	actor_2_facebook_likes	imdb_score	aspect_ratio	movie_facebook_likes
Ratava	Color	James Cameron	723.0	178.0	...	936.0	7.9	1.78	33000
Pirates of the Caribbean: At World's End	Color	Gore Verbinski	302.0	169.0	...	5000.0	7.1	2.35	0
Ertceps	Color	Sam Mendes	602.0	148.0	...	393.0	6.8	2.35	85000
The Dark Knight Rises	Color	Christopher Nolan	813.0	164.0	...	23000.0	8.5	2.35	164000
Star Wars: Episode VII - The Force Awakens	NaN	Doug Walker	NaN	NaN	...	12.0	7.1	NaN	0

How it works...

The `rename` DataFrame method allows for both row and column labels to be renamed at the same time with the `index` and `columns` parameters. Each of these parameters may be set to a dictionary that maps old labels to their new values.

There's more...

There are multiple ways to rename row and column labels. It is possible to reassign the index and column attributes directly to a Python list. This assignment works when the list has the same number of elements as the row and column labels. The following code uses the `tolist` method on each Index object to create a Python list of labels. It then modifies a couple values in the list and reassigns the list to the attributes `index` and `columns`:

```
>>> movie = pd.read_csv('data/movie.csv', index_col='movie_title')
>>> index = movie.index
>>> columns = movie.columns

>>> index_list = index.tolist()
>>> column_list = columns.tolist()

# rename the row and column labels with list assignments
>>> index_list[0] = 'Ratava'
>>> index_list[2] = 'Ertceps'
>>> column_list[1] = 'Director Name'
>>> column_list[2] = 'Critical Reviews'

>>> print(index_list)
['Ratava', "Pirates of the Caribbean: At World's End", 'Ertceps', 'The Dark
Knight Rises', ... ]

>>> print(column_list)
['color', 'Director Name', 'Critical Reviews', 'duration', ...]

# finally reassign the index and columns
>>> movie.index = index_list
>>> movie.columns = column_list
```

Creating and deleting columns

During a data analysis, it is extremely likely that you will need to create new columns to represent new variables. Commonly, these new columns will be created from previous columns already in the dataset. Pandas has a few different ways to add new columns to a DataFrame.

Getting ready

In this recipe, we create new columns in the movie dataset by using the assignment and then delete columns with the `drop` method.

How to do it...

1. The simplest way to create a new column is to assign it a scalar value. Place the name of the new column as a string into the indexing operator. Let's create the `has_seen` column in the movie dataset to indicate whether or not we have seen the movie. We will assign zero for every value. By default, new columns are appended to the end:

```
>>> movie = pd.read_csv('data/movie.csv')
>>> movie['has_seen'] = 0
```

2. There are several columns that contain data on the number of Facebook likes. Let's add up all the actor and director Facebook likes and assign them to the `actor_director_facebook_likes` column:

```
>>> movie['actor_director_facebook_likes'] =   \
        (movie['actor_1_facebook_likes'] +
        movie['actor_2_facebook_likes'] +
        movie['actor_3_facebook_likes'] +
        movie['director_facebook_likes'])
```

3. From the *Calling Series method* recipe in this chapter, we know that this dataset contains missing values. When numeric columns are added to one another as in the preceding step, pandas defaults missing values to zero. But, if all values for a particular row are missing, then pandas keeps the total as missing as well. Let's check if there are missing values in our new column and fill them with 0:

```
>>> movie['actor_director_facebook_likes'].isnull().sum()
122
>>> movie['actor_director_facebook_likes'] = \
    movie['actor_director_facebook_likes'].fillna(0)
```

4. There is another column in the dataset named `cast_total_facebook_likes`. It would be interesting to see what percentage of this column comes from our newly created column, `actor_director_facebook_likes`. Before we create our percentage column, let's do some basic data validation. Let's ensure that `cast_total_facebook_likes` is greater than or equal to `actor_director_facebook_likes`:

```
>>> movie['is_cast_likes_more'] = \
        (movie['cast_total_facebook_likes'] >=
        movie['actor_director_facebook_likes'])
```

5. `is_cast_likes_more` is now a column of boolean values. We can check whether all the values of this column are `True` with the `all` Series method:

```
>>> movie['is_cast_likes_more'].all()
False
```

6. It turns out that there is at least one movie with more `actor_director_facebook_likes` than `cast_total_facebook_likes`. It could be that director Facebook likes are not part of the cast total likes. Let's backtrack and delete column `actor_director_facebook_likes`:

```
>>> movie = movie.drop('actor_director_facebook_likes',
                    axis='columns')
```

7. Let's recreate a column of just the total actor likes:

```
>>> movie['actor_total_facebook_likes'] = \
        (movie['actor_1_facebook_likes'] +
        movie['actor_2_facebook_likes'] +
        movie['actor_3_facebook_likes'])

>>> movie['actor_total_facebook_likes'] = \
        movie['actor_total_facebook_likes'].fillna(0)
```

8. Check again whether all the values in `cast_total_facebook_likes` are greater than the `actor_total_facebook_likes`:

```
>>> movie['is_cast_likes_more'] = \
        (movie['cast_total_facebook_likes'] >=
        movie['actor_total_facebook_likes'])
>>> movie['is_cast_likes_more'].all()
True
```

9. Finally, let's calculate the percentage of the `cast_total_facebook_likes` that come from `actor_total_facebook_likes`:

```
>>> movie['pct_actor_cast_like'] = \
        (movie['actor_total_facebook_likes'] /
          movie['cast_total_facebook_likes'])
```

10. Let's validate that the min and max of this column fall between 0 and 1:

```
>>> (movie['pct_actor_cast_like'].min(),
     movie['pct_actor_cast_like'].max())
(0.0, 1.0)
```

11. We can then output this column as a Series. First, we need to set the index to the movie title so we can properly identify each value.

```
>>> movie.set_index('movie_title')['pct_actor_cast_like'].head()
movie_title
Avatar                                         0.577369
Pirates of the Caribbean: At World's End       0.951396
Spectre                                        0.987521
The Dark Knight Rises                          0.683783
Star Wars: Episode VII - The Force Awakens     0.000000
Name: pct_actor_cast_like, dtype: float64
```

How it works...

Many pandas operations are flexible, and column creation is one of them. This recipe assigns both a scalar value, as seen in Step 1, and a Series, as seen in step 2, to create a new column.

Step 2 adds four different Series together with the plus operator. Step 3 uses method chaining to find and fill missing values. Step 4 uses the greater than or equal comparison operator to return a boolean Series, which is then evaluated with the `all` method in step 5 to check whether every single value is `True` or not.

The `drop` method accepts the name of the row or column to delete. It defaults to dropping rows by the index names. To drop columns you must set the `axis` parameter to either 1 or *columns*. The default value for axis is 0 or the string *index*.

Steps 7 and 8 redo the work of step 3 to step 5 without the `director_facebook_likes` column. Step 9 finally calculates the desired column we wanted since step 4. Step 10 validates that the percentages are between 0 and 1.

There's more...

It is possible to insert a new column into a specific place in a DataFrame besides the end with the `insert` method. The `insert` method takes the integer position of the new column as its first argument, the name of the new column as its second, and the values as its third. You will need to use the `get_loc` Index method to find the integer location of the column name.

The `insert` method modifies the calling DataFrame in-place, so there won't be an assignment statement. The profit of each movie may be calculated by subtracting `budget` from `gross` and inserting it directly after `gross` with the following:

```
>>> profit_index = movie.columns.get_loc('gross') + 1
>>> profit_index
9

>>> movie.insert(loc=profit_index,
                 column='profit',
                 value=movie['gross'] - movie['budget'])
```

An alternative to deleting columns with the drop method is to use the `del` statement:

```
>>> del movie['actor_director_facebook_likes']
```

See also

- Refer to the *Appending new rows to DataFrames* recipe from Chapter 9, *Combining Pandas Objects* for adding and deleting rows, which is a less common operation
- Refer to the *Developing a data analysis routine* recipe from Chapter 3, *Beginning Data Analysis*

2
Essential DataFrame Operations

In this chapter, we will cover the following topics:

- Selecting multiple DataFrame columns
- Selecting columns with methods
- Ordering column names sensibly
- Operating on the entire DataFrame
- Chaining DataFrame methods together
- Working with operators on a DataFrame
- Comparing missing values
- Transposing the direction of a DataFrame operation
- Determining college campus diversity

Introduction

This chapter covers many fundamental operations of the DataFrame. Many of the recipes will be similar to those in Chapter 1, *Pandas Foundations* which primarily covered operations on a Series.

Selecting multiple DataFrame columns

Selecting a single column is accomplished by passing the desired column name as a string to the indexing operator of a DataFrame. This was covered in the *Selecting a Series* recipe in `Chapter 1`, *Pandas Foundations*. It is often necessary to focus on a subset of the current working dataset, which is accomplished by selecting multiple columns.

Getting ready

In this recipe, all the `actor` and `director` columns will be selected from the `movie` dataset.

How to do it...

1. Read in the movie dataset, and pass in a list of the desired columns to the indexing operator:

```
>>> movie_actor_director = movie[['actor_1_name', 'actor_2_name',
                                   'actor_3_name', 'director_name']]
>>> movie_actor_director.head()
```

	actor_1_name	actor_2_name	actor_3_name	director_name
0	CCH Pounder	Joel David Moore	Wes Studi	James Cameron
1	Johnny Depp	Orlando Bloom	Jack Davenport	Gore Verbinski
2	Christoph Waltz	Rory Kinnear	Stephanie Sigman	Sam Mendes
3	Tom Hardy	Christian Bale	Joseph Gordon-Levitt	Christopher Nolan
4	Doug Walker	Rob Walker	NaN	Doug Walker

2. There are instances when one column of a DataFrame needs to be selected. This is done by passing a single element list to the indexing operator:

```
>>> movie[['director_name']].head()
```

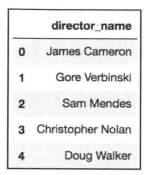

	director_name
0	James Cameron
1	Gore Verbinski
2	Sam Mendes
3	Christopher Nolan
4	Doug Walker

How it works...

The DataFrame indexing operator is very flexible and capable of accepting a number of different objects. If a string is passed, it will return a single-dimensional Series. If a list is passed to the indexing operator, it returns a DataFrame of all the columns in the list in the specified order

Step 2 shows how to select a single column as a DataFrame rather than as a Series. Most commonly, a single column is selected with a string, resulting in a Series. When a DataFrame is the desired output, simply put the column name in a single-element list.

There's more...

Passing a long list inside the indexing operator might cause readability issues. To help with this, you may save all your column names to a list variable first. The following code achieves the same result as step 1:

```
>>> cols = ['actor_1_name', 'actor_2_name',
            'actor_3_name', 'director_name']
>>> movie_actor_director = movie[cols]
```

One of the most common exceptions raised when working with pandas is KeyError. This error is mainly due to mistyping of a column or index name. This same error is raised whenever a multiple column selection is attempted without the use of a list:

```
>>> movie['actor_1_name', 'actor_2_name',
          'actor_3_name', 'director_name']
KeyError: ('actor_1_name', 'actor_2_name',
           'actor_3_name', 'director_name')
```

This is a common error to encounter, as it is easy to forget to place the desired columns in a list. You might be wondering what exactly is going on here. The four string names separated by commas are technically a tuple object. Normally, tuples are written with open and closing parentheses, but it isn't necessary:

```
>>> tuple1 = 1, 2, 3, 'a', 'b'
>>> tuple2 = (1, 2, 3, 'a', 'b')
>>> tuple1 == tuple2
True
```

Pandas is trying to find a column name exactly equal to the tuple, (`'actor_1_name'`, `'actor_2_name'`, `'actor_3_name'`, `'director_name'`). It fails and raises a `KeyError`.

Selecting columns with methods

Although column selection is usually done directly with the indexing operator, there are some DataFrame methods that facilitate their selection in an alternative manner. `select_dtypes` and `filter` are two useful methods to do this.

Getting ready

You need to be familiar with all pandas data types and how to access them. The *Understanding data types* recipe in Chapter 1, *Pandas Foundations*, has a table with all pandas data types.

How it works...

1. Read in the movie dataset, and use the title of the movie to label each row. Use the `get_dtype_counts` method to output the number of columns with each specific data type:

    ```
    >>> movie = pd.read_csv('data/movie.csv',
                            index_col='movie_title')
    >>> movie.get_dtype_counts()
    float64    13
    int64       3
    object     11
    dtype: int64
    ```

2. Use the `select_dtypes` method to select only the integer columns:

```
>>> movie.select_dtypes(include=['int']).head()
```

movie_title	num_voted_users	cast_total_facebook_likes	movie_facebook_likes
Avatar	886204	4834	33000
Pirates of the Caribbean: At World's End	471220	48350	0
Spectre	275868	11700	85000
The Dark Knight Rises	1144337	106759	164000
Star Wars: Episode VII - The Force Awakens	8	143	0

3. If you would like to select all the numeric columns, you may simply pass the string *number* to the `include` parameter:

```
>>> movie.select_dtypes(include=['number']).head()
```

movie_title	num_critic_for_reviews	duration	director_facebook_likes	actor_3_facebook_likes	actor_1_facebook_likes	gross	num_voted_users
Avatar	723.0	178.0	0.0	855.0	1000.0	760505847.0	886204
Pirates of the Caribbean: At World's End	302.0	169.0	563.0	1000.0	40000.0	309404152.0	471220
Spectre	602.0	148.0	0.0	161.0	11000.0	200074175.0	275868
The Dark Knight Rises	813.0	164.0	22000.0	23000.0	27000.0	448130642.0	1144337
Star Wars: Episode VII - The Force Awakens	NaN	NaN	131.0	NaN	131.0	NaN	8

An alternative method to select columns is with the `filter` method. This method is flexible and searches column names (or index labels) based on which parameter is used. Here, we use the `like` parameter to search for all column names that contain the exact string, *facebook*:

```
>>> movie.filter(like='facebook').head()
```

movie_title	director_facebook_likes	actor_3_facebook_likes	actor_1_facebook_likes	cast_total_facebook_likes	actor_2_facebook_likes	movie_facebook_likes
Avatar	0.0	855.0	1000.0	4834	936.0	33000
Pirates of the Caribbean: At World's End	563.0	1000.0	40000.0	48350	5000.0	0
Spectre	0.0	161.0	11000.0	11700	393.0	85000
The Dark Knight Rises	22000.0	23000.0	27000.0	106759	23000.0	164000
Star Wars: Episode VII - The Force Awakens	131.0	NaN	131.0	143	12.0	0

5. The `filter` method allows columns to be searched through regular expressions with the `regex` parameter. Here, we search for all columns that have a digit somewhere in their name:

```
>>> movie.filter(regex='\d').head()
```

movie_title	actor_3_facebook_likes	actor_2_name	actor_1_facebook_likes	actor_1_name	actor_3_name	actor_2_facebook_likes
Avatar	855.0	Joel David Moore	1000.0	CCH Pounder	Wes Studi	936.0
Pirates of the Caribbean: At World's End	1000.0	Orlando Bloom	40000.0	Johnny Depp	Jack Davenport	5000.0
Spectre	161.0	Rory Kinnear	11000.0	Christoph Waltz	Stephanie Sigman	393.0
The Dark Knight Rises	23000.0	Christian Bale	27000.0	Tom Hardy	Joseph Gordon-Levitt	23000.0
Star Wars: Episode VII - The Force Awakens	NaN	Rob Walker	131.0	Doug Walker	NaN	12.0

How it works...

Step 1 lists the frequencies of all the different data types. Alternatively, you may use the dtypes attribute to get the exact data type for each column. The select_dtypes method takes a list of data types in its include parameter and returns a DataFrame with columns of just those given data types. The list values may be either the string name of the data type or the actual Python object.

The filter method selects columns by only inspecting the column names and not the actual data values. It has three mutually exclusive parameters, items, like, and regex, only one of which can be used at a time. The like parameter takes a string and attempts to find all the column names that contain that exact string somewhere in the name. To gain more flexibility, you may use the regex parameter instead to select column names through a regular expression. This particular regular expression, \d, represents all digits from zero to nine and matches any string with at least a single digit in it.

 Regular expressions are character sequences that represent search patterns to be used to select different parts of the text. They allow for very complex and highly specific pattern matching.

There's more...

The filter method comes with another parameter, items, which takes a list of exact column names. This is nearly an exact duplication of the indexing operator, except that a KeyError will not be raised if one of the strings does not match a column name. For instance, movie.filter(items=['actor_1_name', 'asdf']) runs without error and returns a single column DataFrame.

One confusing aspect of select_dtypes is its flexibility to take both strings and Python objects. The following table should clarify all the possible ways to select the many different column data types. There is no standard or preferred method of referring to data types in pandas, so it's good to be aware of both ways:

Python object	String	Notes
np.number	number	Selects both integers and floats regardless of size
np.float64, np.float_, float	float64, float_, float	Selects only 64-bit floats

np.float16, np.float32, np.float128	float16, float32, float128	Respectively selects exactly 16, 32, and 128-bit floats
np.floating	floating	Selects all floats regardless of size
np.int0, np.int64, np.int_, int	int0, int64, int_, int	Selects only 64-bit integers
np.int8, np.int16, np.int32	int8, int16, int32	Respectively selects exactly 8, 16, and 32-bit integers
np.integer	integer	Selects all integers regardless of size
np.object	object, O	Select all object data types
np.datetime64	datetime64, datetime	All datetimes are 64 bits
np.timedelta64	timedelta64, timedelta	All timedeltas are 64 bits
pd.Categorical	category	Unique to pandas; no NumPy equivalent

Because all integers and floats default to 64 bits, you may select them by simply using the string, *int,* or *float* as you can see from the preceding table. If you want to select all integers and floats regardless of their specific size use the string *number*.

See also

- Refer to the *Understanding data types* recipe from Chapter 1, *Pandas Foundations*
- The rarely used select method may also select columns based on their names (http://bit.ly/2fchzhu)

Ordering column names sensibly

One of the first tasks to consider after initially importing a dataset as a DataFrame is to analyze the order of the columns. This basic task is often overlooked but can make a big difference in how an analysis proceeds. Computers have no preference for column order and computations are not affected either. As human beings, we naturally view and read columns left to right, which directly impacts our interpretations of the data. Haphazard column arrangement is similar to haphazard clothes arrangement in a closet. It does no good to place suits next to shirts and pants on top of shorts. It's far easier to find and interpret information when column order is given consideration.

There are no standardized set of rules that dictate how columns should be organized within a dataset. However, it is good practice to develop a set of guidelines that you consistently follow in order to ease the analysis. This is especially true if you work with a group of analysts who share lots of datasets.

Getting ready

The following is a simple guideline to order columns:

- Classify each column as either discrete or continuous
- Group common columns within the discrete and continuous columns
- Place the most important groups of columns first with categorical columns before continuous ones

This recipe shows you how to order the columns with this guideline. There are many possible orderings that are sensible.

How to do it...

1. Read in the movie dataset, and scan the data:

```
>>> movie = pd.read_csv('data/movie.csv')
>>> movie.head()
```

	color	director_name	num_critic_for_reviews	duration	director_facebook_likes	actor_3_facebook_likes	actor_2_name	actor_1_facebook_likes	gross
0	Color	James Cameron	723.0	178.0	0.0	855.0	Joel David Moore	1000.0	760505847.0
1	Color	Gore Verbinski	302.0	169.0	563.0	1000.0	Orlando Bloom	40000.0	309404152.0
2	Color	Sam Mendes	602.0	148.0	0.0	161.0	Rory Kinnear	11000.0	200074175.0
3	Color	Christopher Nolan	813.0	164.0	22000.0	23000.0	Christian Bale	27000.0	448130642.0
4	NaN	Doug Walker	NaN	NaN	131.0	NaN	Rob Walker	131.0	NaN

2. Output all the column names and scan for similar discrete and continuous columns:

```
>>> movie.columns
Index(['color', 'director_name', 'num_critic_for_reviews',
       'duration', 'director_facebook_likes',
       'actor_3_facebook_likes', 'actor_2_name',
       'actor_1_facebook_likes', 'gross', 'genres',
       'actor_1_name', 'movie_title', 'num_voted_users',
       'cast_total_facebook_likes', 'actor_3_name',
       'facenumber_in_poster', 'plot_keywords',
       'movie_imdb_link', 'num_user_for_reviews', 'language',
       'country', 'content_rating', 'budget', 'title_year',
       'actor_2_facebook_likes', 'imdb_score', 'aspect_ratio',
       'movie_facebook_likes'], dtype='object')
```

3. The columns don't appear to have any logical ordering to them. Organize the names sensibly into lists so that the guideline from the previous section is followed:

```
>>> disc_core = ['movie_title', 'title_year',
                 'content_rating', 'genres']
>>> disc_people = ['director_name', 'actor_1_name',
                   'actor_2_name', 'actor_3_name']
>>> disc_other = ['color', 'country', 'language',
                  'plot_keywords', 'movie_imdb_link']

>>> cont_fb = ['director_facebook_likes', 'actor_1_facebook_likes',
               'actor_2_facebook_likes', 'actor_3_facebook_likes',
               'cast_total_facebook_likes', 'movie_facebook_likes']

>>> cont_finance = ['budget', 'gross']
>>> cont_num_reviews = ['num_voted_users', 'num_user_for_reviews',
                        'num_critic_for_reviews']
```

```
>>> cont_other = ['imdb_score', 'duration',
                  'aspect_ratio', 'facenumber_in_poster']
```

4. Concatenate all the lists together to get the final column order. Also, ensure that this list contains all the columns from the original:

```
>>> new_col_order = disc_core + disc_people + \
                    disc_other + cont_fb + \
                    cont_finance + cont_num_reviews + \
                    cont_other
>>> set(movie.columns) == set(new_col_order)
True
```

5. Pass the list with the new column order to the indexing operator of the DataFrame to reorder the columns:

```
>>> movie2 = movie[new_col_order]
>>> movie2.head()
```

	movie_title	title_year	content_rating	genres	director_name	actor_1_name	actor_2_name	actor_3_name	color	country	language
0	Avatar	2009.0	PG-13	Action|Adventure|Fantasy|Sci-Fi	James Cameron	CCH Pounder	Joel David Moore	Wes Studi	Color	USA	English
1	Pirates of the Caribbean: At World's End	2007.0	PG-13	Action|Adventure|Fantasy	Gore Verbinski	Johnny Depp	Orlando Bloom	Jack Davenport	Color	USA	English
2	Spectre	2015.0	PG-13	Action|Adventure|Thriller	Sam Mendes	Christoph Waltz	Rory Kinnear	Stephanie Sigman	Color	UK	English
3	The Dark Knight Rises	2012.0	PG-13	Action|Thriller	Christopher Nolan	Tom Hardy	Christian Bale	Joseph Gordon-Levitt	Color	USA	English
4	Star Wars: Episode VII - The Force Awakens	NaN	NaN	Documentary	Doug Walker	Doug Walker	Rob Walker	NaN	NaN	NaN	NaN

How it works...

To select a subset of columns from a DataFrame, use a list of specific column names. For instance, `movie[['movie_title', 'director_name']]` creates a new DataFrame with only the `movie_title` and `director_name` columns. Selecting columns by name is the default behavior of the indexing operator for a pandas DataFrame.

Step 3 neatly organizes all of the column names into separate lists based on their type (discrete or continuous) and by how similar their data is. The most important columns, such as the title of the movie, are placed first.

Step 4 concatenates all of the lists of column names and validates that this new list contains the same exact values as the original column names. Python sets are unordered and the equality statement checks whether each member of one set is a member of the other. Manually ordering columns in this recipe is susceptible to human error as it's easy to mistakenly forget a column in the new column list.

Step 5 completes the reordering by passing the new column order as a list to the indexing operator. This new order is now much more sensible than the original.

There's more...

There are alternative guidelines for ordering columns besides the simple suggestion mentioned earlier. Hadley Wickham's seminal paper on Tidy Data suggests placing the fixed variables first, followed by measured variables. As this data does not emanate from a controlled experiment, there is some flexibility in determining which variables are fixed and which ones are measured. Good candidates for measured variables are those that we would like to predict such as `gross`, the total revenue, or the `imdb_score`. For instance, in this ordering, we can mix discrete and continuous variables. It might make more sense to place the column for the number of Facebook likes directly after the name of that actor. You can, of course, come up with your own guidelines for column order as the computational parts are unaffected by it.

Quite often, you will be pulling data directly from a relational database. A very common practice for relational databases is to have the primary key (if it exists) as the first column and any foreign keys directly following it.

Primary keys uniquely identify rows in the current table. Foreign keys uniquely identify rows in other tables.

See also

- Hadley Wickham's paper on *Tidy Data* (http://bit.ly/2v1hvH5)

Operating on the entire DataFrame

In the *Calling Series methods* recipe in Chapter 1, *Pandas Foundations*, a variety of methods operated on a single column or Series of data. When these same methods are called from a DataFrame, they perform that operation for each column at once.

Getting ready

In this recipe, we explore a variety of the most common DataFrame attributes and methods with the movie dataset.

How to do it...

1. Read in the movie dataset, and grab the basic descriptive attributes, shape, size, and ndim, along with running the len function:

```
>>> movie = pd.read_csv('data/movie.csv')
>>> movie.shape
(4916, 28)

>>> movie.size
137648

>>> movie.ndim
2

>>> len(movie)
4916
```

2. Use the count method to find the number of non-missing values for each column. The output is a Series that now has the old column names as its index:

```
>>> movie.count()
color                    4897
director_name            4814
```

```
num_critic_for_reviews     4867
duration                   4901
                           ...
actor_2_facebook_likes     4903
imdb_score                 4916
aspect_ratio               4590
movie_facebook_likes       4916
Length: 28, dtype: int64
```

3. The other methods that compute summary statistics such as `min`, `max`, `mean`, `median`, and `std` all return similar Series, with column names in the index and their computational result as the values:

```
>>> movie.min()
num_critic_for_reviews     1.00
duration                   7.00
director_facebook_likes    0.00
actor_3_facebook_likes     0.00
                           ...
actor_2_facebook_likes     0.00
imdb_score                 1.60
aspect_ratio               1.18
movie_facebook_likes       0.00
Length: 16, dtype: float64
```

4. The `describe` method is very powerful and calculates all the descriptive statistics and quartiles in the preceding steps all at once. The end result is a DataFrame with the descriptive statistics as its index:

```
>>> movie.describe()
```

	num_critic_for_reviews	duration	director_facebook_likes	actor_3_facebook_likes	actor_1_facebook_likes	gross
count	4867.000000	4901.000000	4814.000000	4893.000000	4909.000000	4.054000e+03
mean	137.988905	107.090798	691.014541	631.276313	6494.488491	4.764451e+07
std	120.239379	25.286015	2832.954125	1625.874802	15106.986884	6.737255e+07
min	1.000000	7.000000	0.000000	0.000000	0.000000	1.620000e+02
25%	49.000000	93.000000	7.000000	132.000000	607.000000	5.019656e+06
50%	108.000000	103.000000	48.000000	366.000000	982.000000	2.504396e+07
75%	191.000000	118.000000	189.750000	633.000000	11000.000000	6.110841e+07
max	813.000000	511.000000	23000.000000	23000.000000	640000.000000	7.605058e+08

5. It is possible to specify exact quantiles in the `describe` method using the `percentiles` parameter:

```
>>> movie.describe(percentiles=[.01, .3, .99])
```

	num_critic_for_reviews	duration	director_facebook_likes	actor_3_facebook_likes	actor_1_facebook_likes	gross
count	4867.000000	4901.000000	4814.000000	4893.000000	4909.000000	4.054000e+03
mean	137.988905	107.090798	691.014541	631.276313	6494.488491	4.764451e+07
std	120.239379	25.286015	2832.954125	1625.874802	15106.986884	6.737255e+07
min	1.000000	7.000000	0.000000	0.000000	0.000000	1.620000e+02
1%	2.000000	43.000000	0.000000	0.000000	6.080000	8.474800e+03
30%	60.000000	95.000000	11.000000	176.000000	694.000000	7.914069e+06
50%	108.000000	103.000000	48.000000	366.000000	982.000000	2.504396e+07
99%	546.680000	189.000000	16000.000000	11000.000000	44920.000000	3.264128e+08
max	813.000000	511.000000	23000.000000	23000.000000	640000.000000	7.605058e+08

How it works...

Step 1 gives basic information on the size of the dataset. The `shape` attribute returns a two-element tuple of the number of rows and columns. The `size` attribute returns the total number of elements in the DataFrame, which is just the product of the number of rows and columns. The `ndim` attribute returns the number of dimensions, which is two for all DataFrames. Pandas defines the built-in `len` function to return the number of rows.

The methods in step 2 and step 3 aggregate each column down to a single number. Each column name is now the index label in a Series with its aggregated result as the corresponding value.

If you look closely, you will notice that the output from step 3 is missing all the object columns from step 2. The reason for this is that there are missing values in the object columns and pandas does not know how to compare a string value with a missing value. It silently drops all of the columns for which it is unable to compute a minimum.

In this context, silently means that no error was raised and no warning thrown. This is a bit dangerous and requires users to have a good familiarity with pandas.

The numeric columns have missing values as well but have a result returned. By default, pandas handles missing values in numeric columns by skipping them. It is possible to change this behavior by setting the `skipna` parameter to `False`. This will cause pandas to return NaN for all these aggregation methods if there exists at least a single missing value.

The describe method displays the main summarizations all at once and can expand its summary to include more quantiles by passing a list of numbers between 0 and 1 to the percentiles parameter. It defaults to showing information on just the numeric columns. See the *Developing a data analysis routine* recipe for more on the describe method.

There's more...

To see how the skipna parameter affects the outcome, we can set its value to False and rerun step 3 from the preceding recipe. Only numeric columns without missing values will calculate a result:

```
>>> movie.min(skipna=False)
num_critic_for_reviews      NaN
duration                    NaN
director_facebook_likes     NaN
actor_3_facebook_likes      NaN
                            ...
actor_2_facebook_likes      NaN
imdb_score                  1.6
aspect_ratio                NaN
movie_facebook_likes        0.0
Length: 16, dtype: float64
```

Chaining DataFrame methods together

Whether you believe method chaining is a good practice or not, it is quite common to encounter it during data analysis with pandas. The *Chaining Series methods together* recipe in Chapter 1, *Pandas Foundations*, showcased several examples of chaining Series methods together. All the method chains in this chapter will begin from a DataFrame. One of the keys to method chaining is to know the exact object being returned during each step of the chain. In pandas, this will nearly always be a DataFrame, Series, or scalar value.

Getting ready

In this recipe, we count all the missing values in each column of the move dataset.

How to do it...

1. To get a count of the missing values, the `isnull` method must first be called to change each DataFrame value to a boolean. Let's call this method on the movie dataset:

```
>>> movie = pd.read_csv('data/movie.csv')
>>> movie.isnull().head()
```

	color	director_name	num_critic_for_reviews	duration	director_facebook_likes	actor_3_facebook_likes	actor_2_name	actor_1_facebook_likes	gross	genres
0	False	False	False	False	False	False	False	False	False	False
1	False	False	False	False	False	False	False	False	False	False
2	False	False	False	False	False	False	False	False	False	False
3	False	False	False	False	False	False	False	False	False	False
4	True	False	True	True	False	True	False	False	True	False

2. We will chain the `sum` method that interprets `True`/`False` booleans as 1/0. Notice that a Series is returned:

```
>>> movie.isnull().sum().head()
color                       19
director_name              102
num_critic_for_reviews      49
duration                    15
director_facebook_likes    102
dtype: int64
```

3. We can go one step further and take the sum of this Series and return the count of the total number of missing values in the entire DataFrame as a scalar value:

```
>>> movie.isnull().sum().sum()
2654
```

4. A slight deviation is to determine whether there are any missing values in the DataFrame. We use the `any` method here twice in succession to do this:

```
>>> movie.isnull().any().any()
True
```

How it works...

The `isnull` method returns a DataFrame the same size as the calling DataFrame but with all values transformed to booleans. See the counts of the following data types to verify this:

```
>>> movie.isnull().get_dtype_counts()
bool    28
dtype: int64
```

As booleans evaluate numerically as 0/1, it is possible to sum them by column, as done in step 2. The resulting Series itself also has a `sum` method, which gets us the grand total of missing values in the DataFrame.

In step 4, the `any` DataFrame method returns a Series of booleans indicating if there exists at least one `True` for each column. The `any` method is chained again on this resulting Series of booleans to determine if any of the columns have missing values. If step 4 evaluates as `True`, then there is at least one missing value in the entire DataFrame.

There's more...

Most of the columns in the movie dataset with object data type contain missing values. By default, the aggregation methods, `min`, `max`, and `sum`, do not return anything, as seen in the following code snippet, which selects three object columns and attempts to find the maximum value of each one:

```
>>> movie[['color', 'movie_title', 'color']].max()
Series([], dtype: float64)
```

To force pandas to return something for each column, we must fill in the missing values. Here, we choose an empty string:

```
>>> movie.select_dtypes(['object']).fillna('').min()
color                                              Color
director_name                              Etienne Faure
actor_2_name                               Zubaida Sahar
genres                                           Western
actor_1_name                               Oscar Jaenada
```

```
movie_title                                              Æon Flux
actor_3_name                                        Oscar Jaenada
plot_keywords                                   zombie|zombie spoof
movie_imdb_link      http://www.imdb.com/title/tt5574490/?ref_=fn_t...
language                                                     Zulu
country                                              West Germany
content_rating                                                  X
dtype: object
```

For purposes of readability, method chains are often written as one method call per line with the backslash character at the end to escape new lines. This makes it easier to read and insert comments on what is returned at each step of the chain:

```
>>> # rewrite the above chain on multiple lines
>>> movie.select_dtypes(['object']) \
        .fillna('') \
        .min()
```

 It is atypical to aggregate a column of all strings, as the minimum and maximum values are not universally defined. Attempting to call methods that clearly have no string interpretation, such as finding the mean or variance, will not work.

See also

- Refer to the *Chaining Series methods together* recipe in Chapter 1, *Pandas Foundations*

Working with operators on a DataFrame

A primer on operators was given in the *Working with operators on a Series* recipe from Chapter 1, *Pandas Foundations*, which will be helpful here. The Python arithmetic and comparison operators work directly on DataFrames, as they do on Series.

Getting ready

When a DataFrame operates directly with one of the arithmetic or comparison operators, each value of each column gets the operation applied to it. Typically, when an operator is used with a DataFrame, the columns are either all numeric or all object (usually strings). If the DataFrame does not contain homogeneous data, then the operation is likely to fail. Let's see an example of this failure with the college dataset, which contains both numeric and object data types. Attempting to add 5 to each value of the DataFrame raises a TypeError as integers cannot be added to strings:

```
>>> college = pd.read_csv('data/college.csv')
>>> college + 5
TypeError: Could not operate 5 with block values must be str, not int
```

To successfully use an operator with a DataFrame, first select homogeneous data. For this recipe, we will select all the columns that begin with UGDS_. These columns represent the fraction of undergraduate students by race. To get started, we import the data and use the institution name as the label for our index, and then select the columns we desire with the filter method:

```
>>> college = pd.read_csv('data/college.csv', index_col='INSTNM')
>>> college_ugds_ = college.filter(like='UGDS_')
>>> college_ugds_.head()
```

INSTNM	UGDS_WHITE	UGDS_BLACK	UGDS_HISP	UGDS_ASIAN	UGDS_AIAN	UGDS_NHPI	UGDS_2MOR	UGDS_NRA	UGDS_UNKN
Alabama A & M University	0.0333	0.9353	0.0055	0.0019	0.0024	0.0019	0.0000	0.0059	0.0138
University of Alabama at Birmingham	0.5922	0.2600	0.0283	0.0518	0.0022	0.0007	0.0368	0.0179	0.0100
Amridge University	0.2990	0.4192	0.0069	0.0034	0.0000	0.0000	0.0000	0.0000	0.2715
University of Alabama in Huntsville	0.6988	0.1255	0.0382	0.0376	0.0143	0.0002	0.0172	0.0332	0.0350
Alabama State University	0.0158	0.9208	0.0121	0.0019	0.0010	0.0006	0.0098	0.0243	0.0137

This recipe uses multiple operators with a DataFrame to round the undergraduate columns to the nearest hundredth. We will then see how this result is equivalent to the round method.

How to do it...

1. To begin our rounding adventure with operators, we will first add `.00501` to each value of `college_ugds_`:

```
>>> college_ugds_ + .00501
```

INSTNM	UGDS_WHITE	UGDS_BLACK	UGDS_HISP	UGDS_ASIAN	UGDS_AIAN	UGDS_NHPI	UGDS_2MOR	UGDS_NRA	UGDS_UNKN
Alabama A & M University	0.03831	0.94031	0.01051	0.00691	0.00741	0.00691	0.00501	0.01091	0.01881
University of Alabama at Birmingham	0.59721	0.26501	0.03331	0.05681	0.00721	0.00571	0.04181	0.02291	0.01501
Amridge University	0.30401	0.42421	0.01191	0.00841	0.00501	0.00501	0.00501	0.00501	0.27651
University of Alabama in Huntsville	0.70381	0.13051	0.04321	0.04261	0.01931	0.00521	0.02221	0.03821	0.04001
Alabama State University	0.02081	0.92581	0.01711	0.00691	0.00601	0.00561	0.01481	0.02931	0.01871

2. Use the floor division operator, `//`, to round to the nearest whole number percentage:

```
>>> (college_ugds_ + .00501) // .01
```

INSTNM	UGDS_WHITE	UGDS_BLACK	UGDS_HISP	UGDS_ASIAN	UGDS_AIAN	UGDS_NHPI	UGDS_2MOR	UGDS_NRA	UGDS_UNKN
Alabama A & M University	3.0	94.0	1.0	0.0	0.0	0.0	0.0	1.0	1.0
University of Alabama at Birmingham	59.0	26.0	3.0	5.0	0.0	0.0	4.0	2.0	1.0
Amridge University	30.0	42.0	1.0	0.0	0.0	0.0	0.0	0.0	27.0
University of Alabama in Huntsville	70.0	13.0	4.0	4.0	1.0	0.0	2.0	3.0	4.0
Alabama State University	2.0	92.0	1.0	0.0	0.0	0.0	1.0	2.0	1.0

3. To complete the rounding exercise, divide by 100:

```
>>> college_ugds_op_round = (college_ugds_ + .00501) // .01 / 100
>>> college_ugds_op_round.head()
```

INSTNM	UGDS_WHITE	UGDS_BLACK	UGDS_HISP	UGDS_ASIAN	UGDS_AIAN	UGDS_NHPI	UGDS_2MOR	UGDS_NRA	UGDS_UNKN
Alabama A & M University	0.03	0.94	0.01	0.00	0.00	0.0	0.00	0.01	0.01
University of Alabama at Birmingham	0.59	0.26	0.03	0.05	0.00	0.0	0.04	0.02	0.01
Amridge University	0.30	0.42	0.01	0.00	0.00	0.0	0.00	0.00	0.27
University of Alabama in Huntsville	0.70	0.13	0.04	0.04	0.01	0.0	0.02	0.03	0.04
Alabama State University	0.02	0.92	0.01	0.00	0.00	0.0	0.01	0.02	0.01

4. Now use the `round` DataFrame method to do the rounding automatically for us. NumPy rounds numbers that are exactly halfway between either side to the even side. Due to this, we add a small fraction before rounding:

```
>>> college_ugds_round = (college_ugds_ + .00001).round(2)
```

5. Use the `equals` DataFrame method to test the equality of two DataFrames:

```
>>> college_ugds_op_round.equals(college_ugds_round)
True
```

How it works...

Step 1 uses the plus operator, which attempts to add a scalar value to each value of each column of the DataFrame. As the columns are all numeric, this operation works as expected. There are some missing values in each of the columns but they stay missing after the operation.

Mathematically, adding `.005` should be enough so that the floor division in the next step correctly rounds to the nearest whole percentage. The trouble appears because of the inexactness of floating point numbers:

```
>>> .045 + .005
0.049999999999999996
```

There is an extra `.00001` added to each number to ensure that the floating point representation has the first four digits the same as the actual value. This works because the maximum precision of all the points in the dataset is four decimal places.

Step 2 applies the floor division operator, //, to all the values in the DataFrame. As we are dividing by a fraction, in essence, it is multiplying each value by 100 and truncating any decimals. Parentheses are needed around the first part of the expression, as floor division has higher precedence than addition. Step 3 uses the division operator to return the decimal to the correct position.

In step 4, we reproduce the previous steps with the round method. Before we can do this, we must again add an extra .00001 to each DataFrame value for a different reason from step 1. NumPy and Python 3 round numbers that are exactly halfway between either side to the even number. This *ties to the even* (http://bit.ly/2x3V5TU) technique is not usually what is formally taught in schools. It does not consistently bias numbers to the higher side (http://bit.ly/2zhsPy8).

It is necessary here to round up so that both DataFrame values are equal. The equals method determines if all the elements and indexes between two DataFrames are exactly the same and returns a boolean.

There's more...

Just as with Series, DataFrames have method equivalents of the operators. You may replace the operators with their method equivalents:

```
>>> college_ugds_op_round_methods = college_ugds .add(.00501) \
                                                  .floordiv(.01) \
                                                  .div(100)
>>> college_ugds_op_round_methods.equals(college_ugds_op_round)
True
```

See also

- What every computer scientist should know about floating-point arithmetic (http://bit.ly/2vmYZKi)

Comparing missing values

Pandas uses the NumPy NaN (np.nan) object to represent a missing value. This is an unusual object, as it is not equal to itself. Even Python's None object evaluates as True when compared to itself:

```
>>> np.nan == np.nan
False
>>> None == None
True
```

All other comparisons against np.nan also return False, except not equal to:

```
>>> np.nan > 5
False
>>> 5 > np.nan
False
>>> np.nan != 5
True
```

Getting ready

Series and DataFrames use the equals operator, ==, to make element-by-element comparisons that return an object of the same size. This recipe shows you how to use the equals operator, which is very different from the equals method.

As in the previous recipe, the columns representing the fraction of each race of undergraduate students from the college dataset will be used:

```
>>> college = pd.read_csv('data/college.csv', index_col='INSTNM')
>>> college_ugds_ = college.filter(like='UGDS_')
```

How to do it...

1. To get an idea of how the equals operator works, let's compare each element to a scalar value:

```
>>> college_ugds_ == .0019
```

	UGDS_WHITE	UGDS_BLACK	UGDS_HISP	UGDS_ASIAN	UGDS_AIAN	UGDS_NHPI	UGDS_2MOR	UGDS_NRA	UGDS_UNKN
INSTNM									
Alabama A & M University	False	False	False	True	False	True	False	False	False
University of Alabama at Birmingham	False	False	False	False	False	False	False	False	False
Amridge University	False	False	False	False	False	False	False	False	False
University of Alabama in Huntsville	False	False	False	False	False	False	False	False	False
Alabama State University	False	False	False	True	False	False	False	False	False

2. This works as expected but becomes problematic whenever you attempt to compare DataFrames with missing values. This same equals operator may be used to compare two DataFrames with one another on an element-by-element basis. Take, for instance, college_ugds_ compared against itself, as follows:

```
>>> college_self_compare = college_ugds_ == college_ugds_
>>> college_self_compare.head()
```

	UGDS_WHITE	UGDS_BLACK	UGDS_HISP	UGDS_ASIAN	UGDS_AIAN	UGDS_NHPI	UGDS_2MOR	UGDS_NRA	UGDS_UNKN
INSTNM									
Alabama A & M University	True	True	True	True	True	True	True	True	True
University of Alabama at Birmingham	True	True	True	True	True	True	True	True	True
Amridge University	True	True	True	True	True	True	True	True	True
University of Alabama in Huntsville	True	True	True	True	True	True	True	True	True
Alabama State University	True	True	True	True	True	True	True	True	True

3. At first glance, all the values appear to be equal, as you would expect. However, using the `all` method to determine if each column contains only `True` values yields an unexpected result:

```
>>> college_self_compare.all()
UGDS_WHITE      False
UGDS_BLACK      False
UGDS_HISP       False
UGDS_ASIAN      False
UGDS_AIAN       False
UGDS_NHPI       False
UGDS_2MOR       False
UGDS_NRA        False
UGDS_UNKN       False
dtype: bool
```

4. This happens because missing values do not compare equally with one another. If you tried to count missing values using the equal operator and summing up the boolean columns, you would get zero for each one:

```
>>> (college_ugds_ == np.nan).sum()
UGDS_WHITE      0
UGDS_BLACK      0
UGDS_HISP       0
UGDS_ASIAN      0
UGDS_AIAN       0
UGDS_NHPI       0
UGDS_2MOR       0
UGDS_NRA        0
UGDS_UNKN       0
dtype: int64
```

5. The primary way to count missing values uses the `isnull` method:

```
>>> college_ugds_.isnull().sum()
UGDS_WHITE      661
UGDS_BLACK      661
UGDS_HISP       661
UGDS_ASIAN      661
UGDS_AIAN       661
UGDS_NHPI       661
UGDS_2MOR       661
UGDS_NRA        661
UGDS_UNKN       661
dtype: int64
```

6. The correct way to compare two entire DataFrames with one another is not with the equals operator but with the `equals` method:

```
>>> college_ugds_.equals(college_ugds_)
True
```

How it works...

Step 1 compares a DataFrame to a scalar value while step 2 compares a DataFrame with another DataFrame. Both operations appear to be quite simple and intuitive at first glance. The second operation is actually checking whether the DataFrames are identically labeled indexes and thus the same number of elements. The operation will fail if this isn't the case. See the *Producing Cartesian products* recipe from Chapter 6, *Index Alignment*, for more information.

Step 3 verifies that none of the columns in the DataFrames are equivalent to each other. Step 4 further shows the non-equivalence of `np.nan` and itself. Step 5 verifies that there are indeed missing values in the DataFrame. Finally, step 6 shows the correct way to compare DataFrames with `equals` method, which always returns a boolean scalar value.

There's more...

All the comparison operators have method counterparts that allow for more functionality. Somewhat confusingly, the `eq` DataFrame method does element-by-element comparison, just like the equals operator. The `eq` method is not at all the same as the `equals` method. It merely does a similar task as the equals operator. The following code duplicates step 1:

```
>>> college_ugds_.eq(.0019)     # same as college_ugds_ == .0019
```

Inside the `pandas.testing` sub-package, a function exists that developers must use when creating unit tests. The `assert_frame_equal` function raises an `AssertionError` if two DataFrames are not equal. It returns `None` if the two passed frames are equal:

```
>>> from pandas.testing import assert_frame_equal
>>> assert_frame_equal(college_ugds_, college_ugds_)
```

Unit tests are a very important part of software development and ensure that the code is running correctly. Pandas contains many thousands of unit tests that help ensure that it is running properly. To read more on how pandas runs its unit tests, see the *Contributing to pandas* section in the documentation (http://bit.ly/2vmCSU6).

Transposing the direction of a DataFrame operation

Many DataFrame methods have an `axis` parameter. This important parameter controls the direction in which the operation takes place. Axis parameters can only be one of two values, either 0 or 1, and are aliased respectively as the strings *index* and *columns*.

Getting ready

Nearly all DataFrame methods default the `axis` parameter to 0/index. This recipe shows you how to invoke the same method, but with the direction of its operation transposed. To simplify the exercise, only the columns that reference the percentage race of each school from the college dataset will be used.

How to do it...

1. Read in the college dataset; the columns that begin with UGDS_ represent the percentage of the undergraduate students of a particular race. Use the `filter` method to select these columns:

```
>>> college = pd.read_csv('data/college.csv', index_col='INSTNM')
>>> college_ugds_ = college.filter(like='UGDS_')
>>> college_ugds_.head()
```

INSTNM	UGDS_WHITE	UGDS_BLACK	UGDS_HISP	UGDS_ASIAN	UGDS_AIAN	UGDS_NHPI	UGDS_2MOR	UGDS_NRA	UGDS_UNKN
Alabama A & M University	0.0333	0.9353	0.0055	0.0019	0.0024	0.0019	0.0000	0.0059	0.0138
University of Alabama at Birmingham	0.5922	0.2600	0.0283	0.0518	0.0022	0.0007	0.0368	0.0179	0.0100
Amridge University	0.2990	0.4192	0.0069	0.0034	0.0000	0.0000	0.0000	0.0000	0.2715
University of Alabama in Huntsville	0.6988	0.1255	0.0382	0.0376	0.0143	0.0002	0.0172	0.0332	0.0350
Alabama State University	0.0158	0.9208	0.0121	0.0019	0.0010	0.0006	0.0098	0.0243	0.0137

2. Now that the DataFrame contains homogenous column data, operations can be sensibly done both vertically and horizontally. The count method returns the number of non-missing values. By default, its axis parameter is set to 0:

```
>>> college_ugds_.count()
UGDS_WHITE      6874
UGDS_BLACK      6874
UGDS_HISP       6874
UGDS_ASIAN      6874
UGDS_AIAN       6874
UGDS_NHPI       6874
UGDS_2MOR       6874
UGDS_NRA        6874
UGDS_UNKN       6874
```

As the axis parameter is almost always set to 0, it is not necessary to do the following, but for purposes of understanding, Step 2 is equivalent to both college_ugds_.count(axis=0) and college_ugds_.count(axis='index').

3. Changing the axis parameter to 1/columns transposes the operation so that each row of data has a count of its non-missing values:

```
>>> college_ugds_.count(axis='columns').head()
INSTNM
Alabama A & M University                9
University of Alabama at Birmingham     9
Amridge University                      9
University of Alabama in Huntsville     9
Alabama State University                9
```

4. Instead of counting non-missing values, we can sum all the values in each row. Each row of percentages should add up to 1. The `sum` method may be used to verify this:

```
>>> college_ugds_.sum(axis='columns').head()
INSTNM
Alabama A & M University                1.0000
University of Alabama at Birmingham     0.9999
Amridge University                      1.0000
University of Alabama in Huntsville      1.0000
Alabama State University                1.0000
```

5. To get an idea of the distribution of each column, the `median` method can be used:

```
>>> college_ugds_.median(axis='index')
UGDS_WHITE    0.55570
UGDS_BLACK    0.10005
UGDS_HISP     0.07140
UGDS_ASIAN    0.01290
UGDS_AIAN     0.00260
UGDS_NHPI     0.00000
UGDS_2MOR     0.01750
UGDS_NRA      0.00000
UGDS_UNKN     0.01430
```

How it works...

The direction of operation is one of the more confusing aspects of pandas, and threads abound on the internet to discuss its interpretation. Many novice pandas users have difficulty remembering the meaning of the `axis` parameter. Luckily, there are only two potential directions that an operation can complete in pandas. A simple brute force solution of trying both directions until achieving the desired result is one possibility. I remember the meaning of the `axis` parameter by thinking of 1 as looking like a column, and any operation with `axis=1` returns a new column of data (has the same number of items that a column does).

This is confirmed in step 3, where the result (without the `head` method) returns a new column of data and could be easily appended as a column to the DataFrame, if necessary. The other steps with `axis` equal to 1/index return a new row of data.

There's more...

The cumsum method with axis=1 accumulates the race percentages across each row. It gives a slightly different view of the data. For example, it is very easy to see the exact percentage of white, black, and Hispanic together for each school:

```
>> college_ugds_cumsum = college_ugds_.cumsum(axis=1)
>>> college_ugds_cumsum.head()
```

INSTNM	UGDS_WHITE	UGDS_BLACK	UGDS_HISP	UGDS_ASIAN	UGDS_AIAN	UGDS_NHPI	UGDS_2MOR	UGDS_NRA	UGDS_UNKN
Alabama A & M University	0.0333	0.9686	0.9741	0.9760	0.9784	0.9803	0.9803	0.9862	1.0000
University of Alabama at Birmingham	0.5922	0.8522	0.8805	0.9323	0.9345	0.9352	0.9720	0.9899	0.9999
Amridge University	0.2990	0.7182	0.7251	0.7285	0.7285	0.7285	0.7285	0.7285	1.0000
University of Alabama in Huntsville	0.6988	0.8243	0.8625	0.9001	0.9144	0.9146	0.9318	0.9650	1.0000
Alabama State University	0.0158	0.9366	0.9487	0.9506	0.9516	0.9522	0.9620	0.9863	1.0000

See also

- Pandas official documentation for cumsum (http://bit.ly/2v3B6EZ)

Determining college campus diversity

Many articles are written every year on the different aspects and impacts of diversity on college campuses. Various organizations have developed metrics attempting to measure diversity. US News is a leader in providing rankings for many different categories of colleges, with diversity being one of them. Their top 10 diverse colleges with Diversity Index are given as follows:

```
>> pd.read_csv('data/college_diversity.csv', index_col='School')
```

School	Diversity Index
Rutgers University--Newark Newark, NJ	0.76
Andrews University Berrien Springs, MI	0.74
Stanford University Stanford, CA	0.74
University of Houston Houston, TX	0.74
University of Nevada--Las Vegas Las Vegas, NV	0.74
University of San Francisco San Francisco, CA	0.74
San Francisco State University San Francisco, CA	0.73
University of Illinois--Chicago Chicago, IL	0.73
New Jersey Institute of Technology Newark, NJ	0.72
Texas Woman's University Denton, TX	0.72

Getting ready

Our college dataset classifies race into nine different categories. When trying to quantify something without an obvious definition, such as **diversity**, it helps to start with something very simple. In this recipe, our diversity metric will equal the count of the number of races having greater than 15% of the student population.

How to do it...

1. Read in the college dataset, and filter for just the undergraduate race columns:

```
>>> college = pd.read_csv('data/college.csv', index_col='INSTNM')
>>> college_ugds_ = college.filter(like='UGDS_')
```

2. Many of these colleges have missing values for all their race columns. We can count all the missing values for each row and sort the resulting Series from the highest to lowest. This will reveal the colleges that have missing values:

```
>>> college_ugds_.isnull()\
                 .sum(axis=1)\
                 .sort_values(ascending=False)\
                 .head()
INSTNM
Excel Learning Center-San Antonio South     9
Philadelphia College of Osteopathic Medicine  9
Assemblies of God Theological Seminary      9
Episcopal Divinity School                   9
Phillips Graduate Institute                 9
dtype: int64
```

3. Now that we have seen the colleges that are missing all their race columns, we can use the `dropna` method to drop all rows that have all nine race percentages missing. We can then count the remaining missing values:

```
>>> college_ugds_ = college_ugds_.dropna(how='all')
>>> college_ugds_.isnull().sum()
UGDS_WHITE    0
UGDS_BLACK    0
UGDS_HISP     0
UGDS_ASIAN    0
UGDS_AIAN     0
UGDS_NHPI     0
UGDS_2MOR     0
UGDS_NRA      0
UGDS_UNKN     0
dtype: int64
```

4. There are no missing values left in the dataset. We can now calculate our diversity metric. To get started, we will use the greater than or equal DataFrame method, `ge`, to convert each value to a boolean:

```
>>> college_ugds_.ge(.15)
```

INSTNM	UGDS_WHITE	UGDS_BLACK	UGDS_HISP	UGDS_ASIAN	UGDS_AIAN	UGDS_NHPI	UGDS_2MOR	UGDS_NRA	UGDS_UNKN
Alabama A & M University	False	True	False	False	False	False	False	False	False
University of Alabama at Birmingham	True	True	False	False	False	False	False	False	False
Amridge University	True	True	False	False	False	False	False	False	True
University of Alabama in Huntsville	True	False	False	False	False	False	False	False	False
Alabama State University	False	True	False	False	False	False	False	False	False

5. From here, we can use the `sum` method to count the `True` values for each college. Notice that a Series is returned:

```
>>> diversity_metric = college_ugds_.ge(.15).sum(axis='columns')
>>> diversity_metric.head()
INSTNM
Alabama A & M University                 1
University of Alabama at Birmingham      2
Amridge University                       3
University of Alabama in Huntsville       1
Alabama State University                 1
dtype: int64
```

6. To get an idea of the distribution, let's use the `value_counts` method on this Series:

```
>>> diversity_metric.value_counts()
1     3042
2     2884
3      876
4       63
0        7
5        2
dtype: int64
```

7. Amazingly, two schools have more than 15% in five different race categories. Let's sort the `diversity_metric` Series to find out which ones they are:

```
>>> diversity_metric.sort_values(ascending=False).head()
INSTNM
Regency Beauty Institute-Austin          5
Central Texas Beauty College-Temple      5
Sullivan and Cogliano Training Center    4
Ambria College of Nursing                4
Berkeley College-New York                4
dtype: int64
```

8. It seems a little suspicious that schools can be that diverse. Let's look at the raw percentages from these top two schools. The `.loc` indexer is used to specifically select based on the index label:

```
>>> college_ugds_.loc[['Regency Beauty Institute-Austin',
                        'Central Texas Beauty College-Temple']]
```

INSTNM	UGDS_WHITE	UGDS_BLACK	UGDS_HISP	UGDS_ASIAN	UGDS_AIAN	UGDS_NHPI	UGDS_2MOR	UGDS_NRA	UGDS_UNKN
Regency Beauty Institute-Austin	0.1867	0.2133	0.1600	0.0000	0.0	0.0	0.1733	0.0	0.2667
Central Texas Beauty College-Temple	0.1616	0.2323	0.2626	0.0202	0.0	0.0	0.1717	0.0	0.1515

9. It appears that several categories were aggregated into the unknown and two or more races column. Regardless of this, they both appear to be quite diverse. We can see how the top 10 US News schools fared with this basic diversity metric:

```
>>> us_news_top = ['Rutgers University-Newark',
                   'Andrews University',
                   'Stanford University',
                   'University of Houston',
                   'University of Nevada-Las Vegas']
```

```
>>> diversity_metric.loc[us_news_top]
INSTNM
Rutgers University-Newark         4
Andrews University                3
Stanford University               3
University of Houston             3
University of Nevada-Las Vegas    3
dtype: int64
```

How it works...

Step 2 counts and then displays the schools with the highest number of missing values. As there are nine columns in the DataFrame, the maximum number of missing values per school is nine. Many schools are missing values for each column. Step 3 removes rows that have all their values missing. The dropna method in step 3 has the how parameter, which is defaulted to the string any but may also be changed to all. When set to any, it drops rows that contain one or more missing values. When set to all, it only drops rows where all values are missing.

In this case, we conservatively drop rows that are missing all values. This is because it's possible that some missing values simply represent 0 percent. This did not happen to be the case here, as there were no missing values after the dropna was performed. If there were still missing values, we could have run the fillna(0) method to fill all the remaining values with 0.

Step 4 begins our diversity metric calculation using the greater than or equal to method, ge. This results in a DataFrame of all booleans, which is summed horizontally by setting axis='columns'.

The value_counts method is used in step 5 to produce a distribution of our diversity metric. It is quite rare for schools to have three races with 15% or more of the undergraduate student population. Step 7 and step 8 find two schools that are the most diverse based on our metric. Although they are diverse, it appears that many of the races are not fully accounted for and are defaulted into the unknown and two or more categories.

Step 9 selects the top five schools from the US News article. It then selects their diversity metric from our newly created Series. It turns out that these schools also score highly with our simple ranking system.

There's more...

Alternatively, we can find the schools that are least diverse by ordering them by their maximum race percentage:

```
>>> college_ugds .max(axis=1) .sort_values(ascending=False) .head(10)
INSTNM
Dewey University-Manati                        1.0
Yeshiva and Kollel Harbotzas Torah             1.0
Mr Leon's School of Hair Design-Lewiston       1.0
Dewey University-Bayamon                       1.0
Shepherds Theological Seminary                 1.0
```

```
Yeshiva Gedolah Kesser Torah                         1.0
Monteclaro Escuela de Hoteleria y Artes Culinarias   1.0
Yeshiva Shaar Hatorah                                1.0
Bais Medrash Elyon                                   1.0
Yeshiva of Nitra Rabbinical College                  1.0
dtype: float64
```

We can also determine if any school has all nine race categories exceeding 1%:

```
>>> (college_ugds_ > .01).all(axis=1).any()
True
```

See also

- US News Campus Ethnic Diversity 2015-2016 (http://bit.ly/2vmDhWC)

3
Beginning Data Analysis

In this chapter, we will cover the following topics:

- Developing a data analysis routine
- Reducing memory by changing data types
- Selecting the smallest of the largest
- Selecting the largest of each group by sorting
- Replicating `nlargest` with `sort_values`
- Calculating a trailing stop order price

Introduction

It is important to consider the steps that you, as an analyst, take when you first encounter a dataset after importing it into your workspace as a DataFrame. Is there a set of tasks that you usually undertake to first examine the data? Are you aware of all the possible data types? This chapter begins by covering the tasks you might want to undertake when first encountering a new dataseset. The chapter proceeds by answering common questions that are not that trivial to do in pandas.

Developing a data analysis routine

Although there is no standard approach when beginning a data analysis, it is typically a good idea to develop a routine for yourself when first examining a dataset. Similar to common routines that we have for waking up, showering, going to work, eating, and so on, a beginning data analysis routine helps one quickly get acquainted with a new dataset. This routine can manifest itself as a dynamic checklist of tasks that evolves as your familiarity with pandas and data analysis expands.

Exploratory Data Analysis (EDA) is a term used to encompass the entire process of analyzing data without the formal use of statistical testing procedures. Much of EDA involves visually displaying different relationships among the data to detect interesting patterns and develop hypotheses.

Getting ready

This recipe covers a small but fundamental part of EDA: the collection of **metadata** and **univariate descriptive statistics** in a routine and systematic way. It outlines a common set of tasks that can be undertaken when first importing any dataset as a pandas DataFrame. This recipe may help form the basis of the routine that you can implement when first examining a dataset.

Metadata describes the dataset, or more aptly, data about the data. Examples of metadata include the number of columns/rows, column names, data types of each column, the source of the dataset, the date of collection, the acceptable values for different columns, and so on. Univariate descriptive statistics are summary statistics about individual variables (columns) of the dataset, independent of all other variables.

How to do it...

First, some metadata on the `college` dataset will be collected, followed by basic summary statistics of each column:

1. Read in the dataset, and view the first five rows with the `head` method:

```
>>> college = pd.read_college('data/college.csv')
>>> college.head()
```

	INSTNM	CITY	STABBR	HBCU	MENONLY	WOMENONLY	RELAFFIL	SATVRMID	SATMTMID	DISTANCEONLY	...	UGDS_2MOR	UGDS_NRA
0	Alabama A & M University	Normal	AL	1.0	0.0	0.0	0	424.0	420.0	0.0	...	0.0000	0.0059
1	University of Alabama at Birmingham	Birmingham	AL	0.0	0.0	0.0	0	570.0	565.0	0.0	...	0.0368	0.0179
2	Amridge University	Montgomery	AL	0.0	0.0	0.0	1	NaN	NaN	1.0	...	0.0000	0.0000
3	University of Alabama in Huntsville	Huntsville	AL	0.0	0.0	0.0	0	595.0	590.0	0.0	...	0.0172	0.0332
4	Alabama State University	Montgomery	AL	1.0	0.0	0.0	0	425.0	430.0	0.0	...	0.0098	0.0243

2. Get the dimensions of the DataFrame with the `shape` attribute:

```
>>> college.shape
>>> (7535, 27)
```

3. List the data type of each column, number of non-missing values, and memory usage with the `info` method:

```
>>> college.info()
```

```
<class 'pandas.core.frame.DataFrame'>
RangeIndex: 7535 entries, 0 to 7534
Data columns (total 27 columns):
INSTNM                7535 non-null object
CITY                  7535 non-null object
STABBR                7535 non-null object
HBCU                  7164 non-null float64
...
PCTFLOAN              6849 non-null float64
UG25ABV               6718 non-null float64
MD_EARN_WNE_P10       6413 non-null object
GRAD_DEBT_MDN_SUPP    7503 non-null object
dtypes: float64(20), int64(2), object(5)
memory usage: 1.6+ MB
```

4. Get summary statistics for the numerical columns and transpose the DataFrame for more readable output:

```
>>> college.describe(include=[np.number]).T
```

	count	mean	std	min	25%	50%	75%	max
HBCU	7164.0	0.014238	0.118478	0.0	0.0000	0.00000	0.000000	1.0
MENONLY	7164.0	0.009213	0.095546	0.0	0.0000	0.00000	0.000000	1.0
WOMENONLY	7164.0	0.005304	0.072642	0.0	0.0000	0.00000	0.000000	1.0
RELAFFIL	7535.0	0.190975	0.393096	0.0	0.0000	0.00000	0.000000	1.0
...	...	...	...	...	...	...	...	...
CURROPER	7535.0	0.923291	0.266146	0.0	1.0000	1.00000	1.000000	1.0
PCTPELL	6849.0	0.530643	0.225544	0.0	0.3578	0.52150	0.712900	1.0
PCTFLOAN	6849.0	0.522211	0.283616	0.0	0.3329	0.58330	0.745000	1.0
UG25ABV	6718.0	0.410021	0.228939	0.0	0.2415	0.40075	0.572275	1.0

5. Get summary statistics for the object and categorical columns:

```
>>> college.describe(include=[np.object, pd.Categorical]).T
```

	count	unique	top	freq
INSTNM	7535	7535	University of Phoenix-Illinois	1
CITY	7535	2514	New York	87
STABBR	7535	59	CA	773
MD_EARN_WNE_P10	6413	598	PrivacySuppressed	822
GRAD_DEBT_MDN_SUPP	7503	2038	PrivacySuppressed	1510

How it works...

After importing your dataset, a common task is to print out the first few ro
DataFrame for manual inspection with the `head` method. The `shape` attrib
first piece of metadata, a tuple containing the number of rows and columns.

The primary method to get the most metadata at once is the `info` method. It provides each
column name, the number of non-missing values, the data type of each column, and the
approximate memory usage of the DataFrame. For all DataFrames, columns values are
always one data type. The same holds for relational databases. DataFrames, as a whole,
might be composed of columns with different data types.

> Internally, pandas stores columns of the same data type together in blocks.
> For a deeper dive into pandas internals, see Jeff Tratner's slides
> (http://bit.ly/2xHIv1g).

Step 4 and step 5 produce univariate descriptive statistics on different types of columns.
The powerful `describe` method produces different output based on the data types
provided to the `include` parameter. By default, `describe` outputs a summary for all the
numeric (mostly **continuous**) columns and silently drops any **categorical** columns. You
may use `np.number` or the string *number* to include both integers and floats in the
summary. Technically, the data types are part of a hierarchy where number resides above
integers and floats. Take a look at the following diagram to understand the NumPy data
type hierarchy better:

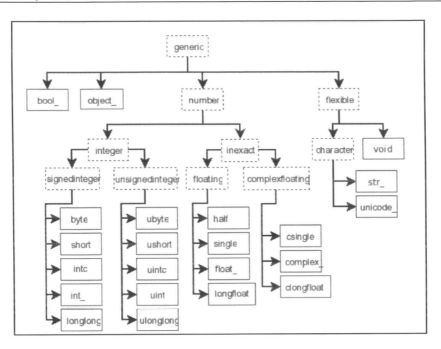

 Broadly speaking, we can classify data as being either continuous or categorical. Continuous data is always numeric and can usually take on an infinite number of possibilities such as height, weight, and salary. Categorical data represents discrete values that take on a finite number of possibilities such as ethnicity, employment status, and car color. Categorical data can be represented numerically or with characters.

Categorical columns are usually going to be either of type `np.object` or `pd.Categorical`. Step 5 ensures that both of these types are represented. In both step 4 and step 5, the output DataFrame is transposed with the `T` attribute. This eases readability for DataFrames with many columns.

There's more...

It is possible to specify the exact quantiles returned from the `describe` method when used with numeric columns:

```
>>> college.describe(include=[np.number],
                     percentiles=[.01, .05, .10, .25, .5,
                                  .75, .9, .95, .99]).T
```

	count	mean	std	min	1%	5%	10%	25%	50%	75%	90%	95%	99%	max
HBCU	7164.0	0.014238	0.118478	0.0	0.0000	0.0000	0.0000	0.0000	0.00000	0.000000	0.00000	0.00000	1.000000	1.0
MENONLY	7164.0	0.009216	0.095520	0.0	0.0000	0.0000	0.0000	0.0000	0.00000	0.000000	0.00000	0.00000	0.000000	1.0
...	...	...	...	...	...	...	...	...	...	...	...	...	...	...
PCTFLOAN	6849.0	0.522211	0.283616	0.0	0.0000	0.0000	0.0000	0.3329	0.58330	0.745000	0.84752	0.89792	0.986368	1.0
UG25ABV	6718.0	0.410021	0.228939	0.0	0.0025	0.0374	0.0899	0.2415	0.40075	0.572275	0.72666	0.80000	0.917383	1.0

Data dictionaries

A crucial part of a data analysis involves creating and maintaining a data dictionary. A data dictionary is a table of metadata and notes on each column of data. One of the primary purposes of a data dictionary is to explain the meaning of the column names. The college dataset uses a lot of abbreviations that are likely to be unfamiliar to an analyst who is inspecting it for the first time.

A data dictionary for the college dataset is provided in the following `college_data_dictionary.csv` file:

```
>>> pd.read_csv('data/collge_data_dictionaray.csv')
```

	column_name	description
0	INSTNM	Institution Name
1	CITY	City Location
2	STABBR	State Abbreviation
3	HBCU	Historically Black College or University
...	...	
23	PCTFLOAN	Percent Students with federal loan
24	UG25ABV	Percent Students Older than 25
25	MD_EARN_WNE_P10	Median Earnings 10 years after enrollment
26	GRAD_DEBT_MDN_SUPP	Median debt of completers

As you can see, it is immensely helpful in deciphering the abbreviated column names. DataFrames are actually not the best place to store data dictionaries. A platform such as Excel or Google Sheets with easy ability to edit values and append columns is a better choice. Minimally, a column to keep track of notes on the data should be included in a data dictionary. A data dictionary is one of the first things that you can share as an analyst to collaborators.

It will often be the case that the dataset you are working with originated from a database whose administrators you will have to contact in order to get more information. Formal electronic databases generally have more formal representations of their data, called **schemas**. If possible, attempt to investigate your dataset with people who have expert knowledge on its design.

See also

- NumPy data hierarchy documentation (http://bit.ly/2yqsg7p)

Reducing memory by changing data types

Pandas does not broadly classify data as either continuous or categorical but has precise technical definitions for many distinct data types.

Getting ready

This recipe changes the data type of one of the object columns from the college dataset to the special pandas Categorical data type to drastically reduce its memory usage.

How to do it...

1. After reading in our college dataset, we select a few columns of different data types that will clearly show how much memory may be saved:

```
>>> college = pd.read_csv('data/college.csv')
>>> different_cols = ['RELAFFIL', 'SATMTMID', 'CURROPER',
                      'INSTNM', 'STABBR']
>>> col2 = college.loc[:, different_cols]
>>> col2.head()
```

	RELAFFIL	SATMTMID	CURROPER	INSTNM	STABBR
0	0	420.0	1	Alabama A & M University	AL
1	0	565.0	1	University of Alabama at Birmingham	AL
2	1	NaN	1	Amridge University	AL
3	0	590.0	1	University of Alabama in Huntsville	AL
4	0	430.0	1	Alabama State University	AL

2. Inspect the data types of each column:

```
>>> col2.dtypes
RELAFFIL        int64
SATMTMID      float64
CURROPER        int64
INSTNM         object
STABBR         object
dtype: object
```

3. Find the memory usage of each column with the `memory_usage` method:

```
>>> original_mem = col2.memory_usage(deep=True)
>>> original_mem
Index            80
RELAFFIL      60280
SATMTMID      60280
CURROPER      60280
INSTNM       660240
STABBR       444565
dtype: int64
```

4. There is no need to use 64 bits for the RELAFFIL column as it contains only 0/1 values. Let's convert this column to an 8-bit (1 byte) integer with the `astype` method:

```
>>> col2['RELAFFIL'] = col2['RELAFFIL'].astype(np.int8)
```

5. Use the `dtypes` attribute to confirm the data type change:

```
>>> col2.dtypes
RELAFFIL          int8
SATMTMID       float64
CURROPER         int64
INSTNM          object
STABBR          object
dtype: object
```

6. Find the memory usage of each column again and note the large reduction:

```
>>> college[different_cols].memory_usage(deep=True)
Index             80
RELAFFIL        7535
SATMTMID       60280
CURROPER       60280
INSTNM        660240
STABBR        444565
```

7. To save even more memory, you will want to consider changing object data types to categorical if they have a reasonably low cardinality (number of unique values). Let's first check the number of unique values for both the object columns:

```
>>> col2.select_dtypes(include=['object']).nunique()
INSTNM     7535
STABBR       59
dtype: int64
```

8. The `STABBR` column is a good candidate to convert to Categorical as less than one percent of its values are unique:

```
>>> col2['STABBR'] = col2['STABBR'].astype('category')
>>> col2.dtypes
RELAFFIL          int8
SATMTMID       float64
CURROPER         int64
INSTNM          object
STABBR        category
dtype: object
```

9. Compute the memory usage again:

```
>>> new_mem = col2.memory_usage(deep=True)
>>> new_mem
Index             80
RELAFFIL        7535
SATMTMID       60280
CURROPER       60280
INSTNM        660699
STABBR         13576
dtype: int64
```

10. Finally, let's compare the original memory usage with our updated memory usage. The RELAFFIL column is, as expected, an eighth of its original, while the STABBR column has shrunk to just three percent of its original size:

```
>>> new_mem / original_mem
Index         1.000000
RELAFFIL      0.125000
SATMTMID      1.000000
CURROPER      1.000000
INSTNM        1.000695
STABBR        0.030538
dtype: float64
```

How it works...

Pandas defaults `integer` and `float` data types to 64 bits regardless of the maximum necessary size for the particular DataFrame. Integers, floats, and even booleans may be coerced to a different data type with the `astype` method and passing it the exact type, either as a string or specific object, as done in step 4.

The RELAFFIL column is a good choice to cast to a smaller integer type as the data dictionary explains that its values must be 0/1. The memory for RELAFFIL is now an eighth of CURROPER, which remains as its former type.

 The memory units displayed are in bytes and not bits. One byte is equivalent to 8 bits, so when RELAFFIL was changed to an 8-bit integer, it uses one 1 byte of memory and as there are 7,535 rows, its memory footprint is equivalent to 7,535 bytes.

Columns that are object data type, such as INSTNM, are not like the other pandas data types. For all the other pandas data types, each value in that column is the same data type. For instance, when a column has the int64 type, every individual column value is also int64. This is not true for columns that are object data type. Each individual column value can be of any type. Object data types can have a mix of strings, numerics, datetimes, or even other Python objects such as lists or tuples. For this reason, the object data type is sometimes referred to as a *catch-all* for a column of data that doesn't match any of the other data types. The vast majority of the time, though, object data type columns will all be strings.

 Relational database management systems such as Microsoft's SQL Server or PostgreSQL have specific data types for characters such as varchar, text, or nchar that also usually specify a maximum number of characters. Pandas object data type is a much broader data type. Every value in an object column can be of any data type.

Therefore, the memory of each individual value in an object data type column is inconsistent. There is no predefined amount of memory for each value like the other data types. For pandas to extract the exact amount of memory of an object data type column, the deep parameter must be set to True in the memory_usage method.

Object columns are targets for the largest memory savings. Pandas has an additional categorical data type that is not available in NumPy. When converting to category, pandas internally creates a mapping from integers to each unique string value. Thus, each string only needs to be kept a single time in memory. As you can see, this simple change of data type reduced memory usage by 97%.

You might also have noticed that the index uses an extremely low amount of memory. If no index is specified during DataFrame creation, as is the case in this recipe, pandas defaults the index to a RangeIndex. The RangeIndex is very similar to the built-in range function. It produces values on demand and only stores the minimum amount of information needed to create an index.

There's more...

To get a better idea of how object data type columns differ from integers and floats, a single value from each one of these columns can be modified and the resulting memory usage displayed. The CURROPER and INSTNM columns are of int64 and object types, respectively:

```
>>> college.loc[0, 'CURROPER'] = 10000000
>>> college.loc[0, 'INSTNM'] = college.loc[0, 'INSTNM'] + 'a'
>>> college[['CURROPER', 'INSTNM']].memory_usage(deep=True)
Index            80
CURROPER      60280
INSTNM       660345
```

Memory usage for CURROPER remained the same since a 64-bit integer is more than enough space for the larger number. On the other hand, the memory usage for INSTNM increased by 105 bytes by just adding a single letter to one value.

Python 3 uses Unicode, a standardized character representation intended to encode all the world's writing systems. Unicode uses up to 4 bytes per character. It seems that pandas has some overhead (100 bytes) when making the first modification to a character value. Afterward, increments of 5 bytes per character are sustained.

Not all columns can be coerced to the desired type. Take a look at the MENONLY column, which from the data dictionary appears to contain only 0/1 values. The actual data type of this column upon import unexpectedly turns out to be float64. The reason for this is that there happen to be missing values, denoted by np.nan. There is no integer representation for missing values. Any numeric column with even a single missing value must be a float. Furthermore, any column of an integer data type will automatically be coerced to a float if one of the values becomes missing:

```
>>> college['MENONLY'].dtype
dtype('float64')

>>> college['MENONLY'].astype(np.int8)
ValueError: Cannot convert non-finite values (NA or inf) to integer
```

Additionally, it is possible to substitute string names in place of Python objects when referring to data types. For instance, when using the `include` parameter in the `describe` DataFame method, it is possible to pass a list of either the formal object NumPy/pandas object or their equivalent string representation. These are available in the table at the beginning of the *Selecting columns with methods* recipe in Chapter 2, *Essential DataFrame Operations,*. For instance, each of the following produces the same result:

```
>>> college.describe(include=['int64', 'float64']).T
>>> college.describe(include=[np.int64, np.float64]).T
>>> college.describe(include=['int', 'float']).T
>>> college.describe(include=['number']).T
```

These strings can be similarly used when changing types:

```
>>> college['MENONLY'] = college['MENONLY'].astype('float16')
>>> college['RELAFFIL'] = college['RELAFFIL'].astype('int8')
```

 The equivalence of a string and the outright pandas or NumPy object occurs elsewhere in the pandas library and can be a source of confusion as there are two different ways to access the same thing.

Lastly, it is possible to see the enormous memory difference between the minimal `RangeIndex` and `Int64Index`, which stores every row index in memory:

```
>>> college.index = pd.Int64Index(college.index)
>>> college.index.memory_usage() # previously was just 80
60280
```

See also

- Pandas official documentation on data types (http://bit.ly/2vxe8ZI)

Selecting the smallest of the largest

This recipe can be used to create catchy news headlines such as *Out of the top 100 best universities, these 5 have the lowest tuition* or *From the top 50 cities to live, these 10 are the most affordable*. During an analysis, it is possible that you will first need to find a grouping of data that contains the top *n* values in a single column and, from this subset, find the bottom *m* values based on a different column.

Getting ready

In this recipe, we find the five lowest budget movies from the top 100 scoring movies by taking advantage of the convenience methods, `nlargest` and `nsmallest`.

How to do it...

1. Read in the movie dataset, and select the columns, `movie_title`, `imdb_score`, and `budget`:

```
>>> movie = pd.read_csv('data/movie.csv')
>>> movie2 = movie[['movie_title', 'imdb_score', 'budget']]
>>> movie2.head()
```

	movie_title	imdb_score	budget
0	Avatar	7.9	237000000.0
1	Pirates of the Caribbean: At World's End	7.1	300000000.0
2	Spectre	6.8	245000000.0
3	The Dark Knight Rises	8.5	250000000.0
4	Star Wars: Episode VII - The Force Awakens	7.1	NaN

the `nlargest` method to select the top 100 movies by `imdb_score`:

```
> movie2.nlargest(100, 'imdb_score').head()
```

	movie_title	imdb_score	budget
2725	Towering Inferno	9.5	NaN
1920	The Shawshank Redemption	9.3	25000000.0
3402	The Godfather	9.2	6000000.0
2779	Dekalog	9.1	NaN
4312	Kickboxer: Vengeance	9.1	17000000.0

3. Chain the `nsmallest` method to return the five lowest budget films among those with a top 100 score:

```
>>> movie2.nlargest(100, 'imdb_score').nsmallest(5, 'budget')
```

	movie_title	imdb_score	budget
4804	Butterfly Girl	8.7	180000.0
4801	Children of Heaven	8.5	180000.0
4706	12 Angry Men	8.9	350000.0
4550	A Separation	8.4	500000.0
4636	The Other Dream Team	8.4	500000.0

How it works...

The first parameter of the `nlargest` method, n, must be an integer and selects the number of rows to be returned. The second parameter, `columns`, takes a column name as a string. Step 2 returns the 100 highest scoring movies. We could have saved this intermediate result as its own variable but instead, we chain the `nsmallest` method to it in step 3, which returns exactly five rows, sorted by budget.

There's more...

It is possible to pass a list of column names to the `columns` parameter of the `nlargest`/`nsmallest` methods. This would only be useful to break ties in the event that there were duplicate values sharing the nth ranked spot in the first column in the list.

Selecting the largest of each group by sorting

One of the most basic and common operations to perform during a data analysis is to select rows containing the largest value of some column within a group. For instance, this would be like finding the highest rated film of each year or the highest grossing film by content rating. To accomplish this task, we need to sort the groups as well as the column used to rank each member of the group, and then extract the highest member of each group.

Getting ready

In this recipe, we will find the highest rated film of each year.

How to do it...

1. Read in the movie dataset and slim it down to just the three columns we care about, `movie_title`, `title_year`, and `imdb_score`:

   ```
   >>> movie = pd.read_csv('data/movie.csv')
   >>> movie2 = movie[['movie_title', 'title_year', 'imdb_score']]
   ```

2. Use the `sort_values` method to sort the DataFrame by `title_year`. The default behavior sorts from the smallest to largest. Use the `ascending` parameter to invert this behavior by setting it equal to `True`:

   ```
   >>> movie2.sort_values('title_year', ascending=False).head()
   ```

	movie_title	title_year	imdb_score
2366	Fight Valley	2016.0	5.0
3817	Yoga Hosers	2016.0	4.8
1367	The 5th Wave	2016.0	5.2
1742	The Boss	2016.0	5.3
519	The Secret Life of Pets	2016.0	6.8

3. Notice how only the year was sorted. To sort multiple columns at once, use a list. Let's look at how to sort both year and score:

```
>>> movie3 = movie2.sort_values(['title_year','imdb_score'],
                                ascending=False)
>>> movie3.head()
```

	movie_title	title_year	imdb_score
4409	Kickboxer: Vengeance	2016.0	9.1
4372	A Beginner's Guide to Snuff	2016.0	8.7
3870	Airlift	2016.0	8.5
27	Captain America: Civil War	2016.0	8.2
98	Godzilla Resurgence	2016.0	8.2

4. Now, we use the drop_duplicates method to keep only the first row of every year:

```
>>> movie_top_year = movie3.drop_duplicates(subset='title_year')
>>> movie_top_year.head()
```

	movie_title	title_year	imdb_score
4409	Kickboxer: Vengeance	2016.0	9.1
3816	Running Forever	2015.0	8.6
4468	Queen of the Mountains	2014.0	8.7
4017	Batman: The Dark Knight Returns, Part 2	2013.0	8.4
3	The Dark Knight Rises	2012.0	8.5

How it works...

In step 1, we slim the dataset down to concentrate on only the columns of importance. This recipe would work the same with the entire DataFrame. Step 2 shows how to sort a DataFrame by a single column, which is not exactly what we wanted. Step 3 sorts multiple columns at the same time. It works by first sorting all of title_year and then, within each distinct value of title_year, sorts by imdb_score.

The default behavior of the drop_duplicates method is to keep the first occurrence of each unique row, which would not drop any rows as each row is unique. However, the subset parameter alters it to only consider the column (or list of columns) given to it. In this example, only one row for each year will be returned. As we sorted by year and score in the last step, the highest scoring movie for each year is what we get.

There's more...

It is possible to sort one column in ascending order while simultaneously sorting another column in descending order. To accomplish this, pass in a list of booleans to the ascending parameter that corresponds to how you would like each column sorted. The following sorts title_year and content_rating in descending order and budget in ascending order. It then finds the lowest budget film for each year and content rating group:

```
>>> movie4 = movie[['movie_title', 'title_year',
                    'content_rating', 'budget']]
>>> movie4_sorted = movie4.sort_values(['title_year',
                                'content_rating', 'budget'],
                            ascending=[False, False, True])
>>> movie4_sorted.drop_duplicates(subset=['title_year',
                                'content_rating']).head(10)
```

	movie_title	title_year	content_rating	budget
4108	Compadres	2016.0	R	3000000.0
4772	Fight to the Finish	2016.0	PG-13	150000.0
4775	Rodeo Girl	2016.0	PG	500000.0
3309	The Wailing	2016.0	Not Rated	NaN
4773	Alleluia! The Devil's Carnival	2016.0	NaN	500000.0
4848	Bizarre	2015.0	Unrated	500000.0
821	The Ridiculous 6	2015.0	TV-14	NaN
4956	The Gallows	2015.0	R	100000.0
4948	Romantic Schemer	2015.0	PG-13	125000.0
3868	R.L. Stine's Monsterville: The Cabinet of Souls	2015.0	PG	4400000.0

By default, `drop_duplicates` keeps the very first appearance, but this behavior may be modified by passing the `keep` parameter *last* to select the last row of each group or `False` to drop all duplicates entirely.

Replicating nlargest with sort_values

The previous two recipes work similarly by sorting values in slightly different manners. Finding the top n values of a column of data is equivalent to sorting the entire column descending and taking the first n values. Pandas has many operations that are capable of doing this in a variety of ways.

Getting ready

In this recipe, we will replicate the *Selecting the smallest from the largest* recipe with the `sort_values` method and explore the differences between the two.

How to do it...

1. Let's recreate the result from the final step of the *Selecting the smallest from the largest* recipe:

```
>>> movie = pd.read_csv('data/movie.csv')
>>> movie2 = movie[['movie_title', 'imdb_score', 'budget']]
>>> movie_smallest_largest = movie2.nlargest(100, 'imdb_score') \
                                   .nsmallest(5, 'budget')
>>> movie_smallest_largest
```

	movie_title	imdb_score	budget
4804	Butterfly Girl	8.7	180000.0
4801	Children of Heaven	8.5	180000.0
4706	12 Angry Men	8.9	350000.0
4550	A Separation	8.4	500000.0
4636	The Other Dream Team	8.4	500000.0

2. Use `sort_values` to replicate the first part of the expression and grab the first 100 rows with the `head` method:

```
>>> movie2.sort_values('imdb_score', ascending=False).head(100)
```

3. Now that we have the top 100 scoring movies, we can use `sort_values` with `head` again to grab the lowest five by `budget`:

```
>>> movie2.sort_values('imdb_score', ascending=False).head(100) \
          .sort_values('budget').head()
```

	movie_title	imdb_score	budget
4815	A Charlie Brown Christmas	8.4	150000.0
4801	Children of Heaven	8.5	180000.0
4804	Butterfly Girl	8.7	180000.0
4706	12 Angry Men	8.9	350000.0
4636	The Other Dream Team	8.4	500000.0

How it works...

The `sort_values` method can nearly replicate `nlargest` by chaining the `head` method after the operation, as seen in step 2. Step 3 replicates `nsmallest` by chaining another `sort_values` and completes the query by taking just the first five rows with the `head` method.

Take a look at the output from the first DataFrame from step 1 and compare it with the output from step 3. Are they the same? No! What happened? To understand why the two results are not equivalent, let's look at the tail of the intermediate steps of each recipe:

```
>>> movie2.nlargest(100, 'imdb_score').tail()
```

	movie_title	imdb_score	budget
4815	A Charlie Brown Christmas	8.4	150000.0
4801	Children of Heaven	8.5	180000.0
4804	Butterfly Girl	8.7	180000.0
4706	12 Angry Men	8.9	350000.0
4636	The Other Dream Team	8.4	500000.0

```
>>> movie2.sort_values('imdb_score', ascending=False) \
        .head(100).tail()
```

	movie_title	imdb_score	budget
3799	Anne of Green Gables	8.4	NaN
3777	Requiem for a Dream	8.4	4500000.0
3935	Batman: The Dark Knight Returns, Part 2	8.4	3500000.0
4636	The Other Dream Team	8.4	500000.0
2455	Aliens	8.4	18500000.0

The issue arises because more than 100 movies exist with a rating of at least 8.4. Each of the methods, nlargest and sort_values, breaks ties differently, which results in a slightly different 100-row DataFrame.

There's more...

If you look at the nlargest documentation, you will see that the keep parameter has three possible values, first, last, and False. From my knowledge of other pandas methods, keep=False should allow all ties to remain part of the result. Unfortunately, pandas raises an error when attempting to do this. I created an issue with pandas development team on GitHub to make this enhancement (http://bit.ly/2fGrCMa).

Calculating a trailing stop order price

There is essentially an infinite number of strategies to trade stocks. One basic type of trade that many investors employ is the stop order. A stop order is an order placed by an investor to buy or sell a stock that executes whenever the market price reaches a certain point. Stop orders are useful to both prevent huge losses and protect gains.

For the purposes of this recipe, we will only be examining stop orders used to sell currently owned stocks. In a typical stop order, the price does not change throughout the lifetime of the order. For instance, if you purchased a stock for $100 per share, you might want to set a stop order at $90 per share to limit your downside to 10%.

A more advanced strategy would be to continually modify the sale price of the stop order to track the value of the stock if it increases in value. This is called a **trailing stop order**. Concretely, if the same $100 stock increases to $120, then a trailing stop order 10% below the current market value would move the sale price to $108.

The trailing stop order never moves down and is always tied to the maximum value since the time of purchase. If the stock fell from $120 to $110, the stop order would still remain at $108. It would only increase if the price moved above $120.

Getting ready

This recipe requires the use of the third party package pandas-datareader which fetches stock market prices online. It does not come pre-installed with the Anaconda distribution. To install this package simply visit the command line and run `conda install pandas-datareader`. If you don't have Anaconda, you can install it by running `pip install pandas-datareader`. This recipe determines the trailing stop order price given an initial purchase price for any stock.

How to do it...

1. To get started, we will work with Tesla Motors (TSLA) stock and presume a purchase on the first trading day of 2017:

```
>>> import pandas_datareader as pdr
>>> tsla = pdr.DataReader('tsla', data_source='google',
                          start='2017-1-1')
>>> tsla.head(8)
```

	Open	High	Low	Close	Volume
Date					
2017-01-03	214.86	220.33	210.96	216.99	5923254
2017-01-04	214.75	228.00	214.31	226.99	11213471
2017-01-05	226.42	227.48	221.95	226.75	5911695
2017-01-06	226.93	230.31	225.45	229.01	5527893
2017-01-09	228.97	231.92	228.00	231.28	3979484
2017-01-10	232.00	232.00	226.89	229.87	3659955
2017-01-11	229.07	229.98	226.68	229.73	3650825
2017-01-12	229.06	230.70	225.58	229.59	3790229

2. For simplicity, we will work with the closing price of each trading day.

```
>>> tsla_close = tsla['Close']
```

3. Use the `cummax` method to track the highest closing price until the current date:

```
>>> tsla_cummax = tsla_close.cummax()
>>> tsla_cummax.head(8)
Date
2017-01-03    216.99
2017-01-04    226.99
2017-01-05    226.99
2017-01-06    229.01
2017-01-09    231.28
2017-01-10    231.28
2017-01-11    231.28
2017-01-12    231.28
Name: Close, dtype: float64
```

4. To limit the downside to 10%, we multiply `tsla_cummax` by 0.9. This creates the trailing stop order:

```
>>> tsla_trailing_stop = tsla_cummax * .9
>>> tsla_trailing_stop.head(8)
Date
2017-01-03    195.291
2017-01-04    204.291
2017-01-05    204.291
2017-01-06    206.109
2017 01 09    208.152
2017-01-10    208.152
2017-01-11    208.152
2017-01-12    208.152
Name: Close, dtype: float64
```

How it works...

The `cummax` method works by retaining the maximum value encountered up to and including the current value. Multiplying this series by 0.9, or whatever cushion you would like to use, creates the trailing stop order. In this particular example, TSLA increased in value and thus, its trailing stop has also increased.

There's more...

This recipe gives just a taste of how useful pandas may be used to trade securities and stops short of calculating a return for if and when the stop order triggers. It is possible to turn this recipe into a function that accepts the ticker symbol, purchase date, and stop percentage and returns the trailing stop prices:

```
>>> def set_trailing_loss(symbol, purchase_date, perc):
        close = pdr.DataReader(symbol, 'google',
                                start=purchase_date)['Close']
        return close.cummax() * perc

>>> msft_trailing_stop = set_trailing_loss('msft', '2017-6-1', .85)
>>> msft_trailing_stop.head()
Date
2017-06-01    59.585
2017-06-02    60.996
2017-06-05    61.438
2017-06-06    61.642
2017-06-07    61.642
Name: Close, dtype: float64
```

A very similar strategy may be used during a weight-loss program. You can set a warning any time you have strayed too far away from your minimum weight. Pandas provides you with the cummin method to track the minimum value. If you keep track of your daily weight in a series, the following code provides a trailing weight loss of 5% above your lowest recorded weight to date:

```
>>> weight.cummin() * 1.05
```

See also

- Pandas official documentation of the two other accumulation methods, cumsum (http://bit.ly/2v3B6EZ) and cumprod (http://bit.ly/2uHBWGt)

4
Selecting Subsets of Data

In this chapter, we will cover the following topics:

- Selecting Series data
- Selecting DataFrame rows
- Selecting DataFrame rows and columns simultaneously
- Selecting data with both integers and labels
- Speeding up scalar selection
- Slicing rows lazily
- Slicing lexicographically

Introduction

Every dimension of data in a Series or DataFrame is labeled through an Index object. It is this Index that separates pandas data structures from NumPy's n-dimensional array. Indexes provide meaningful labels for each row and column of data, and pandas users have the ability to select data through the use of these labels. Additionally, pandas allows its users to select data by the integer location of the rows and columns. This dual selection capability, one using labels and the other using integer location, makes for powerful yet confusing syntax to select subsets of data.

Selecting data through the use of labels or integer location is not unique to pandas. Python dictionaries and lists are built-in data structures that select their data in exactly one of these ways. Both dictionaries and lists have precise instructions and limited use-cases for what may be passed to the indexing operator. A dictionary's key (its label) must be an immutable object, such as a string, integer, or tuple. Lists must either use integers or slice objects for selection. Dictionaries can only select one object at a time by passing the key to the indexing operator. In some sense, pandas is combining the ability to select data using integers, as with lists, and labels, as with dictionaries.

Selecting Series data

Series and DataFrames are complex data containers that have multiple attributes that use the indexing operator to select data in different ways. In addition to the indexing operator itself, the .iloc and .loc attributes are available and use the indexing operator in their own unique ways. Collectively, these attributes are called the **indexers**.

The indexing terminology can get confusing. The term **indexing operator** is used here to distinguish it from the other indexers. It refers to the brackets, [] directly after a Series or DataFrame. For instance, given a Series s, you can select data in the following ways: s[item] and s.loc[item]. The first uses the indexing operator. The second uses the .loc indexer.

Series and DataFrame indexers allow selection by integer location (like Python lists) and by label (like Python dictionaries). The .iloc indexer selects only by integer location and works similarly to Python lists. The .loc indexer selects only by index label, which is similar to how Python dictionaries work.

Getting ready

Both .loc and .iloc work with Series and DataFrames. This recipe shows how to select Series data by integer location with .iloc and by label with .loc. These indexers not only take scalar values, but also lists and slices.

How to do it...

1. Read in the college dataset with the institution name as the index, and select a single column as a Series with the indexing operator:

```
>>> college = pd.read_csv('data/college.csv', index_col='INSTNM')
>>> city = college['CITY']
>>> city.head()
INSTNM
Alabama A & M University                   Normal
University of Alabama at Birmingham        Birmingham
Amridge University                         Montgomery
University of Alabama in Huntsville        Huntsville
Alabama State University                   Montgomery
Name: CITY, dtype: object
```

2. The `.iloc` indexer makes selections only by integer location. Passing an integer to it returns a scalar value:

```
>>> city.iloc[3]
Huntsville
```

3. To select several different integer locations, pass a list to `.iloc`. This returns a Series:

```
>>> city.iloc[[10,20,30]]
INSTNM
Birmingham Southern College                          Birmingham
George C Wallace State Community College-Hanceville   Hanceville
Judson College                                       Marion
Name: CITY, dtype: object
```

4. To select an equally spaced partition of data, use slice notation:

```
>>> city.iloc[4:50:10]
INSTNM
Alabama State University               Montgomery
Enterprise State Community College     Enterprise
Heritage Christian University          Florence
Marion Military Institute              Marion
Reid State Technical College           Evergreen
Name: CITY, dtype: object
```

5. Now we turn to the .loc indexer, which selects only with index labels. Passing a single string returns a scalar value:

```
>>> city.loc['Heritage Christian University']
Florence
```

6. To select several disjoint labels, use a list:

```
>>> np.random.seed(1)
>>> labels = list(np.random.choice(city.index, 4))
>>> labels
['Northwest HVAC/R Training Center',
 'California State University-Dominguez Hills',
 'Lower Columbia College',
 'Southwest Acupuncture College-Boulder']

>>> city.loc[labels]
INSTNM
Northwest HVAC/R Training Center                Spokane
California State University-Dominguez Hills       Carson
Lower Columbia College                          Longview
Southwest Acupuncture College-Boulder            Boulder
Name: CITY, dtype: object
```

7. To select an equally spaced partition of data, use slice notation. Make sure that the start and stop values are strings. You can use an integer to specify the step size of the slice:

```
>>> city.loc['Alabama State University':
             'Reid State Technical College':10]
INSTNM
Alabama State University                     Montgomery
Enterprise State Community College           Enterprise
Heritage Christian University                  Florence
Marion Military Institute                        Marion
Reid State Technical College                  Evergreen
Name: CITY, dtype: object
```

How it works...

The values in a Series are referenced by integers beginning from 0. Step 2 selects the fourth element of the Series with the .loc indexer. Step 3 passes a three-item integer list to the indexing operator, which returns a Series with those integer locations selected. This feature is an enhancement over a Python list, which is incapable of selecting multiple disjoint items in this manner.

In step 4, slice notation with `start`, `stop`, and `step` values specified is used to select an entire section of a Series.

Steps 5 through 7 replicate steps 2 through 4 with the label-based indexer, `.loc`. The labels must be exact matches of values in the index. To ensure our labels are exact, we choose four labels at random from the index in step 6 and store them to a list before selecting their values as a Series. Selections with the `.loc` indexer always include the last element, as seen in step 7.

There's more...

When passing a scalar value to the indexing operator, as with step 2 and step 5, a scalar value is returned. When passing a list or slice, as in the other steps, a Series is returned. This returned value might seem inconsistent, but if we think of a Series as a dictionary-like object that maps labels to values, then returning the value makes sense. To select a single item and retain the item in its Series, pass in as a single-item list rather than a scalar value:

```
>>> city.iloc[[3]]
INSTNM
University of Alabama in Huntsville    Huntsville
Name: CITY, dtype: object
```

Care needs to be taken when using slice notation with `.loc`. If the `start` index appears after the `stop` index, then an empty Series is returned without an exception raised:

```
>>> city.loc['Reid State Technical College':
             'Alabama State University':10]
Series([], Name: CITY, dtype: object)
```

See also

- Pandas official documentation on indexing (`http://bit.ly/2fdtZWu`)

Selecting DataFrame rows

The most explicit and preferred way to select DataFrame rows is with the `.iloc` and `.loc` indexers. They are capable of selecting rows or columns independently and simultaneously.

Getting ready

This recipe shows you how to select rows from a DataFrame using the `.iloc` and `.loc` indexers.

How to do it...

1. Read in the college dataset, and set the index as the institution name:

    ```
    >>> college = pd.read_csv('data/college.csv', index_col='INSTNM')
    >>> college.head()
    ```

INSTNM	CITY	STABBR	HBCU	MENONLY	WOMENONLY	RELAFFIL	SATVRMID	SATMTMID	DISTANCEONLY	UGDS	...	UGDS_2MOR
Alabama A & M University	Normal	AL	1.0	0.0	0.0	0	424.0	420.0	0.0	4206.0	...	0.0000
University of Alabama at Birmingham	Birmingham	AL	0.0	0.0	0.0	0	570.0	565.0	0.0	11383.0	...	0.0368
Amridge University	Montgomery	AL	0.0	0.0	0.0	1	NaN	NaN	1.0	291.0	...	0.0000
University of Alabama in Huntsville	Huntsville	AL	0.0	0.0	0.0	0	595.0	590.0	0.0	5451.0	...	0.0172
Alabama State University	Montgomery	AL	1.0	0.0	0.0	0	425.0	430.0	0.0	4811.0	...	0.0098

2. Pass an integer to the `.iloc` indexer to select an entire row at that position:

    ```
    >>> college.iloc[60]
    CITY                      Anchorage
    STABBR                           AK
    HBCU                              0
                                ...
    UG25ABV                      0.4386
    MD_EARN_WNE_P10               42500
    GRAD_DEBT_MDN_SUPP          19449.5
    Name: University of Alaska Anchorage, Length: 26, dtype: object
    ```

3. To get the same row as the preceding step, pass the index label to the `.loc` indexer:

```
>>> college.loc['University of Alaska Anchorage']
CITY                  Anchorage
STABBR                       AK
HBCU                          0
                        ...
UG25ABV                  0.4386
MD_EARN_WNE_P10           42500
GRAD_DEBT_MDN_SUPP      19449.5
Name: University of Alaska Anchorage, Length: 26, dtype: object
```

4. To select a disjointed set of rows as a DataFrame, pass a list of integers to the `.iloc` indexer:

```
>>> college.iloc[[60, 99, 3]]
```

INSTNM	CITY	STABBR	HBCU	MENONLY	WOMENONLY	RELAFFIL	SATVRMID	SATMTMID	DISTANCEONLY	UGDS	...	UGDS_2MOR
University of Alaska Anchorage	Anchorage	AK	0.0	0.0	0.0	0	NaN	NaN	0.0	12865.0	...	0.0980
International Academy of Hair Design	Tempe	AZ	0.0	0.0	0.0	0	NaN	NaN	0.0	188.0	...	0.0160
University of Alabama in Huntsville	Huntsville	AL	0.0	0.0	0.0	0	595.0	590.0	0.0	5451.0	...	0.0172

5. The same DataFrame from step 4 may be reproduced using `.loc` by passing it a list of the exact institution names:

```
>>> labels = ['University of Alaska Anchorage',
              'International Academy of Hair Design',
              'University of Alabama in Huntsville']
>>> college.loc[labels]
```

6. Use slice notation with `.iloc` to select an entire segment of the data:

```
>>> college.iloc[99:102]
```

INSTNM	CITY	STABBR	HBCU	MENONLY	WOMENONLY	RELAFFIL	SATVRMID	SATMTMID	DISTANCEONLY	UGDS	...	UGDS_2MOR
International Academy of Hair Design	Tempe	AZ	0.0	0.0	0.0	0	NaN	NaN	0.0	188.0	...	0.0160
GateWay Community College	Phoenix	AZ	0.0	0.0	0.0	0	NaN	NaN	0.0	5211.0	...	0.0127
Mesa Community College	Mesa	AZ	0.0	0.0	0.0	0	NaN	NaN	0.0	19055.0	...	0.0205

7. Slice notation also works with the `.loc` indexer and is inclusive of the last label:

```
>>> start = 'International Academy of Hair Design'
>>> stop = 'Mesa Community College'
>>> college.loc[start:stop]
```

How it works...

Passing a scalar value, a list of scalars, or a slice object to the `.iloc` or `.loc` indexers causes pandas to scan the index labels for the appropriate rows and return them. If a single scalar value is passed, a Series is returned. If a list or slice object is passed, then a DataFrame is returned.

There's more...

In step 5, the list of index labels can be selected directly from the DataFrame returned in step 4 without the need for copying and pasting:

```
>>> college.iloc[[60, 99, 3]].index.tolist()
['University of Alaska Anchorage',
 'International Academy of Hair Design',
 'University of Alabama in Huntsville']
```

See also

- Refer to the *Examining the Index object* recipe from Chapter 6, *Index Alignment*

Selecting DataFrame rows and columns simultaneously

Directly using the indexing operator is the correct method to select one or more columns from a DataFrame. However, it does not allow you to select both rows and columns simultaneously. To select rows and columns simultaneously, you will need to pass both valid row and column selections separated by a comma to either the `.iloc` or `.loc` indexers.

Getting ready

The generic form to select rows and columns will look like the following code:

```
>>> df.iloc[rows, columns]
>>> df.loc[rows, columns]
```

The `rows` and `columns` variables may be scalar values, lists, slice objects, or boolean sequences.

Passing a boolean sequence to the indexers is covered in Chapter 5, *Boolean Indexing*.

In this recipe, each step shows a simultaneous row and column selection using `.iloc` and its exact replication using `.loc`.

...

ollege dataset, and set the index as the institution name. Select the
...s and the first four columns with slice notation:

```
>>> college = pd.read_csv('data/college.csv', index_col='INSTNM')
>>> college.iloc[:3, :4]
>>> college.loc[:'Amridge University', :'MENONLY']
```

INSTNM	CITY	STABBR	HBCU	MENONLY
Alabama A & M University	Normal	AL	1.0	0.0
University of Alabama at Birmingham	Birmingham	AL	0.0	0.0
Amridge University	Montgomery	AL	0.0	0.0

2. Select all the rows of two different columns:

```
>>> college.iloc[:, [4,6]].head()
>>> college.loc[:, ['WOMENONLY', 'SATVRMID']].head()
```

INSTNM	WOMENONLY	SATVRMID
Alabama A & M University	0.0	424.0
University of Alabama at Birmingham	0.0	570.0
Amridge University	0.0	NaN
University of Alabama in Huntsville	0.0	595.0
Alabama State University	0.0	425.0

3. Select disjointed rows and columns:

```
>>> college.iloc[[100, 200], [7, 15]]
>>> rows = ['GateWay Community College',
            'American Baptist Seminary of the West']
>>> columns = ['SATMTMID', 'UGDS_NHPI']
>>> college.loc[rows, columns]
```

	SATMTMID	UGDS_NHPI
INSTNM		
GateWay Community College	NaN	0.0029
American Baptist Seminary of the West	NaN	NaN

4. Select a single scalar value:

```
>>> college.iloc[5, -4]
>>> college.loc['The University of Alabama', 'PCTFLOAN']
-.401
```

5. Slice the rows and select a single column:

```
>>> college.iloc[90:80:-2, 5]
>>> start = 'Empire Beauty School-Flagstaff'
>>> stop = 'Arizona State University-Tempe'
>>> college.loc[start:stop:-2, 'RELAFFIL']
INSTNM
Empire Beauty School-Flagstaff      0
Charles of Italy Beauty College     0
Central Arizona College             0
University of Arizona               0
Arizona State University-Tempe      0
Name: RELAFFIL, dtype: int64
```

How it works...

One of the keys to selecting rows and columns simultaneously is to understand the use of the comma in the brackets. The selection to the left of the comma always selects rows based on the row index. The selection to the right of the comma always selects columns based on the column index.

It is not necessary to make a selection for both rows and columns simultaneously. Step 2 shows how to select all the rows and a subset of columns. The colon represents a slice object that simply returns all the values for that dimension.

There's more...

When selecting a subset of rows, along with all the columns, it is not necessary to use a colon following a comma. The default behavior is to select all the columns if there is no comma present. The previous recipe selected rows in exactly this manner. You can, however, use a colon to represent a slice of all the columns. The following lines of code are equivalent:

```
>>> college.iloc[:10]
>>> college.iloc[:10, :]
```

Selecting data with both integers and labels

The .iloc and .loc indexers each select data by either integer or label location but are not able to handle a combination of both input types at the same time. In earlier versions of pandas, another indexer, .ix, was available to select data by both integer and label location. While this conveniently worked for those specific situations, it was ambiguous by nature and was a source of confusion for many pandas users. The .ix indexer has subsequently been deprecated and thus should be avoided.

Getting ready

Before the .ix deprecation, it was possible to select the first five rows and the columns of the college dataset from UGDS_WHITE through UGDS_UNKN using college.ix[:5, 'UGDS_WHITE':'UGDS_UNKN']. This is now impossible to do directly using .loc or .iloc. The following recipe shows how to find the integer location of the columns and then use .iloc to complete the selection.

How to do it...

1. Read in the college dataset and assign the institution name (INSTNM) as the index:

    ```
    >>> college = pd.read_csv('data/college.csv', index_col='INSTNM')
    ```

2. Use the Index method `get_loc` to find the integer position of the desired columns:

```
>>> col_start = college.columns.get_loc('UGDS_WHITE')
>>> col_end = college.columns.get_loc('UGDS_UNKN') + 1
>>> col_start, col_end
```

3. Use `col_start` and `col_end` to select columns by integer location using `.iloc`:

```
>>> college.iloc[:5, col_start:col_end]
```

INSTNM	UGDS_WHITE	UGDS_BLACK	UGDS_HISP	UGDS_ASIAN	UGDS_AIAN	UGDS_NHPI	UGDS_2MOR	UGDS_NRA	UGDS_UNKN
Alabama A & M University	0.0333	0.9353	0.0055	0.0019	0.0024	0.0019	0.0000	0.0059	0.0138
University of Alabama at Birmingham	0.5922	0.2600	0.0283	0.0518	0.0022	0.0007	0.0368	0.0179	0.0100
Amridge University	0.2990	0.4192	0.0069	0.0034	0.0000	0.0000	0.0000	0.0000	0.2715
University of Alabama in Huntsville	0.6988	0.1255	0.0382	0.0376	0.0143	0.0002	0.0172	0.0332	0.0350
Alabama State University	0.0158	0.9208	0.0121	0.0019	0.0010	0.0006	0.0098	0.0243	0.0137

How it works...

Step 2 first retrieves the column index through the `columns` attribute. Indexes have a `get_loc` method, which accepts an index label and returns its integer location. We find both the start and end integer locations for the columns that we wish to slice. We add one because slicing with `.iloc` is exclusive of the last item. Step 3 uses slice notation with the rows and columns.

There's more...

We can do a very similar operation to make `.loc` work with a mixture of integers and positions. The following shows how to select the 10th through 15th (inclusive) rows, along with columns UGDS_WHITE through UGDS_UNKN:

```
>>> row_start = df_college.index[10]
>>> row_end = df_college.index[15]
>>> college.loc[row_start:row_end, 'UGDS_WHITE':'UGDS_UNKN']
```

Doing this same operation with `.ix` (which is deprecated, so don't do this) would look like this:

```
>>> college.ix[10:16, 'UGDS_WHITE':'UGDS_UNKN']
```

It is possible to achieve the same results by chaining `.loc` and `.iloc` together, but chaining indexers is typically a bad idea:

```
>>> college.iloc[10:16].loc[:, 'UGDS_WHITE':'UGDS_UNKN']
```

See also

- Refer to the *Selecting columns with methods* recipe from `Chapter 2`, *Essential DataFrame Operations*

Speeding up scalar selection

Both the `.iloc` and `.loc` indexers are capable of selecting a single element, a scalar value, from a Series or DataFrame. However, there exist the indexers, `.iat` and `.at`, which respectively achieve the same thing at faster speeds. Like `.iloc`, the `.iat` indexer uses integer location to make its selection and must be passed two integers separated by a comma. Similar to `.loc`, the `.at` index uses labels to make its selection and must be passed an index and column label separated by a comma.

Getting ready

This recipe is valuable if computational time is of utmost importance. It shows the performance improvement of `.iat` and `.at` over `.iloc` and `.loc` when using scalar selection.

How to do it...

1. Read in the `college` scoreboard dataset with the institution[...]
   Pass a college name and column name to `.loc` in order to se[...]

   ```
   >>> college = pd.read_csv('data/college.csv', ind[...]
   >>> cn = 'Texas A & M University-College Station'
   >>> college.loc[cn, 'UGDS_WHITE']
   .661
   ```

2. Achieve the same result with `.at`:

   ```
   >>> college.at[cn, 'UGDS_WHITE']
   .661
   ```

3. Use the `%timeit` magic command to find the difference in speed:

   ```
   >>> %timeit college.loc[cn, 'UGDS_WHITE']
   8.97 µs ± 617 ns per loop (mean ± std. dev. of 7 runs, 100000 loops
   each)

   >>> %timeit college.at[cn, 'UGDS_WHITE']
   6.28 µs ± 214 ns per loop (mean ± std. dev. of 7 runs, 100000 loops
   each)
   ```

4. Find the integer locations of the preceding selections and then time the difference between `.iloc` and `.iat`:

   ```
   >>> row_num = college.index.get_loc(cn)
   >>> col_num = college.columns.get_loc('UGDS_WHITE')
   >>> row_num, col_num
   (3765, 10)

   >>> %timeit college.iloc[row_num, col_num]
   9.74 µs ± 153 ns per loop (mean ± std. dev. of 7 runs, 100000 loops
   each)

   >>> %timeit college.iat[row_num, col_num]
   7.29 µs ± 431 ns per loop (mean ± std. dev. of 7 runs, 100000 loops
   each)
   ```

...w it works...

The scalar indexers, `.iat` and `.at`, only accept scalar values. They fail if anything else is passed to them. They are drop-in replacements for `.iloc` and `.loc` when doing scalar selection. The `timeit` magic command times entire blocks of code when preceded by two percentage signs and a single time when preceded by one percentage sign. It shows that about 2.5 microseconds are saved on average by switching to the scalar indexers. This might not be much but can add up quickly if scalar selection is repeatedly done in a program.

There's more...

Both `.iat` and `.at` work with Series as well. Pass them a single scalar value, and they will return a scalar:

```
>>> state = college['STBBR']   # Select a Series
>>> state.iat[1000]
'IL'

>>> state.at['Stanford University']
'CA'
```

Slicing rows lazily

The previous recipes in this chapter showed how the `.iloc` and `.loc` indexers were used to select subsets of both Series and DataFrames in either dimension. A shortcut to select the rows exists with just the indexing operator itself. This is just a shortcut to show additional features of pandas, but the primary function of the indexing operator is actually to select DataFrame columns. If you want to select rows, it is best to use `.iloc` or `.loc`, as they are unambiguous.

Getting ready

In this recipe, we pass a slice object to both the Series and DataFrame indexing operators.

How to do it...

1. Read in the college dataset with the institution name as the index and then select every other row from index 10 to 20:

```
>>> college = pd.read_csv('data/college.csv', index_col='INSTNM')
>>> college[10:20:2]
```

INSTNM	CITY	STABBR	HBCU	MENONLY	WOMENONLY	RELAFFIL	SATVRMID	SATMTMID	DISTANCEONLY	UGDS	...	UGDS_2MOR	UGDS_NR
Birmingham Southern College	Birmingham	AL	0.0	0.0	0.0	1	560.0	560.0	0.0	1180.0	...	0.0051	0.000
Concordia College Alabama	Selma	AL	1.0	0.0	0.0	1	420.0	400.0	0.0	322.0	...	0.0031	0.046
Enterprise State Community College	Enterprise	AL	0.0	0.0	0.0	0	NaN	NaN	0.0	1729.0	...	0.0254	0.001
Faulkner University	Montgomery	AL	0.0	0.0	0.0	1	NaN	NaN	0.0	2367.0	...	0.0173	0.018
New Beginning College of Cosmetology	Albertville	AL	0.0	0.0	0.0	0	NaN	NaN	0.0	115.0	...	0.0000	0.000

2. This same slicing exists with Series:

```
>>> city = college['CITY']
>>> city[10:20:2]
INSTNM
Birmingham Southern College                 Birmingham
Concordia College Alabama                        Selma
Enterprise State Community College          Enterprise
Faulkner University                         Montgomery
New Beginning College of Cosmetology       Albertville
Name: CITY, dtype: object
```

3. Both Series and DataFrames can slice by label as well with just the indexing operator:

```
>>> start = 'Mesa Community College'
>>> stop = 'Spokane Community College'
>>> college[start:stop:1500]
```

INSTNM	CITY	STABBR	HBCU	MENONLY	WOMENONLY	RELAFFIL	SATVRMID	SATMTMID	DISTANCEONLY	UGDS	...	UGDS_2MOR	UGDS_NRA
Mesa Community College	Mesa	AZ	0.0	0.0	0.0	0	NaN	NaN	0.0	19055.0	...	0.0205	0.0257
Hair Academy Inc-New Carrollton	New Carrollton	MD	0.0	0.0	0.0	0	NaN	NaN	0.0	504.0	...	0.0000	0.0000
National College of Natural Medicine	Portland	OR	0.0	0.0	0.0	0	NaN	NaN	0.0	NaN	...	NaN	NaN

4. Here is the same slice by label with a Series:

```
>>> city[start:stop:1500]
INSTNM
Mesa Community College                               Mesa
Hair Academy Inc-New Carrollton            New Carrollton
National College of Natural Medicine             Portland
Name: CITY, dtype: object
```

How it works...

The indexing operator changes behavior based on what type of object is passed to it. The following pseudocode outlines how DataFrame indexing operator handles the object that it is passed:

```
>>> df[item]  # Where `df` is a DataFrame and item is some object

If item is a string then
    Find a column name that matches the item exactly
    Raise KeyError if there is no match
    Return the column as a Series

If item is a list of strings then
    Raise KeyError if one or more strings in item don't match columns
    Return a DataFrame with just the columns in the list

If item is a slice object then
    Works with either integer or string slices
    Raise KeyError if label from label slice is not in index
    Return all ROWS that are selected by the slice

If item is a list, Series or ndarray of booleans then
    Raise ValueError if length of item not equal to length of DataFrame
    Use the booleans to return only the rows with True in same location
```

The preceding logic covers all the most common cases but is not an exhaustive list. The logic for a Series is slightly different and actually more complex than it is for a DataFrame. Due to its complexity, it is probably a good idea to avoid using just the indexing operator itself on a Series and instead use the explicit `.iloc` and `.loc` indexers.

> One acceptable use case of the Series indexing operator is when doing boolean indexing. See `Chapter 6`, *Index Alignment* for more details.

I titled this type of row slicing in this section as *lazy*, as it does not use the more explicit `.iloc` or `.loc`. Personally, I always use these indexers whenever slicing rows, as there is never a question of exactly what I am doing.

There's more...

It is important to be aware that this lazy slicing does not work for columns, just for DataFrame rows and Series.It also cannot be used to select both rows and columns simultaneously. Take, for instance, the following code, which attempts to select the first ten rows and two columns:

```
>>> college[:10, ['CITY', 'STABBR']]
TypeError: unhashable type: 'slice'
```

To make a selection in this manner, you need to use `.loc` or `.iloc`. Here is one possible way that selects all the institution labels first and then uses the label-based indexer `.loc`:

```
>>> first_ten_instnm = college.index[:10]
>>> college.loc[first_ten_instnm, ['CITY', 'STABBR']]
```

Slicing lexicographically

The `.loc` indexer typically selects data based on the exact string label of the index. However, it also allows you to select data based on the lexicographic order of the values in the index. Specifically, `.loc` allows you to select all rows with an index lexicographically using slice notation. This works only if the index is sorted.

Getting ready

In this recipe, you will first sort the index and then use slice notation inside the `.loc` indexer to select all rows between two strings.

How to do it...

1. Read in the college dataset, and set the institution name as the index:

```
>>> college = pd.read_csv('data/college.csv', index_col='INSTNM')
```

2. Attempt to select all colleges with names lexicographically between `'Sp'` and `'Su'`:

```
>>> college.loc['Sp':'Su']
KeyError: 'Sp'
```

3. As the index is not sorted, the preceding command fails. Let's go ahead and sort the index:

```
>>> college = college.sort_index()
```

INSTNM	CITY	STABBR	HBCU	MENONLY	WOMENONLY	RELAFFIL	SATVRMID	SATMTMID	DISTANCEONLY	UGDS	...	UGDS_2MOR
A & W Healthcare Educators	New Orleans	LA	0.0	0.0	0.0	0	NaN	NaN	0.0	40.0	...	0.0000
A T Still University of Health Sciences	Kirksville	MO	0.0	0.0	0.0	0	NaN	NaN	0.0	NaN	...	NaN
ABC Beauty Academy	Garland	TX	0.0	0.0	0.0	0	NaN	NaN	0.0	30.0	...	0.0000
ABC Beauty College Inc	Arkadelphia	AR	0.0	0.0	0.0	0	NaN	NaN	0.0	38.0	...	0.0000
AI Miami International University of Art and Design	Miami	FL	0.0	0.0	0.0	0	NaN	NaN	0.0	2778.0	...	0.0018

4. Now, let's rerun the same command from step 2:

```
>>> college.loc['Sp':'Su']
```

INSTNM	CITY	STABBR	HBCU	MENONLY	WOMENONLY	RELAFFIL	SATVRMID	SATMTMID	DISTANCEONLY	UGDS	...	UGDS_2MOR	UGDS_NRA
Spa Tech Institute-Ipswich	Ipswich	MA	0.0	0.0	0.0	0	NaN	NaN	0.0	37.0	...	0.000	0.0
Spa Tech Institute-Plymouth	Plymouth	MA	0.0	0.0	0.0	0	NaN	NaN	0.0	153.0	...	0.000	0.0
Spa Tech Institute-Westboro	Westboro	MA	0.0	0.0	0.0	0	NaN	NaN	0.0	90.0	...	0.000	0.0
...	...	...	...	...	...	...	...	...	...	...	...	...	...
Stylemaster College of Hair Design	Longview	WA	0.0	0.0	0.0	0	NaN	NaN	0.0	77.0	...	0.013	0.0
Styles and Profiles Beauty College	Selmer	TN	0.0	0.0	0.0	0	NaN	NaN	0.0	31.0	...	0.000	0.0
Styletrends Barber and Hairstyling Academy	Rock Hill	SC	0.0	0.0	0.0	0	NaN	NaN	0.0	45.0	...	0.000	0.0

201 rows × 26 columns

How it works...

The normal behavior of `.loc` is to make selections of data based on the exact labels passed to it. It raises a `KeyError` when these labels are not found in the index. However, one special exception to this behavior exists whenever the index is lexicographically sorted, and a slice is passed to it. Selection is now possible between the `start` and `stop` labels of the slice, even if they are not exact values of the index.

There's more...

With this recipe, it is easy to select colleges between two letters of the alphabet. For instance, to select all colleges that begin with the letter `D` through `S`, you would use `college.loc['D':'T']`. Slicing like this is still inclusive of the last index so this would technically return a college with the exact name `T`.

This type of slicing also works when the index is sorted in the opposite direction. You can determine which direction the index is sorted with the index attribute, is_monotonic_increasing or is_monotonic_decreasing. **Either of these must be** True in order for lexicographic slicing to work. For instance, the following code lexicographically sorts the index from Z to A:

```
>>> college = college.sort_index(ascending=False)
>>> college.index.is_monotonic_decreasing
True
>>> college.loc['E':'B']
```

INSTNM	CITY	STABBR	HBCU	MENONLY	WOMENONLY	RELAFFIL	SATVRMID	SATMTMID	DISTANCEONLY	UGDS	...	UGDS_2MOR
Dyersburg State Community College	Dyersburg	TN	0.0	0.0	0.0	0	NaN	NaN	0.0	2001.0	...	0.0185
Dutchess Community College	Poughkeepsie	NY	0.0	0.0	0.0	0	NaN	NaN	0.0	6885.0	...	0.0446
Dutchess BOCES-Practical Nursing Program	Poughkeepsie	NY	0.0	0.0	0.0	0	NaN	NaN	0.0	155.0	...	0.0581
...	...	...	...	...	...	...	...	...	...	...	...	...
BJ's Beauty & Barber College	Auburn	WA	0.0	0.0	0.0	0	NaN	NaN	0.0	28.0	...	0.0714
BIR Training Center	Chicago	IL	0.0	0.0	0.0	0	NaN	NaN	0.0	2132.0	...	0.0000
B M Spurr School of Practical Nursing	Glen Dale	WV	0.0	0.0	0.0	0	NaN	NaN	0.0	31.0	...	0.0000

1411 rows × 26 columns

Python sorts all capital letters before lowercase and all integers before capital letters.

5
Boolean Indexing

In this chapter, we will cover the following topics:

- Calculating boolean statistics
- Constructing multiple boolean conditions
- Filtering with boolean indexing
- Replicating boolean indexing with index selection
- Selecting with unique and sorted indexes
- Gaining perspective on stock prices
- Translating SQL WHERE clauses
- Determining the normality of stock market returns
- Improving readability of boolean indexing with the query method
- Preserving Series with the `where` method
- Masking DataFrame rows
- Selecting with booleans, integer location, and labels

Introduction

Filtering data from a dataset is one of the most common and basic operations. There are numerous ways to filter (or subset) data in pandas with **boolean indexing**. Boolean indexing (also known as **boolean selection**) can be a confusing term, but for the purposes of pandas, it refers to selecting rows by providing a boolean value (`True` or `False`) for each row. These boolean values are usually stored in a Series or NumPy `ndarray` and are usually created by applying a boolean condition to one or more columns in a DataFrame. We begin by creating boolean Series and calculating statistics on them and then move on to creating more complex conditionals before using boolean indexing in a wide variety of ways to filter data.

Calculating boolean statistics

When first getting introduced to boolean Series, it can be informative to calculate basic summary statistics on them. Each value of a boolean series evaluates to 0 or 1 so all the Series methods that work with numerical values also work with booleans.

Getting ready

In this recipe, we create a boolean Series by applying a condition to a column of data and then calculate summary statistics from it.

How to do it...

1. Read in the `movie` dataset, set the index to the movie title, and inspect the first few rows:

```
>>> movie = pd.read_csv('data/movie.csv', index_col='movie_title')
>>> movie.head()
```

movie_title	color	director_name	num_critic_for_reviews	duration	director_facebook_likes	actor_3_facebook_likes	actor_2_name	actor_1_facebook_likes
Avatar	Color	James Cameron	723.0	178.0	0.0	855.0	Joel David Moore	1000.0
Pirates of the Caribbean: At World's End	Color	Gore Verbinski	302.0	169.0	563.0	1000.0	Orlando Bloom	40000.0
Spectre	Color	Sam Mendes	602.0	148.0	0.0	161.0	Rory Kinnear	11000.0
The Dark Knight Rises	Color	Christopher Nolan	813.0	164.0	22000.0	23000.0	Christian Bale	27000.0
Star Wars: Episode VII - The Force Awakens	NaN	Doug Walker	NaN	NaN	131.0	NaN	Rob Walker	131.0

2. Determine whether the duration of each movie is longer than two hours by using the greater than comparison operator with the `duration` Series:

```
>>> movie_2_hours = movie['duration'] > 120
>>> movie_2_hours.head(10)
movie_title
Avatar                                          True
Pirates of the Caribbean: At World's End        True
Spectre                                         True
The Dark Knight Rises                           True
Star Wars: Episode VII - The Force Awakens      False
John Carter                                     True
Spider-Man 3                                    True
Tangled                                         False
Avengers: Age of Ultron                         True
Harry Potter and the Half-Blood Prince          True
Name: duration, dtype: bool
```

3. We can now use this Series to determine the number of movies that are longer than two hours:

```
>>> movie_2_hours.sum()
1039
```

4. To find the percentage of movies in the dataset longer than two hours, use the `mean` method:

```
>>> movie_2_hours.mean()
0.2114
```

5. Unfortunately, the output from step 4 is misleading. The `duration` column has a few missing values. If you look back at the DataFrame output from step 1, you will see that the last row is missing a value for `duration`. The boolean condition in step 2 returns `False` for this. We need to drop the missing values first, then evaluate the condition and take the mean:

```
>>> movie['duration'].dropna().gt(120).mean()
.2112
```

6. Use the `describe` method to output a few summary statistics on the boolean Series:

```
>>> movie_2_hours.describe()
count      4916
unique        2
top       False
freq       3877
Name: duration, dtype: object
```

How it works...

Most DataFrames will not have columns of booleans like our movie dataset. The most straightforward method to produce a boolean Series is to apply a condition to one of the columns using one of the comparison operators. In step 2, we use the greater than operator to test whether or not the duration of each movie was more than two hours (120 minutes). Steps 3 and 4 calculate two important quantities from a boolean Series, its sum and mean. These methods are possible as Python evaluates `False`/`True` as 0/1.

You can prove to yourself that the mean of a boolean Series represents the percentage of `True` values. To do this, use the `value_counts` method to count with the `normalize` parameter set to `True` to get its distribution:

```
>>> movie_2_hours.value_counts(normalize=True)
False    0.788649
True     0.211351
Name: duration, dtype: float64
```

Step 5 alerts us to the incorrect result from step 4. Even though the `duration` column had missing values, the boolean condition evaluated all these comparisons against missing values as `False`. Dropping these missing values allows us to calculate the correct statistic. This is done in one step through method chaining.

Step 6 shows that pandas treats boolean columns similarly to how it treats object data types by displaying frequency information. This is a natural way to think about boolean Series, rather than display quantiles like it does with numeric data.

There's more...

It is possible to compare two columns from the same DataFrame to produce a boolean Series. For instance, we could determine the percentage of movies that have actor 1 with more Facebook likes than actor 2. To do this, we would select both of these columns and then drop any of the rows that had missing values for either movie. Then we would make the comparison and calculate the mean:

```
>>> actors = movie[['actor_1_facebook_likes',
                     'actor_2_facebook_likes']].dropna()
>>> (actors['actor_1_facebook_likes'] >
     actors['actor_2_facebook_likes']).mean()
.978
```

See also

- Refer to the *Chaining Series methods together* recipe from `Chapter 1`, *Pandas Foundations*
- Refer to the *Working with operators* recipe from `Chapter 1`, *Pandas Foundations*

Constructing multiple boolean conditions

In Python, boolean expressions use the built-in logical operators and, or, and not. These keywords do not work with boolean indexing in pandas and are respectively replaced with &, |, and ~. Additionally, each expression must be wrapped in parentheses or an error will be raised.

Getting ready

Constructing a precise filter for your dataset might have you combining multiple boolean expressions together to extract an exact subset. In this recipe, we construct multiple boolean expressions before combining them together to find all the movies that have an imdb_score greater than 8, a content_rating of PG-13, and a title_year either before 2000 or after 2009.

How to do it...

1. Load in the movie dataset and set the index as the title:

```
>>> movie = pd.read_csv('data/movie.csv', index_col='movie_title')
```

2. Create a variable to hold each set of criteria independently as a boolean Series:

```
>>> criteria1 = movie.imdb_score > 8
>>> criteria2 = movie.content_rating == 'PG-13'
>>> criteria3 = ((movie.title_year < 2000) |
                 (movie.title_year > 2009))

>>> criteria2.head()      # all criteria Series look similar
movie_title
Avatar                                         True
Pirates of the Caribbean: At World's End       True
Spectre                                        True
The Dark Knight Rises                          True
Star Wars: Episode VII - The Force Awakens     False
Name: content_rating, dtype: bool
```

3. Combine all the criteria together into a single boolean Series:

```
>>> criteria_final = criteria1 & criteria2 & criteria3
>>> criteria_final.head()
movie_title
Avatar                                         False
Pirates of the Caribbean: At World's End       False
Spectre                                        False
The Dark Knight Rises                          True
Star Wars: Episode VII - The Force Awakens     False
dtype: bool
```

How it works...

All values in a Series can be compared against a scalar value using the standard comparison operators(<, >, ==, !=, <=, >=). The expression `movie.imdb_score > 8` yields a Series of booleans where all `imdb_score` values prices exceeding 8 are `True` and those less than or equal to 8 are `False`. The index of this boolean Series retains the same index as the original and in this case, is the title of the movie.

The `criteria3` variable is created by two independent boolean expressions. Each expression must be enclosed in parentheses to function properly. The pipe character, |, is used to create a logical `or` condition between each of the values in both Series.

All three criteria need to be `True` to match the requirements of the recipe. They are each combined together with the ampersand character, &, which creates a logical `and` condition between each Series value.

There's more...

A consequence of pandas using different syntax for the logical operators is that operator precedence is no longer the same. The comparison operators have a higher precedence than `and`, `or`, and `not`. However, the new operators for pandas (the bitwise operators &, |, and ~) have a higher precedence than the comparison operators, thus the need for parentheses. An example can help clear this up. Take the following expression:

```
>>> 5 < 10 and 3 > 4
False
```

In the preceding expression, `5 < 10` evaluates first, followed by `3 < 4`, and finally, the `and` evaluates. Python progresses through the expression as follows:

```
>>> 5 < 10 and 3 > 4
>>> True and 3 > 4
>>> True and False
>>> False
```

Let's take a look at what would happen if the expression in `criteria3` was written as follows:

```
>>> movie.title_year < 2000 | movie.title_year > 2009
TypeError: cannot compare a dtyped [float64] array with a scalar of type
[bool]
```

As the bitwise operators have higher precedence than the comparison operators, `2000 | movie.title_year` is evaluated first, which is nonsensical and raises an error. Therefore, parentheses are needed to have the operations evaluated in the correct order.

Why can't pandas use `and`, `or`, and `not`? When these keywords are evaluated, Python attempts to find the **truthiness** of the objects as a whole. As it does not make sense for a Series as a whole to be either True or False--only each element--pandas raises an error.

Many objects in Python have boolean representation. For instance, all integers except 0 are considered True. All strings except the empty string are True. All non-empty sets, tuples, dictionaries, and lists are True. An empty DataFrame or Series does not evaluate as True or False and instead an error is raised. In general, to retrieve the truthiness of a Python object, pass it to the `bool` function.

See also

- Python operator precedence (`http://bit.ly/2vxuqSn`)

Filtering with boolean indexing

Boolean selection for Series and DataFrame objects is virtually identical. Both work by passing a Series of booleans indexed identically to the object being filtered to the indexing operator.

Getting ready

This recipe constructs two complex and independent boolean criteria for different sets of movies. The first set of movies comes from the previous recipe and consists of those with an `imdb_score` greater than 8, a `content_rating` of PG-13, and a `title_year` either before 2000 or after 2009. The second set of movies consists of those with `imdb_score` less than 5, a `content_rating` of R, and a `title_year` between 2000 and 2010.

How to do it...

1. Read in the `movie` dataset, set the index to the `movie_title`, and create the first set of criteria:

```
>>> movie = pd.read_csv('data/movie.csv', index_col='movie_title')
>>> crit_a1 = movie.imdb_score > 8
>>> crit_a2 = movie.content_rating == 'PG-13'
>>> crit_a3 = (movie.title_year < 2000) | (movie.title_year > 2009)
>>> final_crit_a = crit_a1 & crit_a2 & crit_a3
```

2. Create criteria for the second set of movies:

```
>>> crit_b1 = movie.imdb_score < 5
>>> crit_b2 = movie.content_rating == 'R'
>>> crit_b3 = ((movie.title_year >= 2000) &
               (movie.title_year <= 2010))
>>> final_crit_b = crit_b1 & crit_b2 & crit_b3
```

3. Combine the two sets of criteria using the pandas or operator. This yields a boolean Series of all movies that are members of either set:

```
>>> final_crit_all = final_crit_a | final_crit_b
>>> final_crit_all.head()
movie_title
Avatar                                          False
Pirates of the Caribbean: At World's End        False
Spectre                                         False
The Dark Knight Rises                            True
Star Wars: Episode VII - The Force Awakens      False
dtype: bool
```

4. Once you have your boolean Series, you simply pass it to the indexing operator to filter the data:

```
>>> movie[final_crit_all].head()
```

movie_title	color	director_name	num_critic_for_reviews	duration	director_facebook_likes	actor_3_facebook_likes	actor_2_name	actor_1_facebook_likes
The Dark Knight Rises	Color	Christopher Nolan	813.0	164.0	22000.0	23000.0	Christian Bale	27000.0
The Avengers	Color	Joss Whedon	703.0	173.0	0.0	19000.0	Robert Downey Jr.	26000.0
Captain America: Civil War	Color	Anthony Russo	516.0	147.0	94.0	11000.0	Scarlett Johansson	21000.0
Guardians of the Galaxy	Color	James Gunn	653.0	121.0	571.0	3000.0	Vin Diesel	14000.0
Interstellar	Color	Christopher Nolan	712.0	169.0	22000.0	6000.0	Anne Hathaway	11000.0

5. We have successfully filtered the data and all the columns of the DataFrame. We can't easily perform a manual check to determine whether the filter worked correctly. Let's filter both rows and columns with the `.loc` indexer:

```
>>> cols = ['imdb_score', 'content_rating', 'title_year']
>>> movie_filtered = movie.loc[final_crit_all, cols]
>>> movie_filtered.head(10)
```

movie_title	imdb_score	content_rating	title_year
The Dark Knight Rises	8.5	PG-13	2012.0
The Avengers	8.1	PG-13	2012.0
Captain America: Civil War	8.2	PG-13	2016.0
Guardians of the Galaxy	8.1	PG-13	2014.0
Interstellar	8.6	PG-13	2014.0
Inception	8.8	PG-13	2010.0
The Martian	8.1	PG-13	2015.0
Town & Country	4.4	R	2001.0
Sex and the City 2	4.3	R	2010.0
Rollerball	3.0	R	2002.0

How it works...

In step 1 and step 2, each set of criteria is built from simpler boolean expressions. It is not necessary to create a different variable for each boolean expression as done here, but it does make it far easier to read and debug any logic mistakes. As we desire both sets of movies, step 3 uses the pandas logical `or` operator to combine them.

Step 4 shows the exact syntax of how boolean indexing works. You simply pass the Series of booleans created from step 3 directly to the indexing operator. Only the movies with `True` values from `final_crit_all` are selected.

Boolean indexing also works with the `.loc` indexer as seen in step 5 by simultaneously doing boolean indexing and individual column selection. This slimmed DataFrame is far easier to check manually whether the logic was implemented correctly.

Boolean indexing does not quite work with the `.iloc` indexing operator. If you pass in a boolean series to it, an exception will get raised. However, if you pass in a boolean ndarray it will the same as it does in this recipe with the other indexers.

There's more...

As was stated earlier, it is possible to use one long boolean expression in place of several other shorter ones. To replicate the `final_crit_a` variable from step 1 with one long line of code, we can do the following:

```
>>> final_crit_a2 = (movie.imdb_score > 8) & \
                    (movie.content_rating == 'PG-13') & \
                    ((movie.title_year < 2000) |
                     (movie.title_year > 2009))
>>> final_crit_a2.equals(final_crit_a)
True
```

See also

- Pandas official documentation on *boolean indexing* (http://bit.ly/2v1xK77)
- Checking the truth of a Python object (http://bit.ly/2vn8WXX)

Replicating boolean indexing with index selection

It is possible to replicate specific cases of boolean selection by taking advantage of the index. Selection through the index is more intuitive and makes for greater readability.

Getting ready

In this recipe, we use the `college` dataset to select all institutions from a particular state with both boolean indexing and index selection and then compare each of their performance against one another.

How to do it...

1. Read in the `college` dataset and use boolean indexing to select all institutions from the state of Texas (TX):

    ```
    >>> college = pd.read_csv('data/college.csv')
    >>> college[college['STABBR'] == 'TX'].head()
    ```

Pandas official documentation on

	INSTNM	CITY	STABBR	HBCU	MENONLY	WOMENONLY	RELAFFIL	SATVRMID	SATMTMID	DISTANCEONLY
3610	Abilene Christian University	Abilene	TX	0.0	0.0	0.0	1	530.0	545.0	0.0
3611	Alvin Community College	Alvin	TX	0.0	0.0	0.0	0	NaN	NaN	0.0
3612	Amarillo College	Amarillo	TX	0.0	0.0	0.0	0	NaN	NaN	0.0
3613	Angelina College	Lufkin	TX	0.0	0.0	0.0	0	NaN	NaN	0.0
3614	Angelo State University	San Angelo	TX	0.0	0.0	0.0	0	475.0	490.0	0.0

2. To replicate this using index selection, we need to move the STABBR column into the index. We can then use label-based selection with the `.loc` indexer:

    ```
    >>> college2 = college.set_index('STABBR')
    >>> college2.loc['TX'].head()
    ```

STABBR	INSTNM	CITY	HBCU	MENONLY	WOMENONLY	RELAFFIL	SATVRMID	SATMTMID	DISTANCEONLY	UGDS
TX	Abilene Christian University	Abilene	0.0	0.0	0.0	1	530.0	545.0	0.0	3572.0
TX	Alvin Community College	Alvin	0.0	0.0	0.0	0	NaN	NaN	0.0	4682.0
TX	Amarillo College	Amarillo	0.0	0.0	0.0	0	NaN	NaN	0.0	9346.0
TX	Angelina College	Lufkin	0.0	0.0	0.0	0	NaN	NaN	0.0	3825.0
TX	Angelo State University	San Angelo	0.0	0.0	0.0	0	475.0	490.0	0.0	5290.0

3. Let's compare the speed of both methods:

```
>>> %timeit college[college['STABBR'] == 'TX']
1.43 ms ± 53.5 µs per loop (mean ± std. dev. of 7 runs, 1000 loops
each)

>>> %timeit college2.loc['TX']
526 µs ± 6.67 µs per loop (mean ± std. dev. of 7 runs, 1000 loops
each)
```

4. Boolean indexing takes three times as long as index selection. As setting the index does not come for free, let's time that operation as well:

```
>>> %timeit college2 = college.set_index('STABBR')
1.04 ms ± 5.37 µs per loop (mean ± std. dev. of 7 runs, 1000 loops
each)
```

How it works...

Step 1 creates a boolean Series by determining which rows of data have STABBR equal to TX. This Series is passed to the indexing operator, which subsets the data. This process may be replicated by moving that same column to the index and simply using basic label-based index selection with .loc. Selection via the index is much faster than boolean selection.

There's more...

This recipe only selects a single state. It is possible to select multiple states with both boolean and index selection. Let's select **Texas (TX)**, **California (CA)**, and **New York (NY)**. With boolean selection, you can use the isin method but with indexing, just pass a list to .loc:

```
>>> states = ['TX', 'CA', 'NY']
>>> college[college['STABBR'].isin(states)]
>>> college2.loc[states]
```

There is quite a bit more to the story than what this recipe explains. Pandas implements the index differently based on whether the index is unique or sorted. See the following recipe for more details.

Selecting with unique and sorted indexes

Index selection performance drastically improves when the index is unique or sorted. The prior recipe used an unsorted index that contained duplicates, which makes for relatively slow selections.

Getting ready

In this recipe, we use the college dataset to form unique or sorted indexes to increase the performance of index selection. We will continue to compare the performance to boolean indexing as well.

How to do it...

1. Read in the college dataset, create a separate DataFrame with STABBR as the index, and check whether the index is sorted:

```
>>> college = pd.read_csv('data/college.csv')
>>> college2 = college.set_index('STABBR')
>>> college2.index.is_monotonic
False
```

2. Sort the index from college2 and store it as another object:

```
>>> college3 = college2.sort_index()
>>> college3.index.is_monotonic
True
```

3. Time the selection of the state of Texas (TX) from all three DataFrames:

```
>>> %timeit college[college['STABBR'] == 'TX']
1.43 ms ± 53.5 µs per loop (mean ± std. dev. of 7 runs, 1000 loops each)

>>> %timeit college2.loc['TX']
526 µs ± 6.67 µs per loop (mean ± std. dev. of 7 runs, 1000 loops each)

>>> %timeit college3.loc['TX']
183 µs ± 3.67 µs per loop (mean ± std. dev. of 7 runs, 1000 loops each)
```

4. The sorted index performs nearly an order of magnitude faster than boolean selection. Let's now turn towards unique indexes. For this, we use the institution name as the index:

```
>>> college_unique = college.set_index('INSTNM')
>>> college_unique.index.is_unique
True
```

5. Let's select Stanford University with boolean indexing:

```
>>> college[college['INSTNM'] == 'Stanford University']
```

	INSTNM	CITY	STABBR	HBCU	MENONLY	WOMENONLY	RELAFFIL	SATVRMID	SATMTMID	DISTANCEONLY	...	UGDS_2MOR	UGDS_NRA
4217	Stanford University	Stanford	CA	0.0	0.0	0.0	0	730.0	745.0	0.0	...	0.1067	0.0819

6. Let's select Stanford University with index selection:

```
>>> college_unique.loc['Stanford University']
CITY                      Stanford
STABBR                          CA
HBCU                             0
...
UG25ABV                     0.0401
MD_EARN_WNE_P10              86000
GRAD_DEBT_MDN_SUPP          12782
Name: Stanford University, dtype: object
```

7. They both produce the same data, just with different objects. Let's time each approach:

```
>>> %timeit college[college['INSTNM'] == 'Stanford University']
1.3 ms ± 56.8 µs per loop (mean ± std. dev. of 7 runs, 1000 loops
each)

>>> %timeit college_unique.loc['Stanford University']
157 µs ± 682 ns per loop (mean ± std. dev. of 7 runs, 10000 loops
each)
```

How it works...

When the index is not sorted and contains duplicates, as with `college2`, pandas will need to check every single value in the index in order to make the correct selection. When the index is sorted, as with `college3`, pandas takes advantage of an algorithm called **binary search** to greatly improve performance.

In the second half of the recipe, we use a unique column as the index. Pandas implements unique indexes with a hash table, which makes for even faster selection. Each index location can be looked up in nearly the same time regardless of its length.

There's more...

Boolean selection gives much more flexibility than index selection as it is possible to condition on any number of columns. In this recipe, we used a single column as the index. It is possible to concatenate multiple columns together to form an index. For instance, in the following code, we set the index equal to the concatenation of the city and state columns:

```
>>> college.index = college['CITY'] + ', ' + college['STABBR']
>>> college = college.sort_index()
>>> college.head()
```

	INSTNM	CITY	STABBR	HBCU	MENONLY	WOMENONLY	RELAFFIL	SATVRMID	SATMTMID	DISTANCEONLY	...	UGDS_2MOR
ARTESIA, CA	Angeles Institute	ARTESIA	CA	0.0	0.0	0.0	0	NaN	NaN	0.0	...	0.0175
Aberdeen, SD	Presentation College	Aberdeen	SD	0.0	0.0	0.0	1	440.0	480.0	0.0	...	0.0284
Aberdeen, SD	Northern State University	Aberdeen	SD	0.0	0.0	0.0	0	480.0	475.0	0.0	...	0.0219
Aberdeen, WA	Grays Harbor College	Aberdeen	WA	0.0	0.0	0.0	0	NaN	NaN	0.0	...	0.0937
Abilene, TX	Hardin-Simmons University	Abilene	TX	0.0	0.0	0.0	1	508.0	515.0	0.0	...	0.0298

From here, we can select all colleges from a particular city and state combination without boolean indexing. Let's select all colleges from `Miami, FL`:

```
>>> college.loc['Miami, FL'].head()
```

	INSTNM	CITY	STABBR	HBCU	MENONLY	WOMENONLY	RELAFFIL	SATVRMID	SATMTMID	DISTANCEONLY	...	UGDS_2MOR
Miami, FL	New Professions Technical Institute	Miami	FL	0.0	0.0	0.0	0	NaN	NaN	0.0	...	0.0000
Miami, FL	Management Resources College	Miami	FL	0.0	0.0	0.0	0	NaN	NaN	0.0	...	0.0000
Miami, FL	Strayer University-Doral	Miami	FL	NaN	NaN	NaN	1	NaN	NaN	NaN	...	NaN
Miami, FL	Keiser University-Miami	Miami	FL	NaN	NaN	NaN	1	NaN	NaN	NaN	...	NaN
Miami, FL	George T Baker Aviation Technical College	Miami	FL	0.0	0.0	0.0	0	NaN	NaN	0.0	...	0.0046

We can compare the speed of this compound index selection with boolean indexing. There is more than an order of magnitude difference:

```
>>> %%timeit
>>> crit1 = college['CITY'] == 'Miami'
>>> crit2 = college['STABBR'] == 'FL'
>>> college[crit1 & crit2]
2.43 ms ± 80.4 µs per loop (mean ± std. dev. of 7 runs, 100 loops each)

>>> %timeit college.loc['Miami, FL']
197 µs ± 8.69 µs per loop (mean ± std. dev. of 7 runs, 10000 loops each)
```

See also

- The *Binary search algorithm* (http://bit.ly/2wbMq20)

Gaining perspective on stock prices

Investors who have purchased long stock positions would obviously like to sell stocks at or near their all-time highs. This, of course, is very difficult to do in practice, especially if a stock price has only spent a small portion of its history above a certain threshold. We can use boolean indexing to find all points in time that a stock has spent above or below a certain value. This exercise may help us gain perspective as to what a common range for some stock to be trading within.

Getting ready

In this recipe, we examine Schlumberger stock from the start of 2010 until mid-2017. We use boolean indexing to extract a Series of the lowest and highest ten percent of closing prices during this time period. We then plot all points and highlight those that are in the upper and lower ten percent.

How to do it...

1. Read in the Schlumberger stock data, put the `Date` column into the index, and convert it to a `DatetimeIndex`:

```
>>> slb = pd.read_csv('data/slb_stock.csv', index_col='Date',
                      parse_dates=['Date'])
>>> slb.head()
```

	Open	High	Low	Close	Volume
Date					
2010-01-04	66.39	67.20	66.12	67.11	5771234
2010-01-05	66.99	67.62	66.73	67.30	7366270
2010-01-06	67.17	68.94	67.03	68.80	9949946
2010-01-07	68.49	69.81	68.21	69.51	7700297
2010-01-08	69.19	72.00	69.09	70.65	13487621

2. Select the closing price as a Series and use the `describe` method to return summary statistics as a Series:

```
>>> slb_close = slb['Close']
>>> slb_summary = slb_close.describe(percentiles=[.1, .9])
>>> slb_summary
count    1895.000000
mean       79.121905
std        11.767802
min        51.750000
10%        64.892000
50%        78.000000
90%        93.248000
max       117.950000
Name: Close, dtype: float64
```

3. Using boolean selection, select all closing prices in the upper or lower tenth percentile:

```
>>> upper_10 = slb_summary.loc['90%']
>>> lower_10 = slb_summary.loc['10%']
>>> criteria = (slb_close < lower_10) | (slb_close > upper_10)
>>> slb_top_bottom_10 = slb_close[criteria]
```

4. Plot the resulting filtered Series in light gray on top of all closing prices in black. Use the `matplotlib` library to draw horizontal lines at the tenth and ninetieth percentiles:

```
>>> slb_close.plot(color='black', figsize=(12,6))
>>> slb_top_bottom_10.plot(marker='o', style=' ',
                            ms=4, color='lightgray')

>>> xmin = criteria.index[0]
>>> xmax = criteria.index[-1]
>>> plt.hlines(y=[lower_10, upper_10], xmin=xmin,
               xmax=xmax, color='black')
```

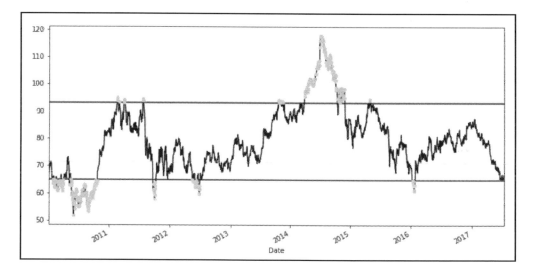

How it works...

The result of the `describe` method in step 2 is itself a Series with the identifying summary statistic as its index labels. This summary Series is used to store the tenth and ninetieth percentiles as their own variables. Step 3 uses boolean indexing to select only those values in the upper and lower tenth of the distribution.

Both Series and DataFrames have direct plotting capabilities through the `plot` method. This first call to the `plot` method comes from the `slb_close` Series, which contains all the SLB closing prices. This is the black line in the plot. The points from `slb_filtered` are plotted as gray markers directly on top of the closing prices. The `style` parameter is set to a single blank space so that no line is drawn. The `ms` parameter sets the marker size.

Matplotlib comes with a convenience function, `hlines`, that plots horizontal lines. It takes a list of `y` values and plots them from `xmin` to `xmax`.

Judging from our new perspective from the plots that we created, it's clear to see that although SLB's all-time high is close to $120 per share, only 10% of the trading days in the last seven years have been above $93 per share.

There's more...

Instead of plotting red points (black points) over the closing prices to indicate the upper and lower tenth percentiles, we can use matplotlib's `fill_between` function. This function fills in all the areas between two lines. It takes an optional `where` parameter that accepts a boolean Series, alerting it to exactly which locations to fill in:

```
>>> slb_close.plot(color='black', figsize=(12,6))
>>> plt.hlines(y=[lower_10, upper_10],
                xmin=xmin, xmax=xmax,color='lightgray')
>>> plt.fill_between(x=criteria.index, y1=lower_10,
                    y2=slb_close.values, color='black')
>>> plt.fill_between(x=criteria.index,y1=lower_10,
                    y2=slb_close.values, where=slb_close < lower_10,
                    color='lightgray')
>>> plt.fill_between(x=criteria.index, y1=upper_10,
                    y2=slb_close.values, where=slb_close > upper_10,
                    color='lightgray')
```

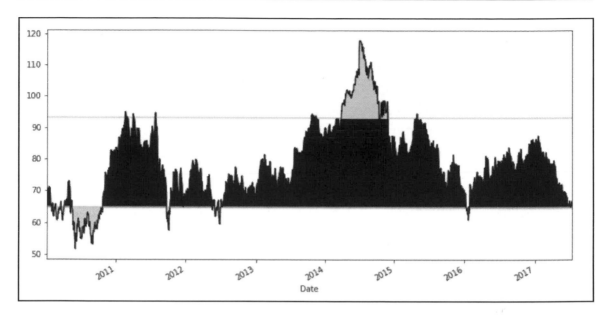

See also

- Refer to `Chapter 11`, *Visualization with Matplotlib, Pandas, and Seaborn*

Translating SQL WHERE clauses

Many pandas users will have a background processing data directly from databases using the ubiquitous **Structured Query Language** (SQL). SQL is a standardized language to define, manipulate, and control data stored in a database. The SELECT statement is the most common way to use SQL to select, filter, aggregate, and order data. Pandas has the ability to connect to databases and send SQL statements to them.

SQL is a very important language to know for data scientists. Much of the world's data is stored in databases that necessitate SQL to retrieve, manipulate, and perform analyses on. SQL syntax is fairly simple and easy to learn. There are many different SQL implementations from companies such as Oracle, Microsoft, IBM, and more. Although the syntax is not compatible between the different implementations, the core of it will look very much the same.

Getting ready

Within a SQL SELECT statement, the WHERE clause is very common and filters data. This recipe will write pandas code that is equivalent to a SQL query that selects a certain subset of the employee dataset.

It is not necessary to understand any SQL syntax to make use of this recipe.

Suppose we are given a task to find all the female employees that work in the police or fire departments that have a base salary between 80 and 120 thousand dollars. The following SQL statement would answer this query for us:

```
SELECT
    UNIQUE_ID,
    DEPARTMENT,
    GENDER,
    BASE_SALARY
FROM
    EMPLOYEE
WHERE
    DEPARTMENT IN ('Houston Police Department-HPD',
                   'Houston Fire Department (HFD)') AND
    GENDER = 'Female' AND
    BASE_SALARY BETWEEN 80000 AND 120000;
```

How to do it...

1. Read in the `employee` dataset as a DataFrame:

   ```
   >>> employee = pd.read_csv('data/employee.csv')
   ```

2. Before filtering out the data, it is helpful to do some manual inspection of each of the filtered columns to know the exact values that will be used in the filter:

   ```
   >>> employee.DEPARTMENT.value_counts().head()
   Houston Police Department-HPD       638
   Houston Fire Department (HFD)       384
   Public Works & Engineering-PWE      343
   Health & Human Services             110
   Houston Airport System (HAS)        106
   Name: DEPARTMENT, dtype: int64

   >>> employee.GENDER.value_counts()
    Male 1397
    Female 603

   >>> employee.BASE_SALARY.describe().astype(int)
   count        1886
   mean        55767
   std         21693
   min         24960
   25%         40170
   50%         54461
   75%         66614
   max        275000
   Name: BASE_SALARY, dtype: int64
   ```

3. Write a single statement for each of the criteria. Use the `isin` method to test equality to one of many values:

   ```
   >>> depts = ['Houston Police Department-HPD',
                'Houston Fire Department (HFD)']
   >>> criteria_dept = employee.DEPARTMENT.isin(depts)
   >>> criteria_gender = employee.GENDER == 'Female'
   >>> criteria_sal = (employee.BASE_SALARY >= 80000) & \
                      (employee.BASE_SALARY <= 120000)
   ```

4. Combine all the boolean Series together:

```
>>> criteria_final = (criteria_dept &
                      criteria_gender &
                      criteria_sal)
```

5. Use boolean indexing to select only the rows that meet the final criteria:

```
>>> select_columns = ['UNIQUE_ID', 'DEPARTMENT',
                      'GENDER', 'BASE_SALARY']
>>> employee.loc[criteria_final, select_columns].head()
```

	UNIQUE_ID	DEPARTMENT	GENDER	BASE_SALARY
61	11087	Houston Fire Department (HFD)	Female	96668.0
136	6146	Houston Police Department-HPD	Female	81239.0
367	7589	Houston Police Department-HPD	Female	86534.0
474	5407	Houston Police Department-HPD	Female	91181.0
513	6252	Houston Police Department-HPD	Female	81239.0

How it works...

Before any filtering is actually done, you will obviously need to know the exact string names that will be used. The Series `value_counts` method is an excellent way to get both the exact string name and number of occurrences of that value.

The `isin` Series method is equivalent to the SQL `IN` operator and accepts a list of all possible values that you would like to keep. It is possible to use a series of `OR` conditions to replicate this expression but it would not be as efficient or idiomatic.

The criteria for salary, `criteria_sal`, is formed by combining two simple inequality expressions. All the criteria are finally combined together with the pandas `and` operator, `&`, to yield a single boolean Series as the filter.

There's more...

For many operations, pandas has multiple ways to do the same thing. In the preceding recipe, the criteria for salary uses two separate boolean expressions. Similarly to SQL, Series have a `between` method, with the salary criteria equivalently written as follows:

```
>>> criteria_sal = employee.BASE_SALARY.between(80000, 120000)
```

Another useful application of `isin` is to provide a sequence of values automatically generated by some other pandas statements. This would avoid any manual investigating to find the exact string names to store in a list. Conversely, let's try to exclude the rows from the top five most frequently occurring departments:

```
>>> top_5_depts = employee.DEPARTMENT.value_counts().index[:5]
>>> criteria = ~employee.DEPARTMENT.isin(top_5_depts)
>>> employee[criteria]
```

The SQL equivalent of this would be as follows:

```
SELECT
    *
FROM
    EMPLOYEE
WHERE
    DEPARTMENT not in
    (
      SELECT
          DEPARTMENT
     FROM (
          SELECT
              DEPARTMENT,
              COUNT(1) as CT
          FROM
              EMPLOYEE
          GROUP BY
              DEPARTMENT
          ORDER BY
              CT DESC
          LIMIT 5
          )
    );
```

Notice the use of the pandas not operator, ~, which negates all boolean values of a Series.

See also

- Pandas official documentation of the isin (http://bit.ly/2v1GPfQ) and between (http://bit.ly/2wq9YPF) Series methods
- Refer to the *Connecting to SQL databases recipe* in Chapter 9, *Combining Pandas Objects*
- A basic introduction to SQL from W3 schools (http://bit.ly/2hsq8Wp)
- The SQL IN operator (http://bit.ly/2v3H7Bg)
- The SQL BETWEEN operator (http://bit.ly/2vn5UTP)

Determining the normality of stock market returns

In elementary statistics textbooks, the normal distribution is heavily relied upon to describe many different populations of data. Although many random processes do appear to look like normal distributions most of the time, real-life tends to be more complex. Stock market returns are a prime example of a distribution that can look fairly normal but in actuality be quite far off.

Getting ready

This recipe describes how to find daily stock market returns of the internet retail giant Amazon and informally test whether they follow a normal distribution.

How to do it...

1. Load Amazon stock data and set the date as the index:

```
>>> amzn = pd.read_csv('data/amzn_stock.csv', index_col='Date',
                       parse_dates=['Date'])
>>> amzn.head()
```

	Open	High	Low	Close	Volume
Date					
2010-01-04	136.25	136.61	133.14	133.90	7600543
2010-01-05	133.43	135.48	131.81	134.69	8856456
2010-01-06	134.60	134.73	131.65	132.25	7180977
2010-01-07	132.01	132.32	128.80	130.00	11030124
2010-01-08	130.56	133.68	129.03	133.52	9833829

2. Create a Series by selecting only the closing price and then using the `pct_change` method to get the daily rate of return:

```
>>> amzn_daily_return = amzn.Close.pct_change()
>>> amzn_daily_return.head()
Date
2010-01-04         NaN
2010-01-05    0.005900
2010-01-06   -0.018116
2010-01-07   -0.017013
2010-01-08    0.027077
Name: Close, dtype: float64
```

3. Drop the missing value and plot a histogram of the returns to visually inspect the distribution:

```
>>> amzn_daily_return = amzn_daily_return.dropna()
>>> amzn_daily_return.hist(bins=20)
```

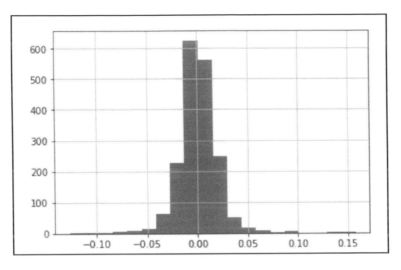

4. Normal distributions approximately follow the 68-95-99.7 rule--meaning that 68% of the data falls between 1 standard deviation of the mean, 95% between 2, and 99.7% between 3. We will now calculate the percentage of daily returns that fall between 1, 2, and 3 standard deviations from the mean. For this, we will need the mean and standard deviation:

```
>>> mean = amzn_daily_return.mean()
>>> std = amzn_daily_return.std()
```

5. Calculate the absolute value of the z-score for each observation. The z-score is the number of standard deviations away from the mean:

```
>>> abs_z_score = amzn_daily_return.sub(mean).abs().div(std)
```

6. Find the percentage of returns that are within 1, 2, and 3 standard deviations:

```
>>> pcts = [abs_z_score.lt(i).mean() for i in range(1,4)]
>>> print('{:.3f} fall within 1 standard deviation. '
          '{:.3f} within 2 and {:.3f} within 3'.format(*pcts))
0.787 fall within 1 standard deviation. 0.957 within 2 and 0.985
within 3
```

How it works...

By default, the `pct_change` Series method calculates the percentage change between the current element and previous element. This transforms the raw stock closing prices into daily percentage returns. The first element of the returned Series is a missing value as there is no previous price.

Histograms are fantastic plots to summarize and visualize one-dimensional numeric data. It is clear from the plot that the distribution is symmetrical but it remains difficult to determine whether it is normal or not. There are formal statistical procedures to determine the normality of a distribution but we will simply find how close the data matches the 68 95 99.7 rule.

Step 5 calculates the number of standard deviations away from the mean for each observation which is referred to as the `z-score`. This step uses the methods and not the symbols (- and /) to do subtraction and division. The method for less than is also used in favor of the symbols in step 6.

It may seem odd that the mean is being taken in step 6. The result of the `abs_z_score.lt(1)` expression is a Series of booleans. As booleans evaluate to 0 or 1, taking the mean of this Series returns the percentage of elements that are `True`, which is what we desired.

We can now more easily determine the normality of the returns by comparing the resulting numbers (78.7-95.7-98.5) to the 68-95-99.7 rule. The percentages deviate greatly from the rule for 1 and 3 standard deviations, and we can conclude that Amazon daily stock returns do not follow a normal distribution.

There's more...

To automate this process, we can write a function that accepts stock data in the and outputs the histogram of daily returns along with the percentages that fall within 1, 2, and 3 standard deviations from the mean. The following function does this and replaces the methods with their symbol counterparts:

```
>>> def test_return_normality(stock_data):
        close = stock_data['Close']
        daily_return = close.pct_change().dropna()
        daily_return.hist(bins=20)
        mean = daily_return.mean()
        std = daily_return.std()

        abs_z_score = abs(daily_return - mean) / std
```

```
        pcts = [abs_z_score.lt(i).mean() for i in range(1,4)]

        print('{:.3f} fall within 1 standard deviation. '
              '{:.3f} within 2 and {:.3f} within 3'.format(*pcts))

>>> slb = pd.read_csv('data/slb_stock.csv', index_col='Date',
                      parse_dates=['Date'])
>>> test_return_normality(slb)
0.742 fall within 1 standard deviation. 0.946 within 2 and 0.986 within 3
```

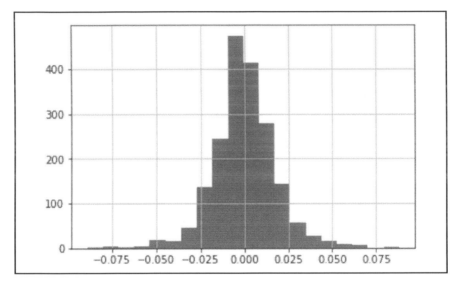

See also

- Pandas official documentation of the pct_change Series method (http://bit. ly/2wcjmqT)

Improving readability of boolean indexing with the query method

Boolean indexing is not necessarily the most pleasant syntax to read or write, especially when using a single line to write a complex filter. Pandas has an alternative string-based syntax through the DataFrame `query` method that can provide more clarity.

> The `query` DataFrame method is experimental and not as capable as boolean indexing and should not be used for production code.

Getting ready

This recipe replicates the earlier recipe in this chapter, *Translating SQL WHERE clauses*, but instead takes advantage of the `query` DataFrame method. The goal here is to filter the employee data for female employees from the police or fire departments that earn a salary between 80 and 120 thousand dollars.

How to do it...

1. Read in the employee data, assign the chosen departments, and import columns to variables:

```
>>> employee = pd.read_csv('data/employee.csv')
>>> depts = ['Houston Police Department-HPD',
            'Houston Fire Department (HFD)']
>>> select_columns = ['UNIQUE_ID', 'DEPARTMENT',
                        'GENDER', 'BASE_SALARY']
```

2. Build the query string and execute the method:

```
>>> qs = "DEPARTMENT in @depts " \
        "and GENDER == 'Female' " \
        "and 80000 <= BASE_SALARY <= 120000"
>>> emp_filtered = employee.query(qs)
>>> emp_filtered[select_columns].head()
```

	UNIQUE_ID	DEPARTMENT	GENDER	BASE_SALARY
61	11087	Houston Fire Department (HFD)	Female	96668.0
136	6146	Houston Police Department-HPD	Female	81239.0
367	7589	Houston Police Department-HPD	Female	86534.0
474	5407	Houston Police Department-HPD	Female	91181.0
513	6252	Houston Police Department-HPD	Female	81239.0

How it works...

Strings passed to the `query` method are going to look more like plain English than normal pandas code. It is possible to reference Python variables using the at symbol (@) as with `depts`. All DataFrame column names are available in the query namespace by simply referencing their name without inner quotes. If a string is needed, such as `Female`, inner quotes will need to wrap it.

Another nice feature of the `query` syntax is the ability to write a double inequality in a single expression and its ability to understand the verbose logical operators `and`, `or`, and `not` instead of their bitwise equivalents as with boolean indexing.

There's more...

Instead of manually typing in a list of department names, we could have programmatically created it. For instance, if we wanted to find all the female employees that were not a member of the top 10 departments by frequency, we can run the following code:

```
>>> top10_depts = employee.DEPARTMENT.value_counts() \
                            .index[:10].tolist()
>>> qs = "DEPARTMENT not in @top10_depts and GENDER == 'Female'"
>>> employee_filtered2 = employee.query(qs)
>>> employee_filtered2.head()
```

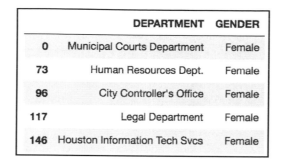

	DEPARTMENT	GENDER
0	Municipal Courts Department	Female
73	Human Resources Dept.	Female
96	City Controller's Office	Female
117	Legal Department	Female
146	Houston Information Tech Svcs	Female

See also

- Pandas official documentation on the `query` method (http://bit.ly/2vnlwXk)

Preserving Series with the where method

Boolean indexing necessarily filters your dataset by removing all the rows that don't match the criteria. Instead of dropping all these values, it is possible to keep them using the `where` method. The `where` method preserves the size of your Series or DataFrame and either sets the values that don't meet the criteria to missing or replaces them with something else.

Getting ready

In this recipe, we pass the `where` method boolean conditions to put a floor and ceiling on the minimum and maximum number of Facebook likes for actor 1 in the `movie` dataset.

How to do it...

1. Read the `movie` dataset, set the movie title as the index, and select all the values in the `actor_1_facebook_likes` column that are not missing:

```
>>> movie = pd.read_csv('data/movie.csv', index_col='movie_title')
>>> fb_likes = movie['actor_1_facebook_likes'].dropna()
>>> fb_likes.head()
movie_title
Avatar                                         1000.0
```

```
Pirates of the Caribbean: At World's End        40000.0
Spectre                                         11000.0
The Dark Knight Rises                           27000.0
Star Wars: Episode VII – The Force Awakens        131.0
Name: actor_1_facebook_likes, dtype: float64
```

2. Let's use the `describe` method to get a sense of the distribution:

```
>>> fb_likes.describe(percentiles=[.1, .25, .5, .75, .9]) \
        .astype(int)
count       4909
mean        6494
std        15106
min            0
10%          240
25%          607
50%          982
75%        11000
90%        18000
max       640000
Name: actor_1_facebook_likes, dtype: int64
```

3. Additionally, we may plot a histogram of this Series to visually inspect the distribution:

```
>>> fb_likes.hist()
```

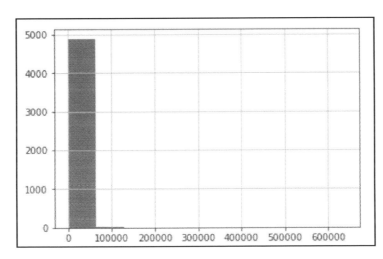

4. This is quite a bad visualization and very difficult to get a sense of the distribution. On the other hand, the summary statistics from step 2 appear to be telling us that it is highly skewed to the right with many observations more than an order of magnitude greater than the median. Let's create criteria to test whether the number of likes is less than 20,000:

```
>>> criteria_high = fb_likes < 20000
>>> criteria_high.mean().round(2)
.91
```

5. About 91% of the movies have an actor 1 with fewer than 20,000 likes. We will now use the `where` method, which accepts a boolean condition. The default behavior is to return a Series the same size as the original but which has all the `False` locations replaced with a missing value:

```
>>> fb_likes.where(criteria_high).head()
movie_title
Avatar                                          1000.0
Pirates of the Caribbean: At World's End           NaN
Spectre                                        11000.0
The Dark Knight Rises                              NaN
Star Wars: Episode VII - The Force Awakens       131.0
Name: actor_1_facebook_likes, dtype: float64
```

6. The second parameter to the `where` method, `other`, allows you to control the replacement value. Let's change all the missing values to 20,000:

```
>>> fb_likes.where(criteria_high, other=20000).head()
movie_title
Avatar                                          1000.0
Pirates of the Caribbean: At World's End       20000.0
Spectre                                        11000.0
The Dark Knight Rises                          20000.0
Star Wars: Episode VII - The Force Awakens       131.0
Name: actor_1_facebook_likes, dtype: float64
```

7. Similarly, we can create criteria to put a floor on the minimum number of likes. Here, we chain another `where` method and replace the values not meeting with the condition to `300`:

```
>>> criteria_low = fb_likes > 300
>>> fb_likes_cap = fb_likes.where(criteria_high, other=20000)\
                           .where(criteria_low, 300)
>>> fb_likes_cap.head()
movie_title
Avatar                                          1000.0
```

```
Pirates of the Caribbean: At World's End       20000.0
Spectre                                        11000.0
The Dark Knight Rises                          20000.0
Star Wars: Episode VII - The Force Awakens       300.0
Name: actor_1_facebook_likes, dtype: float64
```

8. The length of the original Series and modified Series is the same:

```
>>> len(fb_likes), len(fb_likes_cap)
(4909, 4909)
```

9. Let's make a histogram with the modified Series. With the data in a much tighter range, it should produce a better plot:

```
>>> fb_likes_cap.hist()
```

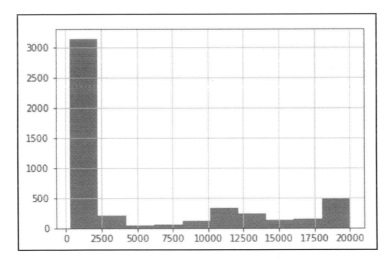

How it works...

The where method again preserves the size and shape of the calling object and does not modify the values where the passed boolean is True. It was important to drop the missing values in step 1 as the where method would have eventually replaced them with a valid number in future steps.

The summary statistics in step 2 give us some intuition where it would make sense to cap our data. The histogram from step 3, on the other hand, appears to clump all the data into one bin. The data has too many outliers for a plain histogram to make a good plot. The `where` method allows us to place a ceiling and floor on our data, which results in a histogram with many more visible bars.

There's more...

Pandas actually has built-in methods `clip`, `clip_lower`, and `clip_upper` that replicate this operation. The `clip` method can set a floor and ceiling at the same time. We also check whether this alternate method produces the exact same Series, which it does:

```
>>> fb_likes_cap2 = fb_likes.clip(lower=300, upper=20000)
>>> fb_likes_cap2.equals(fb_likes_cap)
True
```

See also

- Pandas official documentation on the `where` method (http://bit.ly/2vmW2cv)

Masking DataFrame rows

The `mask` method performs the exact opposite operation that the `where` method does. By default, it creates missing values wherever the boolean condition is `True`. In essence, it is literally masking, or covering up, values in your dataset.

Getting ready

In this recipe, we will mask all rows of the movie dataset that were made after 2010 and then filter all the rows with missing values.

How to do it...

1. Read the `movie` dataset, set the movie title as the index, and create the criteria:

```
>>> movie = pd.read_csv('data/movie.csv', index_col='movie_title')
>>> c1 = movie['title_year'] >= 2010
>>> c2 = movie['title_year'].isnull()
>>> criteria = c1 | c2
```

2. Use the `mask` method on a DataFrame to make all the values in rows with movies that were made from 2010 onward missing. Any movie that originally had a missing value for `title_year` is also masked:

```
>>> movie.mask(criteria).head()
```

movie_title	color	director_name	num_critic_for_reviews	duration	director_facebook_likes	actor_3_facebook_likes	actor_2_name	actor_1_facebook_likes
Avatar	Color	James Cameron	723.0	178.0	0.0	855.0	Joel David Moore	1000.0
Pirates of the Caribbean: At World's End	Color	Gore Verbinski	302.0	169.0	563.0	1000.0	Orlando Bloom	40000.0
Spectre	NaN	NaN	NaN	NaN	NaN	NaN	NaN	NaN
The Dark Knight Rises	NaN	NaN	NaN	NaN	NaN	NaN	NaN	NaN
Star Wars: Episode VII - The Force Awakens	NaN	NaN	NaN	NaN	NaN	NaN	NaN	NaN

3. Notice how all the values in the third, fourth, and fifth rows from the preceding DataFrame are missing. Chain the `dropna` method to remove rows that have all values missing:

```
>>> movie_mask = movie.mask(criteria).dropna(how='all')
>>> movie_mask.head()
```

movie_title	color	director_name	num_critic_for_reviews	duration	director_facebook_likes	actor_3_facebook_likes	actor_2_name	actor_1_facebook_likes
Avatar	Color	James Cameron	723.0	178.0	0.0	855.0	Joel David Moore	1000.0
Pirates of the Caribbean: At World's End	Color	Gore Verbinski	302.0	169.0	563.0	1000.0	Orlando Bloom	40000.0
Star Wars: Episode VII - The Force Awakens	NaN	Doug Walker	NaN	NaN	131.0	NaN	Rob Walker	131.0
Spider-Man 3	Color	Sam Raimi	392.0	156.0	0.0	4000.0	James Franco	24000.0
Harry Potter and the Half-Blood Prince	Color	David Yates	375.0	153.0	282.0	10000.0	Daniel Radcliffe	25000.0

4. The operation in step 3 is just a complex way of doing basic boolean indexing. We can check whether the two methods produce the same DataFrame:

```
>>> movie_boolean = movie[movie['title_year'] < 2010]
>>> movie_mask.equals(movie_boolean)
False
```

5. The `equals` method is telling us that they aren't equal. Something is wrong. Let's do some sanity checking and see if they are the same shape:

```
>>> movie_mask.shape == movie_boolean.shape
True
```

6. When we used the preceding `mask` method, it created many missing values. Missing values are `float` data types so any previous integer column is now a float. The `equals` method returns `False` if the data types of the columns are different, even if the values are the same. Let's check the equality of the data types to see whether this scenario happened:

```
>>> movie_mask.dtypes == movie_boolean.dtypes
color                       True
director_name               True
num_critic_for_reviews      True
duration                    True
director_facebook_likes     True
actor_3_facebook_likes      True
actor_2_name                True
actor_1_facebook_likes      True
```

```
gross                           True
genres                          True
actor_1_name                    True
num_voted_users                 False
cast_total_facebook_likes       False
.....
dtype: bool
```

7. It turns out that a couple of columns don't have the same data type. Pandas has an alternative for these situations. In its testing module, which is primarily used by developers, there is a function, `assert_frame_equal`, that allows you to check the equality of Series and DataFrames without also checking the equality of the data types:

```
from pandas.testing import assert_frame_equal
>>> assert_frame_equal(movie_boolean, movie_mask,
check_dtype=False)
```

How it works...

By default, the `mask` method covers up data with missing values. The first parameter to the `mask` method is the condition which is often a boolean Series such as `criteria`. Because the `mask` method is called from a DataFrame, all the values in each row where the condition is `False` change to missing. Step 3 uses this masked DataFrame to drop the rows that contain all missing values. Step 4 shows how to do this same procedure with boolean indexing.

During a data analysis, it is very important to continually validate results. Checking the equality of Series and DataFrames is an extremely common approach to validation. Our first attempt, in step 4, yielded an unexpected result. Some basic sanity checking, such as ensuring that the number of rows and columns are the same or that the row and column names are the same, are good checks before going deeper.

Step 6 compares the two Series of data types together. It is here where we uncover the reason why the DataFrames were not equivalent. The `equals` method checks that both the values and data types are the same. The `assert_frame_equal` function from step 7 has many available parameters to test equality in a variety of ways. Notice that there is no output after calling `assert_frame_equal`. This method returns None when the two passed DataFrames are equal and raises an error when they are not.

There's more...

Let's compare the speed difference between masking and dropping missing rows and boolean indexing. Boolean indexing is about an order of magnitude faster in this case:

```
>>> %timeit movie.mask(criteria).dropna(how='all')
11.2 ms ± 144 µs per loop (mean ± std. dev. of 7 runs, 100 loops each)

>>> %timeit movie[movie['title_year'] < 2010]
1.07 ms ± 34.9 µs per loop (mean ± std. dev. of 7 runs, 1000 loops each)
```

See also

- Pandas official documentation on `assert_frame_equal` (http://bit.ly/2u5H5Yl)
- Python official documentation of the `assert` statement (http://bit.ly/2v1YKmY)

Selecting with booleans, integer location, and labels

Chapter 4, *Selecting Subsets of Data*, covered a wide range of recipes on selecting different subsets of data through the `.iloc` and `.loc` indexers. Both these indexers select rows and columns simultaneously by either integer location or label. Both these indexers can also do data selection through boolean indexing, even though booleans are not integers and not labels.

Getting ready

In this recipe, we will filter both rows and columns with boolean indexing for both the `.iloc` and `.loc` indexers.

How to do it...

1. Read in the movie dataset, set the index as the title, and then create a boolean Series matching all movies with a content rating of G and an IMDB score less than 4:

    ```
    >>> movie = pd.read_csv('data/movie.csv', index_col='movie_title')
    >>> c1 = movie['content_rating'] == 'G'
    >>> c2 = movie['imdb_score'] < 4
    >>> criteria = c1 & c2
    ```

2. Let's first pass these criteria to the .loc indexer to filter the rows:

    ```
    >>> movie_loc = movie.loc[criteria]
    >>> movie_loc.head()
    ```

movie_title	color	director_name	num_critic_for_reviews	duration	director_facebook_likes	actor_3_facebook_likes	actor_2_name	actor_1_facebook_likes
The True Story of Puss'N Boots	Color	Jérôme Deschamps	4.0	80.0	0.0	0.0	André Wilms	44.0
Doogal	Color	Dave Borthwick	31.0	77.0	3.0	593.0	Kylie Minogue	787.0
Thomas and the Magic Railroad	Color	Britt Allcroft	47.0	85.0	2.0	402.0	Colm Feore	1000.0
Barney's Great Adventure	Color	Steve Gomer	24.0	76.0	9.0	47.0	Kyla Pratt	595.0
Justin Bieber: Never Say Never	Color	Jon M. Chu	84.0	115.0	209.0	41.0	Sean Kingston	569.0

3. Let's check whether this DataFrame is exactly equal to the one generated directly from the indexing operator:

    ```
    >>> movie_loc.equals(movie[criteria])
    True
    ```

4. Now let's attempt the same boolean indexing with the `.iloc` indexer:

```
>>> movie_iloc = movie.iloc[criteria]
ValueError: iLocation based boolean indexing cannot use an
indexable as a mask
```

5. It turns out that we cannot directly use a Series of booleans because of the index. We can, however, use an ndarray of booleans. To extract the array, use the `values` attribute:

```
>>> movie_iloc = movie.iloc[criteria.values]
>>> movie_iloc.equals(movie_loc)
True
```

6. Although not very common, it is possible to do boolean indexing to select particular columns. Here, we select all the columns that have a data type of 64-bit integers:

```
>>> criteria_col = movie.dtypes == np.int64
>>> criteria_col.head()
color                       False
director_name               False
num_critic_for_reviews      False
duration                    False
director_facebook_likes     False
dtype: bool

>>> movie.loc[:, criteria_col].head()
```

movie_title	num_voted_users	cast_total_facebook_likes	movie_facebook_likes
Avatar	886204	4834	33000
Pirates of the Caribbean: At World's End	471220	48350	0
Spectre	275868	11700	85000
The Dark Knight Rises	1144337	106759	164000
Star Wars: Episode VII - The Force Awakens	8	143	0

7. As `criteria_col` is a Series, which always has an index, you must use the underlying ndarray to make it work with `.iloc`. The following produces the same result as step 6.

```
>>> movie.iloc[:, criteria_col.values].head()
```

8. A boolean Series may be used to select rows and then simultaneously select columns with either integers or labels. Remember, you need to put a comma between the row and column selections. Let's keep the row criteria and select `content_rating`, `imdb_score`, `title_year`, and `gross`:

```
>>> cols = ['content_rating', 'imdb_score', 'title_year', 'gross']
>>> movie.loc[criteria, cols].sort_values('imdb_score')
```

movie_title	content_rating	imdb_score	title_year	gross
Justin Bieber: Never Say Never	G	1.6	2011.0	73000942.0
Sunday School Musical	G	2.5	2008.0	NaN
Doogal	G	2.8	2006.0	7382993.0
Barney's Great Adventure	G	2.8	1998.0	11144518.0
The True Story of Puss'N Boots	G	2.9	2009.0	NaN
Thomas and the Magic Railroad	G	3.6	2000.0	15911333.0

9. This same operation may be replicated with `.iloc`, but you need to get the integer location of all the columns:

```
>>> col_index = [movie.columns.get_loc(col) for col in cols]
>>> col_index
[20, 24, 22, 8]

>>> movie.iloc[criteria.values, col_index]
```

How it works...

Boolean indexing may be accomplished with both the `.iloc` and `.loc` indexers with the caveat that `.iloc` cannot be passed a Series but the underlying ndarray. Let's take a look at the one-dimensional ndarray underlying the criteria Series:

```
>>> a = criteria.values
>>> a[:5]
array([False, False, False, False, False], dtype=bool)

>>> len(a), len(criteria)
(4916, 4916)
```

The array is the same length as the Series, which is the same length as the movie DataFrame. The integer location for the boolean array aligns with the integer location of the DataFrame and the filter happens as expected. These arrays also work with the `.loc` operator as well but they are a necessity for `.iloc`.

Steps 6 and 7 show how to filter by columns instead of by rows. The colon, `:`, is needed to indicate the selection of all the rows. The comma following the colon separates the row and column selections. There is actually a much easier way to select columns with integer data types and that is through the `select_dtypes` method.

Steps 8 and 9 show a very common and useful way to do boolean indexing on the row and column selections simultaneously. You simply place a comma between the row and column selections. Step 9 uses a list comprehension to loop through all the desired column names to find their integer location with the index method `get_loc`.

There's more...

It is actually possible to pass arrays and lists of booleans to Series objects that are not the same length as the DataFrame you are doing the indexing on. Let's look at an example of this by selecting the first and third rows, and the first and fourth columns:

```
>>> movie.loc[[True, False, True], [True, False, False, True]]
```

	color	duration
movie_title		
Avatar	Color	178.0
Spectre	Color	148.0

Both of the boolean lists are not the same length as the axis they are indexing. The rest of the rows and columns not explicitly given a boolean value in the lists are dropped.

See also

- Refer to the *Selecting data with both integers and labels* recipe from Chapter 4, *Selecting Subsets of Data*
- Refer to the *Selecting columns with methods* recipe from Chapter 2, *Essential DataFrame Operations*

6
Index Alignment

In this chapter, we will cover the following topics:

- Examining the Index object
- Producing Cartesian products
- Exploding indexes
- Filling values with unequal indexes
- Appending columns from different DataFrames
- Highlighting the maximum value from each column
- Replicating `idxmax` with method chaining
- Finding the most common maximum

Introduction

When multiple Series or DataFrames are combined in some way, each dimension of the data automatically aligns on each axis first before any computation happens. This silent and automatic alignment of axes can cause tremendous confusion for the uninitiated, but it gives great flexibility to the power user. This chapter explores the Index object in-depth before showcasing a variety of recipes that take advantage of its automatic alignment.

Examining the Index object

As was discussed in Chapter 1, *Pandas Foundations*, each axis of Series and DataFrames has an Index object that labels the values. There are many different types of Index objects, but they all share the same common behavior. All Index objects, except for the special MultiIndex, are single-dimensional data structures that combine the functionality and implementation of Python sets and NumPy ndarrays.

Getting ready

In this recipe, we will examine the column index of the college dataset and explore much of its functionality.

How to do it...

1. Read in the college dataset, assign for the column index to a variable, and output it:

```
>>> college = pd.read_csv('data/college.csv')
>>> columns = college.columns
>>> columns
Index(['INSTNM', 'CITY', 'STABBR', 'HBCU', ...], dtype='object')
```

2. Use the `values` attribute to access the underlying NumPy array:

```
>>> columns.values
array(['INSTNM', 'CITY', 'STABBR', 'HBCU', ...], dtype=object)
```

3. Select items from the index by integer location with scalars, lists, or slices:

```
>>> columns[5]
'WOMENONLY'

>>> columns[[1,8,10]]
Index(['CITY', 'SATMTMID', 'UGDS'], dtype='object')

>>> columns[-7:-4]
Index(['PPTUG_EF', 'CURROPER', 'PCTPELL'], dtype='object')
```

4. Indexes share many of the same methods as Series and DataFrames:

```
>>> columns.min(), columns.max(), columns.isnull().sum()
('CITY', 'WOMENONLY', 0)
```

5. Use basic arithmetic and comparison operators directly on `Index` objects:

```
>>> columns + '_A'
Index(['INSTNM_A', 'CITY_A', 'STABBR_A', 'HBCU_A', ...],
dtype='object')

>>> columns > 'G'
array([ True, False,  True,  True, ...], dtype=bool)
```

6. Trying to change an Index value directly after its creation fails. Indexes are immutable objects:

```
>>> columns[1] = 'city'
TypeError: Index does not support mutable operations
```

How it works...

As you can see from many of the Index object operations, it appears to have quite a bit in common with both Series and ndarrays. One of the biggest differences comes in step 6. Indexes are immutable and their values cannot be changed once created.

There's more...

Indexes support the set operations, union, intersection, difference, and symmetric difference:

```
>>> c1 = columns[:4]
>>> c1
Index(['INSTNM', 'CITY', 'STABBR', 'HBCU'], dtype='object')

>>> c2 = columns[2:6]
>>> c2
Index(['STABBR', 'HBCU', 'MENONLY'], dtype='object')

>>> c1.union(c2) # or `c1 | c2`
Index(['CITY', 'HBCU', 'INSTNM', 'MENONLY', 'RELAFFIL', 'STABBR'],
dtype='object')

>>> c1.symmetric_difference(c2) # or `c1 ^ c2`
Index(['CITY', 'INSTNM', 'MENONLY'], dtype='object')
```

Indexes share some of the same operations as Python sets. Indexes are similar to Python sets in another important way. They are (usually) implemented using hash tables, which make for extremely fast access when selecting rows or columns from a DataFrame. As they are implemented using hash tables, the values for the Index object need to be immutable such as a string, integer, or tuple just like the keys in a Python dictionary.

 Indexes support duplicate values, and if there happens to be a duplicate in any Index, then a hash table can no longer be used for its implementation, and object access becomes much slower.

See also

- Pandas official documentation of Index (http://bit.ly/2upfgtr)

Producing Cartesian products

Whenever two Series or DataFrames operate with another Series or DataFrame, the indexes (both the row index and column index) of each object align first before any operation begins. This index alignment happens silently and can be very surprising for those new to pandas. This alignment always creates a Cartesian product between the indexes unless the indexes are identical.

 A Cartesian product is a mathematical term that usually appears in set theory. A Cartesian product between two sets is all the combinations of pairs of both sets. For example, the 52 cards in a standard playing card deck represent a Cartesian product between the 13 ranks (A, 2, 3,..., Q, K) and the four suits.

Getting ready

Producing a Cartesian product isn't always the intended outcome, but it's extremely important to be aware of how and when it occurs to avoid unintended consequences. In this recipe, two Series with overlapping but non-identical indexes are added together, yielding a surprising result.

How to do it...

Follow these steps to create a Cartesian product:

1. Construct two Series that have indexes that are different but contain some of the same values:

```
>>> s1 = pd.Series(index=list('aaab'), data=np.arange(4))
>>> s1
a    0
a    1
a    2
b    3
dtype: int64

>>> s2 = pd.Series(index=list('cababb'), data=np.arange(6))
>>> s2
c    0
a    1
b    2
a    3
```

```
b    4
b    5
dtype: int64
```

2. Add the two Series together to produce a Cartesian product:

```
>>> s1 + s2
a    1.0
a    3.0
a    2.0
a    4.0
a    3.0
a    5.0
b    5.0
b    7.0
b    8.0
c    NaN
dtype: float64
```

How it works...

Each Series was created with the class constructor which accepts a wide variety of inputs with the simplest being a sequence of values for each of the parameters `index` and data.

Mathematical Cartesian products are slightly different from the outcome of operating on two pandas objects. Each a label in `s1` pairs up with each a label in `s2`. This pairing produces six a labels, three b labels, and one c label in the resulting Series. A Cartesian product happens between all identical index labels.

As the element with label c is unique to Series `s2`, pandas defaults its value to missing, as there is no label for it to align to in `s1`. Pandas defaults to a missing value whenever an index label is unique to one object. This has the unfortunate consequence of changing the data type of the Series to a float, whereas each Series had only integers as values. This occurred because of NumPy's missing value object; `np.nan` only exists for floats but not for integers. Series and DataFrame columns must have homogeneous numeric data types; therefore, each value was converted to a float. This makes very little difference for this small dataset, but for larger datasets, this can have a significant memory impact.

There's more...

An exception to the preceding example takes place when the indexes contain the same exact elements in the same order. When this occurs, a Cartesian product does not take place, and the indexes instead align by their position. Notice here that each element aligned exactly by position and that the data type remained an integer:

```
>>> s1 = pd.Series(index=list('aaabb'), data=np.arange(5))
>>> s2 = pd.Series(index=list('aaabb'), data=np.arange(5))
>>> s1 + s2
a    0
a    2
a    4
b    6
b    8
dtype: int64
```

If the elements of the index are identical, but the order is different between the Series, a Cartesian product occurs. Let's change the order of the index in s2 and rerun the same operation:

```
>>> s1 = pd.Series(index=list('aaabb'), data=np.arange(5))
>>> s2 = pd.Series(index=list('bbaaa'), data=np.arange(5))
>>> s1 + s2
a    2
a    3
a    4
a    3
a    4
a    5
a    4
a    5
a    6
b    3
b    4
b    4
b    5
dtype: int64
```

It is quite interesting that pandas has two drastically different outcomes for this same operation. If a Cartesian product was the only choice for pandas, then something as simple as adding DataFrame columns together would explode the number of elements returned.

In this recipe, each Series had a different number of elements. Typically, array-like data structures in Python and other languages do not allow operations to take place when the operating dimensions do not contain the same number of elements. Pandas allows this to happen by aligning the indexes first before completing the operation.

See also

- *Reducing memory by changing data types* recipe in Chapter 3, *Beginning Data Analysis*

Exploding indexes

The previous recipe walked through a trivial example of two small Series being added together with unequal indexes. This problem can produce comically incorrect results when dealing with larger data.

Getting ready

In this recipe, we add two larger Series that have indexes with only a few unique values but in different orders. The result will explode the number of values in the indexes.

How to do it...

1. Read in the employee data and set the index equal to the race column:

```
>>> employee = pd.read_csv('data/employee.csv', index_col='RACE')
>>> employee.head()
```

RACE	UNIQUE_ID	POSITION_TITLE	DEPARTMENT	BASE_SALARY	EMPLOYMENT_TYPE	GENDER	EMPLOYMENT_STATUS	HIRE_DATE
Hispanic/Latino	0	ASSISTANT DIRECTOR (EX LVL)	Municipal Courts Department	121862.0	Full Time	Female	Active	2006-06-12
Hispanic/Latino	1	LIBRARY ASSISTANT	Library	26125.0	Full Time	Female	Active	2000-07-19
White	2	POLICE OFFICER	Houston Police Department-HPD	45279.0	Full Time	Male	Active	2015-02-03
White	3	ENGINEER/OPERATOR	Houston Fire Department (HFD)	63166.0	Full Time	Male	Active	1982-02-08
White	4	ELECTRICIAN	General Services Department	56347.0	Full Time	Male	Active	1989-06-19

2. Select the BASE_SALARY column as two different Series. Check to see whether this operation actually did create two new objects:

```
>>> salary1 = employee['BASE_SALARY']
>>> salary2 = employee['BASE_SALARY']
>>> salary1 is salary2
True
```

3. The salary1 and salary2 variables are actually referring to the same object. This means that any change to one will change the other. To ensure that you receive a brand new copy of the data, use the copy method:

```
>>> salary1 = employee['BASE_SALARY'].copy()
>>> salary2 = employee['BASE_SALARY'].copy()
>>> salary1 is salary2
False
```

4. Let's change the order of the index for one of the Series by sorting it:

```
>>> salary1 = salary1.sort_index()
>>> salary1.head()
RACE
American Indian or Alaskan Native    78355.0
American Indian or Alaskan Native    81239.0
American Indian or Alaskan Native    60347.0
American Indian or Alaskan Native    68299.0
American Indian or Alaskan Native    26125.0
Name: BASE_SALARY, dtype: float64

>>> salary2.head()
RACE
Hispanic/Latino    121862.0
Hispanic/Latino     26125.0
```

```
White                   45279.0
White                   63166.0
White                   56347.0
Name: BASE_SALARY, dtype: float64
```

5. Let's add these `salary` Series together:

```
>>> salary_add = salary1 + salary2
>>> salary_add.head()
RACE
American Indian or Alaskan Native    138702.0
American Indian or Alaskan Native    156710.0
American Indian or Alaskan Native    176891.0
American Indian or Alaskan Native    159594.0
American Indian or Alaskan Native    127734.0
Name: BASE_SALARY, dtype: float64
```

6. The operation completed successfully. Let's create one more Series of `salary1` added to itself and then output the lengths of each Series. We just exploded the index from 2,000 values to more than 1 million:

```
>>> salary_add1 = salary1 + salary1
>>> len(salary1), len(salary2), len(salary_add), len(salary_add1)
(2000, 2000, 1175424, 2000)
```

How it works...

Step 2 appears at first to create two unique objects but in fact, it creates a single object that is referred to by two different variable names. The expression `employee['BASE_SALARY']`, technically creates a **view**, and not a brand new copy. This is verified with the `is` operator.

 In pandas, a view is not a new object but just a reference to another object, usually some subset of a DataFrame. This shared object can be a cause for many issues.

To ensure that both variables reference completely different objects, we use the `copy` Series method and again verify that they are different objects with the `is` operator. Step 4 uses the `sort_index` method to sort the Series by race. Step 5 adds these different Series together to produce some result. By just inspecting the head, it's still not clear what has been produced.

Step 6 adds `salary1` to itself to show a comparison between the two different Series additions. The length of all the Series in this recipe are output and we clearly see that `series_add` has now exploded to over one million values. A Cartesian product took place for each unique value in the index because the indexes were not exactly the same. This recipe dramatically shows how much of an impact the index can have when combining multiple Series or DataFrames.

There's more...

We can verify the number of values of `salary_add` by doing a little mathematics. As a Cartesian product takes place between all of the same index values, we can sum the square of their individual counts. Even missing values in the index produce Cartesian products with themselves:

```
>>> index_vc = salary1.index.value_counts(dropna=False)
>>> index_vc
Black or African American              700
White                                  665
Hispanic/Latino                        480
Asian/Pacific Islander                 107
NaN                                     35
American Indian or Alaskan Native       11
Others                                   2
Name: RACE, dtype: int64

>>> index_vc.pow(2).sum()
1175424
```

Filling values with unequal indexes

When two Series are added together using the plus operator and one of the index labels does not appear in the other, the resulting value is always missing. Pandas offers the `add` method, which provides an option to fill the missing value.

Getting ready

In this recipe, we add together multiple Series from the `baseball` dataset with unequal indexes using the `fill_value` parameter of the `add` method to ensure that there are no missing values in the result.

How to do it...

1. Read in the three `baseball` datasets and set the index as `playerID`:

```
>>> baseball_14 = pd.read_csv('data/baseball14.csv',
                              index_col='playerID')
>>> baseball_15 = pd.read_csv('data/baseball15.csv',
                              index_col='playerID')
>>> baseball_16 = pd.read_csv('data/baseball16.csv',
                              index_col='playerID')
>>> baseball_14.head()
```

playerID	yearID	stint	teamID	lgID	G	AB	R	H	2B	3B	...	RBI	SB	CS	BB	SO	IBB	HBP	SH	SF	GIDP
altuvjo01	2014	1	HOU	AL	158	660	85	225	47	3	...	59.0	56.0	9.0	36	53.0	7.0	5.0	1.0	5.0	20.0
cartech02	2014	1	HOU	AL	145	507	68	115	21	1	...	88.0	5.0	2.0	56	182.0	6.0	5.0	0.0	4.0	12.0
castrja01	2014	1	HOU	AL	126	465	43	103	21	2	...	56.0	1.0	0.0	34	151.0	1.0	9.0	1.0	3.0	11.0
corpoca01	2014	1	HOU	AL	55	170	22	40	6	0	...	19.0	0.0	0.0	14	37.0	0.0	3.0	1.0	2.0	3.0
dominma01	2014	1	HOU	AL	157	564	51	121	17	0	...	57.0	0.0	1.0	29	125.0	2.0	5.0	2.0	7.0	23.0

2. Use the index method `difference` to discover which index labels are in `baseball_14` and not in `baseball_15`, and vice versa:

```
>>> baseball_14.index.difference(baseball_15.index)
Index(['corpoca01', 'dominma01', 'fowlede01', 'grossro01',
       'guzmaje01', 'hoeslj01', 'krausma01', 'preslal01',
       'singljo02'], dtype='object', name='playerID')

>>> baseball_14.index.difference(baseball_16.index)
Index(['congeha01', 'correca01', 'gattiev01', 'gomezca01',
       'lowrije01', 'rasmuco01', 'tuckepr01', 'valbulu01'],
      dtype='object', name='playerID')
```

3. There are quite a few players unique to each index. Let's find out how many hits each player has in total over the three-year period. The H column contains the number of hits:

```
>>> hits_14 = baseball_14['H']
>>> hits_15 = baseball_15['H']
>>> hits_16 = baseball_16['H']
>>> hits_14.head()
playerID
altuvjo01    225
```

```
cartech02    115
castrja01    103
corpoca01     40
dominma01    121
Name: H, dtype: int64
```

4. Let's first add together two Series using the plus operator:

```
>>> (hits_14 + hits_15).head()
playerID
altuvjo01    425.0
cartech02    193.0
castrja01    174.0
congeha01      NaN
corpoca01      NaN
Name: H, dtype: float64
```

5. Even though players congeha01 and corpoca01 have recorded hits for 2015, their result is missing. Let's use the add method and its parameter, fill_value, to avoid missing values:

```
>>> hits_14.add(hits_15, fill_value=0).head()
playerID
altuvjo01    425.0
cartech02    193.0
castrja01    174.0
congeha01     46.0
corpoca01     40.0
Name: H, dtype: float64
```

6. We add hits from 2016 by chaining the `add` method once more:

```
>>> hits_total = hits_14.add(hits_15, fill_value=0) \
                        .add(hits_16, fill_value=0)
>>> hits_total.head()
playerID
altuvjo01    641.0
bregmal01     53.0
cartech02    193.0
castrja01    243.0
congeha01     46.0
Name: H, dtype: float64
```

7. Check for missing values in the result:

```
>>> hits_total.hasnans
False
```

How it works...

The `add` method works similarly to the plus operator but allows for more flexibility by providing the `fill_value` parameter to take the place of a non-matching index. In this problem, it makes sense to default the non-matching index value to 0, but you could have used any other number.

There will be occasions when each Series contains index labels that correspond to missing values. In this specific instance, when the two Series are added, the index label will still correspond to a missing value regardless if the `fill_value` parameter is used. To clarify this, take a look at the following example where the index label a corresponds to a missing value in each Series:

```
>>> s = pd.Series(index=['a', 'b', 'c', 'd'],
                  data=[np.nan, 3, np.nan, 1])
>>> s
a    NaN
b    3.0
c    NaN
d    1.0
dtype: float64

>>> s1 = pd.Series(index=['a', 'b', 'c'], data=[np.nan, 6, 10])
>>> s1
a    NaN
b    6.0
c    10.0
```

```
dtype: float64

>>> s.add(s1, fill_value=5)
a     NaN
b     9.0
c    15.0
d     6.0
dtype: float64
```

There's more...

This recipe shows how to add Series with only a single index together. It is also entirely possible to add DataFrames together. Adding DataFrames together will align both the index and columns before computation and yield missing values for non-matching indexes. Let's start by selecting a few of the columns from the 2014 baseball dataset.

```
>>> df_14 = baseball_14[['G','AB', 'R', 'H']]
>>> df_14.head()
```

	G	AB	R	H
playerID				
altuvjo01	158	660	85	225
cartech02	145	507	68	115
castrja01	126	465	43	103
corpoca01	55	170	22	40
dominma01	157	564	51	121

Let's also select a few of the same and a few different columns from the 2015 baseball dataset:

```
>>> df_15 = baseball_15[['AB', 'R', 'H', 'HR']]
>>> df_15.head()
```

	AB	R	H	HR
playerID				
altuvjo01	638	86	200	15
cartech02	391	50	78	24
castrja01	337	38	71	11
congeha01	201	25	46	11
correca01	387	52	108	22

Adding the two DataFrames together create missing values wherever rows or column labels cannot align. Use the `style` attribute to access the `highlight_null` method to easily see where the missing values are:

```
>>> (df_14 + df_15).head(10).style.highlight_null('yellow')
```

playerID	AB	G	H	HR	R
altuvjo01	1298	nan	425	nan	171
cartech02	898	nan	193	nan	118
castrja01	802	nan	174	nan	81
congeha01	nan	nan	nan	nan	nan
corpoca01	nan	nan	nan	nan	nan
correca01	nan	nan	nan	nan	nan
dominma01	nan	nan	nan	nan	nan
fowlede01	nan	nan	nan	nan	nan
gattiev01	nan	nan	nan	nan	nan
gomezca01	nan	nan	nan	nan	nan

Only the rows with `playerID` appearing in both DataFrames will be non-missing. Similarly, the columns `AB`, `H`, and `R` are the only ones that appear in both DataFrames. Even if we use the `add` method with the `fill_value` parameter specified, we still have missing values. This is because some combinations of rows and columns never existed in our input data. For example, the intersection of `playerID` *congeha01* and column `G`. He only appeared in the 2015 dataset that did not have the `G` column. Therefore, no value was filled with it:

```
>>> df_14.add(df_15, fill_value=0).head(10) \
        .style.highlight_null('yellow')
```

playerID	AB	G	H	HR	R
altuvjo01	1298	158	425	15	171
cartech02	898	145	193	24	118
castrja01	802	126	174	11	81
congeha01	201	nan	46	11	25
corpoca01	170	55	40	nan	22
correca01	387	nan	108	22	52
dominma01	564	157	121	nan	51
fowlede01	434	116	120	nan	61
gattiev01	566	nan	139	27	66
gomezca01	149	nan	36	4	19

Appending columns from different DataFrames

All DataFrames can add new columns to themselves. However, as usual, whenever a DataFrame is adding a new column from another DataFrame or Series, the indexes align first before the new column is created.

Getting ready

This recipe uses the `employee` dataset to append a new column containing the maximum salary of that employee's department.

How to do it...

1. Import the `employee` data and select the DEPARTMENT and BASE_SALARY columns in a new DataFrame:

```
>>> employee = pd.read_csv('data/employee.csv')
>>> dept_sal = employee[['DEPARTMENT', 'BASE_SALARY']]
```

2. Sort this smaller DataFrame by salary within each department:

```
>>> dept_sal = dept_sal.sort_values(['DEPARTMENT', 'BASE_SALARY'],
                                    ascending=[True, False])
```

3. Use the `drop_duplicates` method to keep the first row of each DEPARTMENT:

```
>>> max_dept_sal = dept_sal.drop_duplicates(subset='DEPARTMENT')
>>> max_dept_sal.head()
```

	DEPARTMENT	BASE_SALARY
1494	Admn. & Regulatory Affairs	140416.0
149	City Controller's Office	64251.0
236	City Council	100000.0
647	Convention and Entertainment	38397.0
1500	Dept of Neighborhoods (DON)	89221.0

4. Put the DEPARTMENT column into the index for each DataFrames:

```
>>> max_dept_sal = max_dept_sal.set_index('DEPARTMENT')
>>> employee = employee.set_index('DEPARTMENT')
```

5. Now that the indexes contain matching values, we can append a new column to the `employee` DataFrame:

```
>>> employee['MAX_DEPT_SALARY'] = max_dept_sal['BASE_SALARY']
>>> employee.head()
```

DEPARTMENT	UNIQUE_ID	POSITION_TITLE	BASE_SALARY	...	HIRE_DATE	JOB_DATE	MAX_DEPT_SALARY
Municipal Courts Department	0	ASSISTANT DIRECTOR (EX LVL)	121862.0	...	2006-06-12	2012-10-13	121862.0
Library	1	LIBRARY ASSISTANT	26125.0	...	2000-07-19	2010-09-18	107763.0
Houston Police Department-HPD	2	POLICE OFFICER	45279.0	...	2015-02-03	2015-02-03	199596.0
Houston Fire Department (HFD)	3	ENGINEER/OPERATOR	63166.0	...	1982-02-08	1991-05-25	210588.0
General Services Department	4	ELECTRICIAN	56347.0	...	1989-06-19	1994-10-22	89194.0

6. We can validate our results with the `query` method to check whether there exist any rows where BASE_SALARY is greater than MAX_DEPT_SALARY:

```
>>> employee.query('BASE_SALARY > MAX_DEPT_SALARY')
```

DEPARTMENT	UNIQUE_ID	POSITION_TITLE	BASE_SALARY	...	HIRE_DATE	JOB_DATE	MAX_DEPT_SALARY

0 rows × 10 columns

How it works...

Steps 2 and 3 find the maximum salary for each department. For automatic index alignment to work properly, we set each DataFrame index as the department. Step 5 works because each row index from the left DataFrame; employee aligns with one and only one index from the right DataFrame, max_dept_sal. If max_dept_sal had repeats of any departments in its index, then the operation would fail.

For instance, let's see what happens when we use a DataFrame on the right-hand side of the equality that has repeated index values. We use the `sample` DataFrame method to randomly choose ten rows without replacement:

```
>>> np.random.seed(1234)
>>> random_salary = dept_sal.sample(n=10).set_index('DEPARTMENT')
>>> random_salary
```

	BASE_SALARY
DEPARTMENT	
Public Works & Engineering-PWE	50586.0
Houston Police Department-HPD	66614.0
Houston Police Department-HPD	66614.0
Housing and Community Devp.	78853.0
Houston Police Department-HPD	66614.0
Parks & Recreation	NaN
Public Works & Engineering-PWE	37211.0
Public Works & Engineering-PWE	54683.0
Human Resources Dept.	58474.0
Health & Human Services	47050.0

Notice how there are several repeated departments in the index. Now when we attempt to create a new column, an error is raised alerting us that there are duplicates. At least one index label in the `employee` DataFrame is joining with two or more index labels from `random_salary`:

```
>>> employee['RANDOM_SALARY'] = random_salary['BASE_SALARY']
ValueError: cannot reindex from a duplicate axis
```

There's more...

Not all indexes on the left-hand side of the equal sign need to have a match, but at most can have one. If there is nothing for the left DataFrame index to align to, the resulting value will be missing. Let's create an example where this happens. We will use only the first three rows of the `max_dept_sal` Series to create a new column:

```
>>> employee['MAX_SALARY2'] = max_dept_sal['BASE_SALARY'].head(3)
>>> employee.MAX_SALARY2.value_counts()
110416.0    29
100000.0    11
64251.0      5
Name: MAX_SALARY2, dtype: int64
```

```
>>> employee.MAX_SALARY2.isnull().mean()
```

`.9775`

The operation completed successfully but filled in salaries for only three of the departments. All the other departments that did not appear in the first three rows of the `max_dept_sal` Series resulted in a missing value.

See also

- *Selecting the largest from the smallest* recipe from `Chapter 3`, *Beginning Data Analysis*

Highlighting the maximum value from each column

The `college` dataset has many numeric columns describing different metrics about each school. Many people are interested in schools that perform the best for certain metrics.

Getting ready

This recipe discovers the school that has the maximum value for each numeric column and styles the DataFrame in order to highlight the information so that it is easily consumed by a user.

How to do it...

1. Read the college dataset with the institution name as the index:

```
>>> college = pd.read_csv('data/college.csv', index_col='INSTNM')
>>> college.dtypes
CITY                    object
STABBR                  object
HBCU                    float64
MENONLY                 float64
                         ...
PCTFLOAN                float64
UG25ABV                 float64
MD_EARN_WNE_P10         object
```

```
GRAD_DEBT_MDN_SUPP        object
Length: 26, dtype: object
```

2. All the other columns besides CITY and STABBR appear to be numeric. Examining the data types from the preceding step reveals unexpectedly that the MD_EARN_WNE_P10 and GRAD_DEBT_MDN_SUPP columns are of type object and not numeric. To help get a better idea of what kind of values are in these columns, let's examine their first value:

```
>>> college.MD_EARN_WNE_P10.iloc[0]
'30300'

>>> college.GRAD_DEBT_MDN_SUPP.iloc[0]
'33888'
```

3. These values are strings but we would like them to be numeric. This means that there are likely to be non-numeric characters that appear elsewhere in the Series. One way to check for this is to sort these columns in descending order and examine the first few rows:

```
>>> college.MD_EARN_WNE_P10.sort_values(ascending=False).head()
INSTNM
Sharon Regional Health System School of Nursing
PrivacySuppressed
Northcoast Medical Training Academy
PrivacySuppressed
Success Schools
PrivacySuppressed
Louisiana Culinary Institute
PrivacySuppressed
Bais Medrash Toras Chesed
PrivacySuppressed
Name: MD_EARN_WNE_P10, dtype: object
```

4. The culprit appears to be that some schools have privacy concerns about these two columns of data. To force these columns to be numeric, use the pandas function to_numeric:

```
>>> cols = ['MD_EARN_WNE_P10', 'GRAD_DEBT_MDN_SUPP']
>>> for col in cols:
        college[col] = pd.to_numeric(college[col], errors='coerce')

>>> college.dtypes.loc[cols]
MD_EARN_WNE_P10        float64
GRAD_DEBT_MDN_SUPP     float64
dtype: object
```

5. Use the `select_dtypes` method to filter for only numeric columns. This will exclude `STABBR` and `CITY` columns, where a maximum value doesn't make sense with this problem:

```
>>> college_n = college.select_dtypes(include=[np.number])
>>> college_n.head()
```

INSTNM	HBCU	MENONLY	WOMENONLY	...	UG25ABV	MD_EARN_WNE_P10	GRAD_DEBT_MDN_SUPP
Alabama A & M University	1.0	0.0	0.0	...	0.1049	30300.0	33888.0
University of Alabama at Birmingham	0.0	0.0	0.0	...	0.2422	39700.0	21941.5
Amridge University	0.0	0.0	0.0	...	0.8540	40100.0	23370.0
University of Alabama in Huntsville	0.0	0.0	0.0	...	0.2640	45500.0	24097.0
Alabama State University	1.0	0.0	0.0	...	0.1270	26600.0	33118.5

6. By utilizing the data dictionary, there are several columns that have only binary (0/1) values that will not provide useful information. To programmatically find these columns, we can create boolean Series and find all the columns that have two unique values with the `nunique` method:

```
>>> criteria = college_n.nunique() == 2
>>> criteria.head()
HBCU            True
MENONLY         True
WOMENONLY       True
RELAFFIL        True
SATVRMID        False
dtype: bool
```

7. Pass this boolean Series to the indexing operator of the columns index object and create a list of the binary columns:

```
>>> binary_cols = college_n.columns[criteria].tolist()
>>> binary_cols
['HBCU', 'MENONLY', 'WOMENONLY', 'RELAFFIL', 'DISTANCEONLY',
'CURROPER']
```

8. Remove the binary columns with the `drop` method:

```
>>> college_n2 = college_n.drop(labels=binary_cols, axis='columns')
>>> college_n2.head()
```

INSTNM	SATVRMID	SATMTMID	UGDS	...	UG25ABV	MD_EARN_WNE_P10	GRAD_DEBT_MDN_SUPP
Alabama A & M University	424.0	420.0	4206.0	...	0.1049	30300.0	33888.0
University of Alabama at Birmingham	570.0	565.0	11383.0	...	0.2422	39700.0	21941.5
Amridge University	NaN	NaN	291.0	...	0.8540	40100.0	23370.0
University of Alabama in Huntsville	595.0	590.0	5451.0	...	0.2640	45500.0	24097.0
Alabama State University	425.0	430.0	4811.0	...	0.1270	26600.0	33118.5

9. Use the `idxmax` method to find the index label of the maximum value for each column:

```
>>> max_cols = college_n2.idxmax()
>>> max_cols
SATVRMID                        California Institute of Technology
SATMTMID                        California Institute of Technology
UGDS                                   University of Phoenix-Arizona
UGDS_WHITE              Mr Leon's School of Hair Design-Moscow
                                             ...
PCTFLOAN                                     ABC Beauty College Inc
UG25ABV                           Dongguk University-Los Angeles
MD_EARN_WNE_P10                   Medical College of Wisconsin
GRAD_DEBT_MDN_SUPP      Southwest University of Visual Arts-Tucson
Length: 18, dtype: object
```

10. Call the `unique` method on the `max_cols` Series. This returns an `ndarray` of the unique column names:

```
>>> unique_max_cols = max_cols.unique()
>>> unique_max_cols[:5]
array(['California Institute of Technology',
       'University of Phoenix-Arizona',
       "Mr Leon's School of Hair Design-Moscow",
       'Velvatex College of Beauty Culture',
       'Thunderbird School of Global Management'], dtype=object)
```

11. Use the values of `max_cols` to select only the rows that have schools with a maximum value and then use the `style` attribute to highlight these values:

```
>>> college_n2.loc[unique max_cols].style.highlight_max()
```

INSTNM	SATVRMID	SATMTMID	UGDS	UGDS_WHITE	UGDS_BLACK	UGDS_HISP	UGDS_ASIAN
California Institute of Technology	765	785	983	0.2787	0.0153	0.1221	0.4385
University of Phoenix-Arizona	nan	nan	151558	0.3098	0.1555	0.076	0.0082
Mr Leon's School of Hair Design-Moscow	nan	nan	16	1	0	0	0
Velvatex College of Beauty Culture	nan	nan	25	0	1	0	0
Thunderbird School of Global Management	nan	nan	1	0	0	1	0
Cosmopolitan Beauty and Tech School	nan	nan	110	0.0091	0	0.0182	0.9727

How it works...

The `idxmax` method is very powerful and becomes quite useful when the index is meaningfully labeled. It was unexpected that both `MD_EARN_WNE_P10` and `GRAD_DEBT_MDN_SUPP` were of `object` data type. When importing, pandas coerces all numeric values of columns to strings if the column contains at least one string.

By examining a specific column value in step 2, we were able to see clearly that we had strings in these columns. In step 3, we sort in descending order as numeric characters appear first. This elevates all alphabetical values to the top of the Series. We uncover the `PrivacySuppressed` string causing havoc. Pandas has the ability to force all strings that contain only numeric characters to actual numeric data types with the `to_numeric` function. To override the default behavior of raising an error when `to_numeric` encounters a string that cannot be converted, you must pass *coerce* to the `errors` parameter. This forces all non-numeric character strings to become missing values (`np.nan`).

Several columns don't have useful or meaningful maximum values. They were removed in step 4 through step 6. The `select_dtypes` can be extremely useful for very wide DataFrames with lots of columns.

In step 7, `idxmax` iterates through all the columns to find the index of the maximum value for each column. It outputs the results as a Series. The school with both the highest SAT math and verbal scores is California Institute of Technology. Dongguk University Los Angeles has the highest number of students older than 25.

Although the information provided by `idxmax` is nice, it does not yield the corresponding maximum value. To do this, we gather all the unique school names from the values of the `max_cols` Series.

Finally, in step 8, we use the `.loc` indexer to select rows based on the index label, which we made as school names in the first step. This filters for only schools that have a maximum value. DataFrames have an experimental `style` attribute that itself has some methods to alter the appearance of the displayed DataFrame. Highlighting the maximum value makes the result much clearer.

There's more...

By default, the `highlight_max` method highlights the maximum value of each column. We can use the `axis` parameter to highlight the maximum value of each row instead. Here, we select just the race percentage columns of the `college` dataset and highlight the race with the highest percentage for each school:

```
>>> college = pd.read_csv('data/college.csv', index_col='INSTNM')
>>> college_ugds = college.filter(like='UGDS_').head()
>>> college_ugds.style.highlight_max(axis='columns')
```

INSTNM	UGDS_WHITE	UGDS_BLACK	UGDS_HISP	UGDS_ASIAN	UGDS_AIAN	UGDS_NHPI	UGDS_2MOR	UGDS_NRA	UGDS_UNKN
Alabama A & M University	0.0333	0.9353	0.0055	0.0019	0.0024	0.0019	0	0.0059	0.0138
University of Alabama at Birmingham	0.5922	0.26	0.0283	0.0518	0.0022	0.0007	0.0368	0.0179	0.01
Amridge University	0.299	0.4192	0.0069	0.0034	0	0	0	0	0.2715
University of Alabama in Huntsville	0.6968	0.1255	0.0382	0.0376	0.0143	0.0002	0.0172	0.0332	0.035
Alabama State University	0.0158	0.9208	0.0121	0.0019	0.001	0.0006	0.0098	0.0243	0.0137

Attempting to apply a style on a large DataFrame can cause Jupyter to crash, which is why the style was only applied to the head of the DataFrame.

See also

- Pandas official documentation on Dataframe *Styling* (http://bit.ly/2hsZkVK)

Replicating idxmax with method chaining

It can be a good exercise to attempt an implementation of a built-in DataFrame method on your own. This type of replication can give you a deeper understanding of other pandas methods that you normally wouldn't have come across. `idxmax` is a challenging method to replicate using only the methods covered thus far in the book.

Getting ready

This recipe slowly chains together basic methods to eventually find all the row index values that contain a maximum column value.

How to do it...

1. Load in the college dataset and execute the same operations as the previous recipe to get only the numeric columns that are of interest:

```
>>> college = pd.read_csv('data/college.csv', index_col='INSTNM')
>>> cols = ['MD_EARN_WNE_P10', 'GRAD_DEBT_MDN_SUPP']

>>> for col in cols:
        college[col] = pd.to_numeric(college[col], errors='coerce')

>>> college_n = college.select_dtypes(include=[np.number])
>>> criteria = college_n.nunique() == 2
>>> binary_cols = college_n.columns[criteria].tolist()
>>> college_n = college_n.drop(labels=binary_cols, axis='columns')
```

2. Find the maximum of each column with the `max` method:

```
>>> college_n.max().head()
SATVRMID            765.0
SATMTMID            785.0
UGDS            151558.0
UGDS_WHITE           1.0
UGDS_BLACK           1.0
dtype: float64
```

3. Use the `eq` DataFrame method to test each value with its column `max`. By default, the `eq` method aligns the columns of the column DataFrame with the labels of the passed Series index:

```
>>> college_n.eq(college_n.max()).head()
```

INSTNM	SATVRMID	SATMTMID	UGDS	UGDS_WHITE	UGDS_BLACK	UGDS_HISP	UGDS_ASIAN	UGDS_AIAN	UGDS_NHPI	UGDS_2MOR
Alabama A & M University	False	False	False	False	False	False	False	False	False	False
University of Alabama at Birmingham	False	False	False	False	False	False	False	False	False	False
Amridge University	False	False	False	False	False	False	False	False	False	False
University of Alabama in Huntsville	False	False	False	False	False	False	False	False	False	False
Alabama State University	False	False	False	False	False	False	False	False	False	False

4. All the rows in this DataFrame that have at least one `True` value must contain a column maximum. Let's use the `any` method to find all such rows that have at least one `True` value:

```
>>> has_row_max = college_n.eq(college_n.max()).any(axis='columns')
>>> has_row_max.head()
INSTNM
Alabama A & M University                    False
University of Alabama at Birmingham         False
Amridge University                          False
University of Alabama in Huntsville          False
Alabama State University                    False
dtype: bool
```

5. There are only 18 columns, which means that there should only be at most 18 `True` values in `has_row_max`. Let's find out how many there actually are:

```
>>> college_n.shape
(7535, 18)

>>> has_row_max.sum()
401
```

6. This was a bit unexpected, but it turns out that there are columns with many rows that equal the maximum value. This is common with many of the percentage columns that have a maximum of 1. `idxmax` returns the first occurrence of the maximum value. Let's back up a bit, remove the `any` method, and look at the output from step 3. Let's run the `cumsum` method instead to accumulate all the `True` values. The first and last three rows are shown:

```
>>> college_n.eq(college_n.max()).cumsum()
```

INSTNM	SATVRMID	SATMTMID	UGDS	UGDS_WHITE	UGDS_BLACK	UGDS_HISP	UGDS_ASIAN	UGDS_AIAN	UGDS_NHPI	UGDS_2MOR
Alabama A & M University	0	0	0	0	0	0	0	0	0	0
University of Alabama at Birmingham	0	0	0	0	0	0	0	0	0	0
Amridge University	0	0	0	0	0	0	0	0	0	0
...	...	...	...	...	...	...	...	...	...	...
National Personal Training Institute of Cleveland	1	1	1	109	28	136	1	2	1	1
Bay Area Medical Academy - San Jose Satellite Location	1	1	1	109	28	136	1	2	1	1
Excel Learning Center-San Antonio South	1	1	1	109	28	136	1	2	1	1

7535 rows × 18 columns

7. Some columns have one unique maximum like `SATVRMID` and `SATMTMID`, while others like `UGDS_WHITE` have many. 109 schools have 100% of their undergraduates as white. If we chain the `cumsum` method one more time, the value 1 would only appear once in each column and it would be the first occurrence of the maximum:

```
>>> college_n.eq(college_n.max()).cumsum().cumsum()
```

INSTNM	SATVRMID	SATMTMID	UGDS	UGDS_WHITE	UGDS_BLACK	UGDS_HISP	UGDS_ASIAN	UGDS_AIAN	UGDS_NHPI	UGDS_2MOR	UGDS_NRA
Alabama A & M University	0	0	0	0	0	0	0	0	0	0	0
University of Alabama at Birmingham	0	0	0	0	0	0	0	0	0	0	0
Amridge University	0	0	0	0	0	0	0	0	0	0	0
...	...	...	...	...	...	...	...	...	...	...	...
National Personal Training Institute of Cleveland	7307	7307	417	379968	73163	341375	985	11386	3318	5058	1078
Bay Area Medical Academy - San Jose Satellite Location	7308	7308	418	380077	73191	341511	986	11388	3319	5059	1079
Excel Learning Center-San Antonio South	7309	7309	419	380186	73219	341647	987	11390	3320	5060	1080

8. We can now test the equality of each value against 1 with the `eq` method and then use the `any` method to find rows that have at least one `True` value:

```
>>> has_row_max2 = college_n.eq(college_n.max()) \
                            .cumsum() \
                            .cumsum() \
                            .eq(1) \
                            .any(axis='columns')
>>> has_row_max2.head()
INSTNM
Alabama A & M University                    False
University of Alabama at Birmingham         False
Amridge University                          False
University of Alabama in Huntsville         False
Alabama State University                    False
dtype: bool
```

9. Test that `has_row_max2` has no more `True` values than the number of columns:

```
>>> has_row_max2.sum()
16
```

10. We need all the institutions where `has_row_max2` is True. We can simply use boolean indexing on the Series itself:

```
>>> idxmax_cols = has_row_max2[has_row_max2].index
>>> idxmax_cols
Index(['Thunderbird School of Global Management',
       'Southwest University of Visual Arts-Tucson',
       'ABC Beauty College Inc',
       'Velvatex College of Beauty Culture',
       'California Institute of Technology',
       'Le Cordon Bleu College of Culinary Arts-San Francisco',
       'MTI Business College Inc', 'Dongguk University-Los
Angeles',
       'Mr Leon's School of Hair Design-Moscow',
       'Haskell Indian Nations University', 'LIU Brentwood',
       'Medical College of Wisconsin', 'Palau Community College',
       'California University of Management and Sciences',
       'Cosmopolitan Beauty and Tech School',
       'University of Phoenix-Arizona'], dtype='object',
name='INSTNM')
```

11. All 16 of these institutions are the index of the first maximum occurrence for at least one of the columns. We can check whether they are the same as the ones found with the `idxmax` method:

```
>>> set(college_n.idxmax().unique()) == set(idxmax_cols)
True
```

How it works...

The first step replicates work from the previous recipe by converting two columns to numeric and eliminating the binary columns. We find the maximum value of each column in step 2. Care needs to be taken here as pandas silently drops columns that it cannot produce a maximum. If this happens, then step 3 will still complete but produce all False values for each column without an available maximum.

Step 4 uses the `any` method to scan across each row in search of at least one True value. Any row with at least one True value contains a maximum value for a column. We sum up the resulting boolean Series in step 5 to determine how many rows contain a maximum. Somewhat unexpectedly, there are far more rows than columns. Step 6 gives insight on why this happens. We take a cumulative sum of the output from step 3 and detect the total number of rows that equal the maximum for each column.

Many colleges have 100% of their student population as only a single race. This is by far the largest contributor to the multiple rows with maximums. As you can see, there is only one row with a maximum value for both SAT score columns and undergraduate population, but several of the race columns have a tie for the maximum.

Our goal is to find the first row with the maximum value. We need to take the cumulative sum once more so that each column has only a single row equal to 1. Step 8 formats the code to have one method per line and runs the `any` method exactly as it was done in step 4. If this step is successful, then we should have no more `True` values than the number of columns. Step 9 asserts that this is true.

To validate that we have found the same columns as `idxmax` in the previous columns, we use boolean selection on `has_row_max2` with itself. The columns will be in a different order so we convert the sequence of column names to sets, which are inherently unordered to compare equality.

There's more...

It is possible to complete this recipe in one long line of code chaining the indexing operator with an anonymous function. This little trick removes the need for step 10. We can time the difference between the direct `idxmax` method and our manual effort in this recipe:

```
>>> %timeit college_n.idxmax().values
1.12 ms ± 28.4 µs per loop (mean ± std. dev. of 7 runs, 1000 loops each)

>>> %timeit college_n.eq(college_n.max()) \
                     .cumsum() \
                     .cumsum() \
                     .eq(1) \
                     .any(axis='columns') \
                     [lambda x: x].index
5.35 ms ± 55.2 µs per loop (mean ± std. dev. of 7 runs, 100 loops each)
```

Our effort is, unfortunately, five times as slow as the built-in `idxmax` pandas method but regardless of its performance regression, many creative and practical solutions use the accumulation methods like `cumsum` with boolean Series to find streaks or specific patterns along an axis.

Finding the most common maximum

The college dataset contains the undergraduate population percentage of eight different races for over 7,500 colleges. It would be interesting to find the race with the highest undergrad population for each school and then find the distribution of this result for the entire dataset. We would be able to answer a question like, *What percentage of institutions have more white students than any other race?*

Getting ready

In this recipe, we find the race with the highest percentage of the undergraduate population for each school with the idxmax method and then find the distribution of these maximums.

How to do it...

1. Read in the college dataset and select just those columns with undergraduate race percentage information:

```
>>> college = pd.read_csv('data/college.csv', index_col='INSTNM')
>>> college_ugds = college.filter(like='UGDS_')
>>> college_ugds.head()
```

INSTNM	UGDS_WHITE	UGDS_BLACK	UGDS_HISP	UGDS_ASIAN	UGDS_AIAN	UGDS_NHPI	UGDS_2MOR	UGDS_NRA	UGDS_UNKN
Alabama A & M University	0.0333	0.9353	0.0055	0.0019	0.0024	0.0019	0.0000	0.0059	0.0138
University of Alabama at Birmingham	0.5922	0.2600	0.0283	0.0518	0.0022	0.0007	0.0368	0.0179	0.0100
Amridge University	0.2990	0.4192	0.0069	0.0034	0.0000	0.0000	0.0000	0.0000	0.2715
University of Alabama in Huntsville	0.6988	0.1255	0.0382	0.0376	0.0143	0.0002	0.0172	0.0332	0.0350
Alabama State University	0.0158	0.9208	0.0121	0.0019	0.0010	0.0006	0.0098	0.0243	0.0137

2. Use the `idxmax` method to get the column name with the highest race percentage for each row:

```
>>> highest_percentage_race = college_ugds.idxmax(axis='columns')
>>> highest_percentage_race.head()
INSTNM
Alabama A & M University                    UGDS_BLACK
University of Alabama at Birmingham         UGDS_WHITE
Amridge University                          UGDS_BLACK
University of Alabama in Huntsville         UGDS_WHITE
Alabama State University                    UGDS_BLACK
dtype: object
```

3. Use the `value_counts` method to return the distribution of maximum occurrences:

```
>>> highest_percentage_race.value_counts(normalize=True)
UGDS_WHITE      0.670352
UGDS_BLACK      0.151586
UGDS_HISP       0.129473
UGDS_UNKN       0.023422
UGDS_ASIAN      0.012074
UGDS_AIAN       0.006110
UGDS_NRA        0.004073
UGDS_NHPI       0.001746
UGDS_2MOR       0.001164
dtype: float64
```

How it works...

The key to this recipe is recognizing that the columns all represent the same unit of information. We can compare these columns with each other, which is usually not the case. For instance, it wouldn't make sense to directly compare SAT verbal scores with the undergraduate population. As the data is structured in this manner, we can apply the `idxmax` method to each row of data to find the column with the largest value. We need to alter its default behavior with the `axis` parameter.

Step 2 completes this operation and returns a Series, to which we can now simply apply the `value_counts` method to return the distribution. We pass `True` to the `normalize` parameter as we are interested in the distribution (relative frequency) and not the raw counts.

There's more...

We might want to explore more and answer the question: For the schools with more black students than any other race, what is the distribution of its second highest race percentage?

```
>>> college_black = college_ugds[highest_percentage_race == 'UGDS_BLACK']
>>> college_black = college_black.drop('UGDS_BLACK', axis='columns')
>>> college_black.idxmax(axis='columns').value_counts(normalize=True)
UGDS_WHITE      0.661228
UGDS_HISP       0.230326
UGDS_UNKN       0.071977
UGDS_NRA        0.018234
UGDS_ASIAN      0.009597
UGDS_2MOR       0.006718
UGDS_AIAN       0.000960
UGDS_NHPI       0.000960
dtype: float64
```

We needed to drop the `UGDS_BLACK` column before applying the same method from this recipe. Interestingly, it seems that these schools with higher black populations have a tendency to have higher Hispanic populations.

7
Grouping for Aggregation, Filtration, and Transformation

In this chapter, we will cover the following topics:

- Defining an aggregation
- Grouping and aggregating with multiple columns and functions
- Removing the MultiIndex after grouping
- Customizing an aggregation function
- Customizing aggregating functions with `*args` and `**kwargs`
- Examining the `groupby` object
- Filtering for states with a minority majority
- Transforming through a weight loss bet
- Calculating weighted mean SAT scores per state with apply
- Grouping by continuous variables
- Counting the total number of flights between cities
- Finding the longest streak of on-time flights

Introduction

One of the most fundamental tasks during a data analysis involves splitting data into independent groups before performing a calculation on each group. This methodology has been around for quite some time but has more recently been referred to as **split-apply-combine**. This chapter covers the powerful `groupby` method, which allows you to group your data in any way imaginable and apply any type of function independently to each group before returning a single dataset.

Hadley Wickham coined the term **split-apply-combine** to describe the common data analysis pattern of breaking up data into independent manageable chunks, independently applying functions to these chunks, and then combining the results back together. More details can be found in his paper (http://bit.ly/2isFuL9).

Before we get started with the recipes, we will need to know just a little terminology. All basic groupby operations have **grouping columns**, and each unique combination of values in these columns represents an independent grouping of the data. The syntax looks as follows:

```
>>> df.groupby(['list', 'of', 'grouping', 'columns'])
>>> df.groupby('single_column')  # when grouping by a single column
```

The result of this operation returns a groupby object. It is this groupby object that will be the engine that drives all the calculations for this entire chapter. Pandas actually does very little when creating this groupby object, merely validating that grouping is possible. You will have to chain methods on this groupby object in order to unleash its powers.

Technically, the result of the operation will either be a `DataFrameGroupBy` or `SeriesGroupBy` but for simplicity, it will be referred to as the groupby object for the entire chapter.

Defining an aggregation

The most common use of the `groupby` method is to perform an aggregation. What actually is an aggregation? In our data analysis world, an aggregation takes place when a sequence of many inputs get summarized or combined into a single value output. For example, summing up all the values of a column or finding its maximum are common aggregations applied on a single sequence of data. An aggregation simply takes many values and converts them down to a single value.

In addition to the grouping columns defined during the introduction, most aggregations have two other components, the **aggregating columns** and **aggregating functions**. The aggregating columns are those whose values will be aggregated. The aggregating functions define how the aggregation takes place. Major aggregation functions include `sum`, `min`, `max`, `mean`, `count`, `variance`, `std`, and so on.

Getting ready

In this recipe, we examine the flights dataset and perform the simplest possible aggregation involving only a single grouping column, a single aggregating column, and a single aggregating function. We will find the average arrival delay for each airline. Pandas has quite a few different syntaxes to produce an aggregation and this recipe covers them.

How to do it...

1. Read in the flights dataset, and define the grouping columns (AIRLINE), aggregating columns (ARR_DELAY), and aggregating functions (mean):

    ```
    >>> flights = pd.read_csv('data/flights.csv')
    >>> flights.head()
    ```

	MONTH	WEEKDAY	AIRLINE	ORG_AIR	DEST_AIR	SCHED_DEP	DEP_DELAY	AIR_TIME	DIST	SCHED_ARR	ARR_DELAY	DIVERTED	CANCELLED
0	1	4	WN	LAX	SLC	1625	58.0	94.0	590	1905	65.0	0	0
1	1	4	UA	DEN	IAD	823	7.0	154.0	1452	1333	-13.0	0	0
2	1	4	MQ	DFW	VPS	1305	36.0	85.0	641	1453	35.0	0	0
3	1	4	AA	DFW	DCA	1555	7.0	126.0	1192	1935	-7.0	0	0
4	1	4	WN	LAX	MCI	1720	48.0	166.0	1363	2225	39.0	0	0

2. Place the grouping column in the groupby method and then call the agg method with a dictionary pairing the aggregating column with its aggregating function:

    ```
    >>> flights.groupby('AIRLINE').agg({'ARR_DELAY':'mean'}).head()
    ```

	ARR_DELAY
AIRLINE	
AA	5.542661
AS	-0.833333
B6	8.692593
DL	0.339691
EV	7.034580

3. Alternatively, you may place the aggregating column in the indexing operator and then pass the aggregating function as a string to `agg`:

```
>>> flights.groupby('AIRLINE')['ARR_DELAY'].agg('mean').head()
AIRLINE
AA     5.542661
AS    -0.833333
B6     8.692593
DL     0.339691
EV     7.034580
Name: ARR_DELAY, dtype: float64
```

4. The string names used in the previous step are a convenience pandas offers you to refer to a particular aggregation function. You can pass any aggregating function directly to the `agg` method such as the NumPy `mean` function. The output is the same as the previous step:

```
>>> flights.groupby('AIRLINE')['ARR_DELAY'].agg(np.mean).head()
```

5. It's possible to skip the `agg` method altogether in this case and use the `mean` method directly. This output is also the same as step 3:

```
>>> flights.groupby('AIRLINE')['ARR_DELAY'].mean().head()
```

How it works...

The syntax for the `groupby` method is not as straightforward as other methods. Let's intercept the chain of methods in step 2 by storing the result of the `groupby` method as its own variable

```
>>> grouped = flights.groupby('AIRLINE')
>>> type(grouped)
pandas.core.groupby.DataFrameGroupBy
```

A completely new intermediate object is first produced with its own distinct attributes and methods. No calculations take place at this stage. Pandas merely validates the grouping columns. This groupby object has an `agg` method to perform aggregations. One of the ways to use this method is to pass it a dictionary mapping the aggregating column to the aggregating function, as done in step 2.

There are several different flavors of syntax that produce a similar result, with step 3 showing an alternative. Instead of identifying the aggregating column in the dictionary, place it inside the indexing operator just as if you were selecting it as a column from a DataFrame. The function string name is then passed as a scalar to the `agg` method.

You may pass any aggregating function to the `agg` method. Pandas allows you to use the string names for simplicity but you may also explicitly call an aggregating function as done in step 4. NumPy provides many functions that aggregate values.

Step 5 shows one last syntax flavor. When you are only applying a single aggregating function as in this example, you can often call it directly as a method on the groupby object itself without `agg`. Not all aggregation functions have a method equivalent but many basic ones do. The following is a list of several aggregating functions that may be passed as a string to `agg` or chained directly as a method to the groupby object:

```
min     max     mean    median    sum     count    std    var
size    describe    nunique    idxmin    idxmax
```

There's more...

If you do not use an aggregating function with `agg`, pandas raises an exception. For instance, let's see what happens when we apply the square root function to each group:

```
>>> flights.groupby('AIRLINE')['ARR_DELAY'].agg(np.sqrt)
ValueError: function does not reduce
```

See also

- Pandas official documentation on *Aggregation* (http://bit.ly/2iuf1Nc)

Grouping and aggregating with multiple columns and functions

It is possible to do grouping and aggregating with multiple columns. The syntax is only slightly different than it is for grouping and aggregating with a single column. As usual with any kind of grouping operation, it helps to identify the three components: the grouping columns, aggregating columns, and aggregating functions.

Getting ready

In this recipe, we showcase the flexibility of the `groupby` DataFrame method by answering the following queries:

- Finding the number of cancelled flights for every airline per weekday
- Finding the number and percentage of cancelled and diverted flights for every airline per weekday
- For each origin and destination, finding the total number of flights, the number and percentage of cancelled flights, and the average and variance of the airtime

How to do it...

1. Read in the flights dataset, and answer the first query by defining the grouping columns (AIRLINE, WEEKDAY), the aggregating column (CANCELLED), and the aggregating function (sum):

```
>>> flights.groupby(['AIRLINE', 'WEEKDAY'])['CANCELLED'] \
        .agg('sum').head(7)
AIRLINE  WEEKDAY
AA       1            41
         2             9
         3            16
         4            20
         5            18
         6            21
         7            29
Name: CANCELLED, dtype: int64
```

2. Answer the second query by using a list for each pair of grouping and aggregating columns. Also, use a list for the aggregating functions:

```
>>> flights.groupby(['AIRLINE', 'WEEKDAY']) \
            ['CANCELLED', 'DIVERTED'].agg(['sum', 'mean']).head(7)
```

		CANCELLED		DIVERTED	
		sum	mean	sum	mean
AIRLINE	WEEKDAY				
AA	1	41	0.032106	6	0.004699
	2	9	0.007341	2	0.001631
	3	16	0.011949	2	0.001494
	4	20	0.015004	5	0.003751
	5	18	0.014151	1	0.000786
	6	21	0.018667	9	0.008000
	7	29	0.021837	1	0.000753

3. Answer the third query using a dictionary in the `agg` method to map specific aggregating columns to specific aggregating functions:

```
>>> group_cols = ['ORG_AIR', 'DEST_AIR']
>>> agg_dict = {'CANCELLED':['sum', 'mean', 'size'],
                'AIR_TIME':['mean', 'var']}
>>> flights.groupby(group_cols).agg(agg_dict).head()
```

		CANCELLED			AIR_TIME	
		sum	mean	size	mean	var
ORG_AIR	DEST_AIR					
ATL	ABE	0	0.0	31	96.387097	45.778495
	ABQ	0	0.0	16	170.500000	87.866667
	ABY	0	0.0	19	28.578947	6.590643
	ACY	0	0.0	6	91.333333	11.466667
	AEX	0	0.0	40	78.725000	47.332692

How it works...

To group by multiple columns as in step 1, we pass a list of the string names to the groupby method. Each unique combination of AIRLINE and WEEKDAY forms an independent group. Within each of these groups, the sum of the cancelled flights is found and then returned as a Series.

Step 2, again groups by both AIRLINE and WEEKDAY, but this time aggregates two columns. It applies each of the two aggregation functions, sum and mean, to each column resulting in four returned columns per group.

Step 3 goes even further, and uses a dictionary to map specific aggregating columns to different aggregating functions. Notice that the size aggregating function returns the total number of rows per group. This is different than the count aggregating function, which returns the number of non-missing values per group.

There's more...

There are a few main flavors of syntax that you will encounter when performing an aggregation. The following four blocks of pseudocode summarize the main ways you can perform an aggregation with the groupby method:

1. Using agg with a dictionary is the most flexible and allows you to specify the aggregating function for each column:

```
>>> df.groupby(['grouping', 'columns']) \
       .agg({'agg_cols1':['list', 'of', 'functions'],
             'agg_cols2':['other', 'functions']})
```

2. Using agg with a list of aggregating functions applies each of the functions to each of the aggregating columns:

```
>>> df.groupby(['grouping', 'columns'])['aggregating', 'columns'] \
       .agg([aggregating, functions])
```

3. Directly using a method following the aggregating columns instead of agg, applies just that method to each aggregating column. This way does not allow for multiple aggregating functions:

```
>>> df.groupby(['grouping', 'columns'])['aggregating', 'columns'] \
       .aggregating_method()
```

4. If you do not specify the aggregating columns, then the aggregating method will be applied to all the non-grouping columns:

```
>>> df.groupby(['grouping', 'columns']).aggregating_method()
```

In the preceding four code blocks it is possible to substitute a string for any of the lists when grouping or aggregating by a single column.

Removing the MultiIndex after grouping

Inevitably, when using `groupby`, you will likely create a MultiIndex in the columns or rows or both. DataFrames with MultiIndexes are more difficult to navigate and occasionally have confusing column names as well.

Getting ready

In this recipe, we perform an aggregation with the `groupby` method to create a DataFrame with a MultiIndex for the rows and columns and then manipulate it so that the index is a single level and the column names are descriptive.

How to do it...

1. Read in the flights dataset; write a statement to find the total and average miles flown; and the maximum and minimum arrival delay for each airline for each weekday:

```
>>> flights = pd.read_csv('data/flights.csv')
>>> airline_info = flights.groupby(['AIRLINE', 'WEEKDAY'])\
                          .agg({'DIST':['sum', 'mean'],
                                'ARR_DELAY':['min', 'max']}) \
                          .astype(int)
>>> airline_info.head(7)
```

		DIST		ARR_DELAY	
		sum	mean	min	max
AIRLINE	WEEKDAY				
AA	1	1455386	1139	-60	551
	2	1358256	1107	-52	725
	3	1496665	1117	-45	473
	4	1452394	1089	-46	349
	5	1427749	1122	-41	732
	6	1265340	1124	-50	858
	7	1461906	1100	-49	626

2. Both the rows and columns are labeled by a MultiIndex with two levels. Let's squash it down to just a single level. To address the columns, we use the MultiIndex method, get_level_values. Let's display the output of each level and then concatenate both levels before setting it as the new column values:

```
>>> level0 = airline_info.columns.get_level_values(0)
Index(['DIST', 'DIST', 'ARR_DELAY', 'ARR_DELAY'], dtype='object')

>>> level1 = airline_info.columns.get_level_values(1)
Index(['sum', 'mean', 'min', 'max'], dtype='object')

>>> airline_info.columns = level0 + '_' + level1
>>> airline_info.head(7)
```

		DIST_sum	DIST_mean	ARR_DELAY_min	ARR_DELAY_max
AIRLINE	WEEKDAY				
AA	1	1455386	1139	-60	551
	2	1358256	1107	-52	725
	3	1496665	1117	-45	473
	4	1452394	1089	-46	349
	5	1427749	1122	-41	732
	6	1265340	1124	-50	858
	7	1461906	1100	-49	626

3. Return the row labels to a single level with `reset_index`:

```
>>> airline_info.reset_index().head(7)
```

	AIRLINE	WEEKDAY	DIST_sum	DIST_mean	ARR_DELAY_min	ARR_DELAY_max
0	AA	1	1455386	1139	-60	551
1	AA	2	1358256	1107	-52	725
2	AA	3	1496665	1117	-45	473
3	AA	4	1452394	1089	-46	349
4	AA	5	1427749	1122	-41	732
5	AA	6	1265340	1124	-50	858
6	AA	7	1461906	1100	-49	626

How it works...

When using the `agg` method to perform an aggregation on multiple columns, pandas creates an index object with two levels. The aggregating columns become the top level and the aggregating functions become the bottom level. Pandas displays MultiIndex levels differently than single-level columns. Except for the **innermost** levels, repeated index values do not get displayed on the screen. You can inspect the DataFrame from step 1 to verify this. For instance, the `DIST` column shows up only once but it refers to both of the first two columns.

 The innermost MultiIndex level is the one closest to the data. This would be the bottom-most column level and the right-most index level.

Step 2 defines new columns by first retrieving the underlying values of each of the levels with the MultiIndex method `get_level_values`. This method accepts an integer identifying the index level. They are numbered beginning with zero from the top/left. Indexes support vectorized operations, so we concatenate both levels together with a separating underscore. We assign these new values to the `columns` attribute.

In step 3, we make both index levels as columns with `reset_index`. We could have concatenated the levels together like we did in step 2, but it makes more sense to keep them as separate columns.

There's more...

By default, at the end of a groupby operation, pandas puts all of the grouping columns in the index. The `as_index` parameter in the `groupby` method can be set to `False` to avoid this behavior. You can chain the `reset_index` method after grouping to get the same effect as done in step 3. Let's see an example of this by finding the average distance traveled per flight from each airline:

```
>>> flights.groupby(['AIRLINE'], as_index=False)['DIST'].agg('mean') \
                                                    .round(0)
```

	AIRLINE	DIST
0	AA	1114.0
1	AS	1066.0
2	B6	1772.0
3	DL	866.0
4	EV	460.0
5	F9	970.0
6	HA	2615.0
7	MQ	404.0
8	NK	1047.0
9	OO	511.0
10	UA	1231.0
11	US	1181.0
12	VX	1240.0
13	WN	810.0

Take a look at the order of the airlines in the previous result. By default, pandas sorts the grouping columns. The `sort` parameter exists within the `groupby` method and is defaulted to `True`. You may set it to `False` to keep the order of the grouping columns the same as how they are encountered in the dataset. You also get a small performance improvement by not sorting your data.

Customizing an aggregation function

Pandas provides a number of the most common aggregation functions for you to use with the groupby object. At some point, you will need to write your own customized user-defined functions that don't exist in pandas or NumPy.

Getting ready

In this recipe, we use the college dataset to calculate the mean and standard deviation of the undergraduate student population per state. We then use this information to find the maximum number of standard deviations from the mean that any single population value is per state.

How to do it...

1. Read in the college dataset, and find the mean and standard deviation of the undergraduate population by state:

```
>>> college = pd.read_csv('data/college.csv')
>>> college.groupby('STABBR')['UGDS'].agg(['mean', 'std']) \
                                      .round(0).head()
```

STABBR	mean	std
AK	2493.0	4052.0
AL	2790.0	4658.0
AR	1644.0	3143.0
AS	1276.0	NaN
AZ	4130.0	14894.0

2. This output isn't quite what we desire. We are not looking for the mean and standard deviations of the entire group but the maximum number of standard deviations away from the mean for any one institution. In order to calculate this, we need to subtract the mean undergraduate population by state from each institution's undergraduate population and then divide by the standard deviation. This standardizes the undergraduate population for each group. We can then take the maximum of the absolute value of these scores to find the one that is farthest away from the mean. Pandas does not provide a function capable of doing this. Instead, we will need to create a custom function:

```
>>> def max_deviation(s):
        std_score = (s - s.mean()) / s.std()
        return std_score.abs().max()
```

3. After defining the function, pass it directly to the `agg` method to complete the aggregation:

```
>>> college.groupby('STABBR')['UGDS'].agg(max_deviation) \
                                .round(1).head()
STABBR
AK    2.6
AL    5.8
AR    6.3
AS    NaN
AZ    9.9
Name: UGDS, dtype: float64
```

How it works...

There does not exist a predefined pandas function to calculate the maximum number of standard deviations away from the mean. We were forced to construct a customized function in step 2. Notice that this custom function `max_deviation` accepts a single parameter, s. Looking ahead at step 3, you will notice that the function name is placed inside the `agg` method without directly being called. Nowhere is the parameter s explicitly passed to `max_deviation`. Instead, pandas implicitly passes the UGDS column as a Series to `max_deviation`.

The `max_deviation` function is called once for each group. As s is a Series, all normal Series methods are available. It subtracts the mean of that particular grouping from each of the values in the group before dividing by the standard deviation in a process called **standardization**.

Standardization is a common statistical procedure to understand how greatly individual values vary from the mean. For a normal distribution, 99.7% of the data lies within three standard deviations of the mean.

As we are interested in absolute deviation from the mean, we take the absolute value from all the standardized scores and return the maximum. The `agg` method necessitates that a single scalar value must be returned from our custom function, or else an exception will be raised. Pandas defaults to using the sample standard deviation which is undefined for any groups with just a single value. For instance, the state abbreviation *AS* (American Samoa) has a missing value returned as it has only a single institution in the dataset.

There's more...

It is possible to apply our customized function to multiple aggregating columns. We simply add more column names to the indexing operator. The `max_deviation` function only works with numeric columns:

```
>>> college.groupby('STABBR')['UGDS', 'SATVRMID', 'SATMTMID'] \
        .agg(max_deviation).round(1).head()
```

STABBR	UGDS	SATVRMID	SATMTMID
AK	2.6	NaN	NaN
AL	5.8	1.6	1.8
AR	6.3	2.2	2.3
AS	NaN	NaN	NaN
AZ	9.9	1.9	1.4

You can also use your customized aggregation function along with the prebuilt functions. The following does this and groups by state and religious affiliation:

```
>>> college.groupby(['STABBR', 'RELAFFIL']) \
        ['UGDS', 'SATVRMID', 'SATMTMID'] \
        .agg([max_deviation, 'mean', 'std']).round(1).head()
```

		UGDS			SATVRMID			SATMTMID		
		max_deviation	mean	std	max_deviation	mean	std	max_deviation	mean	std
STABBR	RELAFFIL									
AK	0	2.1	3508.9	4539.5	NaN	NaN	NaN	NaN	NaN	NaN
	1	1.1	123.3	132.9	NaN	555.0	NaN	NaN	503.0	NaN
AL	0	5.2	3248.8	5102.4	1.6	514.9	56.5	1.7	515.8	56.7
	1	2.4	979.7	870.8	1.5	498.0	53.0	1.4	485.6	61.4
AR	0	5.8	1793.7	3401.6	1.9	481.1	37.9	2.0	503.6	39.0

Notice that pandas uses the name of the function as the name for the returned column. You can change the column name directly with the rename method or you can modify the special function attribute __name__:

```
>>> max_deviation.__name__
'max_deviation'

>>> max_deviation.__name__ = 'Max Deviation'
>>> college.groupby(['STABBR', 'RELAFFIL']) \
            ['UGDS', 'SATVRMID', 'SATMTMID'] \
        .agg([max_deviation, 'mean', 'std']).round(1).head()
```

		UGDS			SATVRMID			SATMTMID		
		Max Deviation	mean	std	Max Deviation	mean	std	Max Deviation	mean	std
STABBR	RELAFFIL									
AK	0	2.1	3508.9	4539.5	NaN	NaN	NaN	NaN	NaN	NaN
	1	1.1	123.3	132.9	NaN	555.0	NaN	NaN	503.0	NaN
AL	0	5.2	3248.8	5102.4	1.6	514.9	56.5	1.7	515.8	56.7
	1	2.4	979.7	870.8	1.5	498.0	53.0	1.4	485.6	61.4
AR	0	5.8	1793.7	3401.6	1.9	481.1	37.9	2.0	503.6	39.0

Customizing aggregating functions with *args and **kwargs

When writing your own user-defined customized aggregation function, pandas implicitly passes it each of the aggregating columns one at a time as a Series. Occasionally, you will need to pass more arguments to your function than just the Series itself. To do so, you need to be aware of Python's ability to pass an arbitrary number of arguments to functions. Let's take a look at the signature of the groupby object's agg method with help from the inspect module:

```
>>> college = pd.read_csv('data/college.csv')
>>> grouped = college.groupby(['STABBR', 'RELAFFIL'])

>>> import inspect
>>> inspect.signature(grouped.agg)
<Signature (arg, *args, **kwargs)>
```

The argument `*args` allow you to pass an arbitrary number of non-keyword arguments to your customized aggregation function. Similarly, `**kwargs` allows you to pass an arbitrary number of keyword arguments.

Getting ready

In this recipe, we build a customized function for the college dataset that finds the percentage of schools by state and religious affiliation that have an undergraduate population between two values.

How to do it...

1. Define a function that returns the percentage of schools with an undergraduate population between 1,000 and 3,000:

```
>>> def pct_between_1_3k(s):
        return s.between(1000, 3000).mean()
```

2. Calculate this percentage grouping by state and religious affiliation:

```
>>> college.groupby(['STABBR', 'RELAFFIL'])['UGDS'] \
        .agg(pct_between_1_3k).head(9)
STABBR  RELAFFIL
AK      0              0.142857
        1              0.000000
AL      0              0.236111
        1              0.333333
AR      0              0.279412
        1              0.111111
AS      0              1.000000
AZ      0              0.096774
        1              0.000000
Name: UGDS, dtype: float64
```

3. This function works fine but it doesn't give the user any flexibility to choose the lower and upper bound. Let's create a new function that allows the user to define these bounds:

```
>>> def pct_between(s, low, high):
        return s.between(low, high).mean()
```

4. Pass this new function to the `agg` method along with lower and upper bounds:

```
>>> college.groupby(['STABBR', 'RELAFFIL'])['UGDS'] \
          .agg(pct_between, 1000, 10000).head(9)
STABBR  RELAFFIL
AK      0              0.428571
        1              0.000000
AL      0              0.458333
        1              0.375000
AR      0              0.397059
        1              0.166667
AS      0              1.000000
AZ      0              0.233871
        1              0.111111
Name: UGDS, dtype: float64
```

How it works...

Step 1 creates a function that doesn't accept any extra arguments. The upper and lower bounds must be hardcoded into the function itself, which isn't very flexible. Step 2 shows the results of this aggregation.

We create a more flexible function in step 3 that allows users to define both the lower and upper bounds dynamically. Step 4 is where the magic of `*args` and `**kwargs` come into play. In this particular example, we pass two non-keyword arguments, 1,000 and 10,000, to the `agg` method. Pandas passes these two arguments respectively to the `low` and `high` parameters of `pct_between`.

There are a few ways we could achieve the same result in step 4. We could have explicitly used the parameter names with the following command to produce the same result:

```
>>> college.groupby(['STABBR', 'RELAFFIL'])['UGDS'] \
          .agg(pct_between, high=10000, low=1000).head(9)
```

The order of the keyword arguments doesn't matter as long as they come after the function name. Further still, we can mix non-keyword and keyword arguments as long as the keyword arguments come last:

```
>>> college.groupby(['STABBR', 'RELAFFIL'])['UGDS'] \
          .agg(pct_between, 1000, high=10000).head(9)
```

For ease of understanding, it's probably best to include all the parameter names in the order that they are defined in the function signature.

Technically, when `agg` is called, all the non-keyword arguments get collected into a tuple named `args` and all the keyword arguments get collected into a dictionary named `kwargs`.

There's more...

Unfortunately, pandas does not have a direct way to use these additional arguments when using multiple aggregation functions together. For example, if you wish to aggregate using the `pct_between` and `mean` functions, you will get the following exception:

```
>>> college.groupby(['STABBR', 'RELAFFIL'])['UGDS'] \
        .agg(['mean', pct_between], low=100, high=1000)
TypeError: pct_between() missing 2 required positional arguments: 'low' and
'high'
```

Pandas is incapable of understanding that the extra arguments need to be passed to `pct_between`. In order to use our custom function with other built-in functions and even other custom functions, we can define a special type of nested function called a **closure**. We can use a generic closure to build all of our customized functions:

```
>>> def make_agg_func(func, name, *args, **kwargs):
        def wrapper(x):
            return func(x, *args, **kwargs)
        wrapper.__name__ = name
        return wrapper

>>> my_agg1 = make_agg_func(pct_between, 'pct_1_3k', low=1000, high=3000)
>>> my_agg2 = make_agg_func(pct_between, 'pct_10_30k', 10000, 30000)

>>> college.groupby(['STABBR', 'RELAFFIL'])['UGDS'] \
        .agg(['mean', my_agg1, my_agg2]).head()
```

		mean	pct_1_3k	pct_10_30k
STABBR	**RELAFFIL**			
AK	0	3508.857143	0.142857	0.142857
	1	123.333333	0.000000	0.000000
AL	0	3248.774648	0.236111	0.083333
	1	979.722222	0.333333	0.000000
AR	0	1793.691176	0.279412	0.014706

The make_agg_func function acts as a factory to create customized aggregation functions. It accepts the customized aggregation function that you already built (pct_between in this case), a name argument, and an arbitrary number of extra arguments. It returns a function with the extra arguments already set. For instance, my_agg1 is a specific customized aggregating function that finds the percentage of schools with an undergraduate population between one and three thousand. The extra arguments (*args and **kwargs) specify an exact set of parameters for your customized function (pct_between in this case). The name parameter is very important and must be unique each time make_agg_func is called. It will eventually be used to rename the aggregated column.

A closure is a function that contains a function inside of it (a nested function) and returns this nested function. This nested function must refer to variables in the scope of the outer function in order to be a closure. In this example, make_agg_func is the outer function and returns the nested function wrapper, which accesses the variables func, args, and kwargs from the outer function.

See also

- *Arbitrary Argument Lists* from the official Python documentation (http://bit.ly/2vumbTE)
- A tutorial on *Python Closures* (http://bit.ly/2xFdYga)

Examining the groupby object

The immediate result from using the `groupby` method on a DataFrame will be a groupby object. Usually, we continue operating on this object to do aggregations or transformations without ever saving it to a variable. One of the primary purposes of examining this groupby object is to inspect individual groups.

Getting ready

In this recipe, we examine the groupby object itself by directly calling methods on it as well as iterating through each of its groups.

How to do it...

1. Let's get started by grouping the state and religious affiliation columns from the college dataset, saving the result to a variable and confirming its type:

```
>>> college = pd.read_csv('data/college.csv')
>>> grouped = college.groupby(['STABBR', 'RELAFFIL'])
>>> type(grouped)
pandas.core.groupby.DataFrameGroupBy
```

2. Use the `dir` function to discover all its available functionality:

```
>>> print([attr for attr in dir(grouped) if not
attr.startswith('_')])
['CITY', 'CURROPER', 'DISTANCEONLY', 'GRAD_DEBT_MDN_SUPP', 'HBCU',
'INSTNM', 'MD_EARN_WNE_P10', 'MENONLY', 'PCTFLOAN', 'PCTPELL',
'PPTUG_EF', 'RELAFFIL', 'SATMTMID', 'SATVRMID', 'STABBR',
'UG25ABV', 'UGDS', 'UGDS_2MOR', 'UGDS_AIAN', 'UGDS_ASIAN',
'UGDS_BLACK', 'UGDS_HISP', 'UGDS_NHPI', 'UGDS_NRA', 'UGDS_UNKN',
'UGDS_WHITE', 'WOMENONLY', 'agg', 'aggregate', 'all', 'any',
'apply', 'backfill', 'bfill', 'boxplot', 'corr', 'corrwith',
'count', 'cov', 'cumcount', 'cummax', 'cummin', 'cumprod',
'cumsum', 'describe', 'diff', 'dtypes', 'expanding', 'ffill',
'fillna', 'filter', 'first', 'get_group', 'groups', 'head', 'hist',
'idxmax', 'idxmin', 'indices', 'last', 'mad', 'max', 'mean',
'median', 'min', 'ndim', 'ngroup', 'ngroups', 'nth', 'nunique',
'ohlc', 'pad', 'pct_change', 'plot', 'prod', 'quantile', 'rank',
'resample', 'rolling', 'sem', 'shift', 'size', 'skew', 'std',
'sum', 'tail', 'take', 'transform', 'tshift', 'var']
```

3. Find the number of groups with the `ngroups` attribute:

```
>>> grouped.ngroups
112
```

4. To find the uniquely identifying labels for each group, look in the `groups` attribute, which contains a dictionary of each unique group mapped to all the corresponding index labels of that group:

```
>>> groups = list(grouped.groups.keys())
>>> groups[:6]
[('AK', 0), ('AK', 1), ('AL', 0), ('AL', 1), ('AR', 0), ('AR', 1)]
```

5. Retrieve a single group with the `get_group` method by passing it a tuple of an exact group label. For example, to get all the religiously affiliated schools in the state of Florida, do the following:

```
>>> grouped.get_group(('FL', 1)).head()
```

	CITY	CURROPER	DISTANCEONLY	GRAD_DEBT_MDN_SUPP	HBCU	INSTNM	MD_EARN_WNE_P10	MENONLY	PCTFLOAN	PCTPELL
712	Graceville	1	0.0	20052	0.0	The Baptist College of Florida	30800	0.0	0.5602	0.5878
713	Miami	1	0.0	28250	0.0	Barry University	44100	0.0	0.6733	0.5045
714	Panama City	0	0.0	PrivacySuppressed	0.0	Gooding Institute of Nurse Anesthesia	NaN	0.0	NaN	NaN
715	Daytona Beach	1	0.0	36250	1.0	Bethune-Cookman University	29400	0.0	0.8867	0.7758
724	Kissimmee	1	0.0	20199	0.0	Johnson University Florida	26300	0.0	0.7384	0.6689

6. You may want to take a peek at each individual group. This is possible because groupby objects are iterable:

```
>>> from IPython.display import display
>>> for name, group in grouped:
        print(name)
        display(group.head(3))
```

```
('AK', 0)
```

	INSTNM	CITY	STABBR	HBCU	MENONLY	WOMENONLY	RELAFFIL	SATVRMID	SATMTMID	DISTANCEONLY
60	University of Alaska Anchorage	Anchorage	AK	0.0	0.0	0.0	0	NaN	NaN	0.0
62	University of Alaska Fairbanks	Fairbanks	AK	0.0	0.0	0.0	0	NaN	NaN	0.0

2 rows × 27 columns

```
('AK', 1)
```

	INSTNM	CITY	STABBR	HBCU	MENONLY	WOMENONLY	RELAFFIL	SATVRMID	SATMTMID	DISTANCEONLY	
61	Alaska Bible College	Palmer	AK	0.0	0.0	0.0	1	NaN	NaN	0.0	..
64	Alaska Pacific University	Anchorage	AK	0.0	0.0	0.0	1	555.0	503.0	0.0	..

2 rows × 27 columns

```
('AL', 0)
```

	INSTNM	CITY	STABBR	HBCU	MENONLY	WOMENONLY	RELAFFIL	SATVRMID	SATMTMID	DISTANCEONLY
0	Alabama A & M University	Normal	AL	1.0	0.0	0.0	0	424.0	420.0	0.0
1	University of Alabama at Birmingham	Birmingham	AL	0.0	0.0	0.0	0	570.0	565.0	0.0

2 rows × 27 columns

7. You can also call the head method on your groupby object to get the first rows of each group together in a single DataFrame.

```
>>> grouped.head(2).head(6)
```

	INSTNM	CITY	STABBR	HBCU	MENONLY	WOMENONLY	RELAFFIL	SATVRMID	SATMTMID	DISTANCEONLY	...	UGDS_2MOR	UGDS_NRA
0	Alabama A & M University	Normal	AL	1.0	0.0	0.0	0	424.0	420.0	0.0	...	0.0000	0.0059
1	University of Alabama at Birmingham	Birmingham	AL	0.0	0.0	0.0	0	570.0	565.0	0.0	...	0.0368	0.0179
2	Amridge University	Montgomery	AL	0.0	0.0	0.0	1	NaN	NaN	1.0	...	0.0000	0.0000
10	Birmingham Southern College	Birmingham	AL	0.0	0.0	0.0	1	560.0	560.0	0.0	...	0.0051	0.0000
43	Prince Institute- Southeast	Elmhurst	IL	0.0	0.0	0.0	0	NaN	NaN	0.0	...	0.0000	0.0000
60	University of Alaska Anchorage	Anchorage	AK	0.0	0.0	0.0	0	NaN	NaN	0.0	...	0.0980	0.0181

How it works...

Step 1 formally creates our groupby object. It is useful to display all the public attributes and methods to reveal all the possible functionality as was done in step 2. Each group is uniquely identified by a tuple containing a unique combination of the values in the grouping columns. Pandas allows you to select a specific group as a DataFrame with the `get_group` method shown in step 5.

It is rare that you will need to iterate through your groups and in general, you should avoid doing so if necessary, as it can be quite slow. Occasionally, you will have no other choice. When iterating through a groupby object, you are given a tuple containing the group name and the DataFrame without the grouping columns. This tuple is unpacked into the variables `name` and `group` in the for-loop in step 6.

One interesting thing you can do while iterating through your groups is to display a few of the rows from each group directly in the notebook. To do this, you can either use the print function or the `display` function from the `IPython.display` module. Using the `print` function results in DataFrames that are in plain text without any nice HTML formatting. Using the `display` function will produce DataFrames in their normal easy-to-read format.

There's more...

There are several useful methods that were not explored from the list in step 2. Take for instance the `nth` method, which, when given a list of integers, selects those specific rows from each group. For example, the following operation selects the first and last rows from each group:

```
>>> grouped.nth([1, -1]).head(8)
```

STABBR	RELAFFIL	CITY	CURROPER	DISTANCEONLY	GRAD_DEBT_MDN_SUPP	HBCU	INSTNM	MD_EARN_WNE_P10	MENONLY	PCTFLOAN
AK	0	Fairbanks	1	0.0	19355	0.0	University of Alaska Fairbanks	36200	0.0	0.2550
	0	Barrow	1	0.0	PrivacySuppressed	0.0	Ilisagvik College	24900	0.0	0.0000
	1	Anchorage	1	0.0	23250	0.0	Alaska Pacific University	47000	0.0	0.5297
	1	Soldotna	1	0.0	PrivacySuppressed	0.0	Alaska Christian College	NaN	0.0	0.6792
AL	0	Birmingham	1	0.0	21941.5	0.0	University of Alabama at Birmingham	39700	0.0	0.5214
	0	Dothan	1	0.0	PrivacySuppressed	0.0	Alabama College of Osteopathic Medicine	NaN	0.0	NaN
	1	Birmingham	1	0.0	27000	0.0	Birmingham Southern College	44200	0.0	0.4809
	1	Huntsville	1	NaN	36173.5	NaN	Strayer University-Huntsville Campus	49200	NaN	NaN

See also

- Official documentation of the `display` function from IPython (`http://bit.ly/2iAIogC`)

Filtering for states with a minority majority

In `Chapter 4`, *Selecting Subsets of Data*, we marked every row as `True` or `False` before filtering out the `False` rows. In a similar fashion, it is possible to mark entire groups of data as either `True` or `False` before filtering out the `False` groups. To do this, we first form groups with the `groupby` method and then apply the `filter` method. The `filter` method accepts a function that must return either `True` or `False` to indicate whether a group is kept or not.

 This `filter` method applied after a call to the `groupby` method is completely different than the DataFrame `filter` method covered in the *Selecting columns with methods* recipe from `Chapter 2`, *Essential DataFrame Operations*.

Getting ready

In this recipe, we use the college dataset to find all the states that have more non-white undergraduate students than white. As this is a dataset from the US, whites form the majority and therefore, we are looking for states with a minority majority.

How to do it...

1. Read in the college dataset, group by state, and display the total number of groups. This should equal the number of unique states retrieved from the `nunique` Series method:

```
>>> college = pd.read_csv('data/college.csv', index_col='INSTNM')
>>> grouped = college.groupby('STABBR')
>>> grouped.ngroups
59

>>> college['STABBR'].nunique() # verifying the same number
59
```

2. The `grouped` variable has a `filter` method, which accepts a custom function that determines whether a group is kept or not. The custom function gets implicitly passed a DataFrame of the current group and is required to return a boolean. Let's define a function that calculates the total percentage of minority students and returns `True` if this percentage is greater than a user-defined threshold:

```
>>> def check_minority(df, threshold):
        minority_pct = 1 - df['UGDS_WHITE']
        total_minority = (df['UGDS'] * minority_pct).sum()
        total_ugds = df['UGDS'].sum()
        total_minority_pct = total_minority / total_ugds
        return total_minority_pct > threshold
```

3. Use the `filter` method passed with the `check_minority` function and a threshold of 50% to find all states that have a minority majority:

```
>>> college_filtered = grouped.filter(check_minority, threshold=.5)
>>> college_filtered.head()
```

INSTNM	CITY	STABBR	HBCU	MENONLY	WOMENONLY	RELAFFIL	SATVRMID	SATMTMID	DISTANCEONLY	UGDS
Everest College-Phoenix	Phoenix	AZ	0.0	0.0	0.0	1	NaN	NaN	0.0	4102.0
Collins College	Phoenix	AZ	0.0	0.0	0.0	0	NaN	NaN	0.0	83.0
Empire Beauty School-Paradise Valley	Phoenix	AZ	0.0	0.0	0.0	1	NaN	NaN	0.0	25.0
Empire Beauty School-Tucson	Tucson	AZ	0.0	0.0	0.0	0	NaN	NaN	0.0	126.0
Thunderbird School of Global Management	Glendale	AZ	0.0	0.0	0.0	0	NaN	NaN	0.0	1.0

4. Just looking at the output may not be indicative of what actually happened. The DataFrame starts with state Arizona (AZ) and not Alaska (AK) so we can visually confirm that something changed. Let's compare the `shape` of this filtered DataFrame with the original. Looking at the results, about 60% of the rows have been filtered, and only 20 states remain that have a minority majority:

```
>>> college.shape
(7535, 26)

>>> college_filtered.shape
(3028, 26)

>>> college_filtered['STABBR'].nunique()
20
```

How it works...

This recipe takes a look at the total population of all the institutions on a state-by-state basis. The goal is to keep all the rows from the states, as a whole, that have a minority majority. This requires us to group our data by state, which is done in step 1. We find that there are 59 independent groups.

The `filter` groupby method either keeps all the rows in a group or filters them out. It does not change the number of columns. The `filter` groupby method performs this gatekeeping through a user-defined function, for example, `check_minority` in this recipe. A very important aspect to filter is that it passes the entire DataFrame for that particular group to the user-defined function and returns a single boolean for each group.

Inside of the `check_minority` function, the percentage and the total number of non-white students for each institution are first calculated and then the total number of all students is found. Finally, the percentage of non-white students for the entire state is checked against the given threshold, which produces a boolean.

The final result is a DataFrame with the same columns as the original but with the rows from the states that don't meet the threshold filtered out. As it is possible that the head of the filtered DataFrame is the same as the original, you need to do some inspection to ensure that the operation completed successfully. We verify this by checking the number of rows and number of unique states.

There's more...

Our function, `check_minority`, is flexible and accepts a parameter to lower or raise the percentage of minority threshold. Let's check the shape and number of unique states for a couple of other thresholds:

```
>>> college_filtered_20 = grouped.filter(check_minority, threshold=.2)
>>> college_filtered_20.shape
(7461, 26)

>>> college_filtered_20['STABBR'].nunique()
57

>>> college_filtered_70 = grouped.filter(check_minority, threshold=.7)
>>> college_filtered_70.shape
(957, 26)

>>> college_filtered_70['STABBR'].nunique()
10
```

See also

- Pandas official documentation on *Filtration* (http://bit.ly/2xGUoA7)

Transforming through a weight loss bet

One method to increase motivation to lose weight is to make a bet with someone else. The scenario in this recipe will track weight loss from two individuals over the course of a four-month period and determine a winner.

Getting ready

In this recipe, we use simulated data from two individuals to track the percentage of weight loss over the course of four months. At the end of each month, a winner will be declared based on the individual who lost the highest percentage of body weight for that month. To track weight loss, we group our data by month and person, then call the transform method to find the percentage weight loss at each week from the start of the month.

How to do it...

1. Read in the raw weight_loss dataset, and examine the first month of data from the two people, Amy and Bob. There are a total of four weigh-ins per month:

```
>>> weight_loss = pd.read_csv('data/weight_loss.csv')
>>> weight_loss.query('Month == "Jan"')
```

	Name	Month	Week	Weight
0	Bob	Jan	Week 1	291
1	Amy	Jan	Week 1	197
2	Bob	Jan	Week 2	288
3	Amy	Jan	Week 2	189
4	Bob	Jan	Week 3	283
5	Amy	Jan	Week 3	189
6	Bob	Jan	Week 4	283
7	Amy	Jan	Week 4	190

2. To determine the winner for each month, we only need to compare weight loss from the first week to the last week of each month. But, if we wanted to have weekly updates, we can also calculate weight loss from the current week to the first week of each month. Let's create a function that is capable of providing weekly updates:

```
>>> def find_perc_loss(s):
        return (s - s.iloc[0]) / s.iloc[0]
```

3. Let's test out this function for Bob during the month of January.

```
>>> bob_jan = weight_loss.query('Name=="Bob" and Month=="Jan"')
>>> find_perc_loss(bob_jan['Weight'])
0    0.000000
2   -0.010309
4   -0.027491
6   -0.027491
Name: Weight, dtype: float64
```

 You should ignore the index values in the last output. 0, 2, 4 and 6 simply refer to the original row labels of the DataFrame and have no relation to the week.

4. After the first week, Bob lost 1% of his body weight. He continued losing weight during the second week but made no progress during the last week. We can apply this function to every single combination of person and week to get the weight loss per week in relation to the first week of the month. To do this, we need to group our data by `Name` and `Month`, and then use the `transform` method to apply this custom function:

```
>>> pcnt_loss = weight_loss.groupby(['Name', 'Month'])['Weight'] \
                    .transform(find_perc_loss)
>>> pcnt_loss.head(8)
0    0.000000
1    0.000000
2   -0.010309
3   -0.040609
4   -0.027491
5   -0.040609
6   -0.027491
7   -0.035533
Name: Weight, dtype: float64
```

5. The `transform` method must return an object with the same number of rows as the calling DataFrame. Let's append this result to our original DataFrame as a new column. To help shorten the output, we will select Bob's first two months of data:

```
>>> weight_loss['Perc Weight Loss'] = pcnt_loss.round(3)
>>> weight_loss.query('Name=="Bob" and Month in ["Jan", "Feb"]')
```

	Name	Month	Week	Weight	Perc Weight Loss
0	Bob	Jan	Week 1	291	0.000
2	Bob	Jan	Week 2	288	-0.010
4	Bob	Jan	Week 3	283	-0.027
6	Bob	Jan	Week 4	283	-0.027
8	Bob	Feb	Week 1	283	0.000
10	Bob	Feb	Week 2	275	-0.028
12	Bob	Feb	Week 3	268	-0.053
14	Bob	Feb	Week 4	268	-0.053

6. Notice that the percentage weight loss resets after the new month. With this new column, we can manually determine a winner but let's see if we can find a way to do this automatically. As the only week that matters is the last week, let's select week 4:

```
>>> week4 = weight_loss.query('Week == "Week 4"')
>>> week4
```

	Name	Month	Week	Weight	Perc Weight Loss
6	Bob	Jan	Week 4	283	-0.027
7	Amy	Jan	Week 4	190	-0.036
14	Bob	Feb	Week 4	268	-0.053
15	Amy	Feb	Week 4	173	-0.089
22	Bob	Mar	Week 4	261	-0.026
23	Amy	Mar	Week 4	170	-0.017
30	Bob	Apr	Week 4	250	-0.042
31	Amy	Apr	Week 4	161	-0.053

7. This narrows down the weeks but still doesn't automatically find out the winner of each month. Let's reshape this data with the `pivot` method so that Bob's and Amy's percent weight loss is side-by-side for each month:

```
>>> winner = week4.pivot(index='Month', columns='Name',
                         values='Perc Weight Loss')
>>> winner
```

Name	Amy	Bob
Month		
Apr	-0.053	-0.042
Feb	-0.089	-0.053
Jan	-0.036	-0.027
Mar	-0.017	-0.026

8. This output makes it clearer who has won each month, but we can still go a couple steps farther. NumPy has a vectorized if-then-else function called `where`, which can map a Series or array of booleans to other values. Let's create a column for the name of the winner and highlight the winning percentage for each month:

```
>>> winner['Winner'] = np.where(winner['Amy'] < winner['Bob'],
                                'Amy', 'Bob')
>>> winner.style.highlight_min(axis=1)
```

Name	Amy	Bob	Winner
Month			
Apr	-0.053	-0.042	Amy
Feb	-0.089	-0.053	Amy
Jan	-0.036	-0.027	Amy
Mar	-0.017	-0.026	Bob

9. Use the `value_counts` method to return the final score as the number of months won:

```
>>> winner.Winner.value_counts()
Amy     3
Bob     1
Name: Winner, dtype: int64
```

How it works...

Throughout this recipe, the `query` method is used to filter data instead of boolean indexing. Refer to the *Improving readability of Boolean indexing with the query method* recipe from `Chapter 5`, *Boolean Indexing*, for more information.

Our goal is to find the percentage weight loss for each month for each person. One way to accomplish this task is to calculate each week's weight loss relative to the start of each month. This specific task is perfectly suited to the `transform` groupby method. The `transform` method accepts a function as its one required parameter. This function gets implicitly passed each non-grouping column (or only the columns specified in the indexing operator as was done in this recipe with `Weight`). It must return a sequence of values the same length as the passed group or else an exception will be raised. In essence, all values from the original DataFrame are transforming. No aggregation or filtration takes place.

Step 2 creates a function that subtracts the first value of the passed Series from all of its values and then divides this result by the first value. This calculates the percent loss (or gain) relative to the first value. In step 3 we test this function on one person during one month.

In step 4, we use this function in the same manner over every combination of person and week. In some literal sense, we are *transforming* the `Weight` column into the percentage of weight lost for the current week. The first month of data is outputted for each person. Pandas returns the new data as a Series. This Series isn't all that useful by itself and makes more sense appended to the original DataFrame as a new column. We complete this operation in step 5.

To determine the winner, only week 4 of each month is necessary. We could stop here and manually determine the winner but pandas supplies us functionality to automate this. The `pivot` function in step 7 reshapes our dataset by pivoting the unique values of one column into new column names. The `index` parameter is used for the column that you do not want to pivot. The column passed to the `values` parameter gets tiled over each unique combination of the columns in the `index` and `columns` parameters.

The `pivot` method only works if there is just a single occurrence of each unique combination of the columns in the `index` and `columns` parameters. If there is more than one unique combination, an exception will be raised. You can use the `pivot_table` method in that situation which allows you to aggregate multiple values together.

After pivoting, we utilize the highly effective and fast NumPy `where` function, whose first argument is a condition that produces a Series of booleans. `True` values get mapped to *Amy* and `False` values get mapped to *Bob*. We highlight the winner of each month and tally the final score with the `value_counts` method.

There's more...

Take a look at the DataFrame output from step 7. Did you notice that the months are in alphabetical and not chronological order? Pandas unfortunately, in this case at least, orders the months for us alphabetically. We can solve this issue by changing the data type of `Month` to a categorical variable. Categorical variables map all the values of each column to an integer. We can choose this mapping to be the normal chronological order for the months. Pandas uses this underlying integer mapping during the `pivot` method to order the months chronologically:

```
>>> week4a = week4.copy()
>>> month_chron = week4a['Month'].unique() # or use drop_duplicates
>>> month_chron
array(['Jan', 'Feb', 'Mar', 'Apr'], dtype=object)

>>> week4a['Month'] = pd.Categorical(week4a['Month'],
                                     categories=month_chron,
                                     ordered=True)
>>> week4a.pivot(index='Month', columns='Name',
                 values='Perc Weight Loss')
```

Name	Amy	Bob
Month		
Jan	-0.036	-0.027
Feb	-0.089	-0.053
Mar	-0.017	-0.026
Apr	-0.053	-0.042

To convert the Month column, use the Categorical constructor. Pass it the original column as a Series and a unique sequence of all the categories in the desired order to the categories parameter. As the Month column is already in chronological order, we can simply use the unique method, which preserves order to get the array that we desire. In general, to sort columns of object data type by something other than alphabetical, convert them to categorical.

See also

- Pandas official documentation on groupby *Transformation* (http://bit.ly/2vBkpA7)
- NumPy official documentation on the where function (http://bit.ly/2weT211)

Calculating weighted mean SAT scores per state with apply

The groupby object has four methods that accept a function (or functions) to perform a calculation on each group. These four methods are agg, filter, transform, and apply. Each of the first three of these methods has a very specific output that the function must return. agg must return a scalar value, filter must return a boolean, and transform must return a Series with the same length as the passed group. The apply method, however, may return a scalar value, a Series, or even a DataFrame of any shape, therefore making it very flexible. It is also called only once per group, which contrasts with transform and agg that get called once for each non-grouping column. The apply method's ability to return a single object when operating on multiple columns at the same time makes the calculation in this recipe possible.

Getting ready

In this recipe, we calculate the weighted average of both the math and verbal SAT scores per state from the college dataset. We weight the scores by the population of undergraduate students per school.

How to do it...

1. Read in the college dataset, and drop any rows that have missing values in either the UGDS, SATMTMID, or SATVRMID columns. We must have non-missing values for each of these three columns:

```
>>> college = pd.read_csv('data/college.csv')
>>> subset = ['UGDS', 'SATMTMID', 'SATVRMID']
>>> college2 = college.dropna(subset=subset)
>>> college.shape
(7535, 27)

>>> college2.shape
(1184, 27)
```

2. The vast majority of institutions do not have data for our three required columns, but this is still more than enough data to continue. Next, create a user-defined function to calculate the weighted average of just the SAT math scores:

```
>>> def weighted_math_average(df):
        weighted_math = df['UGDS'] * df['SATMTMID']
        return int(weighted_math.sum() / df['UGDS'].sum())
```

3. Group by state and pass this function to the apply method:

```
>>> college2.groupby('STABBR').apply(weighted_math_average).head()
STABBR
AK    503
AL    536
AR    529
AZ    569
CA    564
dtype: int64
```

4. We successfully returned a scalar value for each group. Let's take a small detour and see what the outcome would have been by passing the same function to the agg method:

```
>>> college2.groupby('STABBR').agg(weighted_math_average).head()
```

STABBR	INSTNM	CITY	HBCU	MENONLY	WOMENONLY	RELAFFIL	SATVRMID	SATMTMID	DISTANCEONLY	UGDS
AK	503	503	503	503	503	503	503	503	503	503
AL	536	536	536	536	536	536	536	536	536	536
AR	529	529	529	529	529	529	529	529	529	529
AZ	569	569	569	569	569	569	569	569	569	569
CA	564	564	564	564	564	564	564	564	564	564

5. The `weighted_math_average` function gets applied to each non-aggregating column in the DataFrame. If you try and limit the columns to just `SATMTMID`, you will get an error as you won't have access to `UGDS`. So, the best way to complete operations that act on multiple columns is with `apply`:

```
>>> college2.groupby('STABBR')['SATMTMID'] \
            .agg(weighted_math_average)
KeyError: 'UGDS'
```

6. A nice feature of `apply` is that you can create multiple new columns by returning a Series. The index of this returned Series will be the new column names. Let's modify our function to calculate the weighted and arithmetic average for both SAT scores along with the count of the number of institutions from each group. We return these five values in a Series:

```
>>> from collections import OrderedDict
>>> def weighted_average(df):
        data = OrderedDict()
        weight_m = df['UGDS'] * df['SATMTMID']
        weight_v = df['UGDS'] * df['SATVRMID']
        wm_avg = weight_m.sum() / df['UGDS'].sum()
        wv_avg = weight_v.sum() / df['UGDS'].sum()

        data['weighted_math_avg'] = wm_avg
        data['weighted_verbal_avg'] = wv_avg
        data['math_avg'] = df['SATMTMID'].mean()
        data['verbal_avg'] = df['SATVRMID'].mean()
        data['count'] = len(df)
        return pd.Series(data, dtype='int')

>>> college2.groupby('STABBR').apply(weighted_average).head(10)
```

STABBR	weighted_math_avg	weighted_verbal_avg	math_avg	verbal_avg	count
AK	503	555	503	555	1
AL	536	533	504	508	21
AR	529	504	515	491	16
AZ	569	557	536	538	6
CA	564	539	562	549	72
CO	553	547	540	537	14
CT	545	533	522	517	14
DC	621	623	588	589	6
DE	569	553	495	486	3
FL	565	565	521	529	38

How it works...

In order for this recipe to complete properly, we need to first filter for institutions that do not have missing values for UGDS, SATMTMID, and SATVRMID. By default, the dropna method drops rows that have one or more missing values. We must use the subset parameter to limit the columns it looks at for missing values.

In step 2, we define a function that calculates the weighted average for just the SATMTMID column. The weighted average differs from an arithmetic mean in that each value is multiplied by some weight. This quantity is then summed and divided by the sum of the weights. In this case, our weight is the undergraduate student population.

In step 3, we pass this function to the apply method. Our function weighted_math_average gets passed a DataFrame of all the original columns for each group. It returns a single scalar value, the weighted average of SATMTMID. At this point, you might think that this calculation is possible using the agg method. Directly replacing apply with agg does not work as agg returns a value for each of its aggregating columns.

It actually is possible to use agg indirectly by precomputing the multiplication of UGDS and SATMTMID.

Step 6 really shows the versatility of `apply`. We build a new function that calculates the weighted and arithmetic average of both SAT columns as well as the number of rows for each group. In order for `apply` to create multiple columns, you must return a Series. The index values are used as column names in the resulting DataFrame. You can return as many values as you want with this method.

Notice that the `OrderedDict` class was imported from the `collections` module, which is part of the standard library. This ordered dictionary is used to store the data. A normal Python dictionary could not have been used to store the data since it does not preserve insertion order.

The constructor, `pd.Series`, does have an index parameter that you can use to specify order but using an `OrderedDict` is cleaner.

There's more...

In this recipe, we returned a single row as a Series for each group. It's possible to return any number of rows and columns for each group by returning a DataFrame. In addition to finding just the arithmetic and weighted means, let's also find the geometric and harmonic means of both SAT columns and return the results as a DataFrame with rows as the name of the type of mean and columns as the SAT type. To ease the burden on us, we use the NumPy function `average` to compute the weighted average and the SciPy functions `gmean` and `hmean` for geometric and harmonic means:

```
>>> from scipy.stats import gmean, hmean
>>> def calculate_means(df):
        df_means = pd.DataFrame(index=['Arithmetic', 'Weighted',
                                       'Geometric', 'Harmonic'])
        cols = ['SATMTMID', 'SATVRMID']
        for col in cols:
            arithmetic = df[col].mean()
            weighted = np.average(df[col], weights=df['UGDS'])
            geometric = gmean(df[col])
            harmonic = hmean(df[col])
            df_means[col] = [arithmetic, weighted,
                             geometric, harmonic]
        df_means['count'] = len(df)
        return df_means.astype(int)

>>> college2.groupby('STABBR').apply(calculate_means).head(12)
```

STABBR		SATMTMID	SATVRMID	count
AK	Arithmetic	503	555	1
	Weighted	503	555	1
	Geometric	503	555	1
	Harmonic	503	555	1
AL	Arithmetic	504	508	21
	Weighted	536	533	21
	Geometric	500	505	21
	Harmonic	497	502	21
AR	Arithmetic	515	491	16
	Weighted	529	504	16
	Geometric	514	489	16
	Harmonic	513	487	16

See also

- Pandas official documentation of the `apply` groupby method (`http://bit.ly/2wmG9ki`)
- Python official documentation of the `OrderedDict` class (`http://bit.ly/2xwtUCa`)
- SciPy official documentation of its stats module (`http://bit.ly/2wHLQ4L`)

Grouping by continuous variables

When grouping in pandas, you typically use columns with discrete repeating values. If there are no repeated values, then grouping would be pointless as there would only be one row per group. Continuous numeric columns typically have few repeated values and are generally not used to form groups. However, if we can transform columns with continuous values into a discrete column by placing each value into a bin, rounding them, or using some other mapping, then grouping with them makes sense.

Getting ready

In this recipe, we explore the flights dataset to discover the distribution of airlines for different travel distances. This allows us, for example, to find the airline that makes the most flights between 500 and 1,000 miles. To accomplish this, we use the pandas `cut` function to discretize the distance of each flight flown.

How to do it...

1. Read in the flights dataset, and output the first five rows:

```
>>> flights = pd.read_csv('data/flights.csv')
>>> flights.head()
```

	MONTH	DAY	WEEKDAY	AIRLINE	ORG_AIR	DEST_AIR	SCHED_DEP	DEP_DELAY	AIR_TIME	DIST	SCHED_ARR	ARR_DELAY	DIVERTED	CANCELLED
0	1	1	4	WN	LAX	SLC	1625	58.0	94.0	590	1905	65.0	0	0
1	1	1	4	UA	DEN	IAD	823	7.0	154.0	1452	1333	-13.0	0	0
2	1	1	4	MQ	DFW	VPS	1305	36.0	85.0	641	1453	35.0	0	0
3	1	1	4	AA	DFW	DCA	1555	7.0	126.0	1192	1935	-7.0	0	0
4	1	1	4	WN	LAX	MCI	1720	48.0	166.0	1363	2225	39.0	0	0

2. If we want to find the distribution of airlines over a range of distances, we need to place the values of the DIST column into discrete bins. Let's use the pandas cut function to split the data into five bins:

```
>>> bins = [-np.inf, 200, 500, 1000, 2000, np.inf]
>>> cuts = pd.cut(flights['DIST'], bins=bins)
>>> cuts.head()
0      (500.0, 1000.0]
1     (1000.0, 2000.0]
2      (500.0, 1000.0]
3     (1000.0, 2000.0]
4     (1000.0, 2000.0]
Name: DIST, dtype: category
Categories (5, interval[float64]): [(-inf, 200.0] < (200.0, 500.0]
< (500.0, 1000.0] < (1000.0, 2000.0] < (2000.0, inf]]
```

3. An ordered categorical Series is created. To help get an idea of what happened, let's count the values of each category:

```
>>> cuts.value_counts()
(500.0, 1000.0]     20659
(200.0, 500.0]      15874
(1000.0, 2000.0]    14186
(2000.0, inf]        4054
(-inf, 200.0]        3719
Name: DIST, dtype: int64
```

4. The cuts Series can now be used to form groups. Pandas allows you to form groups in any way you wish. Pass the cuts Series to the groupby method and then call the value_counts method on the AIRLINE column to find the distribution for each distance group. Notice that SkyWest (*OO*) makes up 33% of flights less than 200 miles but only 16% of those between 200 and 500 miles:

```
>>> flights.groupby(cuts)['AIRLINE'].value_counts(normalize=True) \
                                    .round(3).head(15)
DIST             AIRLINE
(-inf, 200.0]    OO         0.326
                 EV         0.289
                 MQ         0.211
                 DL         0.086
                 AA         0.052
                 UA         0.027
                 WN         0.009
(200.0, 500.0]   WN         0.194
                 DL         0.189
                 OO         0.159
```

```
             EV          0.156
             MQ          0.100
             AA          0.071
             UA          0.062
             VX          0.028
Name: AIRLINE, dtype: float64
```

How it works...

In step 2, the `cut` function places each value of the `DIST` column into one of five bins. The bins are created by a sequence of six numbers defining the edges. You always need one more edge than the number of bins. You can pass the `bins` parameter an integer, which automatically creates that number of equal-width bins. Negative infinity and positive infinity objects are available in NumPy and ensure that all values get placed in a bin. If you have values that are outside of the bin edges, they will be made missing and not be placed in a bin.

The `cuts` variable is now a Series of five ordered categories. It has all the normal Series methods and in step 3, the `value_counts` method is used to get a sense of its distribution.

Very interestingly, pandas allows you to pass the `groupby` method any object. This means that you are able to form groups from something completely unrelated to the current DataFrame. Here, we group by the values in the `cuts` variable. For each grouping, we find the percentage of flights per airline with `value_counts` by setting `normalize` to `True`.

Some interesting insights can be drawn from this result. Looking at the full result, SkyWest is the leading airline for under 200 miles but has no flights over 2,000 miles. In contrast, American Airlines has the fifth highest total for flights under 200 miles but has by far the most flights between 1,000 and 2,000 miles.

There's more...

We can find more results when grouping by the `cuts` variable. For instance, we can find the 25th, 50th, and 75th percentile airtime for each distance grouping. As airtime is in minutes, we can divide by 60 to get hours:

```
>>> flights.groupby(cuts)['AIR_TIME'].quantile(q=[.25, .5, .75]) \
                                      .div(60).round(2)
DIST
(-inf, 200.0]       0.25      0.43
                    0.50      0.50
                    0.75      0.57
```

```
(200.0, 500.0]      0.25    0.77
                    0.50    0.92
                    0.75    1.05
(500.0, 1000.0]     0.25    1.43
                    0.50    1.65
                    0.75    1.92
(1000.0, 2000.0]    0.25    2.50
                    0.50    2.93
                    0.75    3.40
(2000.0, inf]       0.25    4.30
                    0.50    4.70
                    0.75    5.03
Name: AIR_TIME, dtype: float64
```

We can use this information to create informative string labels when using the cut function. These labels replace the interval notation. We can also chain the unstack method which transposes the inner index level to column names:

```
>>> labels=['Under an Hour', '1 Hour', '1-2 Hours',
            '2-4 Hours', '4+ Hours']
>>> cuts2 = pd.cut(flights['DIST'], bins=bins, labels=labels)
>>> flights.groupby(cuts2)['AIRLINE'].value_counts(normalize=True) \
                                     .round(3) \
                                     .unstack() \
                                     .style.highlight_max(axis=1)
```

AIRLINE DIST	AA	AS	B6	DL	EV	F9	HA	MQ	NK	OO	UA	US	VX	WN
Under an Hour	0.052	nan	nan	0.086	0.289	nan	nan	0.211	nan	0.326	0.027	nan	nan	0.009
1 Hour	0.071	0.001	0.007	0.189	0.156	0.005	nan	0.1	0.012	0.159	0.062	0.016	0.028	0.194
1-2 Hours	0.144	0.023	0.003	0.206	0.101	0.038	nan	0.051	0.03	0.106	0.131	0.025	0.004	0.138
2-4 Hours	0.264	0.016	0.003	0.165	0.016	0.031	nan	0.003	0.045	0.046	0.199	0.04	0.012	0.16
4+ Hours	0.212	0.012	0.08	0.171	nan	0.004	0.028	nan	0.019	nan	0.289	0.065	0.074	0.046

See also

- Pandas official documentation on the `cut` function (http://bit.ly/2whcUkJ)
- Refer to `Chapter 8`, *Restructuring Data into Tidy Form*, for many more recipes with unstack

Counting the total number of flights between cities

In the flights dataset, we have data on the origin and destination airport. It is trivial to count the number of flights originating in Houston and landing in Atlanta, for instance. What is more difficult is counting the total number of flights between the two cities, regardless of which one is the origin or destination.

Getting ready

In this recipe, we count the total number of flights between two cities regardless of which one is the origin or destination. To accomplish this, we sort the origin and destination airports alphabetically so that each combination of airports always occurs in the same order. We can then use this new column arrangement to form groups and then to count.

How to do it...

1. Read in the flights dataset, and find the total number of flights between each origin and destination airport:

```
>>> flights = pd.read_csv('data/flights.csv')
>>> flights_ct = flights.groupby(['ORG_AIR', 'DEST_AIR']).size()
>>> flights_ct.head()
ORG_AIR  DEST_AIR
ATL      ABE          31
         ABQ          16
         ABY          19
         ACY           6
         AEX          40
dtype: int64
```

2. Select the total number of flights between Houston (*IAH*) and Atlanta (*ATL*) in both directions:

```
>>> flights_ct.loc[[('ATL', 'IAH'), ('IAH', 'ATL')]]
ORG_AIR  DEST_AIR
ATL      IAH        121
IAH      ATL        148
dtype: int64
```

3. We could simply sum these two numbers together to find the total flights between the cities but there is a more efficient and automated solution that can work for all flights. Let's independently sort the origin and destination cities for each row in alphabetical order:

```
>>> flights_sort = flights[['ORG_AIR', 'DEST_AIR']] \
                       .apply(sorted, axis=1)
>>> flights_sort.head()
```

	ORG_AIR	DEST_AIR
0	LAX	SLC
1	DEN	IAD
2	DFW	VPS
3	DCA	DFW
4	LAX	MCI

4. Now that each row has been independently sorted, the column names are not correct. Let's rename them to something more generic and then again find the total number of flights between all cities:

```
>>> rename_dict = {'ORG_AIR':'AIR1', 'DEST_AIR':'AIR2'}
>>> flights_sort = flights_sort.rename(columns=rename_dict)
>>> flights_ct2 = flights_sort.groupby(['AIR1', 'AIR2']).size()
>>> flights_ct2.head()
AIR1  AIR2
ABE   ATL        31
      ORD        24
ABI   DFW        74
ABQ   ATL        16
      DEN        46
dtype: int64
```

5. Let's select all the flights between Atlanta and Houston and verify that it matches the sum of the values in step 2:

```
>>> flights_ct2.loc[('ATL', 'IAH')]
269
```

6. If we try and select flights with Houston followed by Atlanta, we get an error:

```
>>> flights_ct2.loc[('IAH', 'ATL')]
IndexingError: Too many indexers
```

How it works...

In step 1, we form groups by the origin and destination airport columns and then apply the `size` method to the groupby object, which simply returns the total number of rows for each group. Notice that we could have passed the string `size` to the `agg` method to achieve the same result. In step 2, the total number of flights for each direction between Atlanta and Houston are selected. The Series `flights_count` has a MultiIndex with two levels. One way to select rows from a MultiIndex is to pass the `loc` indexing operator a tuple of exact level values. Here, we actually select two different rows, `('ATL', 'HOU')` and `('HOU', 'ATL')`. We use a list of tuples to do this correctly.

Step 3 is the most pertinent step in the recipe. We would like to have just one label for all flights between Atlanta and Houston and so far we have two. If we alphabetically sort each combination of origin and destination airports, we would then have a single label for flights between airports. To do this, we use the DataFrame `apply` method. This is different from the groupby `apply` method. No groups are formed in step 3.

The DataFrame `apply` method must be passed a function. In this case, it's the built-in `sorted` function. By default, this function gets applied to each column as a Series. We can change the direction of computation by using `axis=1` (or `axis='index'`). The `sorted` function has each row of data passed to it implicitly as a Series. It returns a list of sorted airport codes. Here is an example of passing the first row as a Series to the sorted function:

```
>>> sorted(flights.loc[0, ['ORG_AIR', 'DEST_AIR']])
['LAX', 'SLC']
```

The `apply` method iterates over all rows using `sorted` in this exact manner. After completion of this operation, each row is independently sorted. The column names are now meaningless. We rename the column names in the next step and then perform the same grouping and aggregating as was done in step 2. This time, all flights between Atlanta and Houston fall under the same label.

There's more...

You might be wondering why we can't use the simpler `sort_values` Series method. This method does not sort independently and instead, preserves the row or column as a single record as one would expect while doing a data analysis. Step 3 is a very expensive operation and takes several seconds to complete. There are only about 60,000 rows so this solution would not scale well to larger data. Calling the

Step 3 is a very expensive operation and takes several seconds to complete. There are only about 60,000 rows so this solution would not scale well to larger data. Calling the `apply` method with `axis=1` is one of the least performant operations in all of pandas. Internally, pandas loops over each row and does not provide any speed boosts from NumPy. If possible, avoid using `apply` with `axis=1`.

We can get a massive speed increase with the NumPy `sort` function. Let's go ahead and use this function and analyze its output. By default, it sorts each row independently:

```
>>> data_sorted - np.sort(flights[['ORG_AIR', 'DEST_AIR']])
>>> data_sorted[:10]
array([['LAX', 'SLC'],
       ['DEN', 'IAD'],
       ['DFW', 'VPS'],
       ['DCA', 'DFW'],
       ['LAX', 'MCI'],
       ['IAH', 'SAN'],
       ['DFW', 'MSY'],
       ['PHX', 'SFO'],
       ['ORD', 'STL'],
       ['IAH', 'SJC']], dtype=object)
```

A two-dimensional NumPy array is returned. NumPy does not easily do grouping operations so let's use the DataFrame constructor to create a new DataFrame and check whether it equals the `flights_sorted` DataFrame from step 3:

```
>>> flights_sort2 = pd.DataFrame(data_sorted, columns=['AIR1', 'AIR2'])
>>> fs_orig = flights_sort.rename(columns={'ORG_AIR':'AIR1',
                                          'DEST_AIR':'AIR2'})
>>> flights_sort2.equals(fs_orig)
True
```

As the DataFrames are the same, you can replace step 3 with the previous faster sorting routine. Let's time the difference between each of the different sorting methods:

```
>>> %%timeit
>>> flights_sort = flights[['ORG_AIR', 'DEST_AIR']] \
                          .apply(sorted, axis=1)
7.41 s ± 189 ms per loop (mean ± std. dev. of 7 runs, 1 loop each)

>>> %%timeit
>>> data_sorted = np.sort(flights[['ORG_AIR', 'DEST_AIR']])
>>> flights_sort2 = pd.DataFrame(data_sorted,
                                 columns=['AIR1', 'AIR2'])
10.6 ms ± 453 µs per loop (mean ± std. dev. of 7 runs, 100 loops each)
```

The NumPy solution is an astounding 700 times faster than using `apply` with pandas.

See also

- NumPy official documentation on the `sort` function (http://bit.ly/2vtRt0M)

Finding the longest streak of on-time flights

One of the most important metrics for airlines is their on-time flight performance. The Federal Aviation Administration considers a flight delayed when it arrives at least 15 minutes later than its scheduled arrival time. Pandas has direct methods to calculate the total and percentage of on-time flights per airline. While these basic summary statistics are an important metric, there are other non-trivial calculations that are interesting, such as finding the length of consecutive on-time flights for each airline at each of its origin airports.

Getting ready

In this recipe, we find the longest consecutive streak of on-time flights for each airline at each origin airport. This requires each value in a column to be aware of the value immediately following it. We make clever use of the `diff` and `cumsum` methods in order to find streaks before applying this methodology to each of the groups.

How to do it...

1. Before we get started with the actual flights dataset, let's practice counting streaks of ones with a small sample Series:

```
>>> s = pd.Series([0, 1, 1, 0, 1, 1, 1, 0])
>>> s
0    0
1    1
2    1
3    0
4    1
5    1
6    1
7    0
dtype: int64
```

2. Our final representation of the streaks of ones will be a Series of the same length as the original with an independent count beginning from one for each streak. To get started, let's use the `cumsum` method:

```
>>> s1 = s.cumsum()
>>> s1
0    0
1    1
2    2
3    2
4    3
5    4
6    5
7    5
dtype: int64
```

3. We have now accumulated all the ones going down the Series. Let's multiply this Series by the original:

```
>>> s.mul(s1)
0    0
1    1
2    2
3    0
4    3
5    4
6    5
7    0
dtype: int64
```

4. We have only non-zero values where we originally had ones. This result is fairly close to what we desire. We just need to restart each streak at one instead of where the cumulative sum left off. Let's chain the `diff` method, which subtracts the previous value from the current:

```
>>> s.mul(s1).diff()
0    NaN
1    1.0
2    1.0
3   -2.0
4    3.0
5    1.0
6    1.0
7   -5.0
dtype: float64
```

5. A negative value represents the end of a streak. We need to propagate the negative values down the Series and use them to subtract away the excess accumulation from step 2. To do this, we will make all non-negative values missing with the `where` method:

```
>>> s.mul(s1).diff().where(lambda x: x < 0)
0    NaN
1    NaN
2    NaN
3    2.0
4    NaN
5    NaN
6    NaN
7   -5.0
dtype: float64
```

6. We can now propagate these values down with the `ffill` method:

```
>>> s.mul(s1).diff().where(lambda x: x < 0).ffill()
0    NaN
1    NaN
2    NaN
3   -2.0
4   -2.0
5   -2.0
6   -2.0
7   -5.0
dtype: float64
```

7. Finally, we can add this Series back to `s1` to clear out the excess accumulation:

```
>>> s.mul(s1).diff().where(lambda x: x < 0).ffill() \
        .add(s1, fill_value=0)
0    0.0
1    1.0
2    2.0
3    0.0
4    1.0
5    2.0
6    3.0
7    0.0
dtype: float64
```

8. Now that we have a working consecutive streak finder, we can find the longest streak per airline and origin airport. Let's read in the flights dataset and create a column to represent on-time arrival:

```
>>> flights = pd.read_csv('data/flights.csv')
>>> flights['ON_TIME'] = flights['ARR_DELAY'].lt(15).astype(int)
>>> flights[['AIRLINE', 'ORG_AIR', 'ON_TIME']].head(10)
```

	AIRLINE	ORG_AIR	ON_TIME
0	WN	LAX	0
1	UA	DEN	1
2	MQ	DFW	0
3	AA	DFW	1
4	WN	LAX	0
5	UA	IAH	1
6	AA	DFW	0
7	F9	SFO	1
8	AA	ORD	1
9	UA	IAH	1

9. Use our logic from the first seven steps to define a function that returns the maximum streak of ones for a given Series:

```
>>> def max_streak(s):
        s1 = s.cumsum()
        return s.mul(s1).diff().where(lambda x: x < 0) \
                .ffill().add(s1, fill_value=0).max()
```

10. Find the maximum streak of on-time arrivals per airline and origin airport along with the total number of flights and percentage of on-time arrivals. First, sort the day of the year and scheduled departure time:

```
>>> flights.sort_values(['MONTH', 'DAY', 'SCHED_DEP']) \
        .groupby(['AIRLINE', 'ORG_AIR'])['ON_TIME'] \
        .agg(['mean', 'size', max_streak]).round(2).head()
```

AIRLINE	ORG_AIR	mean	size	max_streak
AA	ATL	0.82	233	15
	DEN	0.74	219	17
	DFW	0.78	4006	64
	IAH	0.80	196	24
	LAS	0.79	374	29

How it works...

Finding streaks in the data is not a straightforward operation in pandas and requires methods that look ahead or behind, such as `diff` or `shift`, or those that remember their current state, such as `cumsum`. The final result from the first seven steps is a Series the same length as the original that keeps track of all consecutive ones. Throughout these steps, we use the `mul` and `add` methods instead of their operator equivalents (*) and (+). In my opinion, this allows for a slightly cleaner progression of calculations from left to right. You, of course, can replace these with the actual operators.

Ideally, we would like to tell pandas to apply the `cumsum` method to the start of each streak and reset itself after the end of each one. It takes many steps to convey this message to pandas. Step 2 accumulates all the ones in the Series as a whole. The rest of the steps slowly remove any excess accumulation. In order to identify this excess accumulation, we need to find the end of each streak and subtract this value from the beginning of the next streak.

To find the end of each streak, we cleverly make all values not part of the streak zero by multiplying `s1` by the original Series of zeros and ones in step 3. The first zero following a non-zero, marks the end of a streak. That's good, but again, we need to eliminate the excess accumulation. Knowing where the streak ends doesn't exactly get us there.

In step 4, we use the `diff` method to find this excess. The `diff` method takes the difference between the current value and any value located at a set number of rows away from it. By default, the difference between the current and the immediately preceding value is returned.

Only negative values are meaningful in step 4. Those are the ones immediately following the end of a streak. These values need to be propagated down until the end of the following streak. To eliminate (make missing) all the values we don't care about, we use the `where` method, which takes a Series of conditionals of the same size as the calling Series. By default, all the `True` values remain the same, while the `False` values become missing. The `where` method allows you to use the calling Series as part of the conditional by taking a function as its first parameter. An anonymous function is used, which gets passed the calling Series implicitly and checks whether each value is less than zero. The result of step 5 is a Series where only the negative values are preserved with the rest changed to missing.

The `ffill` method in step 6 replaces missing values with the last non-missing value going forward/down a Series. As the first three values don't follow a non-missing value, they remain missing. We finally have our Series that removes the excess accumulation. We add our accumulation Series to the result of step 6 to get the streaks all beginning from zero. The `add` method allows us to replace the missing values with the `fill_value` parameter. This completes the process of finding streaks of ones in the dataset. When doing complex logic like this, it is a good idea to use a small dataset where you know what the final output will be. It would be quite a difficult task to start at step 8 and build this streak-finding logic while grouping.

In step 8, we create the ON_TIME column. One item of note is that the cancelled flights have missing values for ARR_DELAY, which do not pass the boolean condition and therefore result in a zero for the ON_TIME column. Canceled flights are treated the same as delayed.

Step 9 turns our logic from the first seven steps into a function and chains the max method to return the longest streak. As our function returns a single value, it is formally an aggregating function and can be passed to the agg method as done in step 10. To ensure that we are looking at actual consecutive flights, we use the sort_values method to sort by date and scheduled departure time.

There's more...

Now that we have found the longest streaks of on-time arrivals, we can easily find the opposite--the longest streak of delayed arrivals. The following function returns two rows for each group passed to it. The first row is the start of the streak, and the last row is the end of the streak. Each row contains the month and day that the streak started/ended, along with the total streak length:

```
>>> def max_delay_streak(df):
        df = df.reset_index(drop=True)
        s = 1 - df['ON_TIME']
        s1 = s.cumsum()
        streak = s.mul(s1).diff().where(lambda x: x < 0) \
                .ffill().add(s1, fill_value=0)
        last_idx = streak.idxmax()
        first_idx = last_idx - streak.max() + 1
        df_return = df.loc[[first_idx, last_idx], ['MONTH', 'DAY']]
        df_return['streak'] = streak.max()
        df_return.index = ['first', 'last']
        df_return.index.name='type'
        return df_return

>>> flights.sort_values(['MONTH', 'DAY', 'SCHED_DEP']) \
        .groupby(['AIRLINE', 'ORG_AIR']) \
        .apply(max_delay_streak) \
        .sort_values('streak', ascending=False).head(10)
```

AIRLINE	ORG_AIR	streak_row	MONTH	DAY	streak
AA	DFW	first	2.0	26.0	38.0
		last	3.0	1.0	38.0
MQ	ORD	first	1.0	6.0	28.0
		last	1.0	12.0	28.0
	DFW	first	2.0	21.0	25.0
		last	2.0	26.0	25.0
NK	ORD	first	6.0	7.0	15.0
		last	6.0	18.0	15.0
DL	ATL	first	12.0	23.0	14.0
		last	12.0	24.0	14.0

As we are using the `apply` groupby method, a DataFrame of each group is passed to the `max_delay_streak` function. Inside this function, the index of the DataFrame is dropped and replaced by a `RangeIndex` in order for us to easily find the first and last row of the streak. The `ON_TIME` column is inverted and then the same logic is used to find streaks of delayed flights. The index of the first and last rows of the streak are stored as variables. These indexes are then used to select the month and day when the streaks ended. We use a DataFrame to return our results. We label and name the index to make the final result clearer.

Our final results show the longest delayed streaks accompanied by the first and last date. Let's investigate to see if we can find out why these delays happened. Inclement weather is a common reason for delayed or canceled flights. Looking at the first row, American Airlines (AA) started a streak of 38 delayed flights in a row from the Dallas Fort-Worth (DFW) airport beginning February 26 until March 1 of 2015. Looking at historical weather data from February 27, 2015, two inches of snow fell, which was a record for that day (`http://bit.ly/2iLGsCg`). This was a major weather event for DFW and caused massive problems for the entire city (`http://bit.ly/2wmsHPj`). Notice that DFW makes another appearance as the third longest streak but this time a few days earlier and for a different airline.

There are many terms that are used to describe the process of data restructuring, with **tidy data** being the most common to data scientists. Tidy data is a term coined by Hadley Wickham to describe a form of data that makes analysis easy to do. This chapter will cover many ideas formulated by Hadley and how to accomplish them with pandas. To learn a great deal more about tidy data, read Hadley's paper (`http://vita.had.co.nz/papers/tidy-data.pdf`).

What is tidy data? Hadley puts forth three simple guiding principles that determine whether a dataset is tidy or not:

- Each variable forms a column
- Each observation forms a row
- Each type of observational unit forms a table

Any dataset that does not meet these guidelines is considered messy. This definition will make more sense once we start restructuring our data into tidy form, but for now, we'll need to know what variables, observations, and observational units are.

To gain intuition about what a variable actually is, it is good to think about the distinction between a variable name and the variable value. The variable names are labels, such as gender, race, salary, and position. The variable values are those things liable to change for every observation, such as male/female for gender or white/black for race. A single observation is the collection of all variable values for a single observational unit. To help understand what an observational unit might be, consider a retail store, which has data for each transaction, employee, customer, item, and the store itself. Each of these can be considered an observational unit and would require its own table. Combining employee information (like the number of hours worked) with customer information (like amount spent) in the same table would break this tidy principle.

The first step to resolving messy data is to recognize it when it exists, and there are boundless possibilities. Hadley explicitly mentions five of the most common types of messy data:

- Column names are values, not variable names
- Multiple variables are stored in column names
- Variables are stored in both rows and columns
- Multiple types of observational units are stored in the same table
- A single observational unit is stored in multiple tables

It is important to understand that tidying data does not typically involve changing the values of your dataset, filling in missing values, or doing any sort of analysis. Tidying data involves changing the shape or structure of the data to meet the tidy principles. Tidy data is akin to having all your tools in the toolbox instead of scattered randomly throughout your house. Having the tools properly in the toolbox allows all other tasks to be completed easily. Once the data is in the correct form, it becomes much easier to perform further analysis.

Once you have spotted messy data, you will use the pandas tools to restructure the data, so that it is tidy. The main tidy tools that pandas has available for you are the DataFrame methods `stack`, `melt`, `unstack`, and `pivot`. More complex tidying involves ripping apart text, which necessitates the `str` accessor. Other helper methods, such as `rename`, `rename_axis`, `reset_index`, and `set_index` will help with applying the final touches to tidy data.

Tidying variable values as column names with stack

To help understand the differences between tidy and messy data, let's take a look at a simple table that may or may not be in tidy form:

```
>>> state_fruit = pd.read_csv('data/state_fruit.csv', index_col=0)
>>> state_fruit
```

	Apple	Orange	Banana
Texas	12	10	40
Arizona	9	7	12
Florida	0	14	190

There does not appear to be anything messy about this table, and the information is easily consumable. However, according to the tidy principles, it isn't actually tidy. Each column name is actually the value of a variable. In fact, none of the variable names are even present in the DataFrame. One of the first steps to transform a messy dataset into tidy data is to identify all of the variables. In this particular dataset, we have variables for **state** and **fruit**. There's also the numeric data that wasn't identified anywhere in the context of the problem. We can label this variable as **weight** or any other sensible name.

Getting ready

This particular messy dataset contains variable values as column names. We will need to transpose these column names into column values. In this recipe, we use the `stack` method to restructure our DataFrame into tidy form.

How to do it...

1. First, take note that the state names are in the index of the DataFrame. These states are correctly placed vertically and do not need to be restructured. It is the column names that are the problem. The `stack` method takes all of the column names and reshapes them to be vertical as a single index level:

```
>>> state_fruit.stack()
Texas      Apple       12
           Orange      10
           Banana      40
Arizona    Apple        9
           Orange       7
           Banana      12
Florida    Apple        0
           Orange      14
           Banana     190
dtype: int64
```

2. Notice that we now have a Series with a MultiIndex. There are now two levels in the index. The original index has been pushed to the left to make room for the old column names. With this one command, we now essentially have tidy data. Each variable, state, fruit, and weight is vertical. Let's use the `reset_index` method to turn the result into a DataFrame:

```
>>> state_fruit_tidy = state_fruit.stack().reset_index()
>>> state_fruit_tidy
```

	level_0	level_1	0
0	Texas	Apple	12
1	Texas	Orange	10
2	Texas	Banana	40
3	Arizona	Apple	9
4	Arizona	Orange	7
5	Arizona	Banana	12
6	Florida	Apple	0
7	Florida	Orange	14
8	Florida	Banana	190

3. Our structure is now correct, but the column names are meaningless. Let's replace them with proper identifiers:

```
>>> state_fruit_tidy.columns = ['state', 'fruit', 'weight']
>>> state_fruit_tidy
```

	state	fruit	weight
0	Texas	Apple	12
1	Texas	Orange	10
2	Texas	Banana	40
3	Arizona	Apple	9
4	Arizona	Orange	7
5	Arizona	Banana	12
6	Florida	Apple	0
7	Florida	Orange	14
8	Florida	Banana	190

4. Instead of directly changing the columns attribute, it's possible to use the lesser-known Series method `rename_axis` to set the names of the index levels before using `reset_index`:

```
>>> state_fruit.stack()\
              .rename_axis(['state', 'fruit'])

state     fruit
Texas     Apple      12
          Orange     10
          Banana     40
Arizona   Apple       9
          Orange      7
          Banana     12
Florida   Apple       0
          Orange     14
          Banana    190
dtype: int64
```

5. From here, we can simply chain the `reset_index` method with the `name` parameter to reproduce the output from step 3:

```
>>> state_fruit.stack()\
              .rename_axis(['state', 'fruit'])\
              .reset_index(name='weight')
```

How it works...

The `stack` method is powerful and it takes time to understand and appreciate fully. It takes all the column names and transposes them, so they become the new innermost index level. Notice how each old column name still labels its original value by being paired with each state. There were nine original values in a 3 x 3 DataFrame, which got transformed into a single Series with the same number of values. The original first row of data became the first three values in the resulting Series.

After resetting the index in step 2, pandas defaults our DataFrame columns to `level_0`, `level_1`, and 0. This is because the Series calling this method has two index levels that were formally unnamed. Pandas also refers to indexes by integer beginning from zero from the outside.

Step 3 shows a simple and intuitive way to rename the columns. You can simply set new columns for the entire DataFrame by setting the columns attribute equal to a list.

Alternatively, it is possible to set the column names in a single step by chaining the `rename_axis` method that, when passing a list as the first argument, uses those values as the index level names. Pandas uses these index level names as the new column names when the index is reset. Additionally, the `reset_index` method has a `name` parameter corresponding to the new column name of the Series values.

 All Series have a `name` attribute that can be set directly or with the `rename` method. It is this attribute that becomes the column name when using `reset_index`.

There's more...

One of the keys to using `stack` is to place all of the columns that you do not wish to transform in the index. The dataset in this recipe was initially read with the states in the index. Let's take a look at what would have happened if we did not read the states into the index:

```
>>> state_fruit2 = pd.read_csv('data/state_fruit2.csv')
>>> state_fruit2
```

	State	Apple	Orange	Banana
0	Texas	12	10	40
1	Arizona	9	7	12
2	Florida	0	14	190

As the state names are not in the index, using `stack` on this DataFrame reshapes all values into one long Series of values:

```
>>> state_fruit2.stack()
0    State     Texas
     Apple        12
     Orange       10
     Banana       40
1    State     Arizona
     Apple         9
     Orange        7
     Banana       12
2    State     Florida
     Apple         0
     Orange       14
     Banana      190
```

```
dtype: object
```

This command reshapes all the columns, this time including the states, and is not at all what we need. In order to reshape this data correctly, you will need to put all the non-reshaped columns into the index first with the set_index method, and then use stack. The following code gives a similar result to step 1:

```
>>> state_fruit2.set_index('State').stack()
```

See also

- Pandas official documentation on *Reshaping and Pivot Tables* (http://bit.ly/2xbnNms)
- Pandas official documentation on the stack method (http://bit.ly/2vWZhH1)

Tidying variable values as column names with melt

Like most large Python libraries, pandas has many different ways to accomplish the same task--the differences usually being readability and performance. Pandas contains a DataFrame method named melt that works similarly to the stack method described in the previous recipe but gives a bit more flexibility.

Before pandas version 0.20, melt was only provided as a function that had to be accessed with pd.melt. Pandas is still an evolving library and you need to expect changes with each new version. Pandas has been making a push to move all functions that only operate on DataFrames to methods, such as they did with melt. This is the preferred way to use melt and the way this recipe uses it. Check the *What's New* part of the pandas documentation to stay up to date with all the changes (http://bit.ly/2xzXIhG).

Getting ready

In this recipe, we use the `melt` method to tidy a simple DataFrame with variable values as column names.

How to do it...

1. Read in the `state_fruit2` dataset and identify which columns need to be transformed and which ones do not:

   ```
   >>> state_fruit2 = pd.read_csv('data/state_fruit2.csv')
   >>> state_fruit2
   ```

	State	Apple	Orange	Banana
0	Texas	12	10	40
1	Arizona	9	7	12
2	Florida	0	14	190

2. Use the `melt` method by passing the appropriate columns to the `id_vars` and `value_vars` parameters:

   ```
   >>> state_fruit2.melt(id_vars=['State'],
                         value_vars=['Apple', 'Orange', 'Banana'])
   ```

	State	variable	value
0	Texas	Apple	12
1	Arizona	Apple	9
2	Florida	Apple	0
3	Texas	Orange	10
4	Arizona	Orange	7
5	Florida	Orange	14
6	Texas	Banana	40
7	Arizona	Banana	12
8	Florida	Banana	190

3. This one step creates tidy data for us. By default, `melt` refers to the transformed former column names as *variable* and the corresponding values as *value*. Conveniently, `melt` has two additional parameters, `var_name` and `value_name`, that give you the ability to rename these two columns:

```
>>> state_fruit2.melt(id_vars=['State'],
                       value_vars=['Apple', 'Orange', 'Banana'],
                       var_name='Fruit',
                       value_name='Weight')
```

	State	Fruit	Weight
0	Texas	Apple	12
1	Arizona	Apple	9
2	Florida	Apple	0
3	Texas	Orange	10
4	Arizona	Orange	7
5	Florida	Orange	14
6	Texas	Banana	40
7	Arizona	Banana	12
8	Florida	Banana	190

How it works...

The `melt` method is powerful and dramatically reshapes your DataFrame. It takes up to five parameters, with two of them being crucial to understanding how to reshape your data correctly:

- `id_vars` is a list of column names that you want to preserve as columns and not reshape
- `value_vars` is a list of column names that you want to reshape into a single column

The `id_vars`, or the identification variables, remain in the same column but repeat for each of the columns passed to `value_vars`. One crucial aspect of `melt` is that it ignores values in the index, and, in fact, it silently drops your index and replaces it with a default `RangeIndex`. This means that if you do have values in your index that you would like to keep, you will need to reset the index first before using `melt`.

It is somewhat common terminology to refer to the transformation of horizontal column names into vertical column values as **melting, stacking,** or **unpivoting**.

There's more...

All the parameters for the `melt` method are optional, and if you desire all your values to be in a single column and their old column labels to be in the other, you may call `melt` with just its defaults:

```
>>> state_fruit2.melt()
```

	variable	value
0	State	Texas
1	State	Arizona
2	State	Florida
3	Apple	12
4	Apple	9
5	Apple	0
6	Orange	10
7	Orange	7
8	Orange	14
9	Banana	40
10	Banana	12
11	Banana	190

More realistically, you might have lots of variables that need melting and would like to specify only the identification variables. In that case, calling `melt` in the following manner will yield the same result as in step 2. You actually don't even need a list when melting a single column and can simply pass its string value:

```
>>> state_fruit2.melt(id_vars='State')
```

See also

- Pandas official documentation on the `melt` method (http://bit.ly/2vcuZNJ)
- Pandas developers discussion of `melt` and other similar functions being converted to methods (http://bit.ly/2iqIQhI)

Stacking multiple groups of variables simultaneously

Some datasets contain multiple groups of variables as column names that need to be stacked simultaneously into their own columns. An example with the `movie` dataset can help clarify this. Let's begin by selecting all columns containing the actor names and their corresponding Facebook likes:

```
>>> movie = pd.read_csv('data/movie.csv')
>>> actor = movie[['movie_title', 'actor_1_name',
                   'actor_2_name', 'actor_3_name',
                   'actor_1_facebook_likes',
                   'actor_2_facebook_likes',
                   'actor_3_facebook_likes']]
>>> actor.head()
```

	movie_title	actor_1_name	actor_2_name	actor_3_name	actor_1_facebook_likes	actor_2_facebook_likes	actor_3_facebook_likes
0	Avatar	CCH Pounder	Joel David Moore	Wes Studi	1000.0	936.0	855.0
1	Pirates of the Caribbean: At World's End	Johnny Depp	Orlando Bloom	Jack Davenport	40000.0	5000.0	1000.0
2	Spectre	Christoph Waltz	Rory Kinnear	Stephanie Sigman	11000.0	393.0	161.0
3	The Dark Knight Rises	Tom Hardy	Christian Bale	Joseph Gordon-Levitt	27000.0	23000.0	23000.0
4	Star Wars: Episode VII - The Force Awakens	Doug Walker	Rob Walker	NaN	131.0	12.0	NaN

If we define our variables as the title of the movie, the actor name, and the number of Facebook likes, then we will need to stack independently two sets of columns, which is not possible using a single call to `stack` or `melt`.

Getting ready

In this recipe, we will tidy our `actor` DataFrame by simultaneously stacking the actor names and their corresponding Facebook likes with the `wide_to_long` function.

How to do it...

1. We will be using the versatile `wide_to_long` function to reshape our data into tidy form. To use this function, we will need to change the column names that we are stacking, so that they end with a digit. We first create a user-defined function to change the column names:

```
>>> def change_col_name(col_name):
        col_name = col_name.replace('_name', '')
        if 'facebook' in col_name:
            fb_idx = col_name.find('facebook')
            col_name = col_name[:5] + col_name[fb_idx - 1:] \
                                    + col_name[5:fb_idx-1]
        return col_name
```

2. Pass this function to the `rename` method to transform all the column names:

```
>>> actor2 = actor.rename(columns=change_col_name)
>>> actor2.head()
```

	movie_title	actor_1	actor_2	actor_3	actor_facebook_likes_1	actor_facebook_likes_2	actor_facebook_likes_3
0	Avatar	CCH Pounder	Joel David Moore	Wes Studi	1000.0	936.0	855.0
1	Pirates of the Caribbean: At World's End	Johnny Depp	Orlando Bloom	Jack Davenport	40000.0	5000.0	1000.0
2	Spectre	Christoph Waltz	Rory Kinnear	Stephanie Sigman	11000.0	393.0	161.0
3	The Dark Knight Rises	Tom Hardy	Christian Bale	Joseph Gordon-Levitt	27000.0	23000.0	23000.0
4	Star Wars: Episode VII - The Force Awakens	Doug Walker	Rob Walker	NaN	131.0	12.0	NaN

3. Use the `wide_to_long` function to stack the actor and Facebook sets of columns simultaneously:

```
>>> stubs = ['actor', 'actor_facebook_likes']
>>> actor2_tidy = pd.wide_to_long(actor2,
                                  stubnames=stubs,
                                  i=['movie_title'],
                                  j='actor_num',
                                  sep='_')
>>> actor2_tidy.head()
```

	movie_title	actor_num	actor	actor_facebook_likes
0	Avatar	1	CCH Pounder	1000.0
1	Pirates of the Caribbean: At World's End	1	Johnny Depp	40000.0
2	Spectre	1	Christoph Waltz	11000.0
3	The Dark Knight Rises	1	Tom Hardy	27000.0
4	Star Wars: Episode VII - The Force Awakens	1	Doug Walker	131.0

How it works...

The `wide_to_long` function works in a fairly specific manner. Its main parameter is `stubnames`, which is a list of strings. Each string represents a single column grouping. All columns that begin with this string will be stacked into a single column. In this recipe, there are two groups of columns: *actor*, and *actor_facebook_likes*. By default, each of these groups of columns will need to end in a digit. This digit will subsequently be used to label the reshaped data. Each of these column groups has an underscore character separating the `stubname` from the ending digit. To account for this, you must use the `sep` parameter.

The original column names do not match the pattern needed for `wide_to_long` to work. The column names could have been changed manually by exactly specifying their values with a list. This could quickly become a lot of typing so instead, we define a function that automatically converts our columns to a format that works. The `change_col_name` function removes **_name** from the actor columns and rearranges the Facebook columns so that now they both end in digits.

To actually accomplish the column renaming, we use the `rename` method in step 2. It accepts many different types of arguments, one of which is a function. When passing it to a function, every column name gets implicitly passed to it one at a time.

We have now correctly created two independent groups of columns, those beginning with **actor** and **actor_facebook_likes** that will be stacked. In addition to this, `wide_to_long` requires a unique column, parameter `i`, to act as an identification variable that will not be stacked. Also required is the parameter `j`, which simply renames the identifying digit stripped from the end of the original column names. By default, the prefix parameter contains the **regular expression**, **\d+** that searches for one more or more digits. The **\d** is a special token that matches the digits 0-9. The plus sign, **+**, makes the expression match for one or more of these digits.

	INSTNM	Race	Percentage
0	Alabama A & M University	UGDS_WHITE	0.0333
1	University of Alabama at Birmingham	UGDS_WHITE	0.5922
2	Amridge University	UGDS_WHITE	0.2990
3	University of Alabama in Huntsville	UGDS_WHITE	0.6988
4	Alabama State University	UGDS_WHITE	0.0158

6. Use the `pivot` method to invert this previous result:

```
>>> melted_inv = college_melted.pivot(index='INSTNM',
                                       columns='Race',
                                       values='Percentage')
>>> melted_inv.head()
```

Race INSTNM	UGDS_2MOR	UGDS_AIAN	UGDS_ASIAN	UGDS_BLACK	UGDS_HISP	UGDS_NHPI	UGDS_NRA	UGDS_UNKN	UGDS_WHITE
A & W Healthcare Educators	0.0000	0.0	0.0000	0.9750	0.0250	0.0	0.0000	0.0000	0.0000
A T Still University of Health Sciences	NaN	NaN	NaN	NaN	NaN	NaN	NaN	NaN	NaN
ABC Beauty Academy	0.0000	0.0	0.9333	0.0333	0.0333	0.0	0.0000	0.0000	0.0000
ABC Beauty College Inc	0.0000	0.0	0.0000	0.6579	0.0526	0.0	0.0000	0.0000	0.2895
AI Miami International University of Art and Design	0.0018	0.0	0.0018	0.0198	0.4773	0.0	0.0025	0.4644	0.0324

7. Notice that the institution names are now shuttled over into the index and are not in their original order. The column names are not in their original order. To get an exact replication of our starting DataFrame from step 4, use the `.loc` indexing operator to select rows and columns simultaneously and then reset the index:

```
>>> college2_replication = melted_inv.loc[college2['INSTNM'],
                                          college2.columns[1:]]\
                                      .reset_index()
>>> college2.equals(college2_replication)
True
```

How it works...

There are multiple ways to accomplish the same thing in step 1. Here, we show the versatility of the `read_csv` function. The `usecols` parameter accepts either a list of the columns that we would like to import or a function that dynamically determines them. We use an anonymous function that checks whether the column name contains `UGDS_` or is equal to `INSTNM`. The function is passed each column name as a string and must return a boolean. A huge amount of memory can be saved in this manner.

The `stack` method in step 2 puts all column names into the innermost index level and returns a Series. In step 3, the `unstack` method inverts this operation by taking all the values in the innermost index level converting them to column names.

 The result from step 3 isn't quite an exact replication of step 1. There are entire rows of missing values, and by default, the `stack` method drops these during step 2. To keep these missing values and create an exact replication, use `dropna=False` in the `stack` method.

Step 4 reads in the same dataset as in step 1 but does not put the institution name in the index because the `melt` method isn't able to access it. Step 5 uses the `melt` method to transpose all the **Race** columns. It does this by leaving the `value_vars` parameter as its default value `None`. When not specified, all the columns not present in the `id_vars` parameter get transposed.

Step 6 inverts the operation from step 5 with the `pivot` method, which accepts three parameters. Each parameter takes a single column as a string. The column referenced by the `index` parameter remains vertical and becomes the new index. The values of the column referenced by the `columns` parameter become the column names. The values referenced by the `values` parameter become tiled to correspond with the intersection of their former index and columns label.

To make an exact replication with `pivot`, we need to sort the rows and columns in the exact order from the original. As the institution name is in the index, we use the `.loc` indexing operator as a way to sort the DataFrame by its original index.

There's more...

To help further understand `stack`/`unstack`, let's use them to **transpose** the `college` DataFrame.

 In this context, we are using the precise mathematical definition of the transposing of a matrix, where the new rows are the old columns of the original data matrix.

If you take a look at the output from step 2, you'll notice that there are two index levels. By default, the `unstack` method uses the innermost index level as the new column values. Index levels are numbered beginning from zero from the outside. Pandas defaults the `level` parameter of the `unstack` method to -1, which refers to the innermost index. We can instead `unstack` the outermost column using `level=0`:

```
>>> college.stack().unstack(0)
```

INSTNM	Alabama A & M University	University of Alabama at Birmingham	Amridge University	University of Alabama in Huntsville	Alabama State University	The University of Alabama	Central Alabama Community College	Athens State University	Auburn University at Montgomery	Auburn University	...
UGDS_WHITE	0.0333	0.5922	0.2990	0.6988	0.0158	0.7825	0.7255	0.7823	0.5328	0.8507	...
UGDS_BLACK	0.9353	0.2600	0.4192	0.1255	0.9208	0.1119	0.2613	0.1200	0.3376	0.0704	...
UGDS_HISP	0.0055	0.0283	0.0069	0.0382	0.0121	0.0348	0.0044	0.0191	0.0074	0.0248	...
UGDS_ASIAN	0.0019	0.0518	0.0034	0.0376	0.0019	0.0106	0.0025	0.0053	0.0221	0.0227	...
UGDS_AIAN	0.0024	0.0022	0.0000	0.0143	0.0010	0.0038	0.0044	0.0157	0.0044	0.0074	...
UGDS_NHPI	0.0019	0.0007	0.0000	0.0002	0.0006	0.0009	0.0000	0.0010	0.0016	0.0000	...
UGDS_2MOR	0.0000	0.0368	0.0000	0.0172	0.0098	0.0261	0.0000	0.0174	0.0297	0.0000	...
UGDS_NRA	0.0059	0.0179	0.0000	0.0332	0.0243	0.0268	0.0000	0.0057	0.0397	0.0100	...
UGDS_UNKN	0.0138	0.0100	0.2715	0.0350	0.0137	0.0026	0.0019	0.0334	0.0246	0.0140	...

There is actually a very simple way to transpose a DataFrame that don't require `stack` or `unstack` by using the `transpose` method or the `T` attribute like this:

```
>>> college.T
>>> college.transpose()
```

See also

- Refer to the *Selecting DataFrame rows and columns simultaneously* recipe from `Chapter 4`, *Selecting Subsets of Data*
- Pandas official documentation of the `unstack` (http://bit.ly/2xIyFvr) and `pivot` (http://bit.ly/2f3qAWP) methods

Unstacking after a groupby aggregation

Grouping data by a single column and performing an aggregation on a single column returns a simple and straightforward result that is easy to consume. When grouping by more than one column, a resulting aggregation might not be structured in a manner that makes consumption easy. Since `groupby` operations by default put the unique grouping columns in the index, the `unstack` method can be extremely useful to rearrange the data so that it is presented in a manner that is more useful for interpretation.

Getting ready

In this recipe, we use the `employee` dataset to perform an aggregation, grouping by multiple columns. We then use the `unstack` method to reshape the result into a format that makes for easier comparisons of different groups.

How to do it...

1. Read in the employee dataset and find the mean salary by race:

```
>>> employee = pd.read_csv('data/employee.csv')
>>> employee.groupby('RACE')['BASE_SALARY'].mean().astype(int)
RACE
American Indian or Alaskan Native    60272
Asian/Pacific Islander               61660
Black or African American            50137
Hispanic/Latino                      52345
Others                               51278
White                                64419
Name: BASE_SALARY, dtype: int64
```

2. This is a very simple `groupby` operation that results in a Series that is easy to read and has no need to reshape. Let's now find the average salary for all races by gender:

```
>>> agg = employee.groupby(['RACE', 'GENDER'])['BASE_SALARY'] \
                  .mean().astype(int)
>>> agg
RACE                                  GENDER
American Indian or Alaskan Native     Female     60238
                                      Male       60305
Asian/Pacific Islander                Female     63226
                                      Male       61033
Black or African American             Female     48915
                                      Male       51082
Hispanic/Latino                       Female     46503
                                      Male       54782
Others                                Female     63785
                                      Male       38771
White                                 Female     66793
                                      Male       63940
Name: BASE_SALARY, dtype: int64
```

3. This aggregation is more complex and can be reshaped to make different comparisons easier. For instance, it would be easier to compare male versus female salaries for each race if they were side by side and not vertical as they are now. Let's unstack the gender index level:

```
>>> agg.unstack('GENDER')
```

GENDER	Female	Male
RACE		
American Indian or Alaskan Native	60238	60305
Asian/Pacific Islander	63226	61033
Black or African American	48915	51082
Hispanic/Latino	46503	54782
Others	63785	38771
White	66793	63940

4. Similarly, we can `unstack` the race index level:

```
>>> agg.unstack('RACE')
```

RACE GENDER	American Indian or Alaskan Native	Asian/Pacific Islander	Black or African American	Hispanic/Latino	Others	White
Female	60238	63226	48915	46503	63785	66793
Male	60305	61033	51082	54782	38771	63940

How it works...

Step 1 has the simplest possible aggregation with a single grouping column (RACE), a single aggregating column (BASE_SALARY), and a single aggregating function (mean). This result is easy to consume and doesn't require any more processing to evaluate. Step 2 slightly increases the complexity by grouping by both race and gender together. The resulting MultiIndex Series contains all the values in a single dimension, which makes comparisons more difficult. To make the information easier to consume, we use the `unstack` method to convert the values in one (or more) of the levels to columns.

By default, `unstack` uses the innermost index level as the new columns. You can specify the exact level you would like to unstack with the `level` parameter, which accepts either the level name as a string or the level integer location. It is preferable to use the level name over the integer location to avoid ambiguity. Steps 3 and 4 unstack each level, which results in a DataFrame with a single-level index. It is now much easier to compare salaries from each race by gender.

There's more...

If there are multiple grouping and aggregating columns, then the immediate result will be a DataFrame and not a Series. For instance, let's calculate more aggregations than just the mean, as was done in step 2:

```
>>> agg2 = employee.groupby(['RACE', 'GENDER'])['BASE_SALARY'] \
              .agg(['mean', 'max', 'min']).astype(int)
>>> agg2
```

RACE	GENDER	mean	max	min
American Indian or Alaskan Native	Female	60238	98536	26125
	Male	60305	81239	26125
Asian/Pacific Islander	Female	63226	130416	26125
	Male	61033	163228	27914
Black or African American	Female	48915	150416	24960
	Male	51082	275000	26125
Hispanic/Latino	Female	46503	126115	26125
	Male	54782	165216	26104
Others	Female	63785	63785	63785
	Male	38771	38771	38771
White	Female	66793	178331	27955
	Male	63940	210588	26125

Unstacking the **Gender** column will result in MultiIndex columns. From here, you can keep swapping row and column levels with both the `unstack` and `stack` methods until you achieve the structure of data you desire:

```
>>> agg2.unstack('GENDER')
```

	mean		max		min	
GENDER	Female	Male	Female	Male	Female	Male
RACE						
American Indian or Alaskan Native	60238	60305	98536	81239	26125	26125
Asian/Pacific Islander	63226	61033	130416	163228	26125	27914
Black or African American	48915	51082	150416	275000	24960	26125
Hispanic/Latino	46503	54782	126115	165216	26125	26104
Others	63785	38771	63785	38771	63785	38771
White	66793	63940	178331	210588	27955	26125

See also

- Refer to the *Grouping and aggregating with multiple columns* recipe and functions from `Chapter 7`, *Grouping for Aggregation, Filtration, and Transformation*

Replicating pivot_table with a groupby aggregation

At first glance, it may seem that the `pivot_table` method provides a unique way to analyze data. However, after a little massaging, it is possible to replicate its functionality exactly with a `groupby` aggregation. Knowing this equivalence can help shrink the universe of pandas functionality.

Getting ready

In this recipe, we use the `flights` dataset to create a pivot table and then recreate it using `groupby` operations.

How to do it...

1. Read in the flights dataset, and use the `pivot_table` method to find the total number of cancelled flights per origin airport for each airline:

```
>>> flights = pd.read_csv('data/flights.csv')
>>> fp = flights.pivot_table(index='AIRLINE',
                             columns='ORG_AIR',
                             values='CANCELLED',
                             aggfunc='sum',
                             fill_value=0).round(2)
>>> fp.head()
```

ORG_AIR	ATL	DEN	DFW	IAH	LAS	LAX	MSP	ORD	PHX	SFO
AIRLINE										
AA	3	4	86	3	3	11	3	35	4	2
AS	0	0	0	0	0	0	0	0	0	0
B6	0	0	0	0	0	0	0	0	0	1
DL	28	1	0	0	1	1	4	0	1	2
EV	18	6	27	36	0	0	6	53	0	0

2. A `groupby` aggregation cannot directly replicate this table. The trick is to group by all the columns in the `index` and `columns` parameters first:

```
>>> fg = flights.groupby(['AIRLINE', 'ORG_AIR'])['CANCELLED'].sum()
>>> fg.head()
AIRLINE   ORG_AIR
AA        ATL          3
          DEN          4
          DFW          86
          IAH          3
          LAS          3
Name: CANCELLED, dtype: int64
```

3. Use the `unstack` method to pivot the `ORG_AIR` index level to column names:

```
>>> fg_unstack = fg.unstack('ORG_AIR', fill_value=0)
>>> fp.equals(fg_unstack)
True
```

How it works...

The `pivot_table` method is very versatile and flexible but performs a rather similar operation to a `groupby` aggregation with step 1 showing a simple example. The `index` parameter takes a column (or columns) that will not be pivoted and whose unique values will be placed in the index. The `columns` parameter takes a column (or columns) that will be pivoted and whose unique values will be made into column names. The `values` parameter takes a column (or columns) that will be aggregated.

There also exists an `aggfunc` parameter that takes an aggregating function (or functions) that determines how the columns in the `values` parameter get aggregated. It defaults to the mean, and, in this example, we change it to calculate the sum. Additionally, some unique combinations of `AIRLINE` and `ORG_AIR` do not exist. These missing combinations will default to missing values in the resulting DataFrame. Here, we use the `fill_value` parameter to change them to zero.

Step 2 begins the replication process using all the columns in the `index` and `columns` parameter as the grouping columns. This is the key to making this recipe work. A pivot table is simply an intersection of all the unique combinations of the grouping columns. Step 3 finishes the replication by pivoting the innermost index level into column names with the `unstack` method. Just like with `pivot_table`, not all combinations of `AIRLINE` and `ORG_AIR` exist; we again use the `fill_value` parameter to force these missing intersections to zero.

There's more...

It is possible to replicate much more complex pivot tables with `groupby` aggregations. For instance, take the following result from `pivot_table`:

```
>>> flights.pivot_table(index=['AIRLINE', 'MONTH'],
                        columns=['ORG_AIR', 'CANCELLED'],
                        values=['DEP_DELAY', 'DIST'],
                        aggfunc=[np.sum, np.mean],
                        fill_value=0)
```

		mean										...	sum								
		DEP_DELAY										...	DIST								
ORG_AIR		ATL		DEN		DFW		IAH		LAS		...	LAX		MSP		ORD		PHX		SFO
CANCELLED		0	1	0	1	0	1	0	1	0	1	...	0	1	0	1	0	1	0	1	0
AIRLINE	MONTH																				
AA	1	-3.250000	0	7.062500	0	11.977591	-3.0	9.750000	0	32.375000	0	...	135921	2475	7281	0	129334	0	21018	0	33483
	2	-3.000000	0	5.461538	0	8.756579	0.0	1.000000	0	-3.055556	0	...	113483	5454	5040	0	120572	5398	17049	868	32110
	3	-0.166667	0	7.666667	0	15.383784	0.0	10.900000	0	12.074074	0	...	131836	1744	14471	0	127072	802	25770	0	43580
	4	0.071429	0	20.266667	0	10.501493	0.0	6.933333	0	27.241379	0	...	170285	0	4541	0	152154	4718	17727	0	51054
	5	5.777778	0	23.466667	0	16.798780	0.0	3.055556	0	2.818182	0	...	167484	0	6298	0	110864	1999	11164	0	40233

To replicate this with a `groupby` aggregation, simply follow the same pattern from the recipe and place all the columns from the `index` and `columns` parameters into the `groupby` method and then `unstack` the columns:

```
>>> flights.groupby(['AIRLINE', 'MONTH', 'ORG_AIR', 'CANCELLED']) \
        ['DEP_DELAY', 'DIST'] \
        .agg(['mean', 'sum']) \
        .unstack(['ORG_AIR', 'CANCELLED'], fill_value=0) \
        .swaplevel(0, 1, axis='columns')
```

There are a few differences. The `pivot_table` method does not accept aggregation functions as strings when passed as a list like the `agg` groupby method. Instead, you must use NumPy functions. The order of the column levels also differs, with `pivot_table` putting the aggregation functions at a level preceding the columns in the `values` parameter. This is equalized with the `swaplevel` method that, in this instance, switches the order of the top two levels.

As of the time of writing this book, there is a bug when unstacking more than one column. The `fill_value` parameter is ignored (http://bit.ly/ 2jCPnWZ). To work around this bug, chain `.fillna(0)` to the end of the code.

Renaming axis levels for easy reshaping

Reshaping with the `stack`/`unstack` methods is far easier when each axis (index/column) level has a name. Pandas allows users to reference each axis level by integer location or by name. Since integer location is implicit and not explicit, you should consider using level names whenever possible. This advice follows from *The Zen of Python* (http://bit.ly/ 2xE83uC), a short list of guiding principles for Python of which the second one is *Explicit is better than implicit.*

Getting ready

When grouping or aggregating with multiple columns, the resulting pandas object will have multiple levels in one or both of the axes. In this recipe, we will name each level of each axis and then use the methods `stack`/`unstack` to dramatically reshape the data to the desired form.

How to do it...

1. Read in the college dataset, and find a few basic summary statistics on the undergraduate population and SAT math scores by institution and religious affiliation:

```
>>> college = pd.read_csv('data/college.csv')
>>> cg = college.groupby(['STABBR', 'RELAFFIL']) \
              ['UGDS', 'SATMTMID'] \
              .agg(['size', 'min', 'max']).head(6)
```

| | | UGDS | | | SATMTMID | | |
| | | count | min | max | count | min | max |
STABBR	RELAFFIL						
AK	0	7	109.0	12865.0	0	NaN	NaN
	1	3	27.0	275.0	1	503.0	503.0
AL	0	71	12.0	29851.0	13	420.0	590.0
	1	18	13.0	3033.0	8	400.0	560.0
AR	0	68	18.0	21405.0	9	427.0	565.0
	1	14	20.0	4485.0	7	495.0	600.0

2. Notice that both index levels have names and are the old column names. The column levels, on the other hand, do not have names. Use the `rename_axis` method to supply level names to them:

```
>>> cg = cg.rename_axis(['AGG_COLS', 'AGG_FUNCS'], axis='columns')
>>> cg
```

		AGG_COLS	UGDS			SATMTMID		
	AGG_FUNCS		count	min	max	count	min	max
STABBR	RELAFFIL							
AK	0		7	109.0	12865.0	0	NaN	NaN
	1		3	27.0	275.0	1	503.0	503.0
AL	0		71	12.0	29851.0	13	420.0	590.0
	1		18	13.0	3033.0	8	400.0	560.0
AR	0		68	18.0	21405.0	9	427.0	565.0
	1		14	20.0	4485.0	7	495.0	600.0

3. Now that each axis level has a name, reshaping is a breeze. Use the `stack` method to move the `AGG_FUNCS` column to an index level:

```
>>> cg.stack('AGG_FUNCS').head()
```

			AGG_COLS	UGDS	SATMTMID
STABBR	RELAFFIL	AGG_FUNCS			
AK	0	count		7.0	0.0
		min		109.0	NaN
		max		12865.0	NaN
	1	count		3.0	1.0
		min		27.0	503.0

4. By default, stacking places the new column level in the innermost position. Use the `swaplevel` method to switch the placement of the levels:

```
>>> cg.stack('AGG_FUNCS').swaplevel('AGG_FUNCS', 'STABBR',
                                    axis='index').head()
```

AGG_FUNCS	RELAFFIL	AGG_COLS STABBR	UGDS	SATMTMID
count	0	AK	7.0	0.0
min	0	AK	109.0	NaN
max	0	AK	12865.0	NaN
count	1	AK	3.0	1.0
min	1	AK	27.0	503.0

5. We can continue to make use of the axis level names by sorting levels with the `sort_index` method:

```
>>> cg.stack('AGG_FUNCS') \
    .swaplevel('AGG_FUNCS', 'STABBR', axis='index') \
    .sort_index(level='RELAFFIL', axis='index') \
    .sort_index(level='AGG_COLS', axis='columns').head(6)
```

AGG_FUNCS	RELAFFIL	AGG_COLS STABBR	SATMTMID	UGDS
count	0	AK	0.0	7.0
		AL	13.0	71.0
		AR	9.0	68.0
min	0	AK	NaN	109.0
		AL	420.0	12.0
		AR	427.0	18.0

6. To completely reshape your data, you might need to stack some columns while unstacking others. Chain the two methods together in a single command:

```
>>> cg.stack('AGG_FUNCS').unstack(['RELAFFIL', 'STABBR'])
```

AGG_COLS	UGDS						SATMTMID					
RELAFFIL	0	1	0	1	0	1	0	1	0	1	0	1
STABBR	AK	AK	AL	AL	AR	AR	AK	AK	AL	AL	AR	AR
AGG_FUNCS												
count	7.0	3.0	71.0	18.0	68.0	14.0	0.0	1.0	13.0	8.0	9.0	7.0
min	109.0	27.0	12.0	13.0	18.0	20.0	NaN	503.0	420.0	400.0	427.0	495.0
max	12865.0	275.0	29851.0	3033.0	21405.0	4485.0	NaN	503.0	590.0	560.0	565.0	600.0

7. Stack all the columns at once to return a Series:

```
>>> cg.stack(['AGG_FUNCS', 'AGG_COLS']).head(12)
STABBR   RELAFFIL   AGG_FUNCS   AGG_COLS
AK       0          count       UGDS            7.0
                                 SATMTMID        0.0
                    min         UGDS          109.0
                    max         UGDS        12865.0
         1          count       UGDS            3.0
                                 SATMTMID        1.0
                    min         UGDS           27.0
                                 SATMTMID      503.0
                    max         UGDS          275.0
                                 SATMTMID      503.0
AL       0          count       UGDS           71.0
                                 SATMTMID       13.0
dtype: float64
```

How it works...

It is common for the result of a `groupby` aggregation to produce a DataFrame or Series with multiple axis levels. The resulting DataFrame from the `groupby` operation in step 1 has multiple levels for each axis. The column levels are not named, which would require us to reference them only by their integer location. To greatly ease our ability to reference the column levels, we rename them with the `rename_axis` method.

The `rename_axis` method is a bit strange in that it can modify both the level names and the level values based on the type of the first argument passed to it. Passing it a list (or a scalar if there is only one level) changes the names of the levels. Passing it a dictionary or a function changes the values of the levels. In step 2, we pass the `rename_axis` method a list and are returned a DataFrame with all axis levels named.

Once all the axis levels have names, we can easily and explicitly control the structure of data. Step 3 stacks the `AGG_FUNCS` column into the innermost index level. The `swaplevel` method in step 4 accepts the name or position of the levels that you want to swap as the first two arguments. The `sort_index` method is called twice and sorts the actual values of each level. Notice that the values of the column level are the column names `SATMTMID` and `UGDS`.

We can get vastly different output by both stacking and unstacking, as done in step 6. It is also possible to stack every single column level into the index to produce a Series.

There's more...

If you wish to dispose of the level values altogether, you may set them to `None`. A case for this can be made when there is a need to reduce clutter in the visual output of a DataFrame or when it is obvious what the column levels represent and no further processing will take place:

```
>>> cg.rename_axis([None, None], axis='index') \
       .rename_axis([None, None], axis='columns')
```

		UGDS			SATMTMID		
		count	min	max	count	min	max
AK	0	7	109.0	12865.0	0	NaN	NaN
	1	3	27.0	275.0	1	503.0	503.0
AL	0	71	12.0	29851.0	13	420.0	590.0
	1	18	13.0	3033.0	8	400.0	560.0
AR	0	68	18.0	21405.0	9	427.0	565.0
	1	14	20.0	4485.0	7	495.0	600.0

Tidying when multiple variables are stored as column names

One particular flavor of messy data appears whenever the column names contain multiple different variables themselves. A common example of this scenario occurs when age and sex are concatenated together. To tidy datasets like this, we must manipulate the columns with the pandas `str` accessor, an attribute that contains additional methods for string processing.

Getting ready...

In this recipe, we will first identify all the variables of which some will be concatenated together as column names. We then reshape the data and parse the text to extract the correct variable values.

How to do it...

1. Read in the men's `weightlifting` dataset, and identify the variables:

   ```
   >>> weightlifting = pd.read_csv('data/weightlifting_men.csv')
   >>> weightlifting
   ```

	Weight Category	M35 35-39	M40 40-44	M45 45-49	M50 50-54	M55 55-59	M60 60-64	M65 65-69	M70 70-74	M75 75-79	M80 80+
0	56	137	130	125	115	102	92	80	67	62	55
1	62	152	145	137	127	112	102	90	75	67	57
2	69	167	160	150	140	125	112	97	82	75	60
3	77	182	172	165	150	135	122	107	90	82	65
4	85	192	182	175	160	142	130	112	95	87	70
5	94	202	192	182	167	150	137	120	100	90	75
6	105	210	200	190	175	157	142	122	102	95	80
7	105+	217	207	197	182	165	150	127	107	100	85

2. The variables are the weight category, sex/age category, and the qualifying total. The age and sex variables have been concatenated together into a single cell. Before we can separate them, let's use the `melt` method to transpose the age and sex column names into a single vertical column:

```
>>> wl_melt = weightlifting.melt(id_vars='Weight Category',
                                 var_name='sex_age',
                                 value_name='Qual Total')
>>> wl_melt.head()
```

	Weight Category	sex_age	Qual Total
0	56	M35 35-39	137
1	62	M35 35-39	152
2	69	M35 35-39	167
3	77	M35 35-39	182
4	85	M35 35-39	192

3. Select the `sex_age` column, and use the `split` method available from the `str` accessor to split the column into two different columns:

```
>>> sex_age = wl_melt['sex_age'].str.split(expand=True)
>>> sex_age.head()
```

	0	1
0	M35	35-39
1	M35	35-39
2	M35	35-39
3	M35	35-39
4	M35	35-39

4. This operation returned a completely separate DataFrame with meaningless column names. Let's rename the columns so that we can explicitly access them:

```
>>> sex_age.columns = ['Sex', 'Age Group']
>>> sex_age.head()
```

	Sex	Age Group
0	M35	35-39
1	M35	35-39
2	M35	35-39
3	M35	35-39
4	M35	35-39

5. Use the indexing operator directly after the str accessor to select the first character from the Sex column:

```
>>> sex_age['Sex'] = sex_age['Sex'].str[0]
>>> sex_age.head()
```

	Sex	Age Group
0	M	35-39
1	M	35-39
2	M	35-39
3	M	35-39
4	M	35-39

6. Use the pd.concat function to concatenate this DataFrame with wl_melt to produce a tidy dataset:

```
>>> wl_cat_total = wl_melt[['Weight Category', 'Qual Total']]
>>> wl_tidy = pd.concat([sex_age, wl_cat_total], axis='columns')
>>> wl_tidy.head()
```

	Sex	Age Group	Weight Category	Qual Total
0	M	35-39	56	137
1	M	35-39	62	152
2	M	35-39	69	167
3	M	35-39	77	182
4	M	35-39	85	192

7. This same result could have been created with the following:

```
>>> cols = ['Weight Category', 'Qual Total']
>>> sex_age[cols] = wl_melt[cols]
```

How it works...

The `weightlifting` dataset, like many datasets, has easily digestible information in its raw form, but technically, it is messy, as all but one of the column names contain information for sex and age. Once the variables are identified, we can begin to tidy the dataset. Whenever column names contain variables, you will need to use the `melt` (or `stack`) method. The `Weight Category` variable is already in the correct position so we keep it as an identifying variable by passing it to the `id_vars` parameter. Note that we don't explicitly need to name all the columns that we are melting with `value_vars`. By default, all the columns not present in `id_vars` get melted.

The `sex_age` column needs to be parsed, and split into two variables. For this, we turn to the extra functionality provided by the `str` accessor, only available to Series (a single DataFrame column). The `split` method is one of the more common methods in this situation, as it can separate different parts of the string into their own column. By default, it splits on an empty space, but you may also specify a string or regular expression with the `pat` parameter. When the `expand` parameter is set to `True`, a new column forms for each independent split character segment. When `False`, a single column is returned, containing a list of all the segments.

After renaming the columns in step 4, we need to use the `str` accessor again. Interestingly enough, the indexing operator is available to select or slice segments of a string. Here, we select the first character, which is the variable for sex. We could go further and split the ages into two separate columns for minimum and maximum age, but it is common to refer to the entire age group in this manner, so we leave it as is.

Step 6 shows one of two different methods to join all the data together. The `concat` function accepts a collection of DataFrames and either concatenates them vertically (`axis='index'`) or horizontally (`axis='columns'`). Because the two DataFrames are indexed identically, it is possible to assign the values of one DataFrame to new columns in the other as done in step 7.

There's more...

Another way to complete this recipe, beginning after step 2, is by directly assigning new columns from the `sex_age` column without using the `split` method. The `assign` method may be used to add these new columns dynamically:

```
>>> age_group = wl_melt.sex_age.str.extract('(\d{2}[-+](?:\d{2})?)',
                                            expand=False)
>>> sex = wl_melt.sex_age.str[0]
>>> new_cols = {'Sex':sex,
                'Age Group': age_group}
>>> wl_tidy2 = wl_melt.assign(**new_cols) \
                      .drop('sex_age',axis='columns')

>>> wl_tidy2.sort_index(axis=1).equals(wl_tidy.sort_index(axis=1))
True
```

The `Sex` column is found in the exact same manner as done in step 5. Because we are not using `split`, the `Age Group` column must be extracted in a different manner. The `extract` method uses a complex regular expression to extract very specific portions of the string. To use `extract` correctly, your pattern must contain capture groups. A capture group is formed by enclosing parentheses around a portion of the pattern. In this example, the entire expression is one large capture group. It begins with `\d{2}`, which searches for exactly two digits, followed by either a literal plus or minus, optionally followed by two more digits. Although the last part of the expression, `(?:\d{2})?`, is surrounded by parentheses, the `?:` denotes that it is not actually a capture group. It is technically a non-capturing group used to express two digits together as optional. The `sex_age` column is no longer needed and is dropped. Finally, the two tidy DataFrames are compared against one another and are found to be equivalent.

See also

- Refer to the site *Regular-Expressions.info* for more on non-capturing groups (http://bit.ly/2f60KSd)

Tidying when multiple variables are stored as column values

Tidy datasets must have a single column for each variable. Occasionally, multiple variable names are placed in a single column with their corresponding value placed in another. The general format for this kind of messy data is as follows:

	attribute	value
0	variable_1	value_1
1	variable_2	value_2
2	variable_3	value_3
3	variable_1	value_1
4	variable_2	value_2
5	variable_3	value_3

In this example, the first and last three rows represent two distinct observations that should each be rows. The data needs to be pivoted such that it ends up like this:

	variable_1	variable_2	variable_3
0	value_1	value_2	value_3
1	value_1	value_2	value_3

Getting ready

In this recipe, we identify the column containing the improperly structured variables and pivot it to create tidy data.

How to do it...

1. Read in the restaurant `inspections` dataset, and convert the `Date` column data type to `datetime64`:

```
>>> inspections = pd.read_csv('data/restaurant_inspections.csv',
                              parse_dates=['Date'])
>>> inspections.head()
```

	Name	Date	Info	Value
0	E & E Grill House	2017-08-08	Borough	MANHATTAN
1	E & E Grill House	2017-08-08	Cuisine	American
2	E & E Grill House	2017-08-08	Description	Non-food contact surface improperly constructe...
3	E & E Grill House	2017-08-08	Grade	A
4	E & E Grill House	2017-08-08	Score	9.0
5	PIZZA WAGON	2017-04-12	Borough	BROOKLYN
6	PIZZA WAGON	2017-04-12	Cuisine	Pizza
7	PIZZA WAGON	2017-04-12	Description	Food contact surface not properly washed, rins...
8	PIZZA WAGON	2017-04-12	Grade	A
9	PIZZA WAGON	2017-04-12	Score	10.0

2. This dataset has two variables, `Name` and `Date`, that are each correctly contained in a single column. The `Info` column itself has five different variables: `Borough`, `Cuisine`, `Description`, `Grade`, and `Score`. Let's attempt to use the `pivot` method to keep the `Name` and `Date` columns vertical, create new columns out of all the values in the `Info` column, and use the `Value` column as their intersection:

```
>>> inspections.pivot(index=['Name', 'Date'],
                      columns='Info', values='Value')
NotImplementedError: > 1 ndim Categorical are not supported at this
time
```

3. Unfortunately, pandas developers have not implemented this functionality for us. There is a good chance that in the future, this line of code is going to work. Thankfully, for the most part, pandas has multiple ways of accomplishing the same task. Let's put `Name`, `Date`, and `Info` into the index:

```
>>> inspections.set_index(['Name','Date', 'Info']).head(10)
```

			Value
Name	**Date**	**Info**	
E & E Grill House	**2017-08-08**	Borough	MANHATTAN
		Cuisine	American
		Description	Non-food contact surface improperly constructe...
		Grade	A
		Score	9.0
PIZZA WAGON	**2017-04-12**	Borough	BROOKLYN
		Cuisine	Pizza
		Description	Food contact surface not properly washed, rins...
		Grade	A
		Score	10.0

4. Use the `unstack` method to pivot all the values in the `Info` column:

```
>>> inspections.set_index(['Name','Date', 'Info']) \
              .unstack('Info').head()
```

		Value				
	Info	Borough	Cuisine	Description	Grade	Score
Name	**Date**					
3 STAR JUICE CENTER	2017-05-10	BROOKLYN	Juice, Smoothies, Fruit Salads	Facility not vermin proof. Harborage or condit...	A	12.0
A & L PIZZA RESTAURANT	2017-08-22	BROOKLYN	Pizza	Facility not vermin proof. Harborage or condit...	A	9.0
AKSARAY TURKISH CAFE AND RESTAURANT	2017-07-25	BROOKLYN	Turkish	Plumbing not properly installed or maintained;...	A	13.0
ANTOJITOS DELI FOOD	2017-06-01	BROOKLYN	Latin (Cuban, Dominican, Puerto Rican, South &...	Live roaches present in facility's food and/or...	A	10.0
BANGIA	2017-06-16	MANHATTAN	Korean	Covered garbage receptacle not provided or ina...	A	9.0

5. Make the index levels into columns with the `reset_index` method:

```
>>> insp_tidy = inspections.set_index(['Name','Date', 'Info']) \
                           .unstack('Info') \
                           .reset_index(col_level=-1)
>>> insp_tidy.head()
```

Info	Name	Date	Borough	Cuisine	Description	Grade	Score
				Value			
0	3 STAR JUICE CENTER	2017-05-10	BROOKLYN	Juice, Smoothies, Fruit Salads	Facility not vermin proof. Harborage or condit...	A	12.0
1	A & L PIZZA RESTAURANT	2017-08-22	BROOKLYN	Pizza	Facility not vermin proof. Harborage or condit...	A	9.0
2	AKSARAY TURKISH CAFE AND RESTAURANT	2017-07-25	BROOKLYN	Turkish	Plumbing not properly installed or maintained;...	A	13.0
3	ANTOJITOS DELI FOOD	2017-06-01	BROOKLYN	Latin (Cuban, Dominican, Puerto Rican, South &...	Live roaches present in facility's food and/or...	A	10.0
4	BANGIA	2017-06-16	MANHATTAN	Korean	Covered garbage receptacle not provided or ina...	A	9.0

6. The dataset is tidy, but there is some annoying leftover pandas debris that needs to be removed. Let's use the MultiIndex method `droplevel` to remove the top column level and then rename the index level to `None`:

```
>>> insp_tidy.columns = insp_tidy.columns.droplevel(0) \
                                         .rename(None)
>>> insp_tidy.head()
```

	Name	Date	Borough	Cuisine	Description	Grade	Score
0	3 STAR JUICE CENTER	2017-05-10	BROOKLYN	Juice, Smoothies, Fruit Salads	Facility not vermin proof. Harborage or condit...	A	12.0
1	A & L PIZZA RESTAURANT	2017-08-22	BROOKLYN	Pizza	Facility not vermin proof. Harborage or condit...	A	9.0
2	AKSARAY TURKISH CAFE AND RESTAURANT	2017-07-25	BROOKLYN	Turkish	Plumbing not properly installed or maintained;...	A	13.0
3	ANTOJITOS DELI FOOD	2017-06-01	BROOKLYN	Latin (Cuban, Dominican, Puerto Rican, South &...	Live roaches present in facility's food and/or...	A	10.0
4	BANGIA	2017-06-16	MANHATTAN	Korean	Covered garbage receptacle not provided or ina...	A	9.0

7. The creation of the column MultiIndex in step 4 could have been avoided by converting that one column DataFrame into a Series with the `squeeze` method. The following code produces the same result as the previous step:

```
>>> inspections.set_index(['Name','Date', 'Info']) \
               .squeeze() \
               .unstack('Info') \
               .reset_index() \
               .rename_axis(None, axis='columns')
```

How it works...

In step 1, we notice that there are five variables placed vertically in the Info column with their corresponding value in the Value column. Because we need to pivot each of these five variables as horizontal column names, it would seem that the pivot method would work. Unfortunately, pandas developers have yet to implement this special case when there is more than one non-pivoted column. We are forced to use a different method.

The unstack method also pivots vertical data, but only for data in the index. Step 3 begins this process by moving both the columns that will and will not be pivoted into the index with the set_index method. Once these columns are in the index, unstack can be put to work as done in step 3.

Notice that as we are unstacking a DataFrame, pandas keeps the original column names (here, it is just a single column, Value) and creates a MultiIndex with the old column names as the upper level. The dataset is now essentially tidy but we go ahead and make our non-pivoted columns normal columns with the reset_index method. Because we have MultiIndex columns, we can choose which level the new column names will belong to with the col_level parameter. By default, the names are inserted into the uppermost level (level 0). We use -1 to indicate the bottommost level.

After all this, we have some excess DataFrame names and indexes that need to be discarded. Unfortunately, there isn't a DataFrame method that can remove levels, so we must drop down into the index and use its droplevel method. Here, we overwrite the old MultiIndex columns with single-level columns. These columns still have a useless name attribute, Info, which is renamed to None.

Cleaning up the MultiIndex columns could have been avoided by forcing the resulting DataFrame from step 3 to a Series. The squeeze method works only on single-column DataFrames and turns them into Series.

There's more...

It is actually possible to use the `pivot_table` method, which has no restrictions on how many non-pivoted columns are allowed. The `pivot_table` method differs from `pivot` by performing an aggregation for all the values that correspond to the intersection between the columns in the `index` and `columns` parameters. Because it is possible that there are multiple values in this intersection, `pivot_table` requires the user to pass it an aggregating function, in order to output a single value. We use the `first` aggregating function, which takes the first of the values of the group. In this particular example, there is exactly one value for each intersection, so there is nothing to be aggregated. The default aggregation function is the mean, which will produce an error here, since some of the values are strings:

```
>>> inspections.pivot_table(index=['Name', 'Date'],
                            columns='Info',
                            values='Value',
                            aggfunc='first') \
           .reset_index() \
           .rename_axis(None, axis='columns')
```

See also

- Pandas official documentation of the `droplevel` (http://bit.ly/2yo5BXf) and `squeeze` (http://bit.ly/2yo5TgN) methods

Tidying when two or more values are stored in the same cell

Tabular data, by nature, is two-dimensional, and thus, there is a limited amount of information that can be presented in a single cell. As a workaround, you will occasionally see datasets with more than a single value stored in the same cell. Tidy data allows for exactly a single value for each cell. To rectify these situations, you will typically need to parse the string data into multiple columns with the methods from the `str` Series accessor.

Getting ready...

In this recipe, we examine a dataset that has a column containing multiple different variables in each cell. We use the `str` accessor to parse these strings into separate columns to tidy the data.

How to do it..

1. Read in the Texas `cities` dataset, and identify the variables:

    ```
    >>> cities = pd.read_csv('data/texas_cities.csv')
    >>> cities
    ```

	City	Geolocation
0	Houston	29.7604° N, 95.3698° W
1	Dallas	32.7767° N, 96.7970° W
2	Austin	30.2672° N, 97.7431° W

2. The `City` column looks good and contains exactly one value. The `Geolocation` column, on the other hand, contains four variables: `latitude`, `latitude direction`, `longitude`, and `longitude direction`. Let's split the `Geolocation` column into four separate columns:

    ```
    >>> geolocations = cities.Geolocation.str.split(pat='. ',
                                                    expand=True)
    >>> geolocations.columns = ['latitude', 'latitude direction',
                                'longitude', 'longitude direction']
    >>> geolocations
    ```

	latitude	latitude direction	longitude	longitude direction
0	29.7604	N	95.3698	W
1	32.7767	N	96.7970	W
2	30.2672	N	97.7431	W

3. Because the original data type for the `Geolocation` was an object, all the new columns are also objects. Let's change `latitude` and `longitude` into floats:

```
>>> geolocations = geolocations.astype({'latitude':'float',
                                        'longitude':'float'})
>>> geolocations.dtypes
latitude                float64
latitude direction       object
longitude               float64
longitude direction      object
dtype: object
```

4. Concatenate these new columns with the `City` column from the original:

```
>>> cities_tidy = pd.concat([cities['City'], geolocations],
                             axis='columns')
>>> cities_tidy
```

	City	latitude	latitude direction	longitude	longitude direction
0	Houston	29.7604	N	95.3698	W
1	Dallas	32.7767	N	96.7970	W
2	Austin	30.2672	N	97.7431	W

How it works...

After reading the data, we decide how many variables there are in the dataset. Here, we chose to split the `Geolocation` column into four variables, but we could have just chosen two for latitude and longitude and used a negative sign to differentiate between west/east and south/north.

There are a few ways to parse the `Geolocation` column with the methods from the `str` accessor. The easiest way is to use the `split` method. We pass it a simple regular expression defined by any character (the period) and a space. When a space follows any character, a split is made, and a new column is formed. The first occurrence of this pattern takes place at the end of the latitude. A space follows the degree character, and a split is formed. The splitting characters are discarded and not kept in the resulting columns. The next split matches the comma and space following directly after the latitude direction.

A total of three splits are made, resulting in four columns. The second line in step 2 provides them with meaningful names. Even though the resulting `latitude` and `longitude` columns appear to be floats, they are not. They were originally parsed from an object column and therefore remain object data types. Step 3 uses a dictionary to map the column names to their new types.

Instead of using a dictionary, which would require a lot of typing if you had many column names, you can use the function `to_numeric` to attempt to convert each column to either integer or float. To apply this function iteratively over each column, use the `apply` method with the following:

```
>>> geolocations.apply(pd.to_numeric, errors='ignore')
```

Step 4 concatenates the city to the front of this new DataFrame to complete the process of making tidy data.

There's more...

The `split` method worked exceptionally well in this example with a simple regular expression. For other examples, some columns might require you to create splits on several different patterns. To search for multiple regular expressions, use the pipe character |. For instance, if we wanted to split only the degree symbol and comma, each followed by a space, we would do the following:

```
>>> cities.Geolocation.str.split(pat='° |, ', expand=True)
```

This returns the same DataFrame from step 2. Any number of additional split patterns may be appended to the preceding string pattern with the pipe character.

The `extract` method is another excellent method which allows you to extract specific groups within each cell. These capture groups must be enclosed in parentheses. Anything that matches outside the parentheses is not present in the result. The following line produces the same output as step 2:

```
>>> cities.Geolocation.str.extract('([0-9.]+). (N|S), ([0-9.]+). (E|W)',
                                   expand=True)
```

This regular expression has four capture groups. The first and third groups search for at least one or more consecutive digits with decimals. The second and fourth groups search for a single character (the direction). The first and third capture groups are separated by any character followed by a space. The second capture group is separated by a comma and then a space.

Tidying when variables are stored in column names and values

One particularly difficult form of messy data to diagnose appears whenever variables are stored both horizontally across the column names and vertically down column values. You will typically encounter this type of dataset, not in a database, but from a summarized report that someone else has already generated.

Getting ready

In this recipe, variables are identified both vertically and horizontally and reshaped into tidy data with the `melt` and `pivot_table` methods.

How to do it...

1. Read in the `sensors` dataset and identify the variables:

```
>>> sensors = pd.read_csv('data/sensors.csv')
>>> sensors
```

	Group	Property	2012	2013	2014	2015	2016
0	A	Pressure	928	873	814	973	870
1	A	Temperature	1026	1038	1009	1036	1042
2	A	Flow	819	806	861	882	856
3	B	Pressure	817	877	914	806	942
4	B	Temperature	1008	1041	1009	1002	1013
5	B	Flow	887	899	837	824	873

2. The only variable placed correctly in a vertical column is Group. The Property column appears to have three unique variables, Pressure, Temperature, and Flow. The rest of the columns 2012 to 2016 are themselves a single variable, which we can sensibly name Year. It isn't possible to restructure this kind of messy data with a single DataFrame method. Let's begin with the melt method to pivot the years into their own column:

```
>>> sensors.melt(id_vars=['Group', 'Property'], var_name='Year') \
        .head(6)
```

	Group	Property	Year	value
0	A	Pressure	2012	928
1	A	Temperature	2012	1026
2	A	Flow	2012	819
3	B	Pressure	2012	817
4	B	Temperature	2012	1008
5	B	Flow	2012	887

3. This takes care of one of our issues. Let's use the pivot_table method to pivot the Property column into new column names:

```
>>> sensors.melt(id_vars=['Group', 'Property'], var_name='Year') \
        .pivot_table(index=['Group', 'Year'],
                     columns='Property', values='value') \
        .reset_index() \
        .rename_axis(None, axis='columns')
```

	Group	Year	Flow	Pressure	Temperature
0	A	2012	819	928	1026
1	A	2013	806	873	1038
2	A	2014	861	814	1009
3	A	2015	882	973	1036
4	A	2016	856	870	1042
5	B	2012	887	817	1008
6	B	2013	899	877	1041
7	B	2014	837	914	1009
8	B	2015	824	806	1002
9	B	2016	873	942	1013

How it works...

Once we have identified the variables in step 1, we can begin our restructuring. Pandas does not have a method to pivot columns simultaneously, so we must take on this task one step at a time. We correct the years by keeping the `Property` column vertical by passing it to the `id_vars` parameter in the `melt` method.

The result is now precisely the pattern of messy data found in the preceding recipe, *Tidying when multiple variables are stored as column values*. As explained in the *There's more* section of that recipe, we must use `pivot_table` to pivot a DataFrame when using more than one column in the `index` parameter. After pivoting, the `Group` and `Year` variables are stuck in the index. We push them back out as columns. The `pivot_table` method preserves the column name used in the `columns` parameter as the name of the column index. After resetting the index, this name is meaningless, and we remove it with `rename_axis`.

There's more...

Whenever a solution involves `melt`, `pivot_table`, or `pivot`, you can be sure that there is an alternative method using `stack` and `unstack`. The trick is first to move the columns that are not currently being pivoted into the index:

```
>>> sensors.set_index(['Group', 'Property']) \
        .stack() \
        .unstack('Property') \
        .rename_axis(['Group', 'Year'], axis='index') \
        .rename_axis(None, axis='columns') \
        .reset_index()
```

Tidying when multiple observational units are stored in the same table

It is generally easier to maintain data when each table contains information from a single observational unit. On the other hand, it can be easier to find insights when all data is in a single table, and in the case of machine learning, all data must be in a single table. The focus of tidy data is not on directly performing analysis. Rather, it is structuring the data so that analysis is easier further down the line, and when there are multiple observational units in one table, they may need to get separated into their own tables.

Getting ready

In this recipe, we use the `movie` dataset to identify the three observational units (movies, actors, and directors) and create separate tables for each. One of the keys to this recipe is understanding that the actor and director Facebook likes are independent of the movie. Each actor and director is mapped to a single value representing their number of Facebook likes. Due to this independence, we can separate the data for the movies, directors, and actors into their own tables. Database folks call this process normalization, which increases data integrity and reduces redundancy.

How to do it...

1. Read in the altered `movie` dataset, and output the first five rows:

    ```
    >>> movie = pd.read_csv('data/movie_altered.csv')
    >>> movie.head()
    ```

	title	rating	year	duration	director_1	director_fb_likes_1	actor_1	actor_2	actor_3	actor_fb_likes_1	actor_fb_likes_2	actor_fb_likes_3
0	Avatar	PG-13	2009.0	178.0	James Cameron	0.0	CCH Pounder	Joel David Moore	Wes Studi	1000.0	936.0	855.0
1	Pirates of the Caribbean: At World's End	PG-13	2007.0	169.0	Gore Verbinski	563.0	Johnny Depp	Orlando Bloom	Jack Davenport	40000.0	5000.0	1000.0
2	Spectre	PG-13	2015.0	148.0	Sam Mendes	0.0	Christoph Waltz	Rory Kinnear	Stephanie Sigman	11000.0	393.0	161.0
3	The Dark Knight Rises	PG-13	2012.0	164.0	Christopher Nolan	22000.0	Tom Hardy	Christian Bale	Joseph Gordon-Levitt	27000.0	23000.0	23000.0
4	Star Wars: Episode VII - The Force Awakens	NaN	NaN	NaN	Doug Walker	131.0	Doug Walker	Rob Walker	NaN	131.0	12.0	NaN

2. This dataset contains information on the movie itself, the director, and actors. These three entities can be considered observational units. Before we start, let's use the `insert` method to create a column to uniquely identify each movie:

    ```
    >>> movie.insert(0, 'id', np.arange(len(movie)))
    >>> movie.head()
    ```

	id	title	rating	year	duration	director_1	director_fb likes_1	actor_1	actor_2	actor_3	actor_fb_likes_1	actor_fb_likes_2	actor_fb_likes_3
0	0	Avatar	PG-13	2009.0	178.0	James Cameron	0.0	CCH Pounder	Joel David Moore	Wes Studi	1000.0	936.0	855.0
1	1	Pirates of the Caribbean: At World's End	PG-13	2007.0	169.0	Gore Verbinski	563.0	Johnny Depp	Orlando Bloom	Jack Davenport	40000.0	5000.0	1000.0
2	2	Spectre	PG-13	2015.0	148.0	Sam Mendes	0.0	Christoph Waltz	Rory Kinnear	Stephanie Sigman	11000.0	393.0	161.0
0	3	The Dark Knight Rises	PG-13	2012.0	164.0	Christopher Nolan	22000.0	Tom Hardy	Christian Bale	Joseph Gordon-Levitt	27000.0	23000.0	23000.0
4	4	Star Wars: Episode VII - The Force Awakens	NaN	NaN	NaN	Doug Walker	131.0	Doug Walker	Rob Walker	NaN	131.0	12.0	NaN

3. Let's attempt to tidy this dataset with the `wide_to_long` function to put all the actors in one column and their corresponding Facebook likes in another, and do the same for the director, even though there is only one per movie:

```
>>> stubnames = ['director', 'director_fb_likes',
                 'actor', 'actor_fb_likes']
>>> movie_long = pd.wide_to_long(movie,
                                 stubnames=stubnames,
                                 i='id',
                                 j='num',
                                 sep='_').reset_index()

>>> movie_long['num'] = movie_long['num'].astype(int)
>>> movie_long.head(9)
```

	id	num	year	duration	rating	title	director	director_fb_likes	actor	actor_fb_likes
0	0	1	2009.0	178.0	PG-13	Avatar	James Cameron	0.0	CCH Pounder	1000.0
1	0	2	2009.0	178.0	PG-13	Avatar	NaN	NaN	Joel David Moore	936.0
2	0	3	2009.0	178.0	PG-13	Avatar	NaN	NaN	Wes Studi	855.0
3	1	1	2007.0	169.0	PG-13	Pirates of the Caribbean: At World's End	Gore Verbinski	563.0	Johnny Depp	40000.0
4	1	2	2007.0	169.0	PG-13	Pirates of the Caribbean: At World's End	NaN	NaN	Orlando Bloom	5000.0
5	1	3	2007.0	169.0	PG-13	Pirates of the Caribbean: At World's End	NaN	NaN	Jack Davenport	1000.0
6	2	1	2015.0	148.0	PG-13	Spectre	Sam Mendes	0.0	Christoph Waltz	11000.0
7	2	2	2015.0	148.0	PG-13	Spectre	NaN	NaN	Rory Kinnear	393.0
8	2	3	2015.0	148.0	PG-13	Spectre	NaN	NaN	Stephanie Sigman	161.0

4. The dataset is now ready to be split into multiple smaller tables:

```
>>> movie_table = movie_long[['id', 'year', 'duration', 'rating']]
>>> director_table = movie_long[['id', 'num',
                                 'director', 'director_fb_likes']]
>>> actor_table = movie_long[['id', 'num',
                              'actor', 'actor_fb_likes']]
```

	id	title	year	duration	rating
0	0	Avatar	2009.0	178.0	PG-13
1	0	Avatar	2009.0	178.0	PG-13
2	0	Avatar	2009.0	178.0	PG-13
3	1	Pirates of the Caribbean: At World's End	2007.0	169.0	PG-13
4	1	Pirates of the Caribbean: At World's End	2007.0	169.0	PG-13
5	1	Pirates of the Caribbean: At World's End	2007.0	169.0	PG-13
6	2	Spectre	2015.0	148.0	PG-13
7	2	Spectre	2015.0	148.0	PG-13
8	2	Spectre	2015.0	148.0	PG-13

	id	director	num	director_fb_likes
0	0	James Cameron	1	0.0
1	0	NaN	2	NaN
2	0	NaN	3	NaN
3	1	Gore Verbinski	1	563.0
4	1	NaN	2	NaN
5	1	NaN	3	NaN
6	2	Sam Mendes	1	0.0
7	2	NaN	2	NaN
8	2	NaN	3	NaN

	id	actor	num	actor_fb_likes
0	0	CCH Pounder	1	1000.0
1	0	Joel David Moore	2	936.0
2	0	Wes Studi	3	855.0
3	1	Johnny Depp	1	40000.0
4	1	Orlando Bloom	2	5000.0
5	1	Jack Davenport	3	1000.0
6	2	Christoph Waltz	1	11000.0
7	2	Rory Kinnear	2	393.0
8	2	Stephanie Sigman	3	161.0

5. There are still several issues with these tables. The `movie` table duplicates each movie three times, the director table has two missing rows for each ID, and a few movies have missing values for some of the actors. Let's take care of these issues:

```
>>> movie_entity = movie_entity.drop_duplicates() \
                        .reset_index(drop=True)
>>> director_entity = director_entity.dropna() \
                        .reset_index(drop=True)
>>> actor_table = actor_table.dropna() \
                        .reset_index(drop=True)
```

	id	title	year	duration	rating
0	0	Avatar	2009.0	178.0	PG-13
1	1	Pirates of the Caribbean: At World's End	2007.0	169.0	PG-13
2	2	Spectre	2015.0	148.0	PG-13
3	3	The Dark Knight Rises	2012.0	164.0	PG-13
4	4	Star Wars: Episode VII - The Force Awakens	NaN	NaN	NaN

	id	director	num	director_fb_likes
0	0	James Cameron	1	0.0
1	1	Gore Verbinski	1	563.0
2	2	Sam Mendes	1	0.0
3	3	Christopher Nolan	1	22000.0
4	4	Doug Walker	1	131.0

6. Now that we have separated the observational units into their own tables, let's compare the memory of the original dataset with these three tables:

```
>>> movie.memory_usage(deep=True).sum()
2318234

>>> movie_table.memory_usage(deep=True).sum() + \
    director_table.memory_usage(deep=True).sum() + \
    actor_table.memory_usage(deep=True).sum()
2627306
```

7. Our new tidier data actually takes up a little more memory. This is to be expected, as all the data in the original columns are simply spread out into the new tables. The new tables also each have an index, and two of them have an extra `num` column, which accounts for the extra memory. We can, however, take advantage of the fact that the count of Facebook likes is independent of the movie, meaning that each actor and director has exactly one count of Facebook likes for all movies. Before we can do this, we need to create another table mapping each movie to each actor/director. Let's first create `id` columns specific to the actor and director tables, uniquely identifying each actor/director:

```
>>> director_cat = pd.Categorical(director_table['director'])
>>> director_table.insert(1, 'director_id', director_cat.codes)

>>> actor_cat = pd.Categorical(actor_table['actor'])
>>> actor_table.insert(1, 'actor_id', actor_cat.codes)
```

	id	actor_id	actor	num	actor_fb_likes
0	0	824	CCH Pounder	1	1000.0
1	0	2867	Joel David Moore	2	936.0
2	0	6099	Wes Studi	3	855.0
3	1	2971	Johnny Depp	1	40000.0
4	1	4536	Orlando Bloom	2	5000.0

	id	director_id	director	num	director_fb_likes
0	0	922	James Cameron	1	0.0
1	1	794	Gore Verbinski	1	563.0
2	2	2020	Sam Mendes	1	0.0
3	3	373	Christopher Nolan	1	22000.0
4	4	600	Doug Walker	1	131.0

8. We can use these tables to form our intermediate tables and unique actor/director tables. Let's first do this with the `director` tables:

```
>>> director_associative = director_table[['id', 'director_id',
                                           'num']]
>>> dcols = ['director_id', 'director', 'director_fb_likes']
>>> director_unique = director_table[dcols].drop_duplicates() \
                                          .reset_index(drop=True)
```

	id	director_id	num
0	0	922	1
1	1	794	1
2	2	2020	1
3	3	373	1
4	4	600	1

	director_id	director	director_fb_likes
0	922	James Cameron	0.0
1	794	Gore Verbinski	563.0
2	2020	Sam Mendes	0.0
3	373	Christopher Nolan	22000.0
4	600	Doug Walker	131.0

9. Let's do the same thing with the `actor` table:

```
>>> actor_associative = actor_table[['id', 'actor_id', 'num']]
>>> acols = ['actor_id', 'actor', 'actor_fb_likes']
>>> actor_unique = actor_table[acols].drop_duplicates() \
                                      .reset_index(drop=True)
```

	id	actor_id	num
0	0	824	1
1	0	2867	2
2	0	6099	3
3	1	2971	1
4	1	4536	2

	actor_id	actor	actor_fb_likes
0	824	CCH Pounder	1000.0
1	2867	Joel David Moore	936.0
2	6099	Wes Studi	855.0
3	2971	Johnny Depp	40000.0
4	4536	Orlando Bloom	5000.0

10. Let's find out how much memory our new tables consume:

```
>>> movie_table.memory_usage(deep=True).sum() + \
    director_associative.memory_usage(deep=True).sum() + \
    director_unique.memory_usage(deep=True).sum() + \
    actor_associative.memory_usage(deep=True).sum() + \
    actor_unique.memory_usage(deep=True).sum()
1833402
```

11. Now that we have normalized our tables, we can build an entity-relationship diagram showing all the tables (entities), columns, and relationships. This diagram was created with the easy to use ERDPlus (https://erdplus.com):

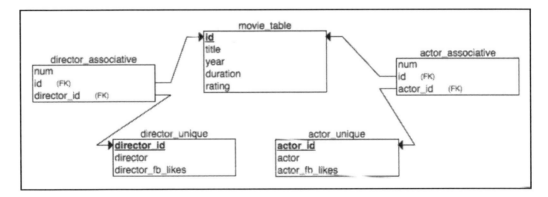

How it works...

After importing the data and identifying the three entities, we must create a unique identifier for each observation so that we can link to the movies, actors and directors together once they have been separated into different tables. In step 2, we simply set the ID column as the row number beginning from zero. In step 3, we use the `wide_to_long` function to simultaneously `melt` the `actor` and `director` columns. It uses the integer suffix of the columns to align the data vertically and places this integer suffix in the index. The parameter `j` is used to control its name. The values in the columns not in the `stubnames` list repeat to align with the columns that were melted.

In step 4, we create our three new tables, keeping the `id` column in each. We also keep the `num` column to identify the exact `director/actor` column from which it was derived. Step 5 condenses each table by removing duplicates and missing values.

After step 5, the three observational units are in their own tables, but they still contain the same amount of data as the original (and a bit more), as seen in step 6. To return the correct number of bytes from the `memory_usage` method for `object` data type columns, you must set the `deep` parameter to `True`.

Each actor/director needs only one entry in his or her respective tables. We can't simply make a table of just actor name and Facebook likes, as there would be no way to link the actors back to the original movie. The relationship between movies and actors is called a **many-to-many relationship**. Each movie is associated with multiple actors, and each actor can appear in multiple movies. To resolve this relationship, an intermediate or associative table is created, which contains the unique identifiers (**primary keys**) of both the movie and actor.

To create associative tables, we must uniquely identify each actor/director. One trick is to create a categorical data type out of each actor/director name with `pd.Categorical`. Categorical data types have an internal map from each value to an integer. This integer is found in the `codes` attribute, which is used as the unique ID. To set up the creation of the associative table, we add this unique ID to the `actor/director` tables.

Step 8 and step 9 create the associative tables by selecting both of the unique identifiers. Now, we can reduce the `actor` and `director` tables to just the unique names and Facebook likes. This new arrangement of tables uses 20% less memory than the original. Formal relational databases have entity-relationship diagrams to visualize the tables. In step 10, we use the simple ERDPlus tool to make the visualization, which greatly eases the understanding of the relationships between the tables.

There's more...

It is possible to recreate the original `movie` table by joining all the tables back together. First, join the associative tables to the `actor`/`director` tables. Then pivot the num column, and add the column prefixes back:

```
>>> actors = actor_associative.merge(actor_unique, on='actor_id') \
                              .drop('actor_id', 1) \
                              .pivot_table(index='id',
                                           columns='num',
                                           aggfunc='first')

>>> actors.columns = actors.columns.get_level_values(0) + '_' + \
                     actors.columns.get_level_values(1).astype(str)

>>> directors = director_associative.merge(director_unique,
                                           on='director_id') \
                                    .drop('director_id', 1) \
                                    .pivot_table(index='id',
                                                 columns='num',
                                                 aggfunc='first')

>>> directors.columns = directors.columns.get_level_values(0) + '_' + \
                        directors.columns.get_level_values(1) \
                                 .astype(str)
```

id	actor_1	actor_2	actor_3	actor_fb_likes_1	actor_fb_likes_2	actor_fb_likes_3
0	CCH Pounder	Joel David Moore	Wes Studi	1000.0	936.0	855.0
1	Johnny Depp	Orlando Bloom	Jack Davenport	40000.0	5000.0	1000.0
2	Christoph Waltz	Rory Kinnear	Stephanie Sigman	11000.0	393.0	161.0
3	Tom Hardy	Christian Bale	Joseph Gordon-Levitt	27000.0	23000.0	23000.0
4	Doug Walker	Rob Walker	None	131.0	12.0	NaN

id	director_1	director_fb_likes_1
0	James Cameron	0.0
1	Gore Verbinski	563.0
2	Sam Mendes	0.0
3	Christopher Nolan	22000.0
4	Doug Walker	131.0

These tables can now be joined together with `movie_table`:

```
>>> movie2 = movie_table.merge(directors.reset_index(),
                               on='id', how='left') \
                        .merge(actors.reset_index(),
                               on='id', how='left')
>>> movie.equals(movie2[movie.columns])
True
```

See also

- More on database normalization (`http://bit.ly/2w8wahQ`), associative tables (`http://bit.ly/2yqE4oh`), and primary and foreign keys (`http://bit.ly/2xgIvEb`)
- Refer to the *Stacking multiple groups of variables simultaneously* recipe in this chapter for more information on the `wide_to_long` function

9
Combining Pandas Objects

In this chapter, we will cover the following topics:

- Appending new rows to DataFrames
- Concatenating multiple DataFrames together
- Comparing President Trump's and Obama's approval ratings
- Understanding the differences between `concat`, `join`, and `merge`
- Connecting to SQL databases

Introduction

A wide variety of options are available to combine two or more DataFrames or Series together. The `append` method is the least flexible and only allows for new rows to be appended to a DataFrame. The `concat` method is very versatile and can combine any number of DataFrames or Series on either axis. The `join` method provides fast lookups by aligning a column of one DataFrame to the index of others. The `merge` method provides SQL-like capabilities to join two DataFrames together.

Appending new rows to DataFrames

When performing a data analysis, it is far more common to create new columns than new rows. This is because a new row of data usually represents a new observation and, as an analyst, it is typically not your job to continually capture new data. Data capture is usually left to other platforms like relational database management systems. Nevertheless, it is a necessary feature to know as it will crop up from time to time.

Getting ready

In this recipe, we will begin by appending rows to a small dataset with the `.loc` indexer and then transition to using the `append` method.

How to do it...

1. Read in the names dataset, and output it:

```
>>> names = pd.read_csv('data/names.csv')
>>> names
```

	Name	Age
0	Cornelia	70
1	Abbas	69
2	Penelope	4
3	Niko	2

2. Let's create a list that contains some new data and use the `.loc` indexer to set a single row label equal to this new data:

```
>>> new_data_list = ['Aria', 1]
>>> names.loc[4] = new_data_list
>>> names
```

	Name	Age
0	Cornelia	70
1	Abbas	69
2	Penelope	4
3	Niko	2
4	Aria	1

3. The `.loc` indexer uses labels to refer to the rows. In this case, the row labels exactly match the integer location. It is possible to append more rows with non-integer labels:

```
>>> names.loc['five'] = ['Zach', 3]
>>> names
```

	Name	Age
0	Cornelia	70
1	Abbas	69
2	Penelope	4
3	Niko	2
4	Aria	1
five	Zach	3

4. To be more explicit in associating variables to values, you may use a dictionary. Also, in this step, we can dynamically choose the new index label to be the length of the DataFrame:

```
>>> names.loc[len(names)] = {'Name':'Zayd', 'Age':2}
>>> names
```

	Name	Age
0	Cornelia	70
1	Abbas	69
2	Penelope	4
3	Niko	2
4	Aria	1
five	Zach	3
6	Zayd	2

5. A Series can hold the new data as well and works exactly the same as a dictionary:

```
>>> names.loc[len(names)] = pd.Series({'Age':32,
                                        'Name':'Dean'})
>>> names
```

	Name	Age
0	Cornelia	70
1	Abbas	69
2	Penelope	4
3	Niko	2
4	Aria	1
five	Zach	3
6	Zayd	2
7	Dean	32

6. The preceding operations all use the `.loc` indexing operator to make changes to the `names` DataFrame in-place. There is no separate copy of the DataFrame that is returned. In the next few steps, we will look at the `append` method, which does not modify the calling DataFrame. Instead, it returns a new copy of the DataFrame with the appended row(s). Let's begin with the original `names` DataFrame and attempt to append a row. The first argument to `append` must be either another DataFrame, Series, dictionary, or a list of these, but not a list like the one in step 2. Let's see what happens when we attempt to use a dictionary with `append`:

```
>>> names = pd.read_csv('data/names.csv')
>>> names.append({'Name':'Aria', 'Age':1})
TypeError: Can only append a Series if ignore_index=True or if the
Series has a name
```

7. This error message appears to be slightly incorrect. We are passing a DataFrame and not a Series but nevertheless, it gives us instructions on how to correct it:

```
>>> names.append({'Name':'Aria', 'Age':1}, ignore_index=True)
```

	Name	Age
0	Cornelia	70
1	Abbas	69
2	Penelope	4
3	Niko	2
4	Aria	1

8. This works but `ignore_index` is a sneaky parameter. When set to `True`, the old index will be removed completely and replaced with a `RangeIndex` from 0 to n-1. For instance, let's specify an index for the `names` DataFrame:

```
>>> names.index = ['Canada', 'Canada', 'USA', 'USA']
>>> names
```

	Name	Age
Canada	Cornelia	70
Canada	Abbas	69
USA	Penelope	4
USA	Niko	2

9. Rerun the code from step 7 and you will get the same result. The original index is completely ignored.

10. Let's continue with this `names` dataset with these country strings in the index and use a Series that has a `name` attribute with the `append` method:

```
>>> s = pd.Series({'Name': 'Zach', 'Age': 3}, name=len(names))
>>> s
Age          3
Name      Zach
Name: 4, dtype: object

>>> names.append(s)
```

	Name	Age
Canada	Cornelia	70
Canada	Abbas	69
USA	Penelope	4
USA	Niko	2
4	Zach	3

11. The `append` method is more flexible than the `.loc` indexer. It supports appending multiple rows at the same time. One way to accomplish this is with a list of Series:

```
>>> s1 = pd.Series({'Name': 'Zach', 'Age': 3}, name=len(names))
>>> s2 = pd.Series({'Name': 'Zayd', 'Age': 2}, name='USA')
>>> names.append([s1, s2])
```

	Name	Age
Canada	Cornelia	70
Canada	Abbas	69
USA	Penelope	4
USA	Niko	2
4	Zach	3
USA	Zayd	2

12. Small DataFrames with only two columns are simple enough to manually write out all the column names and values. When they get larger, this process will be quite painful. For instance, let's take a look at the 2016 baseball dataset:

```
>>> bball_16 = pd.read_csv('data/baseball16.csv')
>>> bball_16.head()
```

	playerID	yearID	stint	teamID	lgID	G	AB	R	H	2B	...	RBI	SB	CS	BB	SO	IBB	HBP	SH	SF	GIDP
0	altuvjo01	2016	1	HOU	AL	161	640	108	216	42	...	96.0	30.0	10.0	60	70.0	11.0	7.0	3.0	7.0	15.0
1	bregmal01	2016	1	HOU	AL	49	201	31	53	13	...	34.0	2.0	0.0	15	52.0	0.0	0.0	0.0	1.0	1.0
2	castrja01	2016	1	HOU	AL	113	329	41	69	16	...	32.0	2.0	1.0	45	123.0	0.0	1.0	1.0	0.0	9.0
3	correca01	2016	1	HOU	AL	153	577	76	158	36	...	96.0	13.0	3.0	75	139.0	5.0	5.0	0.0	3.0	12.0
4	gattiev01	2016	1	HOU	AL	128	447	58	112	19	...	72.0	2.0	1.0	43	127.0	6.0	4.0	0.0	5.0	12.0

13. This dataset contains 22 columns and it would be easy to mistype a column name or forget one altogether if you were manually entering new rows of data. To help protect against these mistakes, let's select a single row as a Series and chain the to_dict method to it to get an example row as a dictionary:

```
>>> data_dict = bball_16.iloc[0].to_dict()
>>> print(data_dict)
{'playerID': 'altuvjo01', 'yearID': 2016, 'stint': 1, 'teamID':
'HOU', 'lgID': 'AL', 'G': 161, 'AB': 640, 'R': 108, 'H': 216, '2B':
42, '3B': 5, 'HR': 24, 'RBI': 96.0, 'SB': 30.0, 'CS': 10.0, 'BB':
60, 'SO': 70.0, 'IBB': 11.0, 'HBP': 7.0, 'SH': 3.0, 'SF': 7.0,
'GIDP': 15.0}
```

14. Clear the old values with a dictionary comprehension assigning any previous string value as an empty string and all others, missing values. This dictionary can now serve as a template for any new data you would like to enter:

```
>>> new_data_dict = {k: '' if isinstance(v, str) else
                          np.nan for k, v in data_dict.items()}
>>> print(new_data_dict)
{'playerID': '', 'yearID': nan, 'stint': nan, 'teamID': '', 'lgID':
'', 'G': nan, 'AB': nan, 'R': nan, 'H': nan, '2B': nan, '3B': nan,
'HR': nan, 'RBI': nan, 'SB': nan, 'CS': nan, 'BB': nan, 'SO': nan,
'IBB': nan, 'HBP': nan, 'SH': nan, 'SF': nan, 'GIDP': nan}
```

How it works...

The `.loc` indexing operator is used to select and assign data based on the row and column labels. The first value passed to it represents the row label. In step 2, `names.loc[4]` refers to the row with a label equal to the integer 4. This label does not currently exist in the DataFrame. The assignment statement creates a new row with data provided by the list. As was mentioned in the recipe, this operation modifies the `names` DataFrame itself. If there was a previously existing row with a label equal to the integer 4, this command would have written over it. This modification in-place makes this indexing operator riskier to use than the `append` method, which never modifies the original calling DataFrame.

Any valid label may be used with the `.loc` indexing operator, as seen in step 3. Regardless of what the new label value actually is, the new row will always be appended at the end. Even though assigning with a list works, for clarity it's best to use a dictionary so that we know exactly which columns are associated with each value, as done in step 4.

Step 5 shows a little trick to dynamically set the new label to be the current number of rows in the DataFrame. Data stored in a Series will also get assigned correctly as long as the index labels match the column names.

The rest of the steps use the `append` method, which is a simple method that only appends new rows to DataFrames. Most DataFrame methods allow both row and column manipulation through an `axis` parameter. One exception is with `append`, which can only append rows to DataFrames.

Using a dictionary of column names mapped to values isn't enough information for append to work, as seen by the error message in step 6. To correctly append a dictionary without a row name, you will have to set the `ignore_index` parameter to `True`. Step 10 shows you how to keep the old index by simply converting your dictionary to a Series. Make sure to use the `name` parameter, which is then used as the new index label. Any number of rows may be added with append in this manner by passing a list of Series as the first argument.

When wanting to append rows in this manner with a much larger DataFrame, you can avoid lots of typing and mistakes by converting a single row to a dictionary with the `to_dict` method and then using a dictionary comprehension to clear out all the old values replacing them with some defaults.

There's more...

Appending a single row to a DataFrame is a fairly expensive operation and if you find yourself writing a loop to append single rows of data to a DataFrame, then you are doing it wrong. Let's first create 1,000 rows of new data as a list of Series:

```
>>> random_data = []
>>> for i in range(1000):
        d = dict()
        for k, v in data_dict.items():
            if isinstance(v, str):
                d[k] = np.random.choice(list('abcde'))
            else:
                d[k] = np.random.randint(10)
        random_data.append(pd.Series(d, name=i + len(bball_16)))

>>> random_data[0].head()
2B    3
3B    9
AB    3
BB    9
CS    4
Name: 16, dtype: object
```

Let's time how long it takes to loop through each item making one append at a time:

```
>>> %%timeit
>>> bball_16_copy = bball_16.copy()
>>> for row in random_data:
        bball_16_copy = bball_16_copy.append(row)
4.88 s ± 190 ms per loop (mean ± std. dev. of 7 runs, 1 loop each)
```

That took nearly five seconds for only 1,000 rows. If we instead pass in the entire list of Series, we get an enormous speed increase:

```
>>> %%timeit
>>> bball_16_copy = bball_16.copy()
>>> bball_16_copy = bball_16_copy.append(random_data)
78.4 ms ± 6.2 ms per loop (mean ± std. dev. of 7 runs, 10 loops each)
```

By passing in the list of Series, the time has been reduced to under one-tenth of a second. Internally, pandas converts the list of Series to a single DataFrame and then makes the append.

Concatenating multiple DataFrames together

The versatile `concat` function enables concatenating two or more DataFrames (or Series) together, both vertically and horizontally. As per usual, when dealing with multiple pandas objects simultaneously, concatenation doesn't happen haphazardly but aligns each object by their index.

Getting ready

In this recipe, we combine DataFrames both horizontally and vertically with the `concat` function and then change the parameter values to yield different results.

How to do it...

1. Read in the 2016 and 2017 stock datasets, and make their ticker symbol the index:

```
>>> stocks_2016 = pd.read_csv('data/stocks_2016.csv',
                              index_col='Symbol')
>>> stocks_2017 = pd.read_csv('data/stocks_2017.csv',
                              index_col='Symbol')
```

Symbol	Shares	Low	High
AAPL	80	95	110
TSLA	50	80	130
WMT	40	55	70

Symbol	Shares	Low	High
AAPL	50	120	140
GE	100	30	40
IBM	87	75	95
SLB	20	55	85
TXN	500	15	23
TSLA	100	100	300

2. Place all the `stock` datasets into a single list, and then call the `concat` function to concatenate them together:

```
>>> s_list = [stocks_2016, stocks_2017]
>>> pd.concat(s_list)
```

Symbol	Shares	Low	High
AAPL	80	95	110
TSLA	50	80	130
WMT	40	55	70
AAPL	50	120	140
GE	100	30	40
IBM	87	75	95
SLB	20	55	85
TXN	500	15	23
TSLA	100	100	300

3. By default, the `concat` function concatenates DataFrames vertically, one on top of the other. One issue with the preceding DataFrame is that there is no way to identify the year of each row. The `concat` function allows each piece of the resulting DataFrame to be labeled with the `keys` parameter. This label will appear in the outermost index level of the concatenated frame and force the creation of a MultiIndex. Also, the `names` parameter has the ability to rename each index level for clarity:

```
>>> pd.concat(s_list, keys=['2016', '2017'],
              names=['Year', 'Symbol'])
```

		Shares	Low	High
Year	**Symbol**			
2016	**AAPL**	80	95	110
	TSLA	50	80	130
	WMT	40	55	70
2017	**AAPL**	50	120	140
	GE	100	30	40
	IBM	87	75	95
	SLB	20	55	85
	TXN	500	15	23
	TSLA	100	100	300

4. It is also possible to concatenate horizontally by changing the `axis` parameter to *columns* or *1*:

```
>>> pd.concat(s_list, keys=['2016', '2017'],
              axis='columns', names=['Year', None])
```

Year	**2016**			**2017**		
	Shares	**Low**	**High**	**Shares**	**Low**	**High**
AAPL	80.0	95.0	110.0	50.0	120.0	140.0
GE	NaN	NaN	NaN	100.0	30.0	40.0
IBM	NaN	NaN	NaN	87.0	75.0	95.0
SLB	NaN	NaN	NaN	20.0	55.0	85.0
TSLA	50.0	80.0	130.0	100.0	100.0	300.0
TXN	NaN	NaN	NaN	500.0	15.0	23.0
WMT	40.0	55.0	70.0	NaN	NaN	NaN

5. Notice that missing values appear whenever a stock symbol is present in one year but not the other. The `concat` function, by default, uses an outer join, keeping all rows from each DataFrame in the list. However, it gives us options to only keep rows that have the same index values in both DataFrames. This is referred to as an inner join. We set the `join` parameter to *inner* to change the behavior:

```
>>> pd.concat(s_list, join='inner', keys=['2016', '2017'],
             axis='columns', names=['Year', None])
```

Year	2016			2017		
	Shares	Low	High	Shares	Low	High
Symbol						
AAPL	80	95	110	50	120	140
TSLA	50	80	130	100	100	300

How it works...

The first argument is the only argument required for the `concat` function and it must be a sequence of pandas objects, typically a list or dictionary of DataFrames or Series. By default, all these objects will be stacked vertically one on top of the other. In this recipe, only two DataFrames are concatenated, but any number of pandas objects work. When we were concatenating vertically, the DataFrames align by their column names.

In this dataset, all the column names were the same so each column in the 2017 data lined up precisely under the same column name in the 2016 data. However, when they were concatenated horizontally, as in step 4, only two of the index labels matched from both years--*AAPL* and *TSLA*. Therefore, these ticker symbols had no missing values for either year. There are two types of alignment possible using `concat`, *outer* (the default) and *inner* referred to by the `join` parameter.

There's more...

The `append` method is a heavily watered down version of `concat` that can only append new rows to a DataFrame. Internally, `append` just calls the `concat` function. For instance, step 2 from this recipe may be duplicated with the following:

```
>>> stocks_2016.append(stocks_2017)
```

Comparing President Trump's and Obama's approval ratings

Public support of the current President of the United States is a topic that frequently makes it into news headlines and is formally measured through opinion polls. In recent years, there has been a rapid increase in the frequency of these polls and lots of new data rolls in each week. There are many different pollsters that each have their own questions and methodology to capture their data, and thus there exists quite a bit of variability among the data. The American Presidency Project from the University of California, Santa Barbara, provides an aggregate approval rating down to a single data point each day.

Unlike most of the recipes in this book, the data is not readily available in a CSV file. Often, as a data analyst, you will need to find data on the web, and use a tool that can scrape it into a format that you can then parse through your local workstation.

Getting ready

In this recipe, we will use the `read_html` function, which comes heavily equipped to scrape data from tables online and turn them into DataFrames. You will also learn how to inspect web pages to find the underlying HTML for certain elements. I used Google Chrome as my browser and suggest you use it, or Firefox, for the web-based steps.

How to do it...

1. Navigate to *The American Presidency Project* approval page for President Donald Trump (`http://www.presidency.ucsb.edu/data/popularity.php?pres=45`). You should get a page that contains a time series plot with the data in a table directly following it:

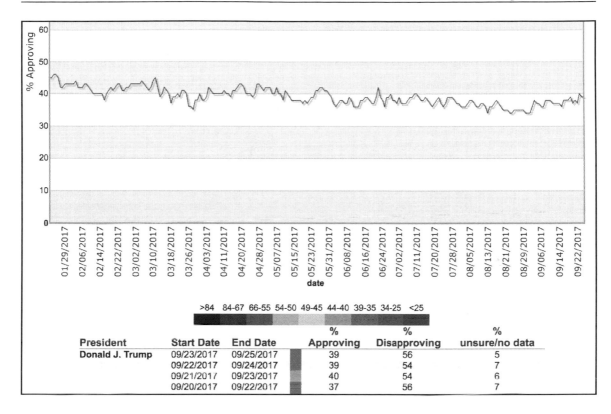

President	Start Date	End Date		% Approving	% Disapproving	% unsure/no data
Donald J. Trump	09/23/2017	09/25/2017		39	56	5
	09/22/2017	09/24/2017		39	54	7
	09/21/2017	09/23/2017		40	54	6
	09/20/2017	09/22/2017		37	56	7

2. The `read_html` function is able to scrape tables off web pages and place their data into DataFrames. It works best with simple HTML tables and provides some useful parameters to select the exact table you desire in case there happen to be multiple tables on the same page. Let's go ahead and use `read_html` with its default values, which will return all the tables as DataFrames in a list:

```
>>> base_url =
'http://www.presidency.ucsb.edu/data/popularity.php?pres={}'
>>> trump_url = base_url.format(45)
>>> df_list = pd.read_html(trump_url)
>>> len(df_list)
14
```

3. The function has returned 14 tables, which seems preposterous at first, as the web page appears to show only a single element that most people would recognize as a table. The `read_html` function formally searches for HTML table elements that begin with <*table*. Let's inspect the HTML page by right-clicking on the approval data table and selecting **inspect** or **inspect element**:

			% Approving	% Disapproving	% unsure/no data
>84 84-67 66-55 54-50 49-45 44-40 39-35 34-25 <25					
President	**Start Date**	**End Date**			
Donald J. Trump	09/23/2017	09/25/2017	39	56	5
	09/22/2017	09/24/2017	39	54	7
	09/21/2017	09/23/2017	40		
	09/20/2017	09/22/2017	37		
	09/19/2017	09/21/2017	38		
	09/18/2017	09/20/2017	37		
	09/17/2017	09/19/2017	39		
	09/16/2017	09/18/2017	38		
	09/15/2017	09/17/2017	38		
	09/14/2017	09/16/2017	38		
	09/13/2017	09/15/2017	36		
	09/12/2017	09/14/2017	37		
	09/11/2017	09/13/2017	37		
	09/10/2017	09/12/2017	37		
	09/09/2017	09/11/2017	37		
	09/08/2017	09/10/2017	38		
	09/07/2017	09/09/2017	38		
	09/06/2017	09/08/2017	38		
	09/05/2017	09/07/2017	36	57	7

Look Up "54"

Copy
Search Google for "54"
Print...

LastPass ▶

Inspect ←

Speech ▶

Add to iTunes as a Spoken Track

4. This opens up the console, which is a very powerful tool for web development. For this recipe, we will only need it for a few tasks. All consoles allow you to search the HTML for a specific word. Let's search for the word `table`. My browser found 15 different HTML tables, very close to the number returned by `read_html`:

```
    <td bgcolor="#ffff
    "listdate">...</td>
    <td bgcolor="#ffff
```

... tbody tr td table tbody tr td table

table   1 of 15 ∧ ∨

Styles Computed Event Listeners DOM Breakpoint

5. Let's begin inspecting the DataFrames in `df_list`:

```
>>> df0 = df_list[0]
>>> df0.shape
(308, 1794)

>>> df0.head(7)
```

	0	1	2	3	4	5	6	7
0	NaN	NaN	NaN	NaN	NaN	NaN	NaN	NaN
1	NaN	NaN	NaN	NaN	NaN	NaN	NaN	NaN
2	NaN	NaN	NaN	NaN	NaN	NaN	NaN	NaN
3	NaN	NaN	NaN	NaN	NaN	NaN	NaN	NaN
4	NaN	NaN	NaN	NaN	NaN	NaN	NaN	NaN
5	NaN	NaN	NaN	NaN	NaN	NaN	NaN	NaN
6	Document Archive • Public Papers of the Presi...	Document Archive • Public Papers of the Presi...	Document Archive • Public Papers of the Presi...	NaN	NaN	Document Archive	• Public Papers of the Presidents	• State of the Union Addresses & Messages

6. Looking back at the web page, there is a row in the approval table for nearly each day beginning January 22, 2017, until the day the data was scraped--September 25, 2017. This is a little more than eight months or 250 rows of data, which is somewhat close to the 308 lines in that first table. Scanning through the rest of the tables, you can see that lots of empty meaningless tables were discovered, as well as tables for different parts of the web page that don't actually resemble tables. Let's use some of the parameters of the `read_html` function to help us select the table we desire. We can use the `match` parameter to search for a specific string in the table. Let's search for a table with the word *Start Date* in it:

```
>>> df_list = pd.read_html(trump_url, match='Start Date')
>>> len(df_list)
3
```

7. By searching for a specific string in the table, we have reduced the number of tables down to just three. Another useful parameter is `attrs`, which accepts a dictionary of HTML attributes paired with their value. We would like to find some unique attributes for our particular table. To do this, let's right-click again in our data table. This time, make sure to click at the very top in one of the table headers. For example, right click on *President,* and select **inspect** or **inspect element** again:

8. The element that you selected should be highlighted. This is actually not the element we are interested in. Keep looking until you come across an HTML tag beginning with *<table.* All the words to the left of the equal signs are the attributes or `attrs` and to the right are the values. Let's use the *align* attribute with its value *center* in our search:

```
>>> df_list = pd.read_html(trump_url, match='Start Date',
                           attrs={'align':'center'})
>>> len(df_list)
1

>>> trump = df_list[0]
>>> trump.shape
(249, 19)

>>> trump.head(8)
```

	0	1	2	3	4	5	6
0	>84 84-67 66-55 54-50 49-45 44-40 39-35 ...	>84	84-67	66-55	54-50	49-45	44-40
1	>84	84-67	66-55	54-50	49-45	44-40	39-35
2	NaN	NaN	NaN	NaN	NaN	NaN	NaN
3	NaN	NaN	NaN	NaN	%	%	%
4	President	Start Date	End Date	NaN	Approving	Disapproving	unsure/no data
5	NaN	NaN	NaN	NaN	NaN	NaN	NaN
6	Donald J. Trump	09/23/2017	09/25/2017	NaN	39	56	5
7	NaN	09/22/2017	09/24/2017	NaN	39	54	7

9. We only matched with one table and the number of rows is very close to the total days between the first and last dates. Looking at the data, it appears that we have indeed found the table we are looking for. The six column names appear to be on line 4. We can go even further and precisely select the rows we want to skip and which row we would like to use for the column names with the skiprows and header parameters. We can also make sure that the start and end dates are coerced correctly to the right data type with the parse_dates parameter:

```
>>> df_list = pd.read_html(trump_url, match='Start Date',
                           attrs={'align':'center'},
                           header=0, skiprows=[0,1,2,3,5],
                           parse_dates=['Start Date',
                                        'End Date'])
>>> trump = df_list[0]
>>> trump.head()
```

	President	Start Date	End Date	Unnamed: 3	Approving	Disapproving	unsure/no data	Unnamed: 7	Unnamed: 8	Unnamed: 9	Unnamed: 10	Unnamed: 11	Unnamed: 12
0	Donald J. Trump	09/23/2017	09/25/2017	NaN	39	56	5	NaN	NaN	NaN	NaN	NaN	NaN
1	NaN	09/22/2017	09/24/2017	NaN	39	54	7	NaN	NaN	NaN	NaN	NaN	NaN
2	NaN	09/21/2017	09/23/2017	NaN	40	54	6	NaN	NaN	NaN	NaN	NaN	NaN
3	NaN	09/20/2017	09/22/2017	NaN	37	56	7	NaN	NaN	NaN	NaN	NaN	NaN
4	NaN	09/19/2017	09/21/2017	NaN	38	56	6	NaN	NaN	NaN	NaN	NaN	NaN

10. This is almost exactly what we want, except for the columns with missing values. Let's use the `dropna` method to drop columns with all values missing:

```
>>> trump = trump.dropna(axis=1, how='all')
>>> trump.head()
```

	President	Start Date	End Date	Approving	Disapproving	unsure/no data
0	Donald J. Trump	2017-09-23	2017-09-25	39	56	5
1	NaN	2017-09-22	2017-09-24	39	54	7
2	NaN	2017-09-21	2017-09-23	40	54	6
3	NaN	2017-09-20	2017-09-22	37	56	7
4	NaN	2017-09-19	2017-09-21	38	56	6

11. Let's fill the missing values in the `President` column in a forward direction with the `ffill` method. Let's first check whether there are any missing values in the other columns:

```
>>> trump.isnull().sum()
President          242
Start Date           0
End Date             0
Approving            0
Disapproving         0
unsure/no data       0
dtype: int64

>>> trump = trump.ffill()
trump.head()
```

	President	Start Date	End Date	Approving	Disapproving	unsure/no data
0	Donald J. Trump	2017-09-23	2017-09-25	39	56	5
1	Donald J. Trump	2017-09-22	2017-09-24	39	54	7
2	Donald J. Trump	2017-09-21	2017-09-23	40	54	6
3	Donald J. Trump	2017-09-20	2017-09-22	37	56	7
4	Donald J. Trump	2017-09-19	2017-09-21	38	56	6

12. Finally, it is important to check the data types to ensure they are correct:

```
>>> trump.dtypes
President                    object
Start Date           datetime64[ns]
End Date             datetime64[ns]
Approving                     int64
Disapproving                  int64
unsure/no data                int64
dtype: object
```

13. Let's build a function with all the steps combined into one to automate the process of retrieving approval data for any President:

```
>>> def get_pres_appr(pres_num):
        base_url = \
'http://www.presidency.ucsb.edu/data/popularity.php?pres={}'
        pres_url = base_url.format(pres_num)
        df_list = pd.read_html(pres_url, match='Start Date',
                               attrs={'align':'center'},
                               header=0, skiprows=[0,1,2,3,5],
                               parse_dates=['Start Date',
                                            'End Date'])
        pres = df_list[0].copy()
        pres = pres.dropna(axis=1, how='all')
        pres['President'] = pres['President'].ffill()
        return pres.sort_values('End Date') \
                   .reset_index(drop=True)
```

14. The only parameter, `pres_num`, denotes the order number of each president. Barack Obama was the 44th President of the United States; pass 44 to the `get_pres_appr` function to retrieve his approval numbers:

```
>>> obama = get_pres_appr(44)
>>> obama.head()
```

	President	Start Date	End Date	Approving	Disapproving	unsure/no data
0	Barack Obama	2009-01-21	2009-01-23	68	12	21
1	Barack Obama	2009-01-22	2009-01-24	69	13	18
2	Barack Obama	2009-01-23	2009-01-25	67	14	19
3	Barack Obama	2009-01-24	2009-01-26	65	15	20
4	Barack Obama	2009-01-25	2009-01-27	64	16	20

15. There is Presidential approval rating data dating back to 1941 during President Franklin Roosevelt's third term. With our custom function along with the `concat` function, it is possible to grab all the presidential approval rating data from this site. For now, let's just grab the approval rating data for the last five presidents and output the first three rows for each President:

```
>>> pres_41_45 = pd.concat([get_pres_appr(x) for x in
range(41,46)],
                            ignore_index=True)
>>> pres_41_45.groupby('President').head(3)
```

	President	Start Date	End Date	Approving	Disapproving	unsure/no data
0	George Bush	1989-01-24	1989-01-26	51	6	43
1	George Bush	1989-02-24	1989-02-27	60	11	27
2	George Bush	1989-02-28	1989-03-02	62	13	24
158	William J. Clinton	1993-01-24	1993-01-26	58	20	22
159	William J. Clinton	1993-01-29	1993-01-31	53	30	16
160	William J. Clinton	1993-02-12	1993-02-14	51	33	15
386	George W. Bush	2001-02-01	2001-02-04	57	25	18
387	George W. Bush	2001-02-09	2001-02-11	57	24	17
388	George W. Bush	2001-02-19	2001-02-21	61	21	16
656	Barack Obama	2009-01-21	2009-01-23	68	12	21
657	Barack Obama	2009-01-22	2009-01-24	69	13	18
658	Barack Obama	2009-01-23	2009-01-25	67	14	19
3443	Donald J. Trump	2017-01-20	2017-01-22	45	45	10
3444	Donald J. Trump	2017-01-21	2017-01-23	45	46	9
3445	Donald J. Trump	2017-01-22	2017-01-24	46	45	9

16. Before continuing, let's determine if there are any dates with multiple approval ratings:

```
>>> pres_41_45['End Date'].value_counts().head(8)
1990-08-26    2
1990-03-11    2
1999-02-09    2
2013-10-10    2
1990-08-12    2
1992-11-22    2
1990-05-22    2
1991-09-30    1
Name: End Date, dtype: int64
```

17. Only a few of the days have duplicate values. To help simplify our analysis, let's keep only the first row where the duplicate date exists:

```
>>> pres_41_45 = pres_41_45.drop_duplicates(subset='End Date')
```

18. Let's get a few summary statistics on the data:

```
>>> pres_41_45.shape
(3679, 6)

>>> pres_41_45['President'].value_counts()
Barack Obama           2786
George W. Bush          270
Donald J. Trump         243
William J. Clinton      227
George Bush             153
Name: President, dtype: int64

>>> pres_41_45.groupby('President', sort=False) \
                 .median().round(1)
```

President	Approving	Disapproving	unsure/no data
George Bush	63.0	22.0	9.0
William J. Clinton	57.0	36.0	0.0
George W. Bush	50.5	45.5	4.0
Barack Obama	47.0	47.0	7.0
Donald J. Trump	39.0	56.0	6.0

19. Let's plot each President's approval rating on the same chart. To do this, we will group by each President, iterate through each group, and individually plot the approval rating for each date:

```
>>> from matplotlib import cm
>>> fig, ax = plt.subplots(figsize=(16,6))

>>> styles = ['-.', '-', ':', '-', ':']
>>> colors = [.9, .3, .7, .3, .9]
>>> groups = pres_41_45.groupby('President', sort=False)

>>> for style, color, (pres, df) in zip(styles, colors, groups):
        df.plot('End Date', 'Approving', ax=ax,
```

```
                      label=pres, style=style, color=cm.Greys(color),
                      title='Presedential Approval Rating')
```

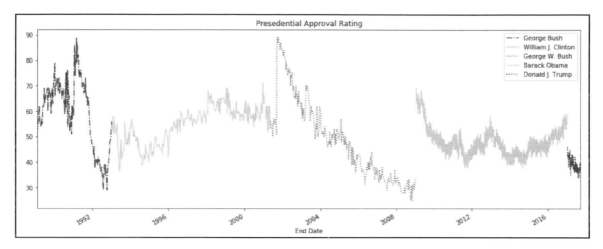

20. This chart places all the Presidents sequentially one after the other. We can compare them on a simpler scale by plotting their approval rating against the number of days in office. Let's create a new variable to represent the number of days in office:

```
>>> days_func = lambda x: x - x.iloc[0]
>>> pres_41_45['Days in Office'] = pres_41_45.groupby('President') \
                                           ['End Date'] \
                                           .transform(days_func)
>>> pres_41_45.groupby('President').head(3)
```

	President	Start Date	End Date	Approving	Disapproving	unsure/no data	Days in Office
0	George Bush	1989-01-24	1989-01-26	51	6	43	0 days
1	George Bush	1989-02-24	1989-02-27	60	11	27	32 days
2	George Bush	1989-02-28	1989-03-02	62	13	24	35 days
158	William J. Clinton	1993-01-24	1993-01-26	58	20	22	0 days
159	William J. Clinton	1993-01-29	1993-01-31	53	30	16	5 days
160	William J. Clinton	1993-02-12	1993-02-14	51	33	15	19 days
386	George W. Bush	2001-02-01	2001-02-04	57	25	18	0 days
387	George W. Bush	2001-02-09	2001-02-11	57	24	17	7 days
388	George W. Bush	2001-02-19	2001-02-21	61	21	16	17 days
656	Barack Obama	2009-01-21	2009-01-23	68	12	21	0 days
657	Barack Obama	2009-01-22	2009-01-24	69	13	18	1 days
658	Barack Obama	2009-01-23	2009-01-25	67	14	19	2 days
3443	Donald J. Trump	2017-01-20	2017-01-22	45	45	10	0 days
3444	Donald J. Trump	2017-01-21	2017-01-23	45	46	9	1 days
3445	Donald J. Trump	2017-01-22	2017-01-24	46	45	9	2 days

21. We have successfully given each row a relative number of days since the start of the presidency. It's interesting that the new column, Days in Office, has a string representation of its value. Let's check its data type:

```
>>> pres_41_45.dtypes
...
Days in Office    timedelta64[ns]
dtype: object
```

22. The Days in Office column is a timedelta64 object with nanosecond precision. This is far more precision than is needed. Let's change the data type to integer by getting just the days:

```
>>> pres_41_45['Days in Office'] = pres_41_45['Days in Office'] \
                                          .dt.days
>>> pres_41_45['Days in Office'].head()
0     0
1    32
2    35
3    43
4    46
Name: Days in Office, dtype: int64
```

23. We could plot this data in a similar fashion to what we did in step 19, but there is a completely different method that doesn't involve any looping. By default, when calling the `plot` method on a DataFrame, pandas attempts to plot each column of data as a line plot and uses the index as the x-axis. Knowing this, let's pivot our data so that each President has his own column for approval rating:

```
>>> pres_pivot = pres_41_45.pivot(index='Days in Office',
                                   columns='President',
                                   values='Approving')
>>> pres_pivot.head()
```

President	Barack Obama	Donald J. Trump	George Bush	George W. Bush	William J. Clinton
Days in Office					
0	68.0	45.0	51.0	57.0	58.0
1	69.0	45.0	NaN	NaN	NaN
2	67.0	46.0	NaN	NaN	NaN
3	65.0	46.0	NaN	NaN	NaN
4	64.0	45.0	NaN	NaN	NaN

24. Now that each President has his own column of approval ratings, we can plot each column directly without grouping. To reduce the clutter in the plot, we will only plot Barack Obama and Donald J. Trump:

```
>>> plot_kwargs = dict(figsize=(16,6), color=cm.gray([.3, .7]),
                       style=['-', '--'], title='Approval Rating')
>>> pres_pivot.loc[:250, ['Donald J. Trump', 'Barack Obama']] \
          .ffill().plot(**plot_kwargs)
```

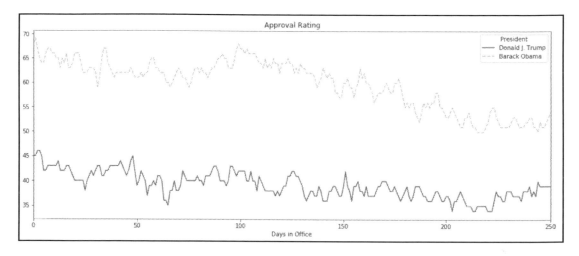

How it works...

It is typical to call `read_html` multiple times before arriving at the table (or tables) that you desire. There are two primary parameters at your disposal to specify a table, `match` and `attrs`. The string provided to `match` is used to find an exact match for the actual text in the table. This is text that will show up on the web page itself. The `attrs` parameter, on the other hand, searches for HTML table attributes found directly after the start of the table tag, `<table`. To see more of the table attributes, visit this page from W3 Schools (`http://bit.ly/2hzUzdD`).

Once we find our table in step 8, we can still take advantage of some other parameters to simplify things. HTML tables don't typically translate directly to nice DataFrames. There are often missing column names, extra rows, and misaligned data. In this recipe, `skiprows` is passed a list of row numbers to skip over when reading the file. They correspond to the rows of missing values in the DataFrame output from step 8. The `header` parameter is also used to specify the location of the column names. Notice that `header` is equal to zero, which may seem wrong at first. Whenever the header parameter is used in conjunction with `skiprows`, the rows are skipped first resulting in a new integer label for each row. The correct column names are in row 4 but as we skipped rows 0 through 3, the new integer label for it is 0.

In step 11, the `ffill` method fills any missing values vertically, going down with the last non-missing value. This method is just a shortcut for `fillna(method='ffill')`.

Step 13 builds a function composed of all the previous steps to automatically get approval ratings from any President, provided you have the order number. There are a few differences in the function. Instead of applying the `ffill` method to the entire DataFrame, we only apply it to the `President` column. In Trump's DataFrame, the other columns had no missing data but this does not guarantee that all the scraped tables will have no missing data in their other columns. The last line of the function sorts the dates in a more natural way for data analysis from the oldest to newest. This changes the order of the index too, so we discard it with `reset_index` to have it begin from zero again.

Step 16 shows a common pandas idiom for collecting multiple, similarly indexed DataFrames into a list before combining them together with the `concat` function. After concatenation into a single DataFrame, we should visually inspect it to ensure its accuracy. One way to do this is to take a glance at the first few rows from each President's section by grouping the data and then using the `head` method on each group.

The summary statistics in step 18 are interesting as each successive President has had lower median approval than the last. Extrapolating the data would lead to naively predicting a negative approval rating within the next several Presidents.

The plotting code in step 19 is fairly complex. You might be wondering why we need to iterate through a `groupby` object, to begin with. In the DataFrame's current structure, it has no ability to plot different groups based on values in a single column. However, step 23 shows you how to set up your DataFrame so that pandas can directly plot each President's data without a loop like this.

To understand the plotting code in step 19, you must first be aware that a `groupby` object is iterable and, when iterating through, yields a tuple containing the current group (here it's just the name of the President) and the sub-DataFrame for just that group. This `groupby` object is zipped together with values controlling the color and linestyle of the plot. We import the colormap module, `cm`, from matplotlib which contains dozens of different colormaps. Passing a float between 0 and 1 chooses a specific color from that colormap and we use it in our `plot` method with the `color` parameter. It is also important to note that we had to create the figure, `fig`, along with a plotting surface, `ax`, to ensure that each approval line was placed on the same plot. At each iteration in the loop, we use the same plotting surface with the identically named parameter, `ax`.

To make a better comparison between Presidents, we create a new column equal to the number of days in office. We subtract the first date from the rest of the dates per President group. When two `datetime64` columns are subtracted, the result is a `timedelta64` object, which represents some length of time, days in this case. If we leave the column with nanosecond precision, the x-axis will similarly display too much precision by using the special `dt` accessor to return the number of days.

A crucial step comes in step 23. We structure the data such that each President has a unique column for their approval rating. Pandas makes a separate line for each column. Finally, in step 24, we use the `.loc` indexer to simultaneously select the first 250 days (rows) along with only the columns for just Trump and Obama. The `ffill` method is used in the rare instances that one of the Presidents has a missing value for a particular day. In Python, it is possible to pass dictionaries that contain the parameter names and their values to functions by preceding them with `**` in a process called **dictionary unpacking**.

There's more...

The plot from step 19 shows quite a lot of noise and the data might be easier to interpret if it were smoothed. One common smoothing method is called the **rolling average**. Pandas offers the `rolling` method for DataFrames and `groupby` objects. It works analogously to the `groupby` method by returning an object waiting for an additional action to be performed on it. When creating it, you must pass the size of the window as the first argument, which can either be an integer or a date offset string.

In this example, we take a 90-day moving average with the date offset string *90D*. The `on` parameter specifies the column from which the rolling window is calculated:

```
>>> pres_rm = pres_41_45.groupby('President', sort=False) \
                  .rolling('90D', on='End Date')['Approving'] \
                  .mean()
>>> pres_rm.head()
President     End Date
George Bush   1989-01-26     51.000000
              1989-02-27     55.500000
              1989-03-02     57.666667
              1989-03-10     58.750000
              1989-03-13     58.200000
Name: Approving, dtype: float64
```

From here, we can restructure the data so that it looks similar to the output from step 23 with the `unstack` method, and then make our plot:

```
>>> styles = ['-.', '-', ':', '-', ':']
>>> colors = [.9, .3, .7, .3, .9]
>>> color = cm.Greys(colors)
>>> title='90 Day Approval Rating Rolling Average'
>>> plot_kwargs = dict(figsize=(16,6), style=styles,
                       color = color, title=title)
>>> correct_col_order = pres_41_45.President.unique()

>>> pres_rm.unstack('President')[correct_col_order].plot(**plot_kwargs)
```

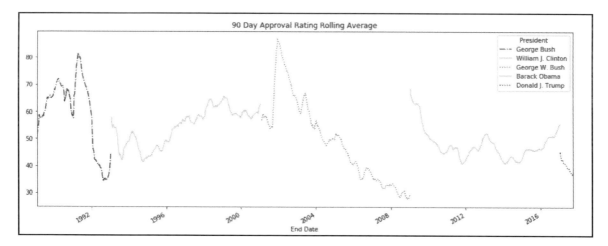

See also

- Colormap references for matplotlib (`http://bit.ly/2yJZOvt`)
- A list of all the date offsets and their aliases (`http://bit.ly/2xO5Yg0`)
- Refer to `chapter 11`, *Visualization with Matplotlib, Pandas, and Seaborn*

Understanding the differences between concat, join, and merge

The merge and join DataFrame (and not Series) methods and the concat function all provide very similar functionality to combine multiple pandas objects together. As they are so similar and they can replicate each other in certain situations, it can get very confusing when and how to use them correctly. To help clarify their differences, take a look at the following outline:

- concat:
  - Pandas function
  - Combines two or more pandas objects vertically or horizontally
  - Aligns only on the index
  - Errors whenever a duplicate appears in the index
  - Defaults to outer join with option for inner

- join:
  - DataFrame method
  - Combines two or more pandas objects horizontally
  - Aligns the calling DataFrame's column(s) or index with the other objects' index (and not the columns)
  - Handles duplicate values on the joining columns/index by performing a cartesian product
  - Defaults to left join with options for inner, outer, and right

- merge:
  - DataFrame method
  - Combines exactly two DataFrames horizontally
  - Aligns the calling DataFrame's column(s)/index with the other DataFrame's column(s)/index
  - Handles duplicate values on the joining columns/index by performing a cartesian product
  - Defaults to inner join with options for left, outer, and right

The first parameter to the join method is `other` which can either be a single DataFrame/Series or a list of any number of DataFrames/Series.

Getting ready

In this recipe, we will do what is required to combine DataFrames. The first situation is simpler with `concat` while the second is simpler with `merge`.

How to do it...

1. Let's read in stock data for 2016, 2017, and 2018 into a list of DataFrames using a loop instead of three different calls to the `read_csv` function. Jupyter notebooks currently only allow a single DataFrame to be displayed on one line. However, there is a way to customize the HTML output with help from the `IPython` library. The user-defined `display_frames` function accepts a list of DataFrames and outputs them all in a single row:

```
>>> from IPython.display import display_html

>>> years = 2016, 2017, 2018
>>> stock_tables = [pd.read_csv('data/stocks_{}.csv'.format(year),
                                index_col='Symbol')
                    for year in years]

>>> def display_frames(frames, num_spaces=0):
        t_style = '<table style="display: inline;"'
        tables_html = [df.to_html().replace('<table', t_style)
                       for df in frames]

        space = ' ' * num_spaces
        display_html(space.join(tables_html), raw=True)

>>> display_frames(stock_tables, 30)
>>> stocks_2016, stocks_2017, stocks_2018 = stock_tables
```

	Shares	Low	High
Symbol			
AAPL	80	95	110
TSLA	50	80	130
WMT	40	55	70

	Shares	Low	High
Symbol			
AAPL	50	120	140
GE	100	30	40
IBM	87	75	95
SLB	20	55	85
TXN	500	15	23
TSLA	100	100	300

	Shares	Low	High
Symbol			
AAPL	40	135	170
AMZN	8	900	1125
TSLA	50	220	400

2. The `concat` function is the only one able to combine DataFrames vertically. Let's do this by passing it the list `stock_tables`:

```
>>> pd.concat(stock_tables, keys=[2016, 2017, 2018])
```

		Shares	Low	High
	Symbol			
2016	AAPL	80	95	110
	TSLA	50	80	130
	WMT	40	55	70
2017	AAPL	50	120	140
	GE	100	30	40
	IBM	87	75	95
	SLB	20	55	85
	TXN	500	15	23
	TSLA	100	100	300
2018	AAPL	40	135	170
	AMZN	8	900	1125
	TSLA	50	220	400

3. It can also combine DataFrames horizontally by changing the `axis` parameter to `columns`:

```
>>> pd.concat(dict(zip(years,stock_tables)), axis='columns')
```

	2016			2017			2018		
	Shares	Low	High	Shares	Low	High	Shares	Low	High
AAPL	80.0	95.0	110.0	50.0	120.0	140.0	40.0	135.0	170.0
AMZN	NaN	NaN	NaN	NaN	NaN	NaN	8.0	900.0	1125.0
GE	NaN	NaN	NaN	100.0	30.0	40.0	NaN	NaN	NaN
IBM	NaN	NaN	NaN	87.0	75.0	95.0	NaN	NaN	NaN
SLB	NaN	NaN	NaN	20.0	55.0	85.0	NaN	NaN	NaN
TSLA	50.0	80.0	130.0	100.0	100.0	300.0	50.0	220.0	400.0
TXN	NaN	NaN	NaN	500.0	15.0	23.0	NaN	NaN	NaN
WMT	40.0	55.0	70.0	NaN	NaN	NaN	NaN	NaN	NaN

4. Now that we have started combining DataFrames horizontally, we can use the `join` and `merge` methods to replicate this functionality of `concat`. Here, we use the `join` method to combine the `stock_2016` and `stock_2017` DataFrames. By default, the DataFrames align on their index. If any of the columns have the same names, then you must supply a value to the `lsuffix` or `rsuffix` parameters to distinguish them in the result:

```
>>> stocks_2016.join(stocks_2017, lsuffix='_2016',
                     rsuffix='_2017', how='outer')
```

Symbol	Shares_2016	Low_2016	High_2016	Shares_2017	Low_2017	High_2017
AAPL	80.0	95.0	110.0	50.0	120.0	140.0
GE	NaN	NaN	NaN	100.0	30.0	40.0
IBM	NaN	NaN	NaN	87.0	75.0	95.0
SLB	NaN	NaN	NaN	20.0	55.0	85.0
TSLA	50.0	80.0	130.0	100.0	100.0	300.0
TXN	NaN	NaN	NaN	500.0	15.0	23.0
WMT	40.0	55.0	70.0	NaN	NaN	NaN

5. To exactly replicate the output of the `concat` function from step 3, we can pass a list of DataFrames to the `join` method:

```
>>> other = [stocks_2017.add_suffix('_2017'),
             stocks_2018.add_suffix('_2018')]
>>> stocks_2016.add_suffix('_2016').join(other, how='outer')
```

	Shares_2016	Low_2016	High_2016	Shares_2017	Low_2017	High_2017	Shares_2018	Low_2018	High_2018
AAPL	80.0	95.0	110.0	50.0	120.0	140.0	40.0	135.0	170.0
AMZN	NaN	NaN	NaN	NaN	NaN	NaN	8.0	900.0	1125.0
GE	NaN	NaN	NaN	100.0	30.0	40.0	NaN	NaN	NaN
IBM	NaN	NaN	NaN	87.0	75.0	95.0	NaN	NaN	NaN
SLB	NaN	NaN	NaN	20.0	55.0	85.0	NaN	NaN	NaN
TSLA	50.0	80.0	130.0	100.0	100.0	300.0	50.0	220.0	400.0
TXN	NaN	NaN	NaN	500.0	15.0	23.0	NaN	NaN	NaN
WMT	40.0	55.0	70.0	NaN	NaN	NaN	NaN	NaN	NaN

6. Let's check whether they actually are exactly equal:

```
>>> stock_join = stocks_2016.add_suffix('_2016').join(other,
                                                      how='outer')
>>> stock_concat = pd.concat(dict(zip(years, stock_tables)),
                             axis='columns')
>>> level_1 = stock_concat.columns.get_level_values(1)
>>> level_0 = stock_concat.columns.get_level_values(0).astype(str)
>>> stock_concat.columns = level_1 + '_' + level_0
>>> stock_join.equals(stock_concat)
True
```

7. Now, let's turn to `merge` that, unlike `concat` and `join`, can combine exactly two DataFrames together. By default, `merge` attempts to align the values in the columns that have the same name for each of the DataFrames. However, you can choose to have it align on the index by setting the boolean parameters `left_index` and `right_index` to `True`. Let's merge the 2016 and 2017 stock data together:

```
>>> stocks_2016.merge(stocks_2017, left_index=True,
                      right_index=True)
```

[375]

Symbol	Shares_x	Low_x	High_x	Shares_y	Low_y	High_y
AAPL	80	95	110	50	120	140
TSLA	50	80	130	100	100	300

8. By default, merge uses an inner join and automatically supplies suffixes for identically named columns. Let's change to an outer join and then perform another outer join of the 2018 data to exactly replicate `concat`:

```
>>> step1 = stocks_2016.merge(stocks_2017, left_index=True,
                              right_index=True, how='outer',
                              suffixes=('_2016', '_2017'))

>>> stock_merge = step1.merge(stocks_2018.add_suffix('_2018'),
                              left_index=True, right_index=True,
                              how='outer')

>>> stock_concat.equals(stock_merge)
True
```

9. Now let's turn our comparison to datasets where we are interested in aligning together the values of columns and not the index or column labels themselves. The `merge` method is built exactly for this situation. Let's take a look at two new small datasets, `food_prices` and `food_transactions`:

```
>>> names = ['prices', 'transactions']
>>> food_tables = [pd.read_csv('data/food_{}.csv'.format(name))
                   for name in names]
>>> food_prices, food_transactions = food_tables
>>> display_frames(food_tables, 30)
```

	item	store	price	Date
0	pear	A	0.99	2017
1	pear	B	1.99	2017
2	peach	A	2.99	2017
3	peach	B	3.49	2017
4	banana	A	0.39	2017
5	banana	B	0.49	2017
6	steak	A	5.99	2017
7	steak	B	6.99	2017
8	steak	B	4.99	2015

	custid	item	store	quantity
0	1	pear	A	5
1	1	banana	A	10
2	2	steak	B	3
3	2	pear	B	1
4	2	peach	B	2
5	2	steak	B	1
6	2	coconut	B	4

10. If we wanted to find the total amount of each transaction, we would need to join these tables on the `item` and `store` columns:

```
>>> food_transactions.merge(food_prices, on=['item', 'store'])
```

	custid	item	store	quantity	price	Date
0	1	pear	A	5	0.99	2017
1	1	banana	A	10	0.39	2017
2	2	steak	B	3	6.99	2017
3	2	steak	B	3	4.99	2015
4	2	steak	B	1	6.99	2017
5	2	steak	B	1	4.99	2015
6	2	pear	B	1	1.99	2017
7	2	peach	B	2	3.49	2017

11. The price is now aligned correctly with its corresponding item and store, but there is a problem. Customer 2 has a total of four `steak` items. As the `steak` item appears twice in each table for store B, a Cartesian product takes place between them, resulting in four rows. Also, notice that the item, `coconut`, is missing because there was no corresponding price for it. Let's fix both of these issues:

```
>>> food_transactions.merge(food_prices.query('Date == 2017'),
                            how='left')
```

	custid	item	store	quantity	price	Date
0	1	pear	A	5	0.99	2017.0
1	1	banana	A	10	0.39	2017.0
2	2	steak	B	3	6.99	2017.0
3	2	pear	B	1	1.99	2017.0
4	2	peach	B	2	3.49	2017.0
5	2	steak	B	1	6.99	2017.0
6	2	coconut	B	4	NaN	NaN

12. We can replicate this with the `join` method but we must first put the joining columns of the `food_prices` DataFrame into the index:

```
>>> food_prices_join = food_prices.query('Date == 2017') \
                                  .set_index(['item', 'store'])
>>> food_prices_join
```

item	store	price	Date
pear	A	0.99	2017
	B	1.99	2017
peach	A	2.99	2017
	B	3.49	2017
banana	A	0.39	2017
	B	0.49	2017
steak	A	5.99	2017
	B	6.99	2017

13. The `join` method only aligns with the index of the passed DataFrame but can use the index or the columns of the calling DataFrame. To use columns for alignment on the calling DataFrame, you will need to pass them to the `on` parameter:

```
>>> food_transactions.join(food_prices join, on=['item', 'store'])
```

14. The output matches the result from step 11 exactly. To replicate this with the `concat` method, you would need to put the item and store columns into the index of both DataFrames. However, in this particular case, an error would be produced as a duplicate index value occurs in at least one of the DataFrames (with item `steak` and store B):

```
>>> pd.concat([food_transactions.set_index(['item', 'store']),
               food_prices.set_index(['item', 'store'])],
              axis='columns')
Exception: cannot handle a non-unique multi-index!
```

How it works...

It can get tedious to repeatedly write the `read_csv` function when importing many DataFrames at the same time. One way to automate this process is to put all the file names in a list and iterate through them with a for loop. This was done in step 1 with a list comprehension.

The rest of this step builds a function to display multiple DataFrames on the same line of output in a Jupyter notebook. All DataFrames have a `to_html` method, which returns a raw HTML string representation of the table. The CSS (cascading style sheet) of each table is changed by altering the `display` attribute to *inline* so that elements get displayed horizontally next to one another rather than vertically. To properly render the table in the notebook, you must use the helper function `read_html` provided by the IPython library.

At the end of step 1, we unpack the list of DataFrames into their own appropriately named variables so that each individual table may be easily and clearly referenced. The nice thing about having a list of DataFrames is that, it is the exact requirement for the `concat` function, as seen in step 2. Notice how step 2 uses the `keys` parameter to name each chunk of data. This can be also be accomplished by passing a dictionary to `concat`, as done in step 3.

In step 4, we must change the type of `join` to `outer` to include all of the rows in the passed DataFrame that do not have an index present in the calling DataFrame. In step 5, the passed list of DataFrames cannot have any columns in common. Although there is an `rsuffix` parameter, it only works when passing a single DataFrame and not a list of them. To work around this limitation, we change the names of the columns beforehand with the `add_suffix` method, and then call the `join` method.

In step 7, we use `merge`, which defaults to aligning on all column names that are the same in both DataFrames. To change this default behavior, and align on the index of either one or both, set the `left_index` or `right_index` parameters to `True`. Step 8 finishes the replication with two calls to merge. As you can see, when you are aligning multiple DataFrames on their index, `concat` is usually going to be a far better choice than merge.

In step 9, we switch gears to focus on a situation where `merge` has the advantage. The `merge` method is the only one capable of aligning both the calling and passed DataFrame by column values. Step 10 shows you how easy it is to merge two DataFrames. The `on` parameter is not necessary but provided for clarity.

Unfortunately, it is very easy to duplicate or drop data when combining DataFrames, as shown in step 10. It is vital to take some time to do some sanity checks after combining data. In this instance, the `food_prices` dataset had a duplicate price for `steak` in store B so we eliminated this row by querying for only the current year in step 11. We also change to a left join to ensure that each transaction is kept regardless if a price is present or not.

It is possible to use join in these instances but all the columns in the passed DataFrame must be moved into the index first. Finally, concat is going to be a poor choice whenever you intend to align data by values in their columns.

There's more...

It is possible to read all files from a particular directory into DataFrames without knowing their names. Python provides a few ways to iterate through directories, with the glob module being a popular choice. The gas prices directory contains five different CSV files, each having weekly prices of a particular grade of gas beginning from 2007. Each file has just two columns--the date for the week and the price. This is a perfect situation to iterate through all the files, read them into DataFrames, and combine them all together with the concat function. The glob module has the glob function, which takes a single parameter--the location of the directory you would like to iterate through as a string. To get all the files in the directory, use the string *. In this example, *.csv returns only files that end in .csv. The result from the glob function is a list of string filenames, which can be directly passed to the read_csv function:

```
>>> import glob

>>> df_list = []
>>> for filename in glob.glob('data/gas prices/*.csv'):
        df_list.append(pd.read_csv(filename, index_col='Week',
                   parse_dates=['Week']))

>>> gas = pd.concat(df_list, axis='columns')
>>> gas.head()
```

Week	All Grades	Diesel	Midgrade	Premium	Regular
2017-09-25	2.701	2.788	2.859	3.105	2.583
2017-09-18	2.750	2.791	2.906	3.151	2.634
2017-09-11	2.800	2.802	2.953	3.197	2.685
2017-09-04	2.794	2.758	2.946	3.191	2.679
2017-08-28	2.513	2.605	2.668	2.901	2.399

Once we have created the engine, selecting entire tables into DataFrames is very easy with the `read_sql_table` function in step 2. Each of the tables in the database has a primary key uniquely identifying each row. It is identified graphically with a key symbol in the diagram. In step 3, we link genres to tracks through `GenreId`. As we only care about the track length, we trim the tracks DataFrame down to just the columns we need before performing the merge. Once the tables have merged, we can answer the query with a basic `groupby` operation.

We go one step further and convert the integer milliseconds into a Timedelta object that is far easier to read. The key is passing in the correct unit of measurement as a string. Now that we have a Timedelta Series, we can use the `dt` attribute to access the `floor` method, which rounds the time down to the nearest second.

The query required to answer step 5 involves three tables. We can trim the tables down significantly to only the columns we need by passing them to the `columns` parameter. When using `merge`, the joining columns are not kept when they have the same name. In step 6, we could have assigned a column for the price times quantity with the following:

```
cust_inv['Total'] = cust_inv['Quantity'] * cust_inv['UnitPrice']
```

There is nothing wrong with assigning columns in this manner. We chose to dynamically create a new column with the assign method to allow a continuous chain of methods.

There's more...

If you are adept with SQL, you can write a SQL query as a string and pass it to the `read_sql_query` function. For example, the following will reproduce the output from step 4:

```
>>> sql_string1 = '''
    select
        Name,
        time(avg(Milliseconds) / 1000, 'unixepoch') as avg_time
    from (
            select
                g.Name,
                t.Milliseconds
            from
                genres as g
            join
                tracks as t
                on
                    g.genreid == t.genreid
        )
```

```
     group by
           Name
     order by
           avg_time
''' 
>>> pd.read_sql_query(sql_string1, engine)
```

	Name	avg_time
0	Rock And Roll	00:02:14
1	Opera	00:02:54
2	Hip Hop/Rap	00:02:58

To reproduce the answer from step 6, use the following SQL query:

```
>>> sql_string2 = '''
    select
            c.customerid,
            c.FirstName,
            c.LastName,
            sum(ii.quantity * ii.unitprice) as Total
    from
        customers as c
    join
        invoices as i
            on c.customerid = i.customerid
    join
        invoice_items as ii
            on i.invoiceid = ii.invoiceid
    group by
        c.customerid, c.FirstName, c.LastName
    order by
        Total desc
''' 
>>> pd.read_sql_query(sql_string2, engine)
```

	CustomerId	FirstName	LastName	Total
0	6	Helena	Holý	49.62
1	26	Richard	Cunningham	47.62
2	57	Luis	Rojas	46.62

See also

- All engine configurations for *SQLAlchemy* (`http://bit.ly/2kb07vV`)
- Pandas official documentation on *SQL Queries* (`http://bit.ly/2fFsOQ8`

10
Time Series Analysis

In this chapter, we will cover the following topics:

- Understanding the difference between Python and pandas date tools
- Slicing time series intelligently
- Using methods that only work with a DatetimeIndex
- Counting the number of weekly crimes
- Aggregating weekly crime and traffic accidents separately
- Measuring crime by weekday and year
- Grouping with anonymous functions with a DatetimeIndex
- Grouping by a Timestamp and another column
- Finding the last time crime was 20% lower with `merge asof`

Introduction

The roots of pandas lay in analyzing financial time series data. The author, Wes McKinney, was not satisfied with the available Python tools at that time, and decided to build pandas to support his own needs at the hedge fund he was working at. Broadly speaking, time series are simply points of data gathered over time. Most typically, the time is evenly spaced between each data point. Pandas has excellent functionality with regards to manipulating dates, aggregating over different time periods, sampling different periods of time, and much more.

Understanding the difference between Python and pandas date tools

Before we get to pandas, it can help to be aware of and understand core Python's date and time functionality. The datetime module provides three distinct data types, date, time, and datetime. Formally, a date is a moment in time consisting of just the year, month, and day. For instance, June 7, 2013 would be a date. A time consists of hours, minutes, seconds, and microseconds (one-millionth of a second) and is unattached to any date. An example of time would be 12 hours and 30 minutes. A datetime consists of both the elements of a date and time together.

On the other hand, pandas has a single object to encapsulate date and time called a Timestamp. It has nanosecond (one-billionth of a second) precision and is derived from NumPy's datetime64 data type. Both Python and pandas each have a timedelta object that is useful when doing date addition/subtraction.

Getting ready

In this recipe, we will first explore Python's datetime module and then turn to the corresponding and superior date tools in pandas.

How to do it...

1. Let's begin by importing the datetime module into our namespace and creating a date, time, and datetime object:

```
>>> import datetime

>>> date = datetime.date(year=2013, month=6, day=7)
>>> time = datetime.time(hour=12, minute=30,
                         second=19, microsecond=463198)
>>> dt = datetime.datetime(year=2013, month=6, day=7,
                           hour=12, minute=30, second=19,
                           microsecond=463198)

>>> print("date is ", date)
>>> print("time is", time)
>>> print("datetime is", dt)

date is 2013-06-07
```

```
time is 12:30:19.463198
datetime is 2013-06-07 12:30:19.463198
```

2. Let's construct and print out a `timedelta` object, the other major data type from the `datetime` module:

```
>>> td = datetime.timedelta(weeks=2, days=5, hours=10,
                            minutes=20, seconds=6.73,
                            milliseconds=99, microseconds=8)
>>> print(td)
19 days, 10:20:06.829008
```

3. Add/subtract this `timedelta` to the `date` and `datetime` objects from step 1:

```
>>> print('new date is', date + td)
>>> print('new datetime is', dt + td)
new date is 2013-06-26
new datetime is 2013-06-26 22:50:26.292206
```

4. Attempting to add a `timedelta` to a `time` object isn't possible:

```
>>> time + td
TypeError: unsupported operand type(s) for +: 'datetime.time' and
'datetime.timedelta'
```

5. Let's turn to pandas and its `Timestamp` object, which is a moment in time with nanosecond precision. The `Timestamp` constructor is very flexible, and handles a wide variety of inputs:

```
>>> pd.Timestamp(year=2012, month=12, day=21, hour=5,
                 minute=10, second=8, microsecond=99)
Timestamp('2012-12-21 05:10:08.000099')

>>> pd.Timestamp('2016/1/10')
Timestamp('2016-01-10 00:00:00')

>>> pd.Timestamp('2014-5/10')
Timestamp('2014-05-10 00:00:00')

>>> pd.Timestamp('Jan 3, 2019 20:45.56')
Timestamp('2019-01-03 20:45:33')

>>> pd.Timestamp('2016-01-05T05:34:43.123456789')
Timestamp('2016-01-05 05:34:43.123456789')
```

6. It's also possible to pass in a single integer or float to the `Timestamp` constructor which returns a date equivalent to the number of nanoseconds after the Unix epoch, which is January 1, 1970:

```
>>> pd.Timestamp(500)
Timestamp('1970-01-01 00:00:00.000000500')

>>> pd.Timestamp(5000, unit='D')
Timestamp('1983-09-10 00:00:00')
```

7. Pandas provides the `to_datetime` function that works fairly similarly to the `Timestamp` constructor, but comes with a few different parameters for special situations. See the following examples:

```
>>> pd.to_datetime('2015-5-13')
Timestamp('2015-05-13 00:00:00')

>>> pd.to_datetime('2015-13-5', dayfirst=True)
Timestamp('2015-05-13 00:00:00')

>>> pd.to_datetime('Start Date: Sep 30, 2017 Start Time: 1:30 pm',
                  format='Start Date: %b %d, %Y Start Time: %I:%M %p')
Timestamp('2017-09-30 13:30:00')

>>> pd.to_datetime(100, unit='D', origin='2013-1-1')
Timestamp('2013-04-11 00:00:00')
```

8. The `to_datetime` function comes equipped with even more functionality. It is capable of converting entire lists or Series of strings or integers to Timestamps. Since we are far more likely to interact with Series or DataFrames and not single scalar values, you are far more likely to use `to_datetime` than `Timestamp`:

```
>>> s = pd.Series([10, 100, 1000, 10000])
>>> pd.to_datetime(s, unit='D')
0    1970-01-11
1    1970-04-11
2    1972-09-27
3    1997-05-19
dtype: datetime64[ns]

>>> s = pd.Series(['12-5-2015', '14-1-2013',
                  '20/12/2017', '40/23/2017'])
>>> pd.to_datetime(s, dayfirst=True, errors='coerce')
0    2015-05-12
1    2013-01-14
2    2017-12-20
```

```
3              NaT
dtype: datetime64[ns]

>>> pd.to_datetime(['Aug 3 1999 3:45:56', '10/31/2017'])
DatetimeIndex(['1999-08-03 03:45:56',
                '2017-10-31 00:00:00'], dtype='datetime64[ns]',
freq=None)
```

9. Analogously to the `Timestamp` constructor and the `to_datetime` function, pandas has `Timedelta` and `to_timedelta` to represent an amount of time. Both the `Timedelta` constructor and the `to_timedelta` function can create a single `Timedelta` object. Like `to_datetime`, `to_timedelta` has quite a bit more functionality and can convert entire lists or Series into `Timedelta` objects.

```
>>> pd.Timedelta('12 days 5 hours 3 minutes 123456789 nanoseconds')
Timedelta('12 days 05:03:00.123456')

>>> pd.Timedelta(days=5, minutes=7.34)
Timedelta('5 days 00:07:20.400000')

>>> pd.Timedelta(100, unit='W')
Timedelta('700 days 00:00:00')

>>> pd.to_timedelta('67:15:45.454')
Timedelta('2 days 19:15:45.454000')

>>> s = pd.Series([10, 100])
>>> pd.to_timedelta(s, unit='s')
0    00:00:10
1    00:01:40
dtype: timedelta64[ns]

>>> time_strings = ['2 days 24 minutes 89.67 seconds',
                    '00:45:23.6']
>>> pd.to_timedelta(time_strings)
TimedeltaIndex(['2 days 00:25:29.670000',
                '0 days 00:45:23.600000'], dtype='timedelta64[ns]',
freq=None)
```

10. Timedeltas may be added or subtracted from Timestamps and from each other. They may even be divided from each other to return a float:

```
>>> pd.Timedelta('12 days 5 hours 3 minutes') * 2
Timedelta('24 days 10:06:00')

>>> pd.Timestamp('1/1/2017') + \
    pd.Timedelta('12 days 5 hours 3 minutes') * 2
```

```
Timestamp('2017 01-25 10:06:00')

>>> td1 = pd.to_timedelta([10, 100], unit='s')
>>> td2 = pd.to_timedelta(['3 hours', '4 hours'])
>>> td1 + td2
TimedeltaIndex(['03:00:10', '04:01:40'],
               dtype='timedelta64[ns]', freq=None)

>>> pd.Timedelta('12 days') / pd.Timedelta('3 days')
4.0
```

11. Both Timestamps and Timedeltas have a large numbera of features available as attributes and methods. Let's sample a few of them:

```
>>> ts = pd.Timestamp('2016-10-1 4:23:23.9')

>>> ts.ceil('h')
Timestamp('2016-10-01 05:00:00'

>>> ts.year, ts.month, ts.day, ts.hour, ts.minute, ts.second
(2016, 10, 1, 4, 23, 23)

>>> ts.dayofweek, ts.dayofyear, ts.daysinmonth
(5, 275, 31)

>>> ts.to_pydatetime()
datetime.datetime(2016, 10, 1, 4, 23, 23, 900000)

>>> td = pd.Timedelta(125.8723, unit='h')
>>> td
Timedelta('5 days 05:52:20.280000')

>>> td.round('min')
Timedelta('5 days 05:52:00')

>>> td.components
Components(days=5, hours=5, minutes=52, seconds=20,
milliseconds=280, microseconds=0, nanoseconds=0)

>>> td.total_seconds()
453140.28
```

How it works...

The datetime module is part of the Python standard library, and is very popular and widely used. For this reason, it is a good idea to have some familiarity with it, as you will likely cross paths with it. The datetime module is actually fairly simple with a total of only six types of objects: date, time, datetime, timedelta along with two others on timezones. The pandas Timestamp and Timedelta objects have all the functionality of their datetime module counterparts and more. It will be possible to remain completely in pandas when working with time series.

Step 1 shows how to create datetimes, dates, times, and timedeltas with the datetime module. Only integers may be used as each component of the date or time, and are passed as separate arguments. Compare this to step 5 where the pandas Timestamp constructor can accept the same components as arguments, as well as a wide variety of date strings. In addition to integer components and strings, step 6 shows how a single numeric scalar can be used as a date. The units of this scalar are defaulted to *nanoseconds* (*ns*) but are changed to *days* (*D*) in the second statement with the other options being *hours* (*h*), *minutes* (*m*), *seconds* (*s*), *milliseconds* (*ms*), and *microseconds* (*μs*).

Step 2 details the construction of the datetime module's timedelta object with all of its parameters. Again, compare this to the pandas Timedelta constructor shown in step 9, which accepts these same parameters along with strings and scalar numerics.

In addition to the Timestamp and Timedelta constructors, which are only capable of creating a single object, the to_datetime and to_timedelta functions can convert entire sequences of integers or strings to the desired type. These functions also provide several more parameters not available with the constructors. One of these parameters is errors, which is defaulted to the string value *raise* but can also be set to *ignore* or *coerce*. Whenever a string date is unable to be converted, the errors parameter determines what action to take. When set to *raise*, an exception is raised and program execution stops. When set to *ignore*, the original sequence gets returned as it was prior to entering the function. When set to *coerce*, the NaT (not a time) object is used to represent the new value. The second statement of step 8 converts all values to a Timestamp correctly, except for the last one, which is forced to become NaT.

Another one of these parameters available only to to_datetime is format, which is particularly useful whenever a string contains a particular date pattern that is not automatically recognized by pandas. In the third statement of step 7, we have a datetime enmeshed inside some other characters. We substitute the date and time pieces of the string with their respective **formatting directives**.

A date formatting directive appears as a single percentage sign, %, followed by a single character. Each directive specifies some part of a date or time. See the official Python documentation for a table of all the directives (`http://bit.ly/2kePoRe`).

There's more...

The date formatting directive can actually make quite a large difference when converting a large sequence of strings to Timestamps. Whenever pandas uses `to_datetime` to convert a sequence of strings to Timestamps, it searches a large number of different string combinations that represent dates. This is true even if all the strings have the same format. With the `format` parameter, we can specify the exact date format, so that pandas doesn't have to search for the correct one each time. Let's create a list of dates as strings and time their conversion to Timestamps both with and without a formatting directive:

```
>>> date_string_list = ['Sep 30 1984'] * 10000

>>> %timeit pd.to_datetime(date_string_list, format='%b %d %Y')
35.6 ms ± 1.47 ms per loop (mean ± std. dev. of 7 runs, 10 loops each)

>>> %timeit pd.to_datetime(date_string_list)
1.31 s ± 63.3 ms per loop (mean ± std. dev. of 7 runs, 1 loop each)
```

Providing the formatting directive resulted in a 40 times improvement in performance.

See also

- Python official documentation of the `datetime` module (`http://bit.ly/2xIjd2b`)
- Pandas official documentation for *Time Series* (`http://bit.ly/2xQcani`)
- Pandas official for *Time Deltas* (`http://bit.ly/2yQTVMQ`)

Slicing time series intelligently

DataFrame selection and slicing was thoroughly covered in Chapter 4, *Selecting Subsets of Data*. When the DataFrame posses a `DatetimeIndex`, even more opportunities arise for selection and slicing.

Getting ready

In this recipe, we will use partial date matching to select and slice a DataFrame with a `DatetimeIndex`.

How to do it...

1. Read in the Denver `crimes` dataset from the `hdf5` file `crimes.h5`, and output the column data types and the first few rows. The `hdf5` file format allows efficient storage of large scientific data and is completely different from a CSV text file.

   ```
   >>> crime = pd.read_hdf('data/crime.h5', 'crime')
   >>> crime.dtypes
   OFFENSE_TYPE_ID                 category
   OFFENSE_CATEGORY_ID             category
   REPORTED_DATE              datetime64[ns]
   GEO_LON                          float64
   GEO_LAT                          float64
   NEIGHBORHOOD_ID                 category
   IS_CRIME                           int64
   IS_TRAFFIC                         int64
   dtype: object
   ```

2. Notice that there are three categorical columns and a `Timestamp` (denoted by NumPy's `datetime64` object). These data types were stored whenever the data file was created, unlike a CSV file, which only stores raw text. Set the `REPORTED_DATE` column as the index in order to make intelligent Timestamp slicing possible:

   ```
   >>> crime = crime.set_index('REPORTED_DATE')
   >>> crime.head()
   ```

REPORTED_DATE	OFFENSE_TYPE_ID	OFFENSE_CATEGORY_ID	GEO_LON	GEO_LAT	NEIGHBORHOOD_ID	IS_CRIME	IS_TRAFFIC
2014-06-29 02:01:00	traffic-accident-dui-duid	traffic-accident	-105.000149	39.745753	cbd	0	1
2014-06-29 01:54:00	vehicular-eluding-no-chase	all-other-crimes	-104.884660	39.738702	east-colfax	1	0
2014-06-29 02:00:00	disturbing-the-peace	public-disorder	-105.020719	39.706674	athmar-park	1	0
2014-06-29 02:18:00	curfew	public-disorder	-105.001552	39.769505	sunnyside	1	0
2014-06-29 04:17:00	aggravated-assault	aggravated-assault	-105.018557	39.679229	college-view-south-platte	1	0

3. As usual, it is possible to select all the rows equal to a single index by passing that value to the `.loc` indexing operator:

```
>>> crime.loc['2016-05-12 16:45:00']
```

REPORTED_DATE	OFFENSE_TYPE_ID	OFFENSE_CATEGORY_ID	GEO_LON	GEO_LAT	NEIGHBORHOOD_ID	IS_CRIME	IS_TRAFFIC
2016-05-12 16:45:00	traffic-accident	traffic-accident	-104.847024	39.779596	montbello	0	1
2016-05-12 16:45:00	traffic-accident	traffic-accident	-105.049180	39.769296	west-highland	0	1
2016-05-12 16:45:00	fraud-identity-theft	white-collar-crime	-104.931971	39.717359	hilltop	1	0

4. With a `Timestamp` in the index, it is possible to select all rows that partially match an index value. For instance, if we wanted all the crimes from May 5, 2016, we would simply select it as follows:

```
>>> crime.loc['2016-05-12']
```

REPORTED_DATE	OFFENSE_TYPE_ID	OFFENSE_CATEGORY_ID	GEO_LON	GEO_LAT	NEIGHBORHOOD_ID	IS_CRIME	IS_TRAFFIC
2016-05-12 23:51:00	criminal-mischief-other	public-disorder	-105.017241	39.705845	athmar-park	1	0
2016-05-12 18:40:00	liquor-possession	drug-alcohol	-104.995692	39.747875	cbd	1	0
...	...	...	...	...	...	...	...
2016-05-12 15:59:00	menacing-felony-w-weap	aggravated-assault	-104.935172	39.723703	hilltop	1	0
2016-05-12 16:39:00	assault-dv	other-crimes-against-persons	-104.974700	39.740555	north-capitol-hill	1	0

243 rows × 7 columns

5. Not only can you select a single date inexactly, but you can do so for an entire month, year, or even hour of the day:

```
>>> crime.loc['2016-05'].shape
(8012, 7)

>>> crime.loc['2016'].shape
(91076, 7)

>>> crime.loc['2016-05-12 03'].shape
(4, 7)
```

6. The selection strings may also contain the name of the month:

```
>>> crime.loc['Dec 2015'].sort_index()
```

REPORTED_DATE	OFFENSE_TYPE_ID	OFFENSE_CATEGORY_ID	GEO_LON	GEO_LAT	NEIGHBORHOOD_ID	IS_CRIME	IS_TRAFFIC
2015-12-01 00:48:00	drug-cocaine-possess	drug-alcohol	-104.891681	39.740155	east-colfax	1	0
2015-12-01 00:48:00	theft-of-motor-vehicle	auto-theft	-104.891681	39.740155	east-colfax	1	0
...	...	...	...	...	...	...	...
2015-12-31 23:45:00	violation-of-restraining-order	all-other-crimes	-105.034887	39.741827	west-colfax	1	0
2015-12-31 23:50:00	weapon-poss-illegal-dangerous	all-other-crimes	-105.032769	39.709188	westwood	1	0

6907 rows × 7 columns

7. Many other string patterns with month name included also work:

```
>>> crime.loc['2016 Sep, 15'].shape
(252, 7)

>>> crime.loc['21st October 2014 05'].shape
(4, 7)
```

8. In addition to selection, you may use the slice notation to select precise ranges of data:

```
>>> crime.loc['2015-3-4':'2016-1-1'].sort_index()
```

	OFFENSE_TYPE_ID	OFFENSE_CATEGORY_ID	GEO_LON	GEO_LAT	NEIGHBORHOOD_ID	IS_CRIME	IS_TRAFFIC
REPORTED_DATE							
2015-03-04 00:11:00	assault-dv	other-crimes-against-persons	-105.021966	39.770883	sunnyside	1	0
2015-03-04 00:19:00	assault-dv	other-crimes-against-persons	-104.978988	39.748799	five-points	1	0
...	...	...	...	...	...	...	...
2016-01-01 23:45:00	drug-cocaine-possess	drug-alcohol	-104.987310	39.753598	five-points	1	0
2016-01-01 23:48:00	drug-poss-paraphernalia	drug-alcohol	-104.986020	39.752541	five-points	1	0

75403 rows × 7 columns

9. Notice that all crimes committed on the end date regardless of the time are included in the returned result. This is true for any result using the label-based .loc indexer. You can provide as much precision (or lack thereof) to any start or end portion of the slice:

```
>>> crime.loc['2015-3-4 22':'2016-1-1 11:45:00'].sort_index()
```

	OFFENSE_TYPE_ID	OFFENSE_CATEGORY_ID	GEO_LON	GEO_LAT	NEIGHBORHOOD_ID	IS_CRIME	IS_TRAFFIC
REPORTED_DATE							
2015-03-04 22:25:00	traffic-accident-hit-and-run	traffic-accident	-104.973896	39.769064	five-points	0	1
2015-03-04 22:30:00	traffic-accident	traffic-accident	-104.906412	39.632816	hampden-south	0	1
...	...	...	...	...	...	...	...
2016-01-01 23:40:00	robbery-business	robbery	-105.039236	39.726157	villa-park	1	0
2016-01-01 23:45:00	drug-cocaine-possess	drug-alcohol	-104.987310	39.753598	five-points	1	0

75175 rows × 7 columns

How it works...

One of the many nice features of hdf5 files is their ability to preserve the data types of each column, which substantially reduces the memory needed. In this case, three of these columns are stored as a pandas category instead of as an object. Storing them as object will lead to a four times increase in memory usage:

```
>>> mem_cat = crime.memory_usage().sum()
>>> mem_obj = crime.astype({'OFFENSE_TYPE_ID':'object',
                            'OFFENSE_CATEGORY_ID':'object',
                            'NEIGHBORHOOD_ID':'object'}) \
                 .memory_usage(deep=True).sum()
>>> mb = 2 ** 20
>>> round(mem_cat / mb, 1), round(mem_obj / mb, 1)
(29.4, 122.7)
```

In order to intelligently select and slice rows by date using the indexing operator, the index must contain date values. In step 2, we move the REPORTED_DATE column into the index and formally create a DatetimeIndex as the new index:

```
>>> crime.index[:2]
DatetimeIndex(['2014-06-29 02:01:00', '2014-06-29 01:54:00'],
dtype='datetime64[ns]', name='REPORTED_DATE', freq=None)
```

With a DatetimeIndex, a huge variety of strings may be used to select rows with the .loc indexer. In fact, all strings that can be sent to the pandas Timestamp constructor will work here. Surprisingly, it is actually not necessary to use the .loc indexer for any of the selections or slices in this recipe. The indexing operator by itself will work in exactly the same manner. For instance, the second statement of step 6 may be written as crime['21st October 2014 05']. The indexing operator is normally reserved for columns but flexibly allows for Timestamps to be used whenever there exists a DatetimeIndex.

Personally, I prefer using the .loc indexer when selecting rows and would always use it over the indexing operator by itself. The .loc indexer is explicit and the first value passed to it is always used to select rows.

Steps 8 and 9 show how slicing works in the same manner as selection from the previous steps. Any date that partially matches either the start or end value of the slice is included in the result.

There's more...

Our original crimes DataFrame was not sorted and slicing still worked as expected. Sorting the index will lead to large gains in performance. Let's see the difference with slicing done from step 8:

```
>>> %timeit crime.loc['2015-3-4':'2016-1-1']
39.6 ms ± 2.77 ms per loop (mean ± std. dev. of 7 runs, 10 loops each)

>>> crime_sort = crime.sort_index()
>>> %timeit crime_sort.loc['2015-3-4':'2016-1-1']
758 µs ± 42.1 µs per loop (mean ± std. dev. of 7 runs, 1000 loops each)
```

The sorted DataFrame provides an impressive 50 times performance improvement over the original.

See also

- Refer to `Chapter 4`, *Selecting Subsets of Data*

Using methods that only work with a DatetimeIndex

There are a number of DataFrame/Series methods that only work with a DatetimeIndex. If the index is of any other type, these methods will fail.

Getting ready

In this recipe, we will first use methods to select rows of data by their time component. We will then learn about the powerful DateOffset objects and their aliases.

How to do it...

1. Read in the crime hdf5 dataset, set the index as `REPORTED_DATE`, and ensure that we have a DatetimeIndex:

```
>>> crime = pd.read_hdf('data/crime.h5', 'crime') \
              .set_index('REPORTED_DATE')
>>> print(type(crime.index))
<class 'pandas.core.indexes.datetimes.DatetimeIndex'>
```

2. Use the `between_time` method to select all crimes that occurred between 2 a.m. and 5 a.m., regardless of the date:

```
>>> crime.between_time('2:00', '5:00', include_end=False).head()
```

REPORTED_DATE	OFFENSE_TYPE_ID	OFFENSE_CATEGORY_ID	GEO_LON	GEO_LAT	NEIGHBORHOOD_ID	IS_CRIME	IS_TRAFFIC
2014-06-29 02:01:00	traffic-accident-dui-duid	traffic-accident	-105.000149	39.745753	cbd	0	1
2014-06-29 02:00:00	disturbing-the-peace	public-disorder	-105.020719	39.706674	athmar-park	1	0
2014-06-29 02:18:00	curfew	public-disorder	-105.001552	39.769505	sunnyside	1	0
2014-06-29 04:17:00	aggravated-assault	aggravated-assault	-105.018557	39.679229	college-view-south-platte	1	0
2014-06-29 04:22:00	violation-of-restraining-order	all-other-crimes	-104.972447	39.739449	cheesman-park	1	0

3. Select all dates at a specific time with `at_time`:

```
>>> crime.at_time('5:47').head()
```

REPORTED_DATE	OFFENSE_TYPE_ID	OFFENSE_CATEGORY_ID	GEO_LON	GEO_LAT	NEIGHBORHOOD_ID	IS_CRIME	IS_TRAFFIC
2013-11-26 05:47:00	criminal-mischief-other	public-disorder	-104.991476	39.751536	cbd	1	0
2017-04-09 05:47:00	criminal-mischief-mtr-veh	public-disorder	-104.959394	39.678425	university	1	0
2017-02-19 05:47:00	criminal-mischief-other	public-disorder	-104.986767	39.741336	north-capitol-hill	1	0
2017-02-16 05:47:00	aggravated-assault	aggravated-assault	-104.934029	39.732320	hale	1	0
2017-02-12 05:47:00	police-interference	all-other-crimes	-104.976306	39.722644	speer	1	0

4. The `first` methods provide an elegant way of selecting the first *n* segments of time, where *n* is an integer. These segments of time are formally represented by DateOffset objects that can be in the `pd.offsets` module. The DataFrame must be sorted on its index to guarantee that this method will work. Let's select the first six months of crime data:

```
>>> crime_sort = crime.sort_index()
>>> crime_sort.first(pd.offsets.MonthBegin(6))
```

REPORTED_DATE	OFFENSE_TYPE_ID	OFFENSE_CATEGORY_ID	GEO_LON	GEO_LAT	NEIGHBORHOOD_ID	IS_CRIME	IS_TRAFFIC
2012-01-02 00:06:00	aggravated-assault	aggravated-assault	-104.816860	39.796717	montbello	1	0
2012-01-02 00:06:00	violation-of-restraining-order	all-other-crimes	-104.816860	39.796717	montbello	1	0
2012-01-02 00:16:00	traffic-accident-dui-duid	traffic-accident	-104.971851	39.736874	cheesman-park	0	1
...	...	...	...	...	...	...	...
2012-06-30 23:50:00	criminal-mischief-mtr-veh	public-disorder	-104.838271	39.788683	montbello	1	0
2012-06-30 23:54:00	traffic-accident-hit-and-run	traffic-accident	-105.014162	39.740439	lincoln-park	0	1
2012-07-01 00:01:00	robbery-street	robbery	-104.924292	39.767585	northeast-park-hill	1	0

27489 rows × 7 columns

5. This captured the data from January through June but also, surprisingly, selected a single row in July. The reason for this is that pandas actually uses the time component of the first element in the index, which, in this example, is 6 minutes. Let's use `MonthEnd`, a slightly different offset:

```
>>> crime_sort.first(pd.offsets.MonthEnd(6))
```

REPORTED_DATE	OFFENSE_TYPE_ID	OFFENSE_CATEGORY_ID	GEO_LON	GEO_LAT	NEIGHBORHOOD_ID	IS_CRIME	IS_TRAFFIC
2012-01-02 00:06:00	aggravated-assault	aggravated-assault	-104.816860	39.796717	montbello	1	0
2012-01-02 00:06:00	violation-of-restraining-order	all-other-crimes	-104.816860	39.796717	montbello	1	0
2012-01-02 00:16:00	traffic-accident-dui-duid	traffic-accident	-104.971851	39.736874	cheesman-park	0	1
...	...	...	...	...	...	...	...
2012-06-29 23:41:00	robbery-street	robbery	-104.991912	39.756163	five-points	1	0
2012-06-29 23:57:00	assault-simple	other-crimes-against-persons	-104.987360	39.715162	speer	1	0
2012-06-30 00:04:00	traffic-accident	traffic-accident	-104.894697	39.628902	hampden-south	0	1

27332 rows × 7 columns

6. This captured nearly the same amount of data but if you look closely, only a single row from June 30th was captured. Again, this is because the time component of the first index was preserved. The exact search went to *2012-06-30 00:06:00*. So, how do we get exactly six months of data? There are a couple of ways. All DateOffsets have a `normalize` parameter that, when set to `True`, sets all the time components to zero. The following should get us very close to what we want:

```
>>> crime_sort.first(pd.offsets.MonthBegin(6, normalize=True))
```

REPORTED_DATE	OFFENSE_TYPE_ID	OFFENSE_CATEGORY_ID	GEO_LON	GEO_LAT	NEIGHBORHOOD_ID	IS_CRIME	IS_TRAFFIC
2012-01-02 00:06:00	aggravated-assault	aggravated-assault	-104.816860	39.796717	montbello	1	0
2012-01-02 00:06:00	violation-of-restraining-order	all-other-crimes	-104.816860	39.796717	montbello	1	0
2012-01-02 00:16:00	traffic-accident-dui-duid	traffic-accident	-104.971851	39.736874	cheesman-park	0	1
...	...	...	...	...	...	...	...
2012-06-30 23:44:00	traffic-accident	traffic-accident	-104.987578	39.711158	baker	0	1
2012-06-30 23:50:00	criminal-mischief-mtr-veh	public-disorder	-104.838271	39.788683	montbello	1	0
2012-06-30 23:54:00	traffic-accident-hit-and-run	traffic-accident	-105.014162	39.740439	lincoln-park	0	1

27488 rows × 7 columns

7. This method has successfully captured all the data for the first six months of the year. With normalize set to `True`, the search went to *2012-07-01 00:00:00*, which would actually include any crimes reported exactly on this date and time. Actually, there is no possible way to use the first method to ensure that only data from January to June is captured. The following very simple slice would yield the exact result:

```
>>> crime_sort.loc[:'2012-06']
```

8. There are a dozen DateOffset objects for very precisely moving forward or backward to the next nearest offset. Instead of hunting down the DateOffset objects in `pd.offsets`, you can use a string called an **offset alias** instead. For instance, the string for MonthEnd is *M* and for MonthBegin is *MS*. To denote the number of these offset aliases, simply place an integer in front of it. Use this table to find all the aliases (`http://bit.ly/2xO5Yg0`). Let's see some examples of offset aliases with the description of what is being selected in the comments:

```
>>> crime_sort.first('5D') # 5 days
>>> crime_sort.first('5B') # 5 business days
>>> crime_sort.first('7W') # 7 weeks, with weeks ending on Sunday
>>> crime_sort.first('3QS') # 3rd quarter start
>>> crime_sort.first('A') # one year end
```

How it works...

Once we ensure that our index is a DatetimeIndex, we can take advantage of all the methods in this recipe. It is impossible to do selection or slicing based on just the time component of a `Timestamp` with the `.loc` indexer. To select all dates by a range of time, you must use the `between_time` method, or to select an exact time, use `at_time`. Make sure that the passed string for start and end times consists of at least the hour and minute. It is also possible to use `time` objects from the `datetime` module. For instance, the following command would yield the same result as in step 2:

```
>>> import datetime
>>> crime.between_time(datetime.time(2,0), datetime.time(5,0),
                       include_end=False)
```

In step 4, we begin using the simple `first` method, but with a complicated parameter `offset`. It must be a DateOffset object or an offset alias as a string. To help understand DateOffset objects, it's best to see what they do to a single `Timestamp`. For example, let's take the first element of the index and add six months to it in two different ways:

```
>>> first_date = crime_sort.index[0]
>>> first_date
Timestamp('2012-01-02 00:06:00')

>>> first_date + pd.offsets.MonthBegin(6)
Timestamp('2012-07-01 00:06:00')

>>> first_date + pd.offsets.MonthEnd(6)
Timestamp('2012-06-30 00:06:00')
```

Both the `MonthBegin` and `MonthEnd` offsets don't add or subtract an exact amount of time but effectively round up to the next beginning or end of the month regardless of what day it is. Internally, the `first` method uses the very first index element of the DataFrame and adds the DateOffset passed to it. It then slices up until this new date. For instance, step 4 is equivalent to the following:

```
>>> step4 = crime_sort.first(pd.offsets.MonthEnd(6))

>>> end_dt = crime_sort.index[0] + pd.offsets.MonthEnd(6)
>>> step4_internal = crime_sort[:end_dt]
>>> step4.equals(step4_internal)
True
```

Steps 5 through 7 follow from this preceding equivalence directly. In step 8, offset aliases make for a much more compact method of referencing DateOffsets.

> The counterpart to the `first` method is the `last` method, which selects the last *n* time segments from a DataFrame given a DateOffset. The groupby object has two methods with the exact same name but with a completely different functionality. They return the first or last element of each group and have nothing to do with having a DatetimeIndex.

There's more...

It is possible to build a custom DateOffset when those available don't exactly suit your needs:

```
>>> dt = pd.Timestamp('2012-1-16 13:40')
>>> dt + pd.DateOffset(months=1)
Timestamp('2012-02-16 13:40:00')
```

Notice that this custom DateOffset increased the `Timestamp` by exactly one month. Let's look at one more example using many more date and time components:

```
>>> do = pd.DateOffset(years=2, months=5, days=3,
                       hours=8, seconds=10)
>>> pd.Timestamp('2012-1-22 03:22') + do
Timestamp('2014-06-25 11:22:10')
```

See also

- Pandas official documentation of *DateOffsets objects* (http://bit.ly/2fOintG)

Counting the number of weekly crimes

The raw Denver crime dataset is huge with over 460,000 rows each marked with a reported date. Counting the number of weekly crimes is one of many queries that can be answered by grouping according to some period of time. The `resample` method provides an easy interface to grouping by any possible span of time.

Getting ready

In this recipe, we will use both the `resample` and `groupby` methods to count the number of weekly crimes.

How to do it...

1. Read in the crime hdf5 dataset, set the index as the REPORTED_DATE, and then sort it to increase performance for the rest of the recipe:

    ```
    >>> crime_sort = pd.read_hdf('data/crime.h5', 'crime') \
                       .set_index('REPORTED_DATE') \
                       .sort_index()
    ```

2. In order to count the number of crimes per week, we need to form a group for each week. The `resample` method takes a DateOffset object or alias and returns an object ready to perform an action on all groups. The object returned from the `resample` method is very similar to the object produced after calling the `groupby` method:

    ```
    >>> crime_sort.resample('W')
    DatetimeIndexResampler [freq=<Week: weekday=6>, axis=0,
    closed=right, label=right, convention=start, base=0]
    ```

3. The offset alias, W, was used to inform pandas that we want to group by each week. There isn't much that happened in the preceding step. Pandas has simply validated our offset and returned an object that is ready to perform an action on each week as a group. There are several methods that we can chain after calling `resample` to return some data. Let's chain the `size` method to count the number of weekly crimes:

    ```
    >>> weekly_crimes = crime_sort.resample('W').size()
    >>> weekly_crimes.head()
    ```

```
REPORTED_DATE
2012-01-08     877
2012-01-15    1071
2012-01-22     991
2012-01-29     988
2012-02-05     888
Freq: W-SUN, dtype: int64
```

4. We now have the weekly crime count as a Series with the new index incrementing one week at a time. There are a few things that happen by default that are very important to understand. Sunday is chosen as the last day of the week and is also the date used to label each element in the resulting Series. For instance, the first index value January 8, 2012 is a Sunday. There were 877 crimes committed during that week ending on the 8th. The week of Monday, January 9th to Sunday, January 15th recorded 1,071 crimes. Let's do some sanity checks and ensure that our resampling is doing exactly this:

```
>>> len(crime_sort.loc[:'2012-1-8'])
877

>>> len(crime_sort.loc['2012-1-9':'2012-1-15'])
1071
```

5. Let's choose a different day to end the week besides Sunday with an **anchored offset**:

```
>>> crime_sort.resample('W-THU').size().head()
REPORTED_DATE
2012-01-05     462
2012-01-12    1116
2012-01-19     924
2012-01-26    1061
2012-02-02     926
Freq: W-THU, dtype: int64
```

6. Nearly all the functionality of `resample` may be reproduced by the `groupby` method. The only difference is that you must pass the offset in the `pd.Grouper` object:

```
>>> weekly_crimes_gby = crime_sort.groupby(pd.Grouper(freq='W')) \
                                  .size()
>>> weekly_crimes_gby.head()
REPORTED_DATE
2012-01-08     877
2012-01-15    1071
2012-01-22     991
```

```
2012-01-29    988
2012-02-05    888
Freq: W-SUN, dtype: int64

>>> weekly_crimes.equal(weekly_crimes_gby)
True
```

How it works...

The `resample` method, by default, works implicitly with a DatetimeIndex, which is why we set it to REPORTED_DATE in step 1. In step 2, we created an intermediate object that helps us understand how to form groups within the data. The first parameter to `resample` is the `rule` determining how the Timestamps in the index will be grouped. In this instance, we use the offset alias `W` to form groups one week in length ending on Sunday. The default ending day is Sunday, but may be changed with an anchored offset by appending a dash and the first three letters of a day of the week.

Once we have formed groups with `resample`, we must chain a method to take action on each of them. In step 3, we use the `size` method to count the number of crimes per week. You might be wondering what are all the possible attributes and methods available to use after calling `resample`. The following examines the `resample` object and outputs them:

```
>>> r = crime_sort.resample('W')
>>> resample_methods = [attr for attr in dir(r) if attr[0].islower()]
>>> print(resample_methods)
['agg', 'aggregate', 'apply', 'asfreq', 'ax', 'backfill', 'bfill', 'count',
'ffill', 'fillna', 'first', 'get_group', 'groups', 'indices',
'interpolate', 'last', 'max', 'mean', 'median', 'min', 'ndim', 'ngroups',
'nunique', 'obj', 'ohlc', 'pad', 'plot', 'prod', 'sem', 'size', 'std',
'sum', 'transform', 'var']
```

Step 4 verifies the accuracy of the count from step 3 by manually slicing the data by week and counting the number of rows. The `resample` method is actually not even necessary to group by `Timestamp` as the functionality is available directly from the `groupby` method itself. However, you must pass an instance of `pd.Grouper` to the `groupby` method using the `freq` parameter for the offset, as done in step 6.

A very similar object called `pd.TimeGrouper` is capable of grouping by time in the exact same fashion as `pd.Grouper`, but as of pandas version 0.21 it is deprecated and should not be used. Unfortunately, there are many examples online that use `pd.TimeGrouper` but do not let them tempt you.

There's more...

It is possible to use `resample` even when the index does not contain a `Timestamp`. You can use the `on` parameter to select the column with Timestamps that will be used to form groups:

```
>>> crime = pd.read_hdf('data/crime.h5', 'crime')
>>> weekly_crimes2 = crime.resample('W', on='REPORTED_DATE').size()
>>> weekly_crimes2.equals(weekly_crimes)
True
```

Similarly, this is possible using `groupby` with `pd.Grouper` by selecting the `Timestamp` column with the `key` parameter:

```
>>> weekly_crimes_gby2 = crime.groupby(pd.Grouper(key='REPORTED_DATE',
                                                  freq='W')).size()
>>> weekly_crimes_gby2.equals(weekly_crimes_gby)
True
```

We can also easily produce a line plot of all the crimes in Denver (including traffic accidents) by calling the `plot` method on our Series of weekly crimes:

```
>>> weekly_crimes.plot(figsize=(16, 4), title='All Denver Crimes')
```

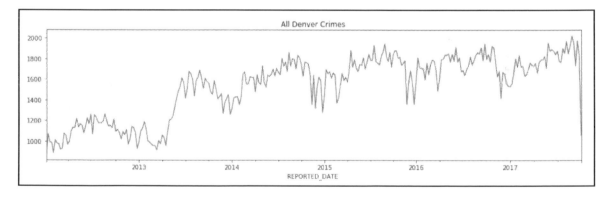

See also

- Pandas official documentation on *Resampling* (http://bit.ly/2yHXrbz)
- Table of all *Anchored Offsets* (http://bit.ly/2xg20h2)

Aggregating weekly crime and traffic accidents separately

The Denver crime dataset has all crime and traffic accidents together in one table, and separates them through the binary columns, IS_CRIME and IS_TRAFFIC. The resample method allows you to group by a period of time and aggregate specific columns separately.

Getting ready

In this recipe, we will use the resample method to group by each quarter of the year and then sum up the number of crimes and traffic accidents separately.

How to do it...

1. Read in the crime hdf5 dataset, set the index as REPORTED_DATE, and then sort it to increase performance for the rest of the recipe:

```
>>> crime_sort = pd.read_hdf('data/crime.h5', 'crime') \
                   .set_index('REPORTED_DATE') \
                   .sort_index()
```

2. Use the resample method to group by each quarter of the year and then sum the IS_CRIME and IS_TRAFFIC columns for each group:

```
>>> crime_quarterly = crime_sort.resample('Q')['IS_CRIME',
                                               'IS_TRAFFIC'].sum()
>>> crime_quarterly.head()
```

REPORTED_DATE	IS_CRIME	IS_TRAFFIC
2012-03-31	7882	4726
2012-06-30	9641	5255
2012-09-30	10566	5003
2012-12-31	9197	4802
2013-03-31	8730	4442

3. Notice that the dates all appear as the last day of the quarter. This is because the offset alias, *Q*, represents the end of the quarter. Let's use the offset alias *QS* to represent the start of the quarter:

```
>>> crime_sort.resample('QS')['IS_CRIME',
'IS_TRAFFIC'].sum().head()
```

	IS_CRIME	IS_TRAFFIC
REPORTED_DATE		
2012-01-01	7882	4726
2012-04-01	9641	5255
2012-07-01	10566	5003
2012-10-01	9197	4802
2013-01-01	8730	4442

4. Let's verify these results by checking whether the second quarter of data is correct:

```
>>> crime_sort.loc['2012-4-1':'2012-6-30',
                   ['IS_CRIME', 'IS_TRAFFIC']].sum()
IS_CRIME       9641
IS_TRAFFIC     5255
dtype: int64
```

5. It is possible to replicate this operation using the `groupby` method:

```
>>> crime_quarterly2 = crime_sort.groupby(pd.Grouper(freq='Q')) \
                                 ['IS_CRIME', 'IS_TRAFFIC'].sum()
>>> crime_quarterly2.equals(crime_quarterly)
True
```

6. Let's make a plot to better analyze the trends in crime and traffic accidents over time:

```
>>> plot_kwargs = dict(figsize=(16,4),
                       color=['black', 'lightgrey'],
                       title='Denver Crimes and Traffic Accidents')
>>> crime_quarterly.plot(**plot_kwargs)
```

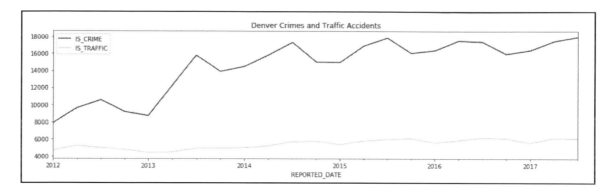

How it works...

After reading in and preparing our data in step 1, we begin grouping and aggregating in step 2. Immediately after calling the `resample` method, we can continue either by chaining a method or by selecting a group of columns to aggregate. We choose to select the `IS_CRIME` and `IS_TRAFFIC` columns to aggregate. If we didn't select just these two, then all of the numeric columns would have been summed with the following outcome:

```
>>> crime_sort.resample('Q').sum().head()
```

	GEO_LON	GEO_LAT	IS_CRIME	IS_TRAFFIC
REPORTED_DATE				
2012-03-31	-1.313006e+06	496960.237747	7882	4726
2012-06-30	-1.547274e+06	585656.789182	9641	5255
2012-09-30	-1.615835e+06	611604.800384	10566	5003
2012-12-31	-1.458177e+06	551923.040048	9197	4802
2013-03-31	-1.368931e+06	518159.721947	8730	4442

By default, the offset alias *Q* technically uses December 31st as the last day of the year. The span of dates that represent a single quarter are all calculated using this ending date. The aggregated result uses the last day of the quarter as its label. Step 3 uses the offset alias *QS*, which, by default, calculates quarters using January 1st as the first day of the year.

Most public businesses report quarterly earnings but they don't all have the same calendar year beginning in January. For instance, if we wanted our quarters to begin March 1st, then we could use *QS-MAR* to anchor our offset alias:

```
>>> crime_sort.resample('QS-MAR')['IS_CRIME', 'IS_TRAFFIC'] \
            .sum().head()
```

REPORTED_DATE	IS_CRIME	IS_TRAFFIC
2011-12-01	5013	3198
2012-03-01	9260	4954
2012-06-01	10524	5190
2012-09-01	9450	4777
2012-12-01	9003	4652

As in the preceding recipe, we verify our results via manual slicing and replicate the result with the `groupby` method using `pd.Grouper` to set our group length. In step 6, we make a single call to the DataFrame `plot` method. By default, a line is plotted for each column of data. The plot clearly shows a sharp increase in reported crimes during the first three quarters of the year. There also appears to be a seasonal component to both crime and traffic, with numbers lower in the cooler months and higher in the warmer months.

There's more...

To get a different visual perspective, we can plot the percentage increase in crime and traffic, instead of the raw count. Let's divide all the data by the first row and plot again:

```
>>> crime_begin = crime_quarterly.iloc[0]
>>> crime_begin
IS_CRIME       7882
IS_TRAFFIC     4726
Name: 2012-03-31 00:00:00, dtype: int64

>>> crime_quarterly.div(crime_begin) \
                .sub(1) \
                .round(2) \
                .plot(**plot_kwargs)
```

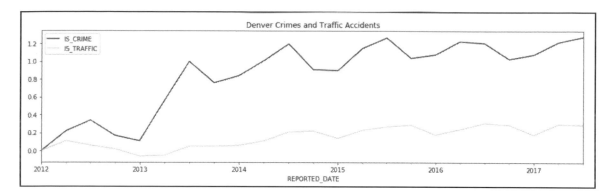

Measuring crime by weekday and year

Measuring crimes by weekday and by year simultaneously necessitate the functionality to pull this information directly from a Timestamp. Thankfully, this functionality is built into any column consisting of Timestamps with the dt accessor.

Getting ready

In this recipe, we will use the dt accessor to provide us with both the weekday name and year of each crime as a Series. We count all of the crimes by forming groups using both of these Series. Finally, we adjust the data to consider partial years and population before creating a heatmap of the total amount of crime.

How to do it...

1. Read in the Denver crime hdf5 dataset leaving the REPORTED_DATE as a column:

```
>>> crime = pd.read_hdf('data/crime.h5', 'crime')
>>> crime.head()
```

	OFFENSE_TYPE_ID	OFFENSE_CATEGORY_ID	REPORTED_DATE	GEO_LON	GEO_LAT	NEIGHBORHOOD_ID	IS_CRIME	IS_TRAFFIC
0	traffic-accident-dui-duid	traffic-accident	2014-06-29 02:01:00	-105.000149	39.745753	cbd	0	1
1	vehicular-eluding-no-chase	all-other-crimes	2014-06-29 01:54:00	-104.884660	39.738702	east-colfax	1	0
2	disturbing-the-peace	public-disorder	2014-06-29 02:00:00	-105.020719	39.706674	athmar-park	1	0
3	curfew	public-disorder	2014-06-29 02:18:00	-105.001552	39.769505	sunnyside	1	0
4	aggravated-assault	aggravated-assault	2014-06-29 04:17:00	-105.018557	39.679229	college-view-south-platte	1	0

2. All Timestamp columns have a special attribute called the dt accessor, which gives access to a variety of extra attributes and methods specifically designed for them. Let's find the weekday name of each REPORTED_DATE and then count these values:

```
>>> wd_counts = crime['REPORTED_DATE'].dt.weekday_name \
                                      .value_counts()
>>> wd_counts
Monday       70024
Friday       69621
Wednesday    69538
Thursday     69287
Tuesday      68394
Saturday     58834
Sunday       55213
Name: REPORTED_DATE, dtype: int64
```

3. The weekends appear to have substantially less crime and traffic accidents. Let's put this data in correct weekday order and make a horizontal bar plot:

```
>>> days = ['Monday', 'Tuesday', 'Wednesday', 'Thursday',
            'Friday', 'Saturday', 'Sunday']
>>> title = 'Denver Crimes and Traffic Accidents per Weekday'
>>> wd_counts.reindex(days).plot(kind='barh', title=title)
```

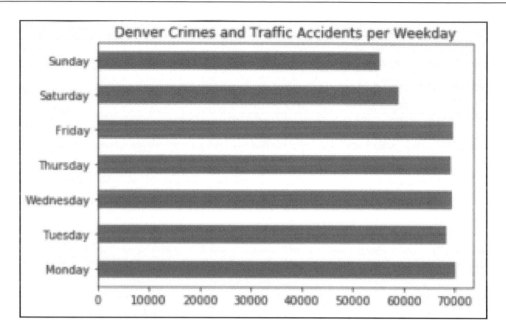

4. We can do a very similar procedure to plot the count by year:

```
>>> title = 'Denver Crimes and Traffic Accidents per Year'
>>> crime['REPORTED_DATE'].dt.year.value_counts() \
                    .sort_index() \
                    .plot(kind='barh', title=title)
```

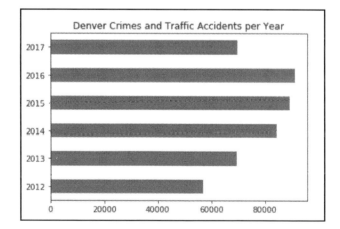

5. We need to group by both weekday and year. One way of doing this is saving the weekday and year Series to separate variables and then using these variables with the `groupby` method:

```
>>> weekday = crime['REPORTED_DATE'].dt.weekday_name
>>> year = crime['REPORTED_DATE'].dt.year

>>> crime_wd_y = crime.groupby([year, weekday]).size()
>>> crime_wd_y.head(10)
REPORTED_DATE   REPORTED_DATE
2012            Friday            8549
                Monday            8786
                Saturday          7442
                Sunday            7189
                Thursday          8440
                Tuesday           8191
                Wednesday         8440
2013            Friday           10380
                Monday           10627
                Saturday          8875
dtype: int64
```

6. We have aggregated the data correctly but the structure isn't exactly conducive to make comparisons easily. Let's first rename those meaningless index level names and then `unstack` the weekday level to get us a more readable table:

```
>>> crime_table = crime_wd_y.rename_axis(['Year', 'Weekday']) \
                            .unstack('Weekday')
>>> crime_table
```

Weekday Year	Friday	Monday	Saturday	Sunday	Thursday	Tuesday	Wednesday
2012	8549	8786	7442	7189	8440	8191	8440
2013	10380	10627	8875	8444	10431	10416	10354
2014	12683	12813	10950	10278	12309	12440	12948
2015	13273	13452	11586	10624	13512	13381	13320
2016	14059	13708	11467	10554	14050	13338	13900
2017	10677	10638	8514	8124	10545	10628	10576

7. We now have a nicer representation that is easier to read but noticeably, the 2017 numbers are incomplete. To help make a fairer comparison, we can make a simple linear extrapolation to estimate the final number of crimes. Let's first find the last day that we have data for in 2017:

```
>>> criteria = crime['REPORTED_DATE'].dt.year == 2017
>>> crime.loc[criteria, 'REPORTED_DATE'].dt.dayofyear.max()
272
```

8. A naive estimate would be to assume a constant rate of crime throughout the year and simply multiply all values in the 2017 table by 365/272. However, we can do a little better and look at our historical data and calculate the average percentage of crimes that have taken place through the first 272 days of the year:

```
>>> round(272 / 365, 3)
.745

>>> crime_pct = crime['REPORTED_DATE'].dt.dayofyear.le(272) \
                                       .groupby(year) \
                                       .mean() \
                                       .round(3)
>>> crime_pct
REPORTED_DATE
2012    0.748
2013    0.725
2014    0.751
2015    0.748
2016    0.752
2017    1.000
Name: REPORTED_DATE, dtype: float64

>>> crime_pct.loc[2012:2016].median()
.748
```

9. It turns out, perhaps very coincidentally, that the percentage of crimes that happen during the first 272 days of the year is almost exactly proportional to the percentage of days passed in the year. Let's now update the row for 2017 and change the column order to match the weekday order:

```
>>> crime_table.loc[2017] = crime_table.loc[2017].div(.748) \
                                                  .astype('int')
>>> crime_table = crime_table.reindex(columns=days)
>>> crime_table
```

Weekday Year	Monday	Tuesday	Wednesday	Thursday	Friday	Saturday	Sunday
2012	8786	8191	8440	8440	8549	7442	7189
2013	10627	10416	10354	10431	10380	8875	8444
2014	12813	12440	12948	12309	12683	10950	10278
2015	13452	13381	13320	13512	13273	11586	10624
2016	13708	13338	13900	14050	14059	11467	10554
2017	14221	14208	14139	14097	14274	11382	10860

10. We could make a bar or line plot but this is also a good situation for a heatmap, which is available with the seaborn library:

```
>>> import seaborn as sns
>>> sns.heatmap(crime_table, cmap='Greys')
```

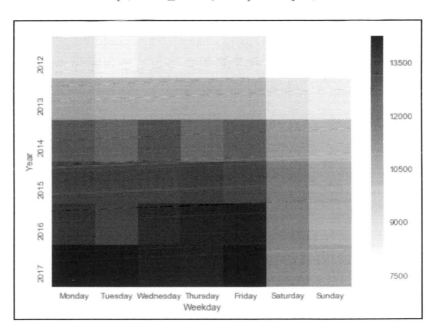

11. Crime seems to be rising every year but this data does not account for rising population. Let's read in a table for the Denver population for each year that we have data:

```
>>> denver_pop = pd.read_csv('data/denver_pop.csv',
                             index_col='Year')
>>> denver_pop
```

Year	Population
2017	705000
2016	693000
2015	680000
2014	662000
2013	647000
2012	634000

12. Many crime metrics are reported as rates per 100,000 residents. Let's divide the population by 100,000 and then divide the raw crime counts by this number to get the crime rate per 100,000 residents:

```
>>> den_100k = denver_pop.div(100000).squeeze()
>>> crime_table2 = crime_table.div(den_100k, axis='index') \
                              .astype('int')
>>> crime_table2
```

Weekday / Year	Monday	Tuesday	Wednesday	Thursday	Friday	Saturday	Sunday
2012	1385	1291	1331	1331	1348	1173	1133
2013	1642	1609	1600	1612	1604	1371	1305
2014	1935	1879	1955	1859	1915	1654	1562
2015	1978	1967	1958	1987	1951	1703	1562
2016	1978	1924	2005	2027	2028	1654	1522
2017	2017	2015	2005	1999	2024	1614	1540

13. Once again, we can make a heatmap that, even after adjusting for population increase, looks nearly identical to the first one:

```
>>> sns.heatmap(crime_table2, cmap='Greys')
```

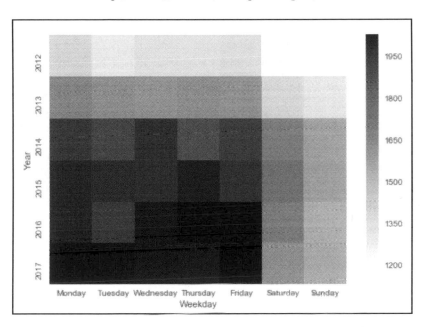

How it works...

All DataFrame columns containing Timestamps have access to numerous other attributes and methods with the dt accessor. In fact, all of these methods and attributes available from the dt accessor are also available directly from a single Timestamp object.

In step 2, we use the dt accessor, which only works on a Series, to extract the weekday name and simply count the occurrences. Before making a plot in step 3, we manually rearrange the order of the index with the reindex method, which, in its most basic use case, accepts a list containing the desired order. This task could have also been accomplished with the .loc indexer like this:

```
>>> wd_counts.loc[days]
Monday       70024
Tuesday      68394
Wednesday    69538
Thursday     69287
Friday       69621
```

```
Saturday        58834
Sunday          55213
Name: REPORTED_DATE, dtype: int64
```

The `reindex` method is actually more performant and has many parameters for more diverse situations than `.loc`. We then use the `weekday_name` attribute of the `dt` accessor to retrieve the name of each day of the week, and count the occurrences before making a horizontal bar plot.

In step 4, we do a very similar procedure, and retrieve the year using the `dt` accessor again, and then count the occurrences with the `value_counts` method. In this instance, we use `sort_index` over `reindex`, as years will naturally sort in the desired order.

The goal of the recipe is to group by both weekday and year together so this is exactly what we do in step 5. The `groupby` method is very flexible and can form groups in multiple ways. In this recipe, we pass it two Series, `year` and `weekday`, from which all unique combinations form a group. We then chain the `size` method to it, which returns a single value, the length of each group.

After step 5, our Series is long with only a single column of data, which makes it difficult to make comparisons by year and weekday. To ease the readability, we pivot the weekday level into horizontal column names with `unstack`.

In step 7, we use boolean indexing to select only the crimes in 2017 and then use `dayofyear` from the `dt` accessor again to find the total elapsed days from the beginning of the year. The maximum of this Series should tell us how many days we have data for in 2017.

Step 8 is quite complex. We first create a boolean Series by testing whether each crime was committed on or before the 272nd day of the year with `crime['REPORTED_DATE'].dt.dayofyear.le(272)`. From here, we again use the flexible `groupby` method to form groups by the previously calculated `year` Series and then use the `mean` method to find the percentage of crimes committed on or before the 272nd day for each year.

The `.loc` indexer selects the entire 2017 row of data in step 9. We adjust this row by dividing by the median percentage found in step 8.

Lots of crime visualizations are done with heatmaps and one is done here in step 10 with the help of the `seaborn` visualization library. The `cmap` parameter takes a string name of the several dozen available matplotlib colormaps (http://bit.ly/2yJZOvt).

In step 12, we create a crime rate per 100k residents by dividing by the population of that year. This is actually a fairly tricky operation. Normally, when you divide one DataFrame by another, they align on their columns and index. However, in this step, crime_table has no columns in common denver_pop so no values will align if we try and divide them. To work around this, we create the den_100k Series with the squeeze method. We still can't simply divide these two objects as, by default, division between a DataFrame and a Series aligns the columns of the DataFrame with the index of the Series, like this:

```
>>> crime_table / den_100k
```

Year	Monday	Tuesday	Wednesday	Thursday	Friday	Saturday	Sunday	2017	2016	2015	2014	2013	2012
2012	NaN	NaN	NaN	NaN	NaN	NaN	NaN	NaN	NaN	NaN	NaN	NaN	NaN
2013	NaN	NaN	NaN	NaN	NaN	NaN	NaN	NaN	NaN	NaN	NaN	NaN	NaN
2014	NaN	NaN	NaN	NaN	NaN	NaN	NaN	NaN	NaN	NaN	NaN	NaN	NaN
2015	NaN	NaN	NaN	NaN	NaN	NaN	NaN	NaN	NaN	NaN	NaN	NaN	NaN
2016	NaN	NaN	NaN	NaN	NaN	NaN	NaN	NaN	NaN	NaN	NaN	NaN	NaN
2017	NaN	NaN	NaN	NaN	NaN	NaN	NaN	NaN	NaN	NaN	NaN	NaN	NaN

We need the index of the DataFrame to align with the index of Series and to do this, we use the div method, which allows us to change the direction of alignment with the axis parameter. A heatmap of the adjusted crime rate is plotted in step 13.

There's more...

Let's finalize this analysis by writing a function to complete all the steps of this recipe at once and add the ability to choose a specific type of crime:

```
>>> ADJ_2017 = .748

>>> def count_crime(df, offense_cat):
        df = df[df['OFFENSE_CATEGORY_ID'] == offense_cat]
        weekday = df['REPORTED_DATE'].dt.weekday_name
        year = df['REPORTED_DATE'].dt.year

        ct = df.groupby([year, weekday]).size().unstack()
        ct.loc[2017] = ct.loc[2017].div(ADJ_2017).astype('int')

        pop = pd.read_csv('data/denver_pop.csv', index_col='Year')
```

```
        pop = pop.squceze().div(100000)

        ct = ct.div(pop, axis=0).astype('int')
        ct = ct.reindex(columns=days)
        sns.heatmap(ct, cmap='Greys')
        return ct

>>> count_crime(crime, 'auto-theft')
```

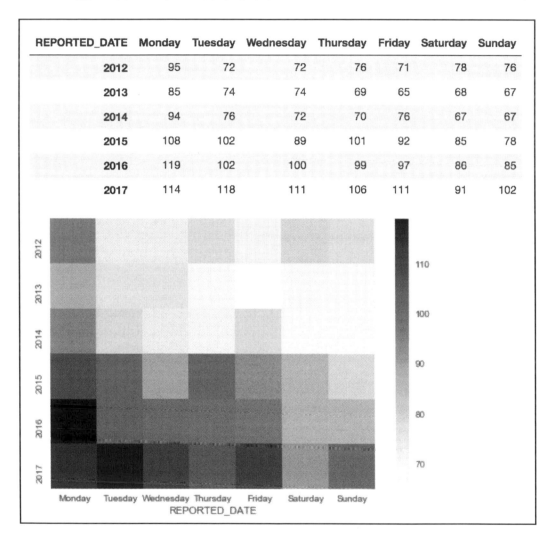

REPORTED_DATE	Monday	Tuesday	Wednesday	Thursday	Friday	Saturday	Sunday
2012	95	72	72	76	71	78	76
2013	85	74	74	69	65	68	67
2014	94	76	72	70	76	67	67
2015	108	102	89	101	92	85	78
2016	119	102	100	99	97	86	85
2017	114	118	111	106	111	91	102

See also

- Pandas official documentation of the `reindex` method (http://bit.ly/2y40eyE)
- The seaborn official documentation of the `heatmap` function (http://bit.ly/2ytbMNe)

Grouping with anonymous functions with a DatetimeIndex

Using DataFrames with a `DatetimeIndex` opens the door to many new and different operations as seen with several recipes in this chapter.

Getting ready

In this recipe, we will show the versatility of using the `groupby` method for DataFrames that have a `DatetimeIndex`.

How to do it...

1. Read in the Denver `crime hdf5` file, place the `REPORTED_DATE` column in the index, and sort it:

```
>>> crime_sort = pd.read_hdf('data/crime.h5', 'crime') \
                   .set_index('REPORTED_DATE') \
                   .sort_index()
```

2. The `DatetimeIndex` itself has many of the same attributes and methods as a pandas `Timestamp`. Let's take a look at some that they have in common:

```
>>> common_attrs = set(dir(crime_sort.index)) & \
                   set(dir(pd.Timestamp))
>>> print([attr for attr in common_attrs if attr[0] != '_'])

['to_pydatetime', 'normalize', 'day', 'dayofyear', 'freq', 'ceil',
'microsecond', 'tzinfo', 'weekday_name', 'min', 'quarter', 'month',
'tz_convert', 'tz_localize', 'is_month_start', 'nanosecond', 'tz',
'to_datetime', 'dayofweek', 'year', 'date', 'resolution',
'is_quarter_end',
```

```
'weekofyear', 'is_quarter_start', 'max', 'is_year_end', 'week',
'round',
'strftime', 'offset', 'second', 'is_leap_year', 'is_year_start',
'is_month_end', 'to_period', 'minute', 'weekday', 'hour',
'freqstr',
'floor', 'time', 'to_julian_date', 'days_in_month', 'daysinmonth']
```

3. We can then use the index to find weekday names, similarly to what was done in step 2 of the preceding recipe:

```
>>> crime_sort.index.weekday_name.value_counts()
Monday       70024
Friday       69621
Wednesday    69538
Thursday     69287
Tuesday      68394
Saturday     58834
Sunday       55213
Name: REPORTED_DATE, dtype: int64
```

4. Somewhat surprisingly, the `groupby` method has the ability to accept a function as an argument. This function will be implicitly passed the index and its return value is used to form groups. Let's see this in action by grouping with a function that turns the index into a weekday name and then counts the number of crimes and traffic accidents separately:

```
>>> crime_sort.groupby(lambda x: x.weekday_name) \
             ['IS_CRIME', 'IS_TRAFFIC'].sum()
```

	IS_CRIME	IS_TRAFFIC
Friday	48833	20814
Monday	52158	17895
Saturday	43363	15516
Sunday	42315	12968
Thursday	49470	19845
Tuesday	49658	18755
Wednesday	50054	19508

5. You can use a list of functions to group by both the hour of day and year, and then reshape the table to make it more readable:

```
>>> funcs = [lambda x: x.round('2h').hour, lambda x: x.year]
>>> cr_group = crime_sort.groupby(funcs) \
                         ['IS_CRIME', 'IS_TRAFFIC'].sum()
>>> cr_final = cr_group.unstack()
>>> cr_final.style.highlight_max(color='lightgrey')
```

	IS_CRIME						IS_TRAFFIC					
	2012	2013	2014	2015	2016	2017	2012	2013	2014	2015	2016	2017
0	2422	4040	5649	5649	5377	3811	919	792	978	1136	980	782
2	1888	3214	4245	4050	4091	3041	718	652	779	773	718	537
4	1472	2181	2956	2959	3044	2255	399	378	424	471	464	313
6	1067	1365	1750	2167	2108	1567	411	399	479	494	593	462
8	2998	3445	3727	4161	4488	3251	1957	1955	2210	2331	2372	1828
10	4305	5035	5658	6205	6218	4993	1979	1901	2139	2320	2303	1873
12	4496	5524	6434	6841	7226	5463	2200	2138	2379	2631	2760	1986
14	4266	5698	6708	7218	6896	5396	2241	2245	2630	2840	2763	1990
16	4113	5889	7351	7643	7926	6338	2714	2562	3002	3160	3527	2784
18	3660	5094	6586	7015	7407	6157	3118	2704	3217	3412	3608	2718
20	3521	4895	6130	6360	6963	5272	1787	1806	1994	2071	2184	1491
22	3078	4318	5496	5626	5637	4358	1343	1330	1532	1671	1472	1072

How it works...

In step 1, we read in our data and place a column of Timestamps into the index to create a DatetimeIndex. In step 2, we see that a DatetimeIndex has lots of the same functionality that a single Timestamp object has. In step 3, we directly use these extra features of the DatetimeIndex to extract the weekday name.

In step 4, we take advantage of the special ability of the `groupby` method to accept a function that is passed the DatetimeIndex. The `x` in the anonymous function is literally the DatetimeIndex and we use it to retrieve the weekday name. It is possible to pass `groupby` a list of any number of custom functions, as done in step 5. Here, the first function uses the `round` DatetimeIndex method to round each value to the nearest second hour. The second function retrieves the year. After the grouping and aggregating, we `unstack` the years as columns. We then highlight the maximum value of each column. Crime is reported most often between 3 and 5 p.m. Most traffic accidents occur between 5 p.m. and 7 p.m.

There's more...

The final result of this recipe is a DataFrame with MultiIndex columns. Using this DataFrame, it is possible to select just the crime or traffic accidents separately. The `xs` method allows you to select a single value from any index level. Let's see an example where we select only the section of data dealing with traffic:

```
>>> cr_final.xs('IS_TRAFFIC', axis='columns', level=0).head()
```

	2012	2013	2014	2015	2016	2017
0	919	792	978	1136	980	782
2	718	652	779	773	718	537
4	399	378	424	471	464	313
6	411	399	479	494	593	462
8	1957	1955	2210	2331	2372	1828

This is referred to as taking a cross section in pandas. We must use the `axis` and `level` parameters to specifically denote where our value is located. Let's use `xs` again to select only data from 2016, which is in a different level:

```
>>> cr_final.xs(2016, axis='columns', level=1).head()
```

	IS_CRIME	IS_TRAFFIC
0	5377	980
2	4091	718
4	3044	464
6	2108	593
8	4488	2372

See also

- Pandas official documentation of the cross section method xs (http://bit.ly/2xkLzLv)

Grouping by a Timestamp and another column

The resample method on its own, is unable to group by anything other than periods of time. The groupby method, however, has the ability to group by both periods of time and other columns.

Getting ready

In this recipe, we will show two very similar but different approaches to group by Timestamps and another column.

How to do it...

1. Read in the employee dataset, and create a DatetimeIndex with the HIRE_DATE column:

```
>>> employee = pd.read_csv('data/employee.csv',
                           parse_dates=['JOB_DATE', 'HIRE_DATE'],
                           index_col='HIRE_DATE')
>>> employee.head()
```

HIRE_DATE	UNIQUE_ID	POSITION_TITLE	DEPARTMENT	BASE_SALARY	RACE	EMPLOYMENT_TYPE	GENDER	EMPLOYMENT_STATUS	JOB_DATE
2006-06-12	0	ASSISTANT DIRECTOR (EX LVL)	Municipal Courts Department	121862.0	Hispanic/Latino	Full Time	Female	Active	2012-10-13
2000-07-19	1	LIBRARY ASSISTANT	Library	26125.0	Hispanic/Latino	Full Time	Female	Active	2010-09-18
2015-02-03	2	POLICE OFFICER	Houston Police Department-HPD	45279.0	White	Full Time	Male	Active	2015-02-03
1982-02-08	3	ENGINEER/OPERATOR	Houston Fire Department (HFD)	63166.0	White	Full Time	Male	Active	1991-05-25
1989-06-19	4	ELECTRICIAN	General Services Department	56347.0	White	Full Time	Male	Active	1994-10-22

2. Let's first do a simple grouping by just gender, and find the average salary for each:

```
>>> employee.groupby('GENDER')['BASE_SALARY'].mean().round(-2)
GENDER
Female    52200.0
Male      57400.0
Name: BASE_SALARY, dtype: float64
```

3. Let's find the average salary based on hire date, and group everyone into 10-year buckets:

```
>>> employee.resample('10AS')['BASE_SALARY'].mean().round(-2)
HIRE_DATE
1958-01-01     81200.0
1968-01-01    106500.0
1978-01-01     69600.0
1988-01-01     62300.0
1998-01-01     58200.0
2008-01-01     47200.0
Freq: 10AS-JAN, Name: BASE_SALARY, dtype: float64
```

4. If we wanted to group by both gender and a five-year time span, we can call `resample` directly after calling `groupby`:

```
>>> employee.groupby('GENDER').resample('10AS')['BASE_SALARY'] \
        .mean().round(-2)
GENDER   HIRE_DATE
Female   1975-01-01     51600.0
         1985-01-01     57600.0
         1995-01-01     55500.0
         2005-01-01     51700.0
         2015-01-01     38600.0
Male     1958-01-01     81200.0
         1968-01-01    106500.0
         1978-01-01     72300.0
         1988-01-01     64600.0
         1998-01-01     59700.0
         2008-01-01     47200.0
Name: BASE_SALARY, dtype: float64
```

5. Now, this does what we set out to do, but we run into a slight issue whenever we want to compare female to male salaries. Let's `unstack` the gender level and see what happens:

```
>>> sal_avg.unstack('GENDER')
```

GENDER HIRE_DATE	Female	Male
1958-01-01	NaN	81200.0
1968-01-01	NaN	106500.0
1975-01-01	51600.0	NaN
1978-01-01	NaN	72300.0
1985-01-01	57600.0	NaN
1988-01-01	NaN	64600.0
1995-01-01	55500.0	NaN
1998-01-01	NaN	59700.0
2005-01-01	51700.0	NaN
2008-01-01	NaN	47200.0
2015-01-01	38600.0	NaN

6. The 10-year periods for males and females do not begin on the same date. This happened because the data was first grouped by gender and then, within each gender, more groups were formed based on hire dates. Let's verify that the first hired male was in 1958 and the first hired female was in 1975:

```
>>> employee[employee['GENDER'] == 'Male'].index.min()
Timestamp('1958-12-29 00:00:00')

>>> employee[employee['GENDER'] == 'Female'].index.min()
Timestamp('1975-06-09 00:00:00')
```

7. To resolve this issue, we must group the date together with the gender, and this is only possible with the `groupby` method:

```
>>> sal_avg2 = employee.groupby(['GENDER',
                            pd.Grouper(freq='10AS')]) \
                    ['BASE_SALARY'].mean().round(-2)
>>> sal_avg2
GENDER  HIRE_DATE
Female  1968-01-01         NaN
        1978-01-01     57100.0
        1988-01-01     57100.0
        1998-01-01     54700.0
        2008-01-01     47300.0
Male    1958-01-01     81200.0
        1968-01-01    106500.0
        1978-01-01     72300.0
        1988-01-01     64600.0
        1998-01-01     59700.0
        2008-01-01     47200.0
Name: BASE_SALARY, dtype: float64
```

8. Now we can `unstack` the gender and get our rows aligned perfectly:

```
>>> sal_final = sal_avg2.unstack('GENDER')
>>> sal_final
```

GENDER	Female	Male
HIRE_DATE		
1958-01-01	NaN	81200.0
1968-01-01	NaN	106500.0
1978-01-01	57100.0	72300.0
1988-01-01	57100.0	64600.0
1998-01-01	54700.0	59700.0
2008-01-01	47300.0	47200.0

How it works...

The `read_csv` function in step 1 allows to both convert columns into Timestamps and put them in the index at the same time creating a DatetimeIndex. Steps 2 does a simple `groupby` operation with a single grouping column, gender. Step 3 uses the `resample` method with the offset alias *10AS* to form groups in 10-year increments of time. The *A* is the alias for year and the *S* informs us that the beginning of the period is used as the label. For instance, the data for the label *1988-01-01* spans that date until December 31, 1997.

Interestingly, the object returned from a call to the `groupby` method has its own `resample` method, but the reverse is not true:

```
>>> 'resample' in dir(employee.groupby('GENDER'))
True

>>> 'groupby' in dir(employee.resample('10AS'))
False
```

In step 4, for each gender, male and female, completely different starting dates for the 10-year periods are calculated based on the earliest hired employee. Step 6 verifies that the year of the earliest hired employee for each gender matches the output from step 4. Step 5 shows how this causes misalignment when we try to compare salaries of females to males. They don't have the same 10-year periods.

To alleviate this issue, we must group both the gender and Timestamp together. The `resample` method is only capable of grouping by a single column of Timestamps. We can only complete this operation with the `groupby` method. With `pd.Grouper`, we can replicate the functionality of `resample`. We simply pass the offset alias to the `freq` parameter and then place the object in a list with all the other columns that we wish to group, as done in step 7. As both males and females now have the same starting dates for the 10-year period, the reshaped data in step 8 will align for each gender making comparisons much easier. It appears that male salaries tend to be higher given a longer length of employment, though both genders have the same average salary with under 10 years of employment.

There's more...

From an outsider's perspective, it would not be obvious that the rows from the output in step 8 represented 10-year intervals. One way to improve the index labels would be to show the beginning and end of each time interval. We can achieve this by concatenating the current index year with 9 added to itself:

```
>>> years = sal_final.index.year
>>> years_right = years + 9
>>> sal_final.index = years.astype(str) + '-' + years_right.astype(str)
>>> sal_final
```

GENDER	Female	Male
1958-1967	NaN	81200.0
1968-1977	NaN	106500.0
1978-1987	57100.0	72300.0
1988-1997	57100.0	64600.0
1998-2007	54700.0	59700.0
2008-2017	47300.0	47200.0

There is actually a completely different way to do this recipe. We can use the `cut` function to create equal-width intervals based on the year that each employee was hired and form groups from it:

```
>>> cuts = pd.cut(employee.index.year, bins=5, precision=0)
>>> cuts.categories.values
array([Interval(1958.0, 1970.0, closed='right'),
       Interval(1970.0, 1981.0, closed='right'),
       Interval(1981.0, 1993.0, closed='right'),
       Interval(1993.0, 2004.0, closed='right'),
       Interval(2004.0, 2016.0, closed='right')], dtype=object)

>>> employee.groupby([cuts, 'GENDER'])['BASE_SALARY'] \
            .mean().unstack('GENDER').round(-2)
```

GENDER	Female	Male
(1958.0, 1970.0]	NaN	85400.0
(1970.0, 1981.0]	54400.0	72700.0
(1981.0, 1993.0]	55700.0	69300.0
(1993.0, 2004.0]	56500.0	62300.0
(2004.0, 2016.0]	49100.0	49800.0

Finding the last time crime was 20% lower with merge_asof

There are frequently times where we would like to know when the last time something happened. For example, we might be interested in the last time unemployment was below 5% or the last time the stock market went up five days in a row or the last time you had eight hours of sleep. The `merge_asof` function provides answers to these types of questions.

Getting ready

In this recipe, we will find the current month's total number of crimes for each offense category and then find the last time there were 20% fewer incidences.

How to do it...

1. Read in the Denver crime dataset, place the REPORTED_DATE in the index, and sort it:

```
>>> crime_sort = pd.read_hdf('data/crime.h5', 'crime') \
                   .set_index('REPORTED_DATE') \
                   .sort_index()
```

2. Find the last full month of data:

```
>>> crime_sort.index.max()
Timestamp('2017-09-29 06:16:00')
```

3. As we don't quite have all of September's data, let's drop it from our dataset:

```
>>> crime_sort = crime_sort[:'2017-8']
>>> crime_sort.index.max()
Timestamp('2017-08-31 23:52:00')
```

4. Let's count the number of crimes and traffic accidents for every month:

```
>>> all_data = crime_sort.groupby([pd.Grouper(freq='M'),
                                   'OFFENSE_CATEGORY_ID']).size()
>>> all_data.head()
REPORTED_DATE   OFFENSE_CATEGORY_ID
2012-01-31      aggravated-assault     113
                all-other-crimes       124
                arson                    5
                auto-theft             275
                burglary               343
dtype: int64
```

5. Although the merge_asof function can work with the index, it will be easier to just reset it:

```
>>> all_data = all_data.sort_values().reset_index(name='Total')
>>> all_data.head()
```

	REPORTED_DATE	OFFENSE_CATEGORY_ID	Total
0	2014-12-31	murder	1
1	2013-01-31	arson	1
2	2016-05-31	murder	1
3	2012-12-31	murder	1
4	2016-12-31	murder	1

6. Let's get the current month's crime count and make a new column to represent the goal:

```
>>> goal = all_data[all_data['REPORTED_DATE'] == '2017-8-31'] \
                  .reset_index(drop=True)
>>> goal['Total_Goal'] = goal['Total'].mul(.8).astype(int)
>>> goal.head()
```

	REPORTED_DATE	OFFENSE_CATEGORY_ID	Total	Total_Goal
0	2017-08-31	murder	7	5
1	2017-08-31	arson	7	5
2	2017-08-31	sexual-assault	57	45
3	2017-08-31	robbery	108	86
4	2017-08-31	white-collar-crime	138	110

7. Now use the `merge_asof` function to find the last time a monthly crime total was less than the column `Total_Goal` for each offense category:

```
>>> pd.merge_asof(goal, all_data, left_on='Total_Goal',
                 right_on='Total', by='OFFENSE_CATEGORY_ID',
                 suffixes=('_Current', '_Last'))
```

	REPORTED_DATE_Current	OFFENSE_CATEGORY_ID	Total_Current	Total_Goal	REPORTED_DATE_Last	Total_Last
0	2017-08-31	murder	7	5	2017-01-31	5
1	2017-08-31	arson	7	5	2012-01-31	5
2	2017-08-31	sexual-assault	57	45	2013-01-31	45
3	2017-08-31	robbery	108	86	2015-03-31	86
4	2017-08-31	white-collar-crime	138	110	2016-10-31	110
5	2017-08-31	aggravated-assault	195	156	2016-05-31	154
6	2017-08-31	other-crimes-against-persons	376	300	2014-04-30	285
7	2017-08-31	burglary	432	345	2012-01-31	343
8	2017-08-31	auto-theft	599	479	2017-07-31	477
9	2017-08-31	drug-alcohol	636	508	2015-05-31	505
10	2017-08-31	theft-from-motor-vehicle	675	540	2015-03-31	535
11	2017-08-31	larceny	877	701	2015-01-31	697
12	2017-08-31	public-disorder	878	702	2015-12-31	699
13	2017-08-31	all-other-crimes	1583	1266	2016-11-30	1264
14	2017-08-31	traffic-accident	2126	1700	2013-12-31	1697

How it works...

After reading in our data, we decide not to include the 2017 September data, as it is not quite a complete month. We use a partial date string to slice all the way up to and including any crimes in August of 2017. In step 4, we tally all the crimes for each offense category per month, and in step 5, we sort by this total, which is required for `merge_asof`.

In step 6, we select the most recent data into a separate DataFrame. We will use this month of August as our baseline and create a column, `Total_Goal`, that is 20% less than the current. In step 7, we use `merge_asof` to find the last time a monthly crime count was less than the `Total_Goal` column.

There's more...

In addition to the Timestamp and Timedelta data types, pandas offers the Period type to represent an exact time period. For example, *2012-05* would represent the entire month of May, 2012. You can manually construct a Period in the following manner:

```
>>> pd.Period(year=2012, month=5, day=17, hour=14, minute=20, freq='T')
Period('2012-05-17 14:20', 'T')
```

This object represents the entire minute of May 17, 2012 at 2:20 p.m. It is possible to use these Periods in step 4 instead of grouping by date with `pd.Grouper`. DataFrames with a DatetimeIndex have the `to_period` method to convert Timestamps to Periods. It accepts an offset alias to determine the exact length of the time period.

```
>>> ad_period = crime_sort.groupby([lambda x: x.to_period('M'),
                                    'OFFENSE_CATEGORY_ID']).size()
>>> ad_period = ad_period.sort_values() \
                         .reset_index(name='Total') \
                         .rename(columns={'level_0':'REPORTED_DATE'})
>>> ad_period.head()
```

	REPORTED_DATE	OFFENSE_CATEGORY_ID	Total
0	2014-12	murder	1
1	2013-01	arson	1
2	2016-05	murder	1
3	2012-12	murder	1
4	2016-12	murder	1

Let's verify that the last two columns from this DataFrame are equivalent to `all_data` from step 5:

```
>>> cols = ['OFFENSE_CATEGORY_ID', 'Total']
>>> all_data[cols].equals(ad_period[cols])
True
```

Steps 6 and 7 can now be replicated in almost the exact same manner with the following code:

```
>>> aug_2018 = pd.Period('2017-8', freq='M')
>>> goal_period = ad_period[ad_period['REPORTED_DATE'] == aug_2018] \
                       .reset_index(drop=True)
>>> goal_period['Total_Goal'] = goal_period['Total'].mul(.8).astype(int)

>>> pd.merge_asof(goal_period, ad_period, left_on='Total_Goal',
```

```
right_on='Total', by='OFFENSE_CATEGORY_ID',
suffixes=('_Current', '_Last')).head()
```

	REPORTED_DATE_Current	OFFENSE_CATEGORY_ID	Total_Current	Total_Goal	REPORTED_DATE_Last	Total_Last
0	2017-08	murder	7	5	2017-01	5
1	2017-08	arson	7	5	2012-01	5
2	2017-08	sexual-assault	57	45	2013-01	45
3	2017-08	robbery	108	86	2015-03	86
4	2017-08	white-collar-crime	138	110	2016-10	110

11
Visualization with Matplotlib, Pandas, and Seaborn

In this chapter, we will cover the following topics:

- Getting started with matplotlib
- Visualizing data with matplotlib
- Plotting basics with pandas
- Visualizing the flights dataset
- Stacking area charts to discover emerging trends
- Understanding the differences between seaborn and pandas
- Doing multivariate analysis with seaborn grids
- Uncovering Simpson's paradox in the diamonds dataset with seaborn

Introduction

Visualization is a critical component in exploratory data analysis, as well as presentations and applications. During exploratory data analysis, you are usually working alone or in small groups and need to create plots quickly to help you better understand your data. It can help you identify outliers and missing data, or it can spark other questions of interest that will lead to further analysis and more visualizations. This type of visualization is usually not done with the end user in mind. It is strictly to help you better your current understanding. The plots don't have to be perfect.

When preparing visualizations for a report or application, a different approach must be used. Attention to small details must be paid. In addition, you usually will have to narrow down all possible visualizations to only the select few that best represent your data. Good data visualizations have the viewer enjoying the experience of extracting information. Almost like movies that make viewers get lost in, good visualizations will have lots of information that really sparks interest.

The primary data visualization library in Python is matplotlib, a project begun in the early 2000s, that was built to mimic the plotting capabilities from Matlab. Matplotlib is enormously capable of plotting most things you can imagine and it gives its users tremendous power to control every aspect of the plotting surface. That said, it isn't quite the friendliest library for beginners to grasp. Thankfully, pandas makes visualizing data very easy for us and usually plots what we want with a single call to the `plot` method. Pandas actually does no plotting on its own. It internally calls matplotlib functions to create the plots. Pandas also adds its own style that, in my opinion, is a bit nicer than the defaults from matplotlib.

Seaborn is also a visualization library that internally calls matplotlib functions and does not do any actual plotting itself. Seaborn makes beautiful plots very easily and allows for the creation of many new types of plots that are not available directly from matplotlib or pandas. Seaborn works with tidy (long) data, while pandas works best with aggregated (wide) data. Seaborn also accepts pandas DataFrame objects in its plotting functions.

Although it is possible to create plots without ever directly running any matplotlib code, from time to time it will be necessary to use it to tweak finer plot details manually. For this reason, the first two recipes will cover some basics of matplotlib that will come in handy if you need to use it directly. Other than the first two recipes, all plotting examples will use pandas or seaborn.

Visualization in Python does not have to rely on matplotlib necessarily. Bokeh is quickly becoming a very popular interactive visualization library targeted for the web. It is completely independent of matplotlib, and it's capable of producing entire applications.

Getting started with matplotlib

For many data scientists, the vast majority of their plotting commands will come directly from pandas or seaborn, which both rely completely on matplotlib to do the actual plotting. However, neither pandas nor seaborn offers a complete replacement for matplotlib, and occasionally you will need to use it directly. For this reason, this recipe will offer a short introduction to the most crucial aspects of matplotlib.

Getting ready

Let's begin our introduction with a look at the anatomy of a matplotlib plot in the following figure:

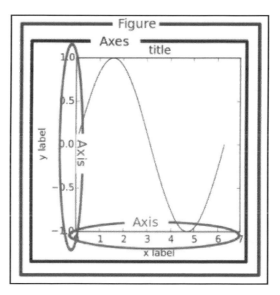

Matplotlib uses a hierarchy of objects to display all of its plotting items in the output. This hierarchy is key to understanding everything about matplotlib. The **Figure** and **Axes** objects are the two main components of the hierarchy. The Figure object is at the top of the hierarchy. It is the container for everything that will be plotted. Contained within the Figure is one or more Axes object(s). The Axes is the primary object that you will interact with when using matplotlib and can be more commonly thought of as the actual plotting surface. The Axes contains the x/y axis, points, lines, markers, labels, legends, and any other useful item that is plotted.

In early 2017, matplotlib underwent a major change when it released version 2.0. Much of the default plotting parameters were changed. The anatomy figure is actually from the documentation of version 1 but does a better job at distinguishing between the Figure and the Axes than the updated anatomy figure from version 2 (http://bit.ly/2gmNV7h).

A very clear distinction needs to be made between an Axes object and an axis. They are completely separate objects. An Axes object, using matplotlib terminology, is not the plural of axis but instead, as mentioned earlier, the object that creates and controls most of the useful plotting elements. An axis simply refers to the x or y (or even z) axis of a plot.

It is unfortunate that matplotlib chose to use axes, the plural of the word axis, to refer to a completely different object, but it is central to the library and unlikely to be changed at this point.

All of these useful plotting elements created by an Axes object are called **artists**. Even the Figure and the Axes objects themselves are artists. This distinction for artists won't be critical to this recipe but will be useful when doing more advanced matplotlib plotting and especially when reading through the documentation.

Object-oriented guide to matplotlib

Matplotlib provides two distinct interfaces for users to develop plots with. The **stateful** interface makes all of its calls directly with the pyplot module. This interface is called **stateful** because matplotlib implicitly keeps track of the current state of the plotting environment. Whenever a plot is created in the stateful interface, matplotlib finds the current Figure or current Axes and makes changes to it. This approach is fine to plot a few things quickly but can become unwieldy when dealing with multiple Figures and Axes.

Matplotlib also offers a stateless, or **object-oriented**, interface in which you explicitly use variables that reference specific plotting objects. Each variable can then be used to change some property of the plot. The object-oriented approach is explicit, and you are always aware of exactly what object is being modified.

Unfortunately, having both options has lead to lots of confusion, and matplotlib has a reputation for being difficult to learn. The documentation has examples using both approaches. Tutorials, blog posts, and Stack Overflow posts abound on the web, perpetuating the confusion. This recipe focuses solely on the object-oriented approach, as it is much more Pythonic and much more similar to how we interact with pandas.

If you are new to matplotlib, you might not know how to recognize the difference between each approach. With the stateful interface, all commands will be given directly from `pyplot`, which is usually aliased `plt`. Making a simple line plot and adding some labels to each axis would look like this:

```
>>> import matplotlib.pyplot as plt

>>> x = [-3, 5, 7]
>>> y = [10, 2, 5]

>>> plt.figure(figsize=(15,3))
>>> plt.plot(x, y)
>>> plt.xlim(0, 10)
>>> plt.ylim(-3, 8)
>>> plt.xlabel('X Axis')
>>> plt.ylabel('Y axis')
>>> plt.title('Line Plot')
>>> plt.suptitle('Figure Title', size=20, y=1.03)
```

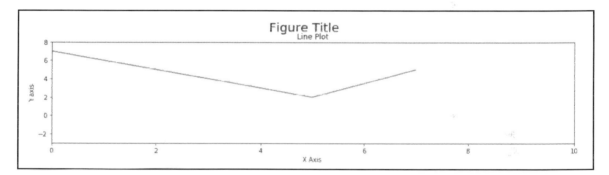

The object-oriented approach still uses `pyplot`, but typically, it is only to create the Figure and Axes objects during the first step. After creation, methods from these objects are called directly to alter the plot. The following code uses the object-oriented approach to make an exact replication of the previous plot:

```
>>> fig, ax = plt.subplots(figsize=(15,3))
>>> ax.plot(x, y)
>>> ax.set_xlim(0, 10)
>>> ax.set_ylim(-3, 8)
>>> ax.set_xlabel('X axis')
>>> ax.set_ylabel('Y axis')
>>> ax.set_title('Line Plot')
>>> fig.suptitle('Figure Title', size=20, y=1.03)
```

In this simple example, we directly use only two objects, the Figure, and Axes, but in general, plots can have many hundreds of objects; each one can be used to make modifications in an extremely finely-tuned manner, not easily doable with the stateful interface. In this chapter, we build an empty plot and modify several of its basic properties using the object-oriented interface.

How to do it...

1. To get started with matplotlib using the object-oriented approach, you will need to import the `pyplot` module and alias `plt`:

    ```
    >>> import matplotlib.pyplot as plt
    ```

2. Typically, when using the object-oriented approach, we will create a Figure and one or more Axes objects. Let's use the `subplots` function to create a Figure with a single Axes:

    ```
    >>> fig, ax = plt.subplots(nrows=1, ncols=1)
    ```

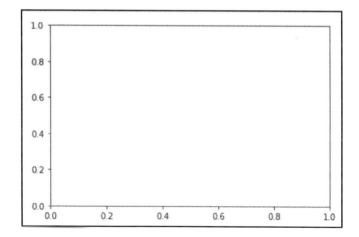

3. The `subplots` function returns a two-item tuple object containing the Figure and one or more Axes objects (here it is just one), which is unpacked into the variables `fig` and `ax`. From here on out, we will directly use these objects by calling methods in a normal object-oriented approach. Let's take a look at the type of each of these objects to ensure that we are actually working with a Figure and an Axes:

```
>>> type(fig)
matplotlib.figure.Figure

>>> type(ax)
matplotlib.axes._subplots.AxesSubplot
```

4. Although you will be calling more Axes than Figure methods, you might still need to interact with them. Let's find the size of the Figure and then enlarge it:

```
>>> fig.get_size_inches()
array([ 6.,   4.])

>>> fig.set_size_inches(14, 4)
>>> fig
```

5. Before we start plotting, let's examine the matplotlib hierarchy. You can collect all the Axes of the Figure with the `axes` attribute:

```
>>> fig.axes
[<matplotlib.axes._subplots.AxesSubplot at 0x112705ba8>]
```

6. This command returns a list of all the Axes objects. However, we already have our Axes object stored in the `ax` variable. Let's verify that they are actually the same object:

```
>>> fig.axes[0] is ax
True
```

7. To help visibly differentiate the Figure from the Axes, we can give each one a unique `facecolor`. Matplotlib accepts a variety of different input types for color. Approximately 140 HTML colors are supported by their string name (see this list: `http://bit.ly/2y52Ut0`). You may also use a string containing a float from zero to one to represent shades of gray:

```
>>> fig.set_facecolor('.9')
>>> ax.set_facecolor('.7')
>>> fig
```

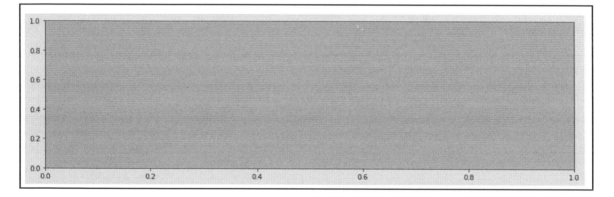

8. Now that we have differentiated between the Figure and the Axes, let's take a look at all of the immediate children of the Axes with the `get_children` method:

```
>>> ax_children = ax.get_children()
>>> ax_children
[<matplotlib.spines.Spine at 0x11145b358>,
 <matplotlib.spines.Spine at 0x11145b0f0>,
 <matplotlib.spines.Spine at 0x11145ae80>,
 <matplotlib.spines.Spine at 0x11145ac50>,
 <matplotlib.axis.XAxis at 0x11145aa90>,
 <matplotlib.axis.YAxis at 0x110fa8d30>,
 ...]
```

9. Every basic plot has four spines and two axis objects. The spines represent the data boundaries and are the four physical lines that you see bordering the darker gray rectangle (the Axes). The *x* and *y* axis objects contain more plotting objects such as the ticks and their labels and the label of the entire axis. We can select the spines from this list, but that isn't generally how it's done. We can access them directly with the `spines` attribute:

```
>>> spines = ax.spines
>>> spines
OrderedDict([('left', <matplotlib.spines.Spine at 0x11279e320>),
            ('right', <matplotlib.spines.Spine at 0x11279e0b8>),
            ('bottom', <matplotlib.spines.Spine at 0x11279e048>),
            ('top', <matplotlib.spines.Spine at 0x1127eb5c0>)])
```

10. The spines are contained in an ordered dictionary. Let's select the left spine and change its position and width so that it is more prominent and also make the bottom spine invisible:

```
>>> spine_left = spines['left']
>>> spine_left.set_position(('outward', -100))
>>> spine_left.set_linewidth(5)

>>> spine_bottom = spines['bottom']
>>> spine_bottom.set_visible(False)
>>> fig
```

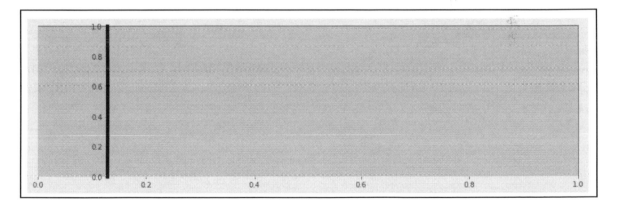

11. Now, let's focus on the axis objects. We can access each axis directly through the `xaxis` and `yaxis` attributes. Some axis properties are also available directly with the `Axes` object. In this step, we change some properties of each axis in both manners:

```
>>> ax.xaxis.grid(True, which='major', linewidth=2,
                    color='black', linestyle='--')
>>> ax.xaxis.set_ticks([.2, .4, .55, .93])
>>> ax.xaxis.set_label_text('X Axis', family='Verdana',
fontsize=15)

>>> ax.set_ylabel('Y Axis', family='Calibri', fontsize=20)
>>> ax.set_yticks([.1, .9])
>>> ax.set_yticklabels(['point 1', 'point 9'], rotation=45)
>>> fig
```

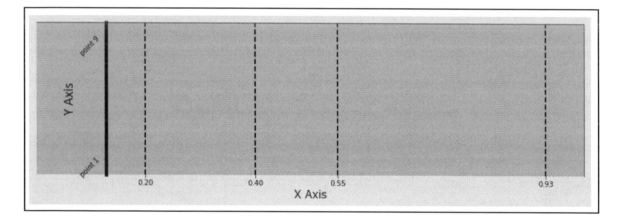

How it works...

One of the crucial ideas to grasp with the object-oriented approach is that each plotting element has both **getter** and **setter** methods. The getter methods all begin with `get_` and either retrieve a specific property or retrieve other plotting objects. For instance, `ax.get_yscale()` retrieves the type of scale that the *y* axis is plotted with as a string (default is *linear*), while `ax.get_xticklabels()` retrieves a list of matplotlib text objects that each have their own getter and setter methods. Setter methods modify a specific property or an entire group of objects. A lot of matplotlib boils down to latching onto a specific plotting element and then examining and modifying it via the getter and setter methods.

It might be useful to make an analogy of the matplotlib hierarchy as a home. The home and all of its contents would be the Figure. Each individual room would be the Axes and the contents of the room would be the artists.

The easiest way to begin using the object-oriented interface is with the `pyplot` module, which is commonly aliased `plt`, as done in step 1. Step 2 shows one of the most common methods to initiate the object-oriented approach. The `plt.subplots` function creates a single Figure, along with a grid of Axes objects. The first two parameters, `nrows` and `ncols`, define a uniform grid of Axes objects. For example, `plt.subplots(2, 4)` creates eight total Axes objects of the same size inside one Figure.

The `plt.subplots` function is somewhat of an oddity in that it returns a two-item tuple. The first element is the Figure, and the second element is the Axes object. This tuple gets unpacked as two distinct variables, `fig` and `ax`. If you are not accustomed to tuple unpacking, it may help to see step 2 written like this:

```
>>> plot_objects = plt.subplots(nrows=1, ncols=1)
>>> type(plot_objects)
tuple

>>> fig = plot_objects[0]
>>> ax = plot_objects[1]
```

If you create more than one Axes with `plt.subplots`, then the second item in the tuple is a NumPy array containing all the Axes. Let's demonstrate that here:

```
>>> plot_objects = plt.subplots(2, 4)
```

The `plot_objects` variable is a tuple containing a Figure as its first element and a Numpy array as its second:

```
>>> plot_objects[1]
array([[<matplotlib.axes._subplots.AxesSubplot object at 0x133b70a20>,
        <matplotlib.axes._subplots.AxesSubplot object at 0x135d6f9e8>,
        <matplotlib.axes._subplots.AxesSubplot object at 0x1310e4668>,
        <matplotlib.axes._subplots.AxesSubplot object at 0x133565ac8>],
       [<matplotlib.axes._subplots.AxesSubplot object at 0x133f67898>,
        <matplotlib.axes._subplots.AxesSubplot object at 0x1326d30b8>,
        <matplotlib.axes._subplots.AxesSubplot object at 0x1335d5eb8>,
        <matplotlib.axes._subplots.AxesSubplot object at 0x133f78f28>]],
      dtype=object)
```

Step 3 verifies that we indeed have Figure and Axes objects referenced by the appropriate variables. In step 4, we come across the first example of getter and setter methods. Matplotlib defaults all Figures to 6 inches in width by 4 inches in height, which is not the actual size of it on the screen, but would be the exact size if you saved the Figure to a file.

Step 5 shows that, in addition to the getter method, you can sometimes directly access another plotting object by its attribute. Often, there exist both an attribute and a getter method to retrieve the same object. For instance, look at these examples:

```
>>> fig.axes == fig.get_axes()
True

>>> ax.xaxis == ax.get_xaxis()
True

>>> ax.yaxis == ax.get_yaxis()
True
```

Many artists have a `facecolor` property that can be set to cover the entire surface one particular color, as in step 7. In step 8, the `get_children` method can be used to get a better understanding of the object hierarchy. A list of all the objects directly below the Axes is returned. It is possible to select all of the objects from this list and start using the setter methods to modify properties, but this isn't customary. We usually collect our objects directly from the attributes or getter methods.

Often, when retrieving a plotting object, they will be returned in a container like a list or a dictionary. This is what happens when collecting the spines in step 9. You will have to select the individual objects from their respective containers in order to use the getter or setter methods on them, as done in step 10. It is also common to use a for-loop to iterate through each of them one at a time.

Step 11 adds grid lines in a peculiar way. We would expect there to be a `get_grid` and `set_grid` method, but instead, there is just a `grid` method, which accepts a boolean as the first argument to turn on/off the grid lines. Each axis has both major and minor ticks, though by default the minor ticks are turned off. The `which` parameter is used to select which type of tick has a grid line.

Notice that the first three lines of step 11 select the `xaxis` attribute and call methods from it, while the last three lines call equivalent methods directly from the Axes object itself. This second set of methods is a convenience provided by matplotlib to save a few keystrokes. Normally, most objects can only set their own properties, not those of their children. Many of the axis-level properties are not able to be set from the Axes, but in this step, some are. Either method is acceptable.

When adding the grid lines with the first line in step 11, we set the properties `linewidth`, `color`, and `linestyle`. These are all properties of a matplotlib line, formally a Line2D object. You can view all of the available properties here: `http://bit.ly/2kE6MiG`. The `set_ticks` method accepts a sequence of floats and draws tick marks for only those locations. Using an empty list will completely remove all ticks.

Each axis may be labeled with some text, for which matplotlib formally uses a `Text` object. Only a few of all the available text properties (`http://bit.ly/2yXIZfP`) are changed. The `set_yticklabels` Axes method takes in a list of strings to use as the labels for each of the ticks. You may set any number of text properties along with it.

There's more...

To help find all the possible properties of each of your plotting objects, simply make a call to the properties method, which displays all of them as a dictionary. Let's see a curated list of the properties of an axis object:

```
>>> ax.xaxis.properties()
{'alpha': None,
 'gridlines': <a list of 4 Line2D gridline objects>,
 'label': Text(0.5,22.2,'X Axis'),
 'label_position': 'bottom',
 'label_text': 'X Axis',
 'tick_padding': 3.5,
 'tick_space': 26,
 'ticklabels': <a list of 4 Text major ticklabel objects>,
 'ticklocs': array([ 0.2 , 0.4 , 0.55, 0.93]),
 'ticks_position': 'bottom',
 'visible': True}
```

See also

- Matplotlib official documentation of its usage guide (http://bit.ly/2xrKjeE)
- Categorized list of all the methods of an Axes object (http://bit.ly/2kEhi9w)
- *Anatomy of Matplotlib* tutorial by key contributor, Ben Root (http://bit.ly/2y86c1M)
- Matplotlib official documentation of the stateful pyplot module and the object-oriented approach (http://bit.ly/2xqYnVR)
- Matplotlib official documentation of the *Artist tutorial* (http://bit.ly/2kwS2SI)

Visualizing data with matplotlib

Matplotlib has a few dozen plotting methods that make nearly any kind of plot imaginable. Line, bar, histogram, scatter, box, violin, contour, pie, and many more plots are available as methods from the Axes object. It was only in version 1.5 (released in 2015) that matplotlib began accepting data from pandas DataFrames. Before this, data had to be passed to it from NumPy arrays or Python lists.

Getting ready

In this recipe, we will visualize the trend in movie budgets over time by reducing our data from pandas DataFrames down to NumPy arrays, which we will then pass to matplotlib plotting functions.

How to do it...

1. Now that we know how to select plotting elements and change their attributes, let's actually create a data visualization. Let's read in the movie dataset, calculate the median budget for each year, and then find the five year rolling average to smooth the data:

```
>>> movie = pd.read_csv('data/movie.csv')
>>> med_budget = movie.groupby('title_year')['budget'].median() /
1e6
>>> med_budget_roll = med_budget.rolling(5, min_periods=1).mean()
>>> med_budget_roll.tail()
title_year
```

```
2012.0    20.893
2013.0    19.893
2014.0    19.100
2015.0    17.980
2016.0    17.780
Name: budget, dtype: float64
```

2. Let's get our data into NumPy arrays:

```
>>> years = med_budget_roll.index.values
>>> years[-5:]
array([ 2012.,  2013.,  2014.,  2015.,  2016.])

>>> budget = med_budget_roll.values
>>> budget[-5:]
array([ 20.893,  19.893,  19.1  ,  17.98 ,  17.78 ])
```

3. The `plot` method is used to create line plots. Let's use it to plot the rolling median of budgets over time in a new Figure:

```
>>> fig, ax = plt.subplots(figsize=(14,4), linewidth=5,
                           edgecolor='.5')
>>> ax.plot(years, budget, linestyle='--',
            linewidth=3, color='.2', label='All Movies')

>>> text_kwargs=dict(fontsize=20, family='cursive')
>>> ax.set_title('Median Movie Budget', **text_kwargs)
>>> ax.set_ylabel('Millions of Dollars', **text_kwargs)
```

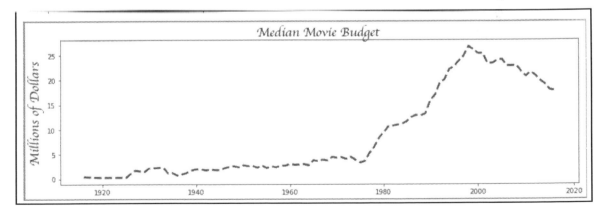

4. It's quite interesting that the median movie budget peaked in the year 2000 and has subsequently fallen. Perhaps this is just an artifact of the dataset, in which we have more data in recent years of all the movies, not just the most popular ones. Let's find the count of the number of movies per year:

```
>>> movie_count = movie.groupby('title_year')['budget'].count()
>>> movie_count.tail()
title_year
2012.0    191
2013.0    208
2014.0    221
2015.0    192
2016.0     86
Name: budget, dtype: int64
```

5. Any number of plots may be put on a single Axes, and these counts can be plotted directly with the median budget as a bar chart. As the units for both plots are completely different (dollars versus count), we can either create a secondary y axis or scale the counts to be in the same range as the budget. We choose the latter and label each bar with its value as text, directly preceding it. As the vast majority of the data is contained in recent years, we can also limit the data to those movies made from 1970 onward:

```
>>> ct = movie_count.values
>>> ct_norm = ct / ct.max() * budget.max()

>>> fifth_year = (years % 5 == 0) & (years >= 1970)
>>> years_5 = years[fifth_year]
>>> ct_5 = ct[fifth_year]
>>> ct_norm_5 = ct_norm[fifth_year]

>>> ax.bar(years_5, ct_norm_5, 3, facecolor='.5',
           alpha=.3, label='Movies per Year')
>>> ax.set xlim(1968, 2017)
>>> for x, y, v in zip(years    _5, ct_norm_5, ct_5):
        ax.text(x, y + .5, str(v), ha='center')
>>> ax.legend()
>>> fig
```

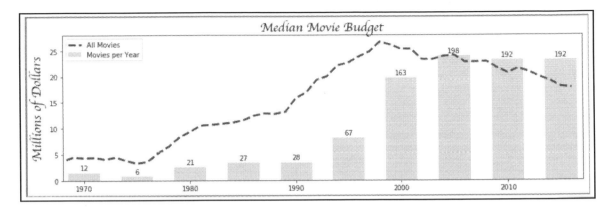

6. This trend might not hold if we just look at the top 10 budgeted movies per year. Let's find the five year rolling median for just the top 10 movies per year:

```
>>> top10 = movie.sort_values('budget', ascending=False) \
                 .groupby('title_year')['budget'] \
                 .apply(lambda x: x.iloc[:10].median() / 1e6)
>>> top10_roll = top10.rolling(5, min_periods=1).mean()
>>> top10_roll.tail()
title_year
2012.0    192.9
2013.0    195.9
2014.0    191.7
2015.0    186.8
2016.0    189.1
Name: budget, dtype: float64
```

7. These numbers represent an order of a magnitude higher than those found in step 13 for all the data. Plotting both lines on the same scale would not look good. Let's create an entirely new Figure with two subplots (Axes) and plot the data from the previous step in the second Axes:

```
>>> fig2, ax_array = plt.subplots(2, 1, figsize=(14,8),
sharex=True)
>>> ax1 = ax_array[0]
>>> ax2 = ax_array[1]

>>> ax1.plot(years, budget, linestyle='--', linewidth=3,
             color='.2', label='All Movies')
>>> ax1.bar(years_5, ct_norm_5, 3, facecolor='.5',
            alpha=.3, label='Movies per Year')
>>> ax1.legend(loc='upper left')
>>> ax1.set_xlim(1968, 2017)
>>> plt.setp(ax1.get_xticklines(), visible=False)
```

```
>>> for x, y, v in zip(years_5, ct_norm_5, ct_5):
        ax1.text(x, y + .5, str(v), ha='center')

>>> ax2.plot(years, top10_roll.values, color='.2',
            label='Top 10 Movies')
>>> ax2.legend(loc='upper left')

>>> fig2.tight_layout()
>>> fig2.suptitle('Median Movie Budget', y=1.02, **text_kwargs)
>>> fig2.text(0, .6, 'Millions of Dollars', rotation='vertical',
            ha='center', **text_kwargs)

>>> import os
>>> path = os.path.expanduser('~/Desktop/movie_budget.png')
>>> fig2.savefig(path, bbox_inches='tight')
```

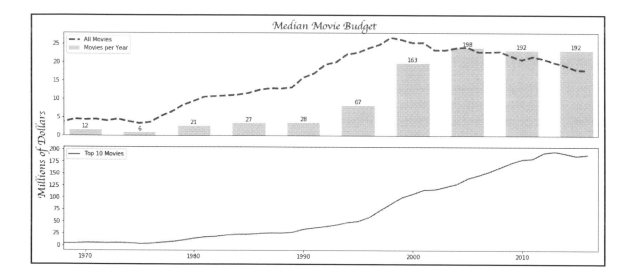

How it works...

In step 1, we begin with a quest to analyze movie budgets by finding the median budget per year in millions of dollars. After finding the median budget for each year, we decided to smooth it out, as there is going to be quite a lot of variability from year to year. We choose to smooth the data because we are looking for a general trend and are not necessarily interested in the exact value of any one year.

In this step, we use the `rolling` method to calculate a new value for each year based on the average of the last five years of data. For example, the median budgets from the years 2011 through 2015 are grouped together and averaged. The result is the new value for the year 2015. The only required parameter for the `rolling` method is the size of the window, which, by default, ends at the current year.

The `rolling` method returns a groupby-like object that must have its groups acted on with another function to produce a result. Let's manually verify that the `rolling` method works as expected for a few of the previous years:

```
>>> med_budget.loc[2012:2016].mean()
17.78

>>> med_budget.loc[2011:2015].mean()
17.98

>>> med_budget.loc[2010:2014].mean()
19.1
```

These values are the same as the output from step 1. In step 2, we get ready to use matplotlib by putting our data into NumPy arrays. In step 3, we create our Figure and Axes to set up the object-oriented interface. The `plt.subplots` method supports a large number of inputs. See the documentation to view all possible parameters for both this and for the `figure` function (`http://bit.ly/2ydM8ZU` and `http://bit.ly/2ycno4U`).

The first two parameters in the `plot` method represent the x and y values for a line plot. All of the line properties are available to be changed inside the call to `plot`. The `set_title` Axes method provides a title and can set all the available text properties inside its call. The same goes for the `set_ylablel` method. If you are setting the same properties for many objects, you can pack them together into a dictionary and pass this dictionary as one of the arguments, as done with `**text_kwargs`.

In step 4, we notice an unexpected downward trend in median budget beginning around the year 2000 and suspect that the number of movies collected per year might play an explanatory role. We choose to add this dimension to the graph by creating a bar plot of every fifth year of data beginning from 1970. We use boolean selection on our NumPy data arrays in the same manner as we do for the pandas Series in step 5.

The `bar` method takes the x-value the height, and the width of the bars as its first three arguments and places the center of the bars directly at each x-value. The bar height was derived from the movie count that was first scaled down to be between zero and one, and then multiplied by the maximum median budget. These bar heights are stored in the variable `ct_norm_5`. To label each bar correctly, we first zip together the bar center, its height, and the actual movie count. We then loop through this zipped object and place the count preceding the bar with the `text` method, which accepts an x-value, y-value, and a string. We adjust the y-value slightly upwards and use the horizontal alignment parameter, `ha`, to center the text.

Look back at step 3, and you will notice the `plot` method with the `label` parameter equal to `All Movies`. This is the value that matplotlib uses when you create a legend for your plot. A call to the `legend` Axes method puts all the plots with assigned labels in the legend.

To investigate the unexpected dip in the median budget, we can focus on just the top 10 budgeted movies for each year. Step 6 uses a custom aggregation function after grouping by year to do so, and then smooths the result in the same manner as before. These results could be plotted directly on the same graph, but because the values are so much greater, we opt to create an entire new Figure with two Axes.

We start step 7 by creating a Figure with two subplots in a two row by one column grid. Remember that when creating more than one subplot, all the Axes get stored in a NumPy array. The final result from step 5 is recreated in the top Axes. We plot the top 10 budgeted movies in the bottom Axes. Notice that the years align for both the bottom and top Axes because the `sharex` parameter was set to `True` in the Figure creation. When sharing an axis, matplotlib removes the labels for all the ticks but keeps those tiny vertical lines for each tick. To remove these tick lines, we use the `setp` pyplot function. Although this isn't directly object-oriented, it is explicit and very useful when we want to set properties for an entire sequence of plotting objects. We set all the tick lines to invisible with this useful function.

Finally, we then make several calls to Figure methods. This is a departure from our normal calling of Axes methods. The `tight_layout` method adjusts the subplots to look much nicer by removing extra space and ensuring that different Axes don't overlap. The `suptitle` method creates a title for the entire Figure, as opposed to the `set_title` Axes method, which creates titles for individual Axes. It accepts an x and y location to represent a place in the **figure coordinate system**, in which (0, 0) represents the bottom left and (1, 1) represents the top right. By default, the y-value is 0.98, but we move it up a few points to 1.02.

Each Axes also has a coordinate system in which (0, 0) is used for the bottom left and (1, 1) for the top right. In addition to those coordinate system, each Axes also has a data coordinate system, which is more natural to most people and represents the bounds of the *x* and *y-axis*. These bounds may be retrieved with `ax.get_xlim()` and `ax.get_ylim()` respectively. All the plotting before this used the data coordinate system. See the *Transformations tutorial* to learn more about the coordinate systems (`http://bit.ly/2gxDkX3`).

As both Axes use the same units for the *y* axis, we use the `text` Figure method to place a custom *y* axis label directly between each Axes, using the figure coordinate system. Finally, we save the Figure to our desktop. The tilde, ~, in the path represents the home directory, but the `savefig` method won't understand what this means. You must use the `expanduser` function from the `os` library to create the full path. For instance, the `path` variable becomes the following on my machine:

```
>>> os.path.expanduser('~/Desktop/movie_budget.png')
'/Users/Ted/Desktop/movie_budget.png'
```

The `savefig` method can now create the file in the correct location. By default, `savefig` will save only what is plotted within (0, 0) to (1, 1) of the figure coordinate system. As our title is slightly outside of this area, some of it will be cropped. Setting the `bbox_inches` parameter to *tight* will have matplotlib include any titles or labels that are extending outside of this region.

There's more...

Matplotlib began accepting pandas DataFrames for all of its plotting functions after the release of version 1.5. The DataFrame gets passed to the plotting method through the `data` parameter. Doing so allows you to reference the columns with string names. The following script creates a scatter plot of the IMDB score against the year for a random selection of 100 movies made from 2000 onwards. The sizes of each point are proportional to the budget:

```
>>> cols = ['budget', 'title_year', 'imdb_score', 'movie_title']
>>> m = movie[cols].dropna()
>>> m['budget2'] = m['budget'] / 1e6
>>> np.random.seed(0)
>>> movie_samp = m.query('title_year >= 2000').sample(100)

>>> fig, ax = plt.subplots(figsize=(14,6))
>>> ax.scatter(x='title_year', y='imdb_score',
                s='budget2', data=movie_samp)
```

```
>>> idx_min = movie_samp['imdb_score'].idxmin()
>>> idx_max = movie_samp['imdb_score'].idxmax()
>>> for idx, offset in zip([idx_min, idx_max], [.5, -.5]):
        year = movie_samp.loc[idx, 'title_year']
        score = movie_samp.loc[idx, 'imdb_score']
        title = movie_samp.loc[idx, 'movie_title']
        ax.annotate(xy=(year, score),
        xytext=(year + 1, score + offset),
        s=title + ' ({})'.format(score),
        ha='center',
        size=16,
        arrowprops=dict(arrowstyle="fancy"))
>>> ax.set_title('IMDB Score by Year', size=25)
>>> ax.grid(True)
```

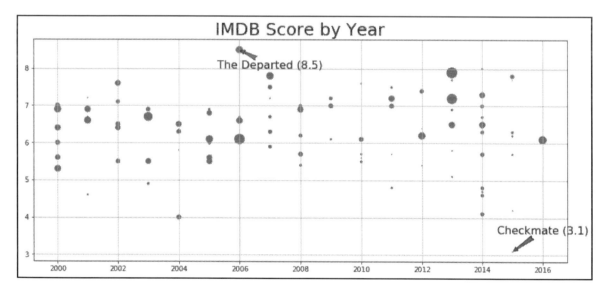

After creating the scatter plot, the highest and lowest scoring movies are labeled with the `annotate` method. The `xy` parameter is a tuple of the point that we would like to annotate. The `xytext` parameter is another tuple coordinate of the text location. The text is centered there due to `ha` being set to `center`.

See also

- Matplotlib official *Legend guide* (`http://bit.ly/2yGvKUu`)
- Matplotlib official documentation of the `scatter` method (`http://bit.ly/2i3N2nI`)
- Matplotlib official *Annotation* guide (`http://bit.ly/2yhYHoP`)

Plotting basics with pandas

Pandas makes plotting quite easy by automating much of the procedure for you. All pandas plotting is handled internally by matplotlib and is publicly accessed through the DataFrame or Series `plot` method. We say that the pandas `plot` method is a *wrapper* around matplotlib. When you create a plot in pandas, you will be returned a matplotlib Axes or Figure. You can use the full power of matplotlib to modify this object until you get the desired result.

Pandas is only able to produce a small subset of the plots available with matplotlib, such as line, bar, box, and scatter plots, along with **kernel density estimates** (KDEs) and histograms. Pandas excels at the plots it does create by making the process very easy and efficient, usually taking just a single line of code, saving lots of time when exploring data.

Getting ready

One of the keys to understanding plotting in pandas is to know whether the plotting method requires one or two variables to make the plot. For instance, line and scatter plots require two variables to plot each point. The same holds true for bar plots, which require some x-coordinates to locate the bar and another variable for the height of the bar. Boxplots, histograms, and KDEs use only a single variable to make their plots.

The two-variable line and scatter plots, by default, use the index as the x axis and the values of the columns as the y axis. The one-variable plots ignore the index and apply a transformation or aggregation to each variable to make their plots. In this recipe, we will look at the differences between two-variable and one-variable plots in pandas.

How to do it..

1. Create a small DataFrame with a meaningful index:

```
>>> df = pd.DataFrame(index=['Atiya', 'Abbas', 'Cornelia',
                             'Stephanie', 'Monte'],
                  data={'Apples':[20, 10, 40, 20, 50],
                        'Oranges':[35, 40, 25, 19, 33]})
```

	Apples	Oranges
Atiya	20	35
Abbas	10	40
Cornelia	40	25
Stephanie	20	19
Monte	50	33

2. Bar plots use the index of the labels for the *x* axis and the column values as the bar heights. Use the `plot` method with the `kind` parameter set to `bar`:

```
>>> color = ['.2', '.7']
>>> df.plot(kind='bar', color=color, figsize=(16,4))
```

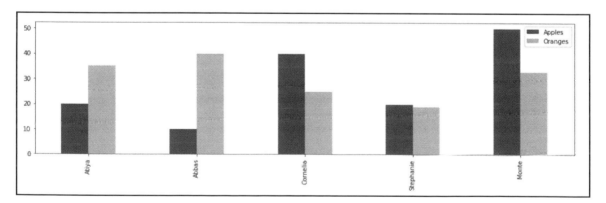

3. A KDE plot ignores the index and uses the values of each column as the x axis and calculates a probability density for the y values:

```
>>> df.plot(kind='kde', color=color, figsize=(16,4))
```

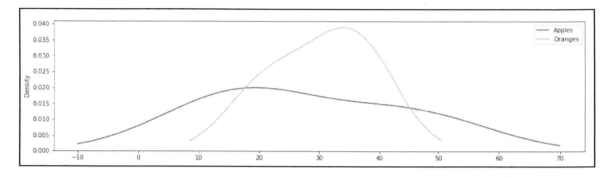

4. Let's plot all two-variable plots together in a single Figure. The scatter plot is the only one that requires you to specify columns for the x and y values. If you wish to use the index for a scatter plot, you will have to use the `reset_index` method to make it a column. The other two plots use the index for the x axis and make a new set of lines/bars for every single numeric column:

```
>>> fig, (ax1, ax2, ax3) = plt.subplots(1, 3, figsize=(16,4))
>>> fig.suptitle('Two Variable Plots', size=20, y=1.02)
>>> df.plot(kind='line', color=color, ax=ax1, title='Line plot')
>>> df.plot(x='Apples', y='Oranges', kind='scatter', color=color,
            ax=ax2, title='Scatterplot')
>>> df.plot(kind='bar', color=color, ax=ax3, title='Bar plot')
```

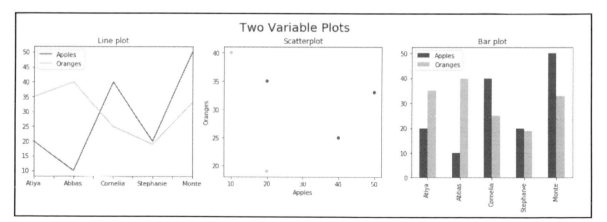

5. Let's put all the one-variable plots in the same Figure as well:

```
>>> fig, (ax1, ax2, ax3) = plt.subplots(1, 3, figsize=(16,4))
>>> fig.suptitle('One Variable Plots', size=20, y=1.02)
>>> df.plot(kind='kde', color=color, ax=ax1, title='KDE plot')
>>> df.plot(kind='box', ax=ax2, title='Boxplot')
>>> df.plot(kind='hist', color=color, ax=ax3, title='Histogram')
```

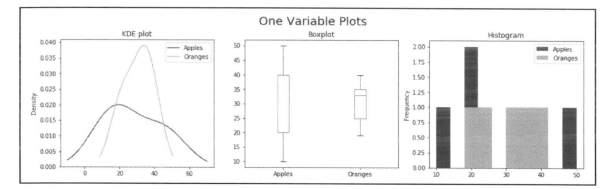

How it works...

Step 1 creates a small sample DataFrame that will help us illustrate the differences between two and one-variable plotting with pandas. By default, pandas will use each numeric column of the DataFrame to make a new set of bars, lines, KDEs, boxplots, or histograms and use the index as the x values when it is a two-variable plot. One of the exceptions is the scatter plot, which must be explicitly given a single column for the x and y values.

The pandas `plot` method is very versatile and has a large number of parameters that allow you to customize the result to your liking. For instance, you can set the Figure size, turn the gridlines on and off, set the range of the x and y axis, color the plot, rotate the tick marks, and much more.

You can also use any of the arguments available to the specific matplotlib plotting method. The extra arguments will be collected by the `**kwds` parameter from the `plot` method and correctly passed to the underlying matplotlib function. For example, In step 2, we create a bar plot. This means that we can use all of the parameters available in the matplotlib `bar` function as well as the ones available in the pandas `plot` method (http://bit.ly/2z213rJ).

In step 3, we create a single-variable KDE plot, which creates a density estimate for each numeric column in the DataFrame. Step 4 places all the two-variable plots in the same Figure. Likewise, step 5 places all the one-variable plots together. Each of steps 4 and 5 creates a Figure with three Axes objects. The command `plt.subplots(1, 3)` creates a Figure with three Axes spread over a single row and three columns. It returns a two-item tuple consisting of the Figure and a one-dimensional NumPy array containing the Axes. The first item of the tuple is unpacked into the variable `fig`. The second item of the tuple is unpacked into three more variables, one for each Axes. The pandas `plot` method handily comes with an `ax` parameter, allowing us to place the result of the plot into a specific Axes in the Figure.

There's more...

With the exception of the scatter plot, all the plots did not specify the columns to be used. Pandas defaulted to using every single numeric column, as well as the index in the case of two-variable plots. You can, of course, specify the exact columns that you would like to use for each x or y value:

```
>>> fig, (ax1, ax2, ax3) = plt.subplots(1, 3, figsize=(16,4))
>>> df.sort_values('Apples').plot(x='Apples', y='Oranges',
                                  kind='line', ax=ax1)
>>> df.plot(x='Apples', y='Oranges', kind='bar', ax=ax2)
>>> df.plot(x='Apples', kind='kde', ax=ax3)
```

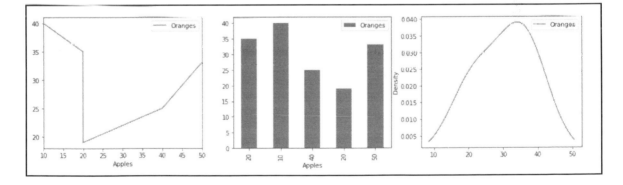

See also

- Pandas official documentation on *Visualization* (http://bit.ly/2zhUqQv)

Visualizing the flights dataset

Exploratory data analysis is mainly guided by visualizations, and pandas provides a great interface for quickly and effortlessly creating them. A simple strategy when beginning a visualization of any dataset is to focus only on univariate plots. The most popular univariate plots tend to be bar charts for categorical data (usually strings) and histograms, boxplots, or KDEs for continuous data (always numeric). Attempting to analyze multiple variables at the same time, directly at the start of a project, can be quite overwhelming.

Getting ready

In this recipe, we do some basic exploratory data analysis on the flights dataset by creating univariate and multivariate plots directly with pandas.

How to do it...

1. Read in the flights dataset, and output the first five rows:

```
>>> flights = pd.read_csv('data/flights.csv')
>>> flights.head()
```

	MONTH	DAY	WEEKDAY	AIRLINE	ORG_AIR	DEST_AIR	SCHED_DEP	DEP_DELAY	AIR_TIME	DIST	SCHED_ARR	ARR_DELAY	DIVERTED	CANCELLED
0	1	1	4	WN	LAX	SLC	1625	58.0	94.0	590	1905	65.0	0	0
1	1	1	4	UA	DEN	IAD	823	7.0	154.0	1452	1333	-13.0	0	0
2	1	1	4	MQ	DFW	VPS	1305	36.0	85.0	641	1453	35.0	0	0
3	1	1	4	AA	DFW	DCA	1555	7.0	126.0	1192	1935	-7.0	0	0
4	1	1	4	WN	LAX	MCI	1720	48.0	166.0	1363	2225	39.0	0	0

2. Before we start plotting, let's calculate the number of diverted, cancelled, delayed, and ontime flights. We already have binary columns for diverted and cancelled. Flights are considered delayed whenever they arrive 15 minutes or more later than scheduled. Let's create two new binary columns to track delayed and on-time arrivals:

```
>>> flights['DELAYED'] = flights['ARR_DELAY'].ge(15).astype(int)
>>> cols = ['DIVERTED', 'CANCELLED', 'DELAYED']
>>> flights['ON_TIME'] = 1 - flights[cols].any(axis=1)

>>> cols.append('ON_TIME')
>>> status = flights[cols].sum()
>>> status
DIVERTED        137
CANCELLED       881
DELAYED       11685
ON_TIME       45789
dtype: int64
```

3. Let's now make several plots on the same Figure for both categorical and continuous columns:

```
>>> fig, ax_array = plt.subplots(2, 3, figsize=(18,8))
>>> (ax1, ax2, ax3), (ax4, ax5, ax6) = ax_array
>>> fig.suptitle('2015 US Flights - Univariate Summary', size=20)

>>> ac = flights['AIRLINE'].value_counts()
>>> ac.plot(kind='barh', ax=ax1, title='Airline')

>>> oc = flights['ORG_AIR'].value_counts()
>>> oc.plot(kind='bar', ax=ax2, rot=0, title='Origin City')

>>> dc = flights['DEST_AIR'].value_counts().head(10)
>>> dc.plot(kind='bar', ax=ax3, rot=0, title='Destination City')

>>> status.plot(kind='bar', ax=ax4, rot=0,
                log=True, title='Flight Status')
>>> flights['DIST'].plot(kind='kde', ax=ax5, xlim=(0, 3000),
                         title='Distance KDE')
>>> flights['ARR_DELAY'].plot(kind='hist', ax=ax6,
                              title='Arrival Delay',
                              range=(0,200))
```

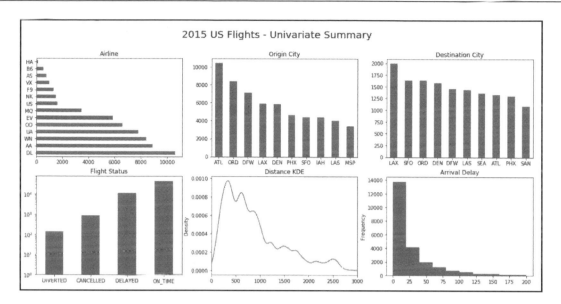

4. This is not an exhaustive look at all the univariate statistics but gives us a good amount of detail on some of the variables. Before we move on to multivariate plots, let's plot the number of flights per week. This is the right situation to use a time series plot with the dates on the *x* axis. Unfortunately, we don't have pandas Timestamps in any of the columns, but we do have the month and day. The `to_datetime` function has a nifty trick that identifies column names that match Timestamp components. For instance, if you have a DataFrame with exactly three columns titled `year`, `month`, and `day`, then passing this DataFrame to the `to_datetime` function will return a sequence of Timestamps. To prepare our current DataFrame, we need to add a column for the year and use the scheduled departure time to get the hour and minute:

```
>>> hour = flights['SCHED_DEP'] // 100
>>> minute = flights['SCHED_DEP'] % 100
>>> df_date = flights[['MONTH', 'DAY']].assign(YEAR=2015,
HOUR=hour,
                                                MINUTE=minute)
>>> df_date.head()
```

	MONTH	DAY	HOUR	MINUTE	YEAR
0	1	1	16	25	2015
1	1	1	8	23	2015
2	1	1	13	5	2015
3	1	1	15	55	2015
4	1	1	17	20	2015

5. Then, almost by magic, we can turn this DataFrame into a proper Series of Timestamps with the to_datetime function:

```
>>> flight_dep = pd.to_datetime(df_date)
>>> flight_dep.head()
0    2015-01-01 16:25:00
1    2015-01-01 08:23:00
2    2015-01-01 13:05:00
3    2015-01-01 15:55:00
4    2015-01-01 17:20:00
dtype: datetime64[ns]
```

6. Let's use this result as our new index and then find the count of flights per week with the resample method:

```
>>> flights.index = flight_dep
>>> fc = flights.resample('W').size()
>>> fc.plot(figsize=(12,3), title='Flights per Week', grid=True)
```

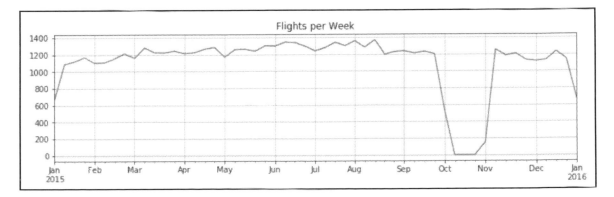

7. This plot is quite revealing. It appears that we have no data for the month of October. Due to this missing data, it's quite difficult to analyze any trend visually, if one exists. The first and last weeks are also lower than normal, likely because there isn't a full week of data for them. Let's make any week of data with fewer than 1,000 flights missing. Then, we can use the `interpolate` method to fill in this missing data:

```
>>> fc_miss = fc.where(fc > 1000)
>>> fc_intp = fc_miss.interpolate(limit_direction='both')

>>> ax = fc_intp.plot(color='black', figsize=(16,4))
>>> fc_intp[fc < 500].plot(linewidth=10, grid=True,
                           color='.8', ax=ax)

>>> ax.annotate(xy=(.8, .55), xytext=(.8, .77),
                xycoords='axes fraction', s='missing data',
                ha='center', size=20, arrowprops=dict())
>>> ax.set_title('Flights per Week (Interpolated Missing Data)')
```

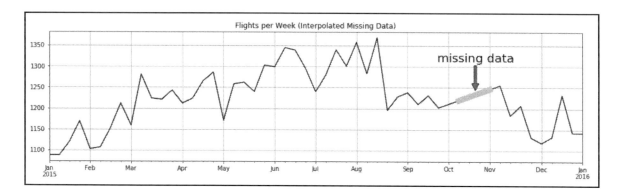

8. Let's change directions and focus on multivariable plotting. Let's find the 10 airports that:

- Have the longest average distance traveled for inbound flights
- Have a minimum of 100 total flights:

```
>>> flights.groupby('DEST_AIR')['DIST'] \
        .agg(['mean', 'count']) \
        .query('count > 100') \
        .sort_values('mean') \
        .tail(10) \
        .plot(kind='bar', y='mean', rot=0, legend=False,
              title='Average Distance per Destination')
```

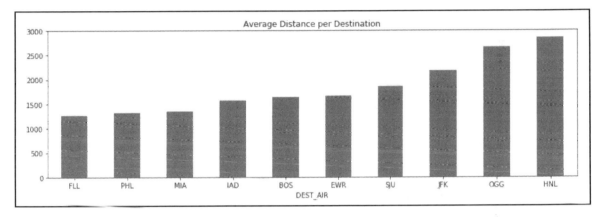

9. It's no surprise that the top two destination airports are in Hawaii. Now let's analyze two variables at the same time by making a scatter plot between distance and airtime for all flights under 2,000 miles:

```
>>> fs = flights.reset_index(drop=True)[['DIST', 'AIR_TIME']] \
        .query('DIST <= 2000').dropna()
>>> fs.plot(x='DIST', y='AIR_TIME', kind='scatter',
            s=1, figsize=(16,4))
```

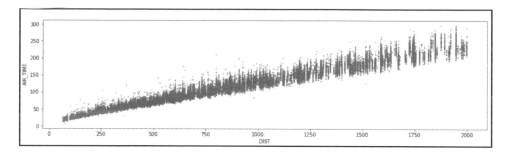

10. As expected, a tight linear relationship exists between distance and airtime, though the variance seems to increase as the number of miles increases. There are a few flights that are quite far outside the trendline. Let's try and identify them. A linear regression model may be used to formally identify them, but as pandas doesn't directly support linear regression, we will take a more manual approach. Let's use the `cut` function to place the flight distances into one of eight groups:

```
>>> fs['DIST_GROUP'] = pd.cut(fs['DIST'], bins=range(0, 2001, 250))
>>> fs['DIST_GROUP'].value_counts().sort_index()
(0, 250]         6529
(250, 500]      12631
(500, 750]      11506
(750, 1000]      8832
(1000, 1250]     5071
(1250, 1500]     3198
(1500, 1750]     3885
(1750, 2000]     1815
Name: DIST_GROUP, dtype: int64
```

11. We will assume that all flights within each group should have similar flight times, and thus calculate for each flight the number of standard deviations if the flight time deviates from the mean of that group:

```
>>> normalize = lambda x: (x - x.mean()) / x.std()
>>> fs['TIME_SCORE'] = fs.groupby('DIST_GROUP')['AIR_TIME'] \
                          .transform(normalize)
>>> fs.head()
```

	DIST	AIR_TIME	DIST_GROUP	TIME_SCORE
0	590	94.0	(500, 750]	0.490966
1	1452	154.0	(1250, 1500]	-1.267551
2	641	85.0	(500, 750]	-0.296749
3	1192	126.0	(1000, 1250]	-1.211020
4	1363	166.0	(1250, 1500]	-0.521999

12. We now need a way to discover the outliers. A box plot provides a nice visual for detecting outliers. Unfortunately, a bug exists when attempting to make a box plot with the `plot` method, but thankfully, there is a DataFrame `boxplot` method that works:

```
>>> ax = fs.boxplot(by='DIST_GROUP', column='TIME_SCORE',
                     figsize=(16,4))
>>> ax.set_title('Z-Scores for Distance Groups')
>>> ax.figure.suptitle('')
```

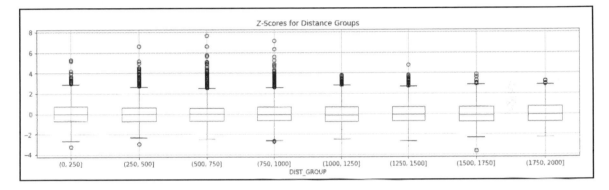

13. Let's arbitrarily choose to examine the points that are greater than six standard deviations away from the mean. Because we reset the index in the `fs` DataFrame in step 9, we can use it to identify each unique row in the flights DataFrame. Let's create a separate DataFrame with just the outliers:

```
>>> outliers = flights.iloc[fs[fs['TIME_SCORE'] > 6].index]
>>> outliers = outliers[['AIRLINE','ORG_AIR', 'DEST_AIR',
'AIR_TIME',
                         'DIST', 'ARR_DELAY', 'DIVERTED']]
>>> outliers['PLOT_NUM'] = range(1, len(outliers) + 1)
>>> outliers
```

	AIRLINE	ORG_AIR	DEST_AIR	AIR_TIME	DIST	ARR_DELAY	DIVERTED	PLOT_NUM
2015-04-08 09:40:00	DL	ATL	CVG	121.0	373	54.0	0	1
2015-05-25 16:30:00	F9	MSP	ATL	199.0	907	79.0	0	2
2015-09-10 20:00:00	UA	IAH	MCI	176.0	643	76.0	0	3
2015-12-10 19:53:00	OO	PHX	SFO	164.0	651	146.0	0	4
2015-12-26 09:15:00	NK	ORD	DFW	210.0	802	98.0	0	5

14. We can use this table to identify the outliers on the plot from step 9. Pandas also provides a way to attach tables to the bottom of the graph:

```
>>> ax = fs.plot(x='DIST', y='AIR_TIME',
                 kind='scatter', s=1,
                 figsize=(16,4), table=outliers)
>>> outliers.plot(x='DIST', y='AIR_TIME',
                  kind='scatter', s=25, ax=ax, grid=True)

>>> outs = outliers[['AIR_TIME', 'DIST', 'PLOT_NUM']]
>>> for t, d, n in outs.itertuples(index=False):
        ax.text(d + 5, t + 5, str(n))
>>> plt.setp(ax.get_xticklabels(), y=.1)
>>> plt.setp(ax.get_xticklines(), visible=False)
>>> ax.set_xlabel('')
>>> ax.set_title('Flight Time vs Distance with Outliers')
```

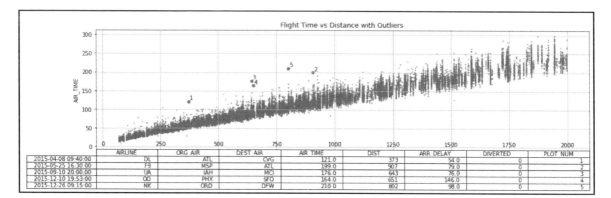

How it works...

After reading in our data in step 1 and calculating columns for delayed and on-time flights, we are ready to begin making univariate plots. The call to the subplots function in step 3 creates a 2 x 3 grid of equal-sized Axes. We unpack each Axes into its own variable to reference it. Each of the calls to the plot method references the specific Axes in the Figure with the ax parameter. The value_counts method is used to create the three Series that form the plots in the top row. The rot parameter rotates the tick labels to the given angle.

The plot in the bottom left-hand corner uses a logarithmic scale for the *y* axis, as the number of on-time flights is about two orders of magnitude greater than the number of cancelled flights. Without the log scale, the left two bars would be difficult to see. By default, KDE plots may result in positive areas for impossible values, such as negative miles in the plot on the bottom row. For this reason, we limit the range of the x values with the `xlim` parameter.

The histogram created in the bottom right-hand corner on arrival delays was passed the `range` parameter. This is not directly part of the method signature of the pandas `plot` method. Instead, this parameter gets collected by the `**kwds` argument and then passed along to the matplotlib `hist` function. Using `xlim`, as done in the previous plot would not work in this case. The plot would simply be cropped without recalculating the new bin widths for just that portion of the graph. The `range` parameter, however, both limits the x-axis and calculates the bin widths for just that range.

Step 4 creates a special extra DataFrame to hold columns with only datetime components so that we can instantly turn each row into a Timestamp with the `to_datetime` function in step 5. The `resample` method, by default, uses the index to form groups based on the date offset passed. We return the number of flights per week (W) as a Series and then call the `plot` method on it, which nicely formats the index as the x-axis. A glaring hole for the month of October appears.

To fill this hole, we use the `where` method to set only value less than 1,000 to missing in the first line of step 7. We then fill in the missing data through linear interpolation. By default, the `interpolate` method only interpolates in a forward direction, so any missing values at the start of the DataFrame will remain. By setting the `limit_direction` parameter to `both`, we ensure that there are no missing values. The new data, now stored in `fc_intp`, is plotted. To show the missing data more clearly, we select the points that were missing from the original and make a line plot on the same Axes directly on top of the previous line. Typically, when we annotate the plot, we can use the data coordinates, but in this instance, it isn't obvious what the coordinates of the *x-axis* are. To use the Axes coordinate system (the one that ranges from (0,0), to (1,1)), the `xycoords` parameter is set to `axes fraction`. This new plot now excludes the erroneous data and it makes it is much easier to spot a trend. The summer months have much more air traffic than any other time of the year.

In step 8, we use a long chain of methods to group by each destination airport and apply two functions, mean and count, to the distance column. The query method is especially nice when for use in a method chain, as it clearly and succinctly selects the desired rows of data of a given condition. We have two columns in our DataFrame when we get to the plot method, which, by default, would make a bar plot for each column. We are not interested in the count column and therefore select only the mean column to form the bars. Also, when plotting with a DataFrame, each column name appears in the legend. This would put the word mean in the legend, which would not be useful, so we remove it by setting the legend parameter to False.

Step 9 begins a new analysis by looking at the relationship between distance traveled and flight airtime. Due to the huge number of points, we shrink their size with the s parameter. To find the flights that took much longer on average to reach their destination, we group each flight into 250 mile chunks in step 10 and find the number of standard deviations from their group mean in step 11.

In step 12, a new box plot is created in the same Axes for every unique value of the by parameter. We capture the Axes object by saving it to a variable after the call to boxplot. This method creates an unnecessary title over the Figure, which is erased by first accessing the Figure and then setting the suptitle to an empty string.

In step 13, the current DataFrame, fs, contains the information we need to find the slowest flights, but it does not possess all of the original data that we might want to investigate further. Because we reset the index of fs in step 9, we can use it to identify the same row from the original. The first line in this step does this for us. We also give each of the outlier rows a unique integer to identify it later on when plotting.

In step 14, we begin with the same scatter plot as in step 9 but use the table parameter to append the outlier table to the bottom of the plot. We then plot our outliers as a scatter plot directly on top and ensure that their points are larger to identify them easily. The itertuples method loops through each DataFrame row and returns its values as a tuple. We unpack the corresponding x and y values for our plot and label it with the number we assigned to it.

As the table is placed directly underneath of the plot, it interferes with the plotting objects on the *x* axis. We move the tick labels to the inside of the axis and remove the tick lines and axis label. This table provides some nice information to anyone who is interested in these outlying events.

See also

- Pandas official documentation of plotting with tables (`http://bit.ly/2yhdBd7`)

Stacking area charts to discover emerging trends

Stacked area charts are great visualizations to discover emerging trends, especially in the marketplace. It is a common choice to show the percentage of the market share for things such as internet browsers, cell phones, or vehicles.

Getting ready

In this recipe, we will use data gathered from the popular website meetup.com. Using a stacked area chart, we will show membership distribution between five data science-related meetup groups.

How to do it...

1. Read in the meetup dataset, convert the `join_date` column into a Timestamp, place it in the index, and output the first five rows:

```
>>> meetup = pd.read_csv('data/meetup_groups.csv',
                         parse_dates=['join_date'],
                         index_col='join_date')
>>> meetup.head()
```

	group	city	state	country
join_date				
2016-11-18 02:41:29	houston machine learning	Houston	TX	us
2017-05-09 14:16:37	houston machine learning	Houston	TX	us
2016-12-30 02:34:16	houston machine learning	Houston	TX	us
2016-07-18 00:48:17	houston machine learning	Houston	TX	us
2017-05-25 12:58:16	houston machine learning	Houston	TX	us

2. Let's get the number of people who joined each group each week:

```
>>> group_count = meetup.groupby([pd.Grouper(freq='W'), 'group']) \
                        .size()
>>> group_count.head()
join_date    group
2010-11-07   houstonr     5
2010-11-14   houstonr    11
2010-11-21   houstonr     2
2010-12-05   houstonr     1
2011-01-16   houstonr     2
dtype: int64
```

3. Unstack the group level so that each meetup group has its own column of data:

```
>>> gc2 = group_count.unstack('group', fill_value=0)
>>> gc2.tail()
```

group	houston data science	houston data visualization	houston energy data science	houston machine learning	houstonr
join_date					
2017-09-17	16	2	6	5	0
2017-09-24	19	4	16	12	7
2017-10-01	20	6	6	20	1
2017-10-08	22	10	10	4	2
2017-10-15	14	13	9	11	2

4. This data represents the number of members who joined that particular week. Let's take the cumulative sum of each column to get the grand total number of members:

```
>>> group_total = gc2.cumsum()
>>> group_total.tail()
```

group	houston data science	houston data visualization	houston energy data science	houston machine learning	houstonr
join_date					
2017-09-17	2105	1708	1886	708	1056
2017-09-24	2124	1712	1902	720	1063
2017-10-01	2144	1718	1908	740	1064
2017-10-08	2166	1728	1918	744	1066
2017-10-15	2180	1741	1927	755	1068

5. Many stacked area charts use the percentage of the total so that each row always adds up to 100 percent. Let's divide each row by the row total to find this percentage:

```
>>> row_total = group_total.sum(axis='columns')
>>> group_cum_pct = group_total.div(row_total, axis='index')
>>> group_cum_pct.tail()
```

group join_date	houston data science	houston data visualization	houston energy data science	houston machine learning	houstonr
2017-09-17	0.282058	0.228862	0.252713	0.094868	0.141498
2017-09-24	0.282409	0.227629	0.252892	0.095732	0.141338
2017-10-01	0.283074	0.226829	0.251914	0.097703	0.140481
2017-10-08	0.284177	0.226712	0.251640	0.097612	0.139858
2017-10-15	0.284187	0.226959	0.251206	0.098423	0.139226

6. We can now create our stacked area plot, which will continually accumulate the columns, one on top of the other:

```
>>> ax = group_cum_pct.plot(kind='area', figsize=(18,4),
                            cmap='Greys', xlim=('2013-6', None),
                            ylim=(0, 1), legend=False)
>>> ax.figure.suptitle('Houston Meetup Groups', size=25)
>>> ax.set_xlabel('')
>>> ax.yaxis.tick_right()

>>> plot_kwargs = dict(xycoords='axes fraction', size=15)
>>> ax.annotate(xy=(.1, .7), s='R Users',
                color='w', **plot_kwargs)
>>> ax.annotate(xy=(.25, .16), s='Data Visualization',
                color='k', **plot_kwargs)
>>> ax.annotate(xy=(.5, .55), s='Energy Data Science',
                color='k', **plot_kwargs)
>>> ax.annotate(xy=(.83, .07), s='Data Science',
                color='k', **plot_kwargs)
>>> ax.annotate(xy=(.86, .78), s='Machine Learning',
                color='w', **plot_kwargs)
```

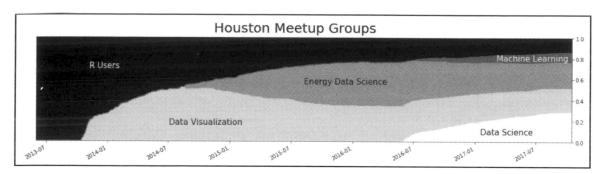

How it works...

Our goal is to determine the distribution of members among the five largest data science meetup groups in Houston over time. To do this, we need to find the total membership at every point in time since each group began. We have the exact date and time when each person joined each group. In step 2, we group by each week (offset alias W) and meetup group and return the number of sign-ups for that week with the size method.

The resulting Series is not suitable to make plots with pandas. Each meetup group needs its own column, so we reshape the group index level as columns. We set the option fill_value to zero so that groups with no memberships during a particular week will not have missing values.

We are in need of the total number of members each week. The cumsum method in step 4 provides this for us. We could create our stacked area plot directly after this step, which would be a nice way to visualize the raw total membership. In step 5, we find the distribution of each group as a percentage of the total members in all groups by dividing each value by its row total. By default, pandas automatically aligns objects by their columns, so we cannot use the division operator. Instead, we must use the div method to change the axis of alignment to the index

The data is now perfectly suited for a stacked area plot, which we create in step 6. Notice that pandas allows you to set the axis limits with a datetime string. This will not work if done directly in matplotlib using the ax.set_xlim method. The starting date for the plot is moved up a couple years because the Houston R Users group began much earlier than any of the other groups.

There's more...

Although typically frowned upon by data visualization gurus, pandas can create pie charts. In this instance, we use them to see snapshots of the total group distribution over time. Let's first select every third month of data, beginning 18 months prior to the end of data collection. We use the `asfreq` method, which only works on DataFrames with datetime values in the index. The offset alias `3MS` is used to represent the start of every third month. Because `group_cum_pct` is aggregated by week, the first day of the month is not always present. We set the `method` parameter to `bfill`, which stands for backfill; it will look back in time to find the first day of the month that has data in it. We then use the `to_period` method (which also only works with datetimes in the index) to change the values in the index to a pandas period of time. Finally, we transpose the data so that each column represents the distribution of members in the meetup group for that month:

```
>>> pie_data = group_cum_pct.asfreq('3MS', method='bfill') \
                    .tail(6).to_period('M').T
>>> pie_data
```

join_date group	2016-06	2016-09	2016-12	2017-03	2017-06	2017-09
houston data science	0.016949	0.110375	0.171245	0.212289	0.244033	0.280162
houston data visualization	0.337827	0.306052	0.277244	0.261103	0.242085	0.230332
houston energy data science	0.416025	0.354467	0.312271	0.288859	0.267576	0.253758
houston machine learning	0.000000	0.037176	0.051969	0.071593	0.087839	0.093026
houstonr	0.229199	0.191931	0.187271	0.166156	0.158467	0.142722

From here, we can use the `plot` method to create the pie charts:

```
>>> from matplotlib.cm import Greys
>>> greys = Greys(np.arange(50,250,40))

>>> ax_array = pie_data.plot(kind='pie', subplots=True,
                        layout=(2,3), labels=None,
                        autopct='%1.0f%%', pctdistance=1.22,
                        colors=greys)
>>> ax1 = ax_array[0, 0]
>>> ax1.figure.legend(ax1.patches, pie_data.index, ncol=3)
>>> for ax in ax_array.flatten():
        ax.xaxis.label.set_visible(True)
```

```
        ax.set_xlabel(ax.get_ylabel())
        ax.set_ylabel('')
>>> ax1.figure.subplots_adjust(hspace=.3)
```

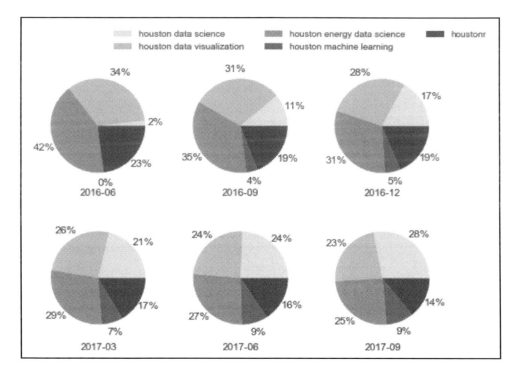

Understanding the differences between seaborn and pandas

Outside of pandas, the seaborn library is one of the most popular in the Python data science community to create visualizations. Like pandas, it does not do any actual plotting itself and is completely reliant on matplotlib for the heavy lifting. Seaborn plotting functions work directly with pandas DataFrames to create aesthetically pleasing visualizations.

While seaborn and pandas both reduce the overhead of matplotlib, the way they approach data is completely different. Nearly all of the seaborn plotting functions require tidy (or long) data. When data is in tidy form, it is not ready for consumption or interpretation until some function is applied to it to yield a result. Tidy data is the raw building blocks that makes all other analysis possible. Processing tidy data during data analysis often creates aggregated or wide data. This data, in wide format, is what pandas uses to make its plots.

Getting ready

In this recipe, we will build similar plots with both seaborn and matplotlib to show definitively that they accept tidy versus wide data.

How to do it...

1. Read in the employee dataset, and output the first five rows:

```
>>> employee = pd.read_csv('data/employee.csv',
                           parse_dates=['HIRE_DATE', 'JOB_DATE'])
>>> employee.head()
```

UNIQUE_ID	POSITION_TITLE	DEPARTMENT	BASE_SALARY	RACE	EMPLOYMENT_TYPE	GENDER	EMPLOYMENT_STATUS	HIRE_DATE	JOB_DATE
0	ASSISTANT DIRECTOR (EX LVL)	Municipal Courts Department	121862.0	Hispanic/Latino	Full Time	Female	Active	2006-06-12	2012-10-13
1	LIBRARY ASSISTANT	Library	26125.0	Hispanic/Latino	Full Time	Female	Active	2000-07-19	2010-09-18
2	POLICE OFFICER	Houston Police Department-HPD	45279.0	White	Full Time	Male	Active	2015-02-03	2015-02-03
3	ENGINEER/OPERATOR	Houston Fire Department (HFD)	63166.0	White	Full Time	Male	Active	1982-02-08	1991-05-25
4	ELECTRICIAN	General Services Department	56347.0	White	Full Time	Male	Active	1989-06-19	1994-10-22

2. Import the seaborn library, and alias it sns:

```
>>> import seaborn as sns
```

3. Let's make a bar chart of the count of each department with seaborn:

```
>>> sns.countplot(y='DEPARTMENT', data=employee)
```

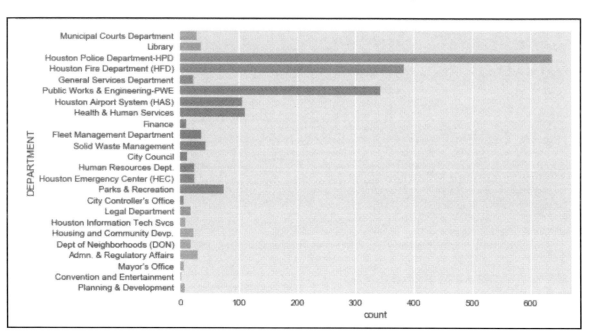

4. To reproduce this plot with pandas, we will need to aggregate the data beforehand:

```
>>> employee['DEPARTMENT'].value_counts().plot('barh')
```

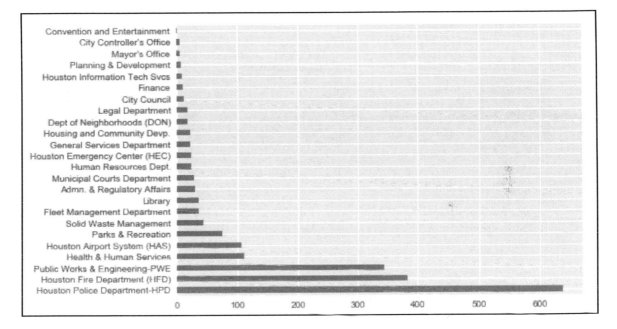

5. Now, let's find the average salary for each race with seaborn:

```
>>> ax = sns.barplot(x='RACE', y='BASE_SALARY', data=employee)
>>> ax.figure.set_size_inches(16, 4)
```

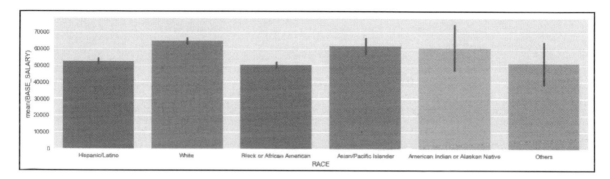

6. To replicate this with pandas, we will need to group by each race first:

```
>>> avg_sal = employee.groupby('RACE', sort=False) \
                      ['BASE_SALARY'].mean()
>>> ax = avg_sal.plot(kind='bar', rot=0, figsize=(16,4), width=.8)
>>> ax.set_xlim(-.5, 5.5)
>>> ax.set_ylabel('Mean Salary')
```

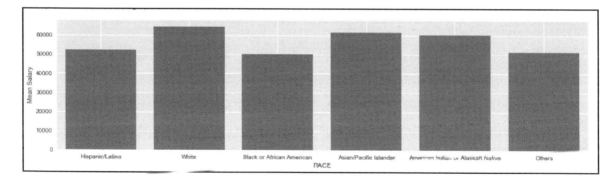

7. Seaborn also has the ability to distinguish groups within the data through a third variable, `hue`, in most of its plotting functions. Let's find the mean salary by race and gender:

```
>>> ax = sns.barplot(x='RACE', y='BASE_SALARY', hue='GENDER',
                     data=employee, palette='Greys')
>>> ax.figure.set_size_inches(16,4)
```

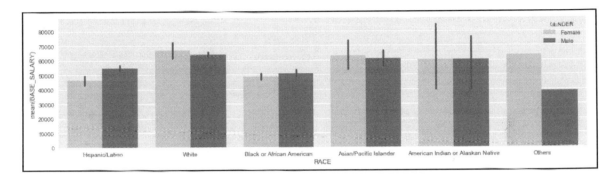

8. With pandas, we will have to group by both race and gender and then unstack the genders as column names:

```
>>> employee.groupby(['RACE', 'GENDER'], sort=False) \
           ['BASE_SALARY'].mean().unstack('GENDER') \
           .plot(kind='bar', figsize=(16,4), rot=0,
                 width=.8, cmap='Greys')
```

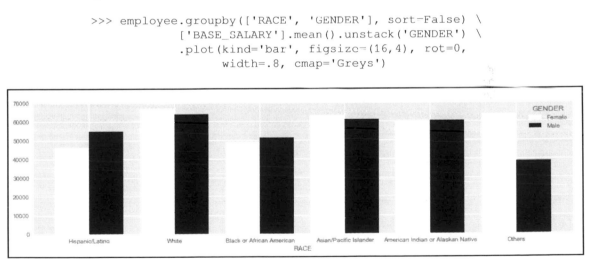

9. A box plot is another type of plot that seaborn and pandas have in common. Let's create a box plot of salary by race and gender with seaborn:

```
>>> sns.boxplot(x='GENDER', y='BASE_SALARY', data=employee,
                hue='RACE', palette='Greys')
>>> ax.figure.set_size_inches(14,4)
```

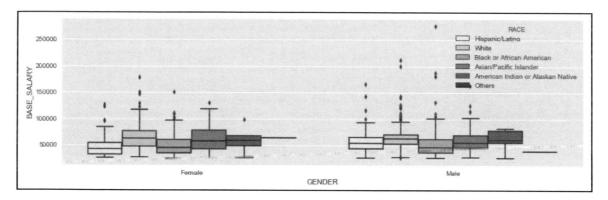

10. Pandas is not easily able to produce an exact replication for this box plot. It can create two separate Axes for gender and then make box plots of the salary by race:

```
>>> fig, ax_array = plt.subplots(1, 2, figsize=(14,4), sharey=True)
>>> for g, ax in zip(['Female', 'Male'], ax_array):
        employee.query('GENDER== @g') \
                .boxplot(by='RACE', column='BASE_SALARY',
                        ax=ax, rot=20)
        ax.set_title(g + ' Salary')
        ax.set_xlabel('')
>>> fig.suptitle('')
```

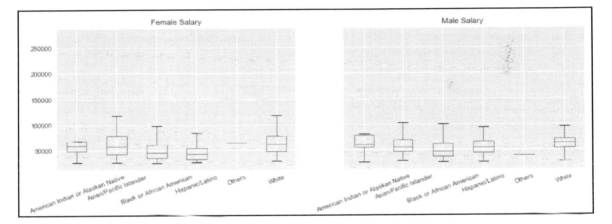

How it works...

Importing seaborn in step 2 changes many of the default properties of matplotlib. There are about 300 default plotting parameters that can be accessed within the dictionary-like object `plt.rcParams`. To restore the matplotlib defaults, call the `plt.rcdefaults` function with no arguments. The style of pandas plots will also be affected when importing seaborn. Our employee dataset meets the requirements for tidy data and thus makes it perfect to use for nearly all seaborn's plotting functions.

Seaborn will do all the aggregation; you just need to supply your DataFrame to the `data` parameter and refer to the columns with their string names. For instance, in step 3, the `countplot` function effortlessly counts each occurrence of a DEPARTMENT to create a bar chart. All seaborn plotting functions have x and y parameters. We could have made a vertical bar plot using x instead of y. Pandas forces you to do a bit more work to get the same plot. In step 4, we must precalculate the height of the bins using the `value_counts` method.

Seaborn is able to do more complex aggregations, as seen in steps 5 and 7, with the `barplot` function. The `hue` parameter further splits each of the groups on the *x* axis. Pandas is capable of nearly replicating these plots by grouping by the x and hue variables in steps 6 and 8.

Box plots are available in both seaborn and pandas and can be plotted directly with tidy data without any aggregation. Even though no aggregation is necessary, seaborn still has the upper hand, as it can split data neatly into separate groups using the `hue` parameter. Pandas cannot easily replicate this function from seaborn, as seen in step 10. Each group needs to be split with the `query` method and plotted on its own Axes. It is actually possible for pandas to split on multiple variables, passing a list to the `by` parameter, but the result is not nearly as elegant:

```
>>> ax = employee.boxplot(by=['GENDER', 'RACE'],
                    column='BASE_SALARY',
                    figsize=(16,4), rot=15)
>>> ax.figure.suptitle('')
```

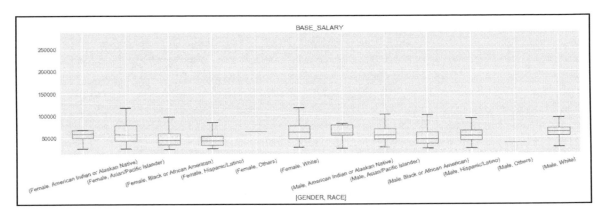

See also

- Seaborn official tutorial (`http://bit.ly/2yhwuPy`)
- Seaborn complete API (`http://bit.ly/2ghWN0T`)

Doing multivariate analysis with seaborn Grids

To understand seaborn further, it is helpful to be aware of the hierarchy between the functions that return multiple Axes as a seaborn Grid and those that return single Axes:

Grid type	Grid function	Axes functions	Variable type
FacetGrid	factorplot	stripplot, swarmplot, boxplot, violinplot, lvplot, pointplot, barplot, countplot	Categorical
FacetGrid	lmplot	regplot	Continuous
PairGrid	pairplot	regplot, distplot, kdeplot	Continuous
JointGrid	jointplot	regplot, kdeplot, residplot	Continuous
ClusterGrid	clustermap	heatmap	Continuous

The seaborn Axes functions may all be called independently to produce a single plot. The Grid functions, for the most part, use the Axes functions to build the grid. The final objects returned from the Grid functions are of Grid type, of which there are four different kinds. Advanced use cases necessitate the direct use of Grid types, but the vast majority of the time, you will call the underlying Grid functions to produce the actual Grid and not the constructor itself.

Getting ready

In this recipe, we will examine the relationship between years of experience and salary by gender and race. We will begin by creating a simple regression plot with a seaborn Axes function and then add more dimensions to the plot with Grid functions.

How to do it...

1. Read in the employee dataset, and create a column for years of experience:

```
>>> employee = pd.read_csv('data/employee.csv',
                     parse_dates=['HIRE_DATE', 'JOB_DATE'])
>>> days_hired = pd.to_datetime('12-1-2016') -
employee['HIRE_DATE']

>>> one_year = pd.Timedelta(1, unit='Y')
>>> employee['YEARS_EXPERIENCE'] = days_hired / one_year
>>> employee[['HIRE_DATE', 'YEARS_EXPERIENCE']].head()
```

	HIRE_DATE	YEARS_EXPERIENCE
0	2006-06-12	10.472494
1	2000-07-19	16.369946
2	2015-02-03	1.826184
3	1982-02-08	34.812488
4	1989-06-19	27.452994

2. Let's create a basic scatter plot with a fitted regression line to represent the relationship between years of experience and salary:

```
>>> ax = sns.regplot(x='YEARS_EXPERIENCE', y='BASE_SALARY',
                     data=employee)
>>> ax.figure.set_size_inches(14,4)
```

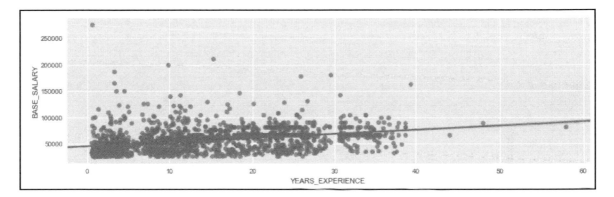

3. The `regplot` function cannot plot multiple regression lines for different levels of a third variable. Let's use its parent function, `lmplot`, to plot a seaborn Grid that adds the same regression lines for males and females:

```
>>> g = sns.lmplot('YEARS_EXPERIENCE', 'BASE_SALARY',
                   hue='GENDER', palette='Greys',
                   scatter_kws={'s':10}, data=employee)
>>> g.fig.set_size_inches(14, 4)
>>> type(g)
seaborn.axisgrid.FacetGrid
```

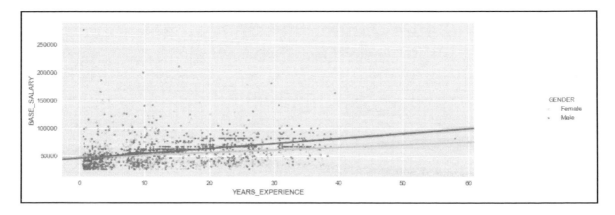

4. The real power of the seaborn Grid functions is their ability to add more Axes based on another variable. Each seaborn Grid has the `col` and `row` parameters available to divide the data further into different groups. For instance, we can create a separate plot for each unique race in the dataset and still fit the regression lines by gender:

```
>>> grid = sns.lmplot(x='YEARS_EXPERIENCE', y='BASE_SALARY',
                      hue='GENDER', col='RACE', col_wrap=3,
                      palette='Greys', sharex=False,
                      line_kws = {'linewidth':5},
                      data=employee)
>>> grid.set(ylim=(20000, 120000))
```

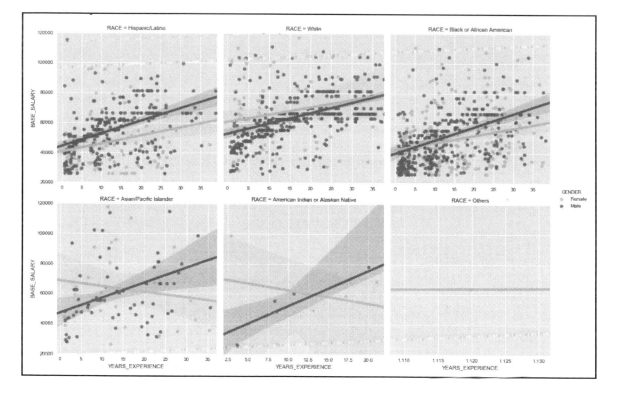

How it works...

In step 1, we create another continuous variable by using pandas date functionality. This data was collected from the city of Houston on December 1, 2016. We use this date to determine how long each employee has worked for the city. When we subtract dates, as done in the second line of code, we are returned a Timedelta object whose largest unit is days. We could have simply divided this number by 365 to calculate the years of experience. Instead, we use `Timedelta(1, unit='Y')` to get a more precise measurement, which happens to be 365 days, 5 hours, 42 minutes and 19 seconds if you are counting at home.

Step 2 uses the seaborn Axes function `regplot` to create a scatter plot with the estimated regression line. It returns an Axes, which we use to change the size of the Figure. In order to create two separate regression lines for each gender, we must use its parent function, `lmplot`. It contains the `hue` parameter, which creates a new regression line for each unique value of that variable. At the end of step 3, we verify that `lmplot` does indeed return a seaborn Grid object.

The seaborn Grid is essentially a wrapper around the entire Figure, with a few convenience methods to alter its elements. All seaborn Grids may access the underlying Figure with their `fig` attribute. Step 4 shows a common use-case for seaborn Grid functions, which is to create multiple plots based on a third or even fourth variable. We set the `col` parameter to *RACE*. Six regression plots are created for each of the six unique races in the dataset. Normally, this would return a grid consisting of 1 row and 6 columns, but we use the `col_wrap` parameter to limit the number of columns to 3.

There are several more available parameters to control most of the important aspects of the Grid. It is possible to change use parameters from the underlying line and scatter plot matplotlib functions. To do so, set the `scatter_kws` or the `line_kws` parameters equal to a dictionary that has the matplotlib parameter as a string paired to the value you want it to be.

There's more...

We can do a similar type of analysis when we have categorical features. First, let's reduce the number of levels in the categorical variables race and department to the top two and three most common, respectively:

```
>>> deps = employee['DEPARTMENT'].value_counts().index[:2]
>>> races = employee['RACE'].value_counts().index[:3]
>>> is_dep = employee['DEPARTMENT'].isin(deps)
>>> is_race = employee['RACE'].isin(races)
```

```
>>> emp2 = employee[is_dep & is_race].copy()
>>> emp2['DEPARTMENT'] = emp2['DEPARTMENT'].str.extract('(HPD|HFD)',
                                                        expand=True)
>>> emp2.shape
(968, 11)

>>> emp2['DEPARTMENT'].value_counts()
HPD     591
HFD     377
Name: DEPARTMENT, dtype: int64

>>> emp2['RACE'].value_counts()
White                        478
Hispanic/Latino              250
Black or African American    240
Name: RACE, dtype: int64
```

Let's use one of the simpler Axes-level functions, such as a violin plot to view the distribution of years of experience by gender:

```
>>> common_depts = employee.groupby('DEPARTMENT') \
                      .filter(lambda x: len(x) > 50)
>>> ax = sns.violinplot(x='YEARS_EXPERIENCE', y='GENDER',
                       data=common_depts)
>>> ax.figure.set_size_inches(10,4)
```

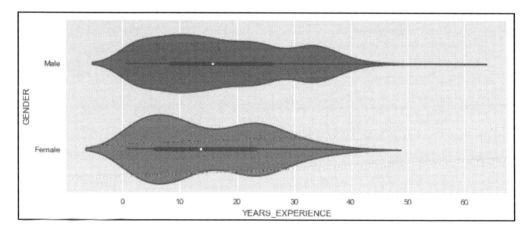

We can then use the Grid function `factorplot` to add a violin plot for each unique combination of department and race with the `col` and `row` parameters:

```
>>> sns.factorplot(x='YEARS_EXPERIENCE', y='GENDER',
                   col='RACE', row='DEPARTMENT',
                   size=3, aspect=2,
                   data=emp2, kind='violin')
```

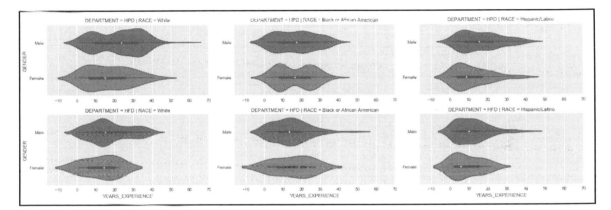

Take a look at the table from the beginning of the recipe. The `factorplot` function must use one of those eight seaborn Axes functions. To do so, you pass its name as a string to the `kind` parameter.

Uncovering Simpson's paradox in the diamonds dataset with seaborn

It is unfortunately quite easy to report erroneous results when doing data analysis. Simpson's paradox is one of the more common phenomena a that can appear in a data analysis. It occurs when one group shows a higher result than another group, when all the data is aggregated, but it shows the opposite when the data is subdivided into different segments. For instance, let's say we have two students, A and B, who have each been given a test with 100 questions on it. Student A answers 50% of the questions correct, while Student B gets 80% correct. This obviously suggests Student B has greater aptitude:

	Raw Score	Percent Correct
Student A	50/100	50
Student B	80/100	80

Let's say that the two tests were very different. Student A's test consisted of 95 problems that were difficult and only five that were easy. Student B was given a test with the exact opposite ratio.

	Difficult	Easy	Difficult Percent	Easy Percent	Total Percent
Student A	45/95	5/5	47	100	50
Student B	2/5	78/95	40	82	80

This paints a completely different picture. Student A now has a higher percentage of both the difficult and easy problems but has a much lower percentage as a whole. This is a quintessential example of Simpson's paradox. The aggregated whole shows the opposite of each individual segment.

Getting ready

In this recipe, we will first reach a perplexing result that appears to suggest that higher quality diamonds are worth less than lower quality ones. We uncover Simpson's paradox by taking more finely grained glimpses into the data that suggest the opposite is actually true.

How to do it...

1. Read in the diamonds dataset, and output the first five rows:

    ```
    >>> diamonds = pd.read_csv('data/diamonds.csv')
    >>> diamonds.head()
    ```

	carat	cut	color	clarity	depth	table	price	x	y	z
0	0.23	Ideal	E	SI2	61.5	55.0	326	3.95	3.98	2.43
1	0.21	Premium	E	SI1	59.8	61.0	326	3.89	3.84	2.31
2	0.23	Good	E	VS1	56.9	65.0	327	4.05	4.07	2.31
3	0.29	Premium	I	VS2	62.4	58.0	334	4.20	4.23	2.63
4	0.31	Good	J	SI2	63.3	58.0	335	4.34	4.35	2.75

2. Before we begin analysis, let's change the `cut`, `color`, and `clarity` columns into ordered categorical variables:

    ```
    >>> cut_cats = ['Fair', 'Good', 'Very Good', 'Premium', 'Ideal']
    >>> color_cats = ['J', 'I', 'H', 'G', 'F', 'E', 'D']
    >>> clarity_cats = ['I1', 'SI2', 'SI1', 'VS2',
                        'VS1', 'VVS2', 'VVS1', 'IF']
    >>> diamonds['cut'] = pd.Categorical(diamonds['cut'],
                                         categories=cut_cats,
                                         ordered=True)

    >>> diamonds['color'] = pd.Categorical(diamonds['color'],
                                           categories=color_cats,
                                           ordered=True)

    >>> diamonds['clarity'] = pd.Categorical(diamonds['clarity'],
                                             categories=clarity_cats,
                                             ordered=True)
    ```

3. Seaborn uses category orders for its plots. Let's make a bar plot of the mean price for each level of cut, color, and clarity:

```
>>> import seaborn as sns
>>> fig, (ax1, ax2, ax3) = plt.subplots(1, 3, figsize=(14,4))
>>> sns.barplot(x='color', y='price', data=diamonds, ax=ax1)
>>> sns.barplot(x='cut', y='price', data=diamonds, ax=ax2)
>>> sns.barplot(x='clarity', y='price', data=diamonds, ax=ax3)
>>> fig.suptitle('Price Decreasing with Increasing Quality?')
```

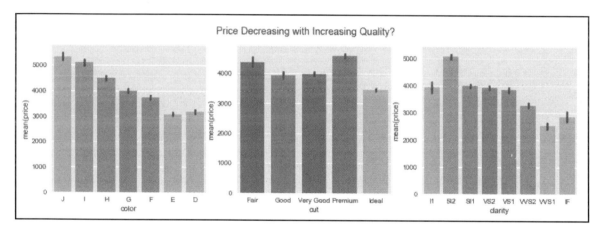

4. There seems to be a decreasing trend for color and price. The highest quality cut and clarity levels also have low prices. How can this be? Let's dig a little deeper and plot the price for each diamond color again, but make a new plot for each level of clarity:

```
>>> sns.factorplot(x='color', y='price', col='clarity',
                   col_wrap=4, data=diamonds, kind='bar')
```

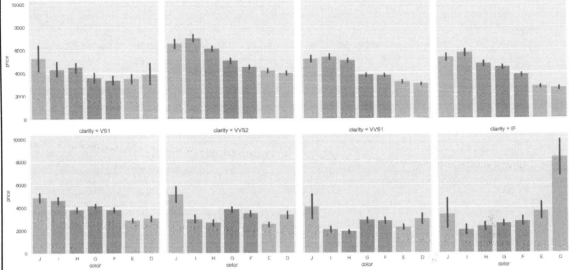

5. This plot is a little more revealing. Although price appears to decrease as the quality of color increases, it does not do so when clarity is at its highest level. There is actually a substantial increase in price. We have yet to look at just the price of the diamond without paying any attention to its size. Let's recreate the plot from step 3 but use the carat size in place of price:

```
>>> fig, (ax1, ax2, ax3) = plt.subplots(1, 3, figsize=(14,4))
>>> sns.barplot(x='color', y='carat', data=diamonds, ax=ax1)
>>> sns.barplot(x='cut', y='carat', data=diamonds, ax=ax2)
>>> sns.barplot(x='clarity', y='carat', data=diamonds, ax=ax3)
>>> fig.suptitle('Diamond size decreases with quality')
```

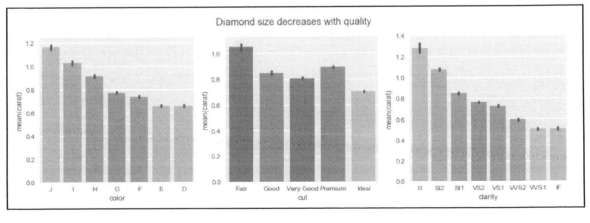

6. Now our story is starting to make a bit more sense. Higher quality diamonds appear to be smaller in size, which intuitively makes sense. Let's create a new variable that segments the `carat` values into five distinct sections, and then create a point plot. The plot that follows accurately reveals that higher quality diamonds do, in fact, cost more money when they are segmented based on size:

```
>>> diamonds['carat_category'] = pd.qcut(diamonds.carat, 5)

>>> from matplotlib.cm import Greys
>>> greys = Greys(np.arange(50,250,40))

>>> g = sns.factorplot(x='clarity', y='price', data=diamonds,
                       hue='carat_category', col='color',
                       col_wrap=4, kind='point', palette=greys)
>>> g.fig.suptitle('Diamond price by size, color and clarity',
                   y=1.02, size=20)
```

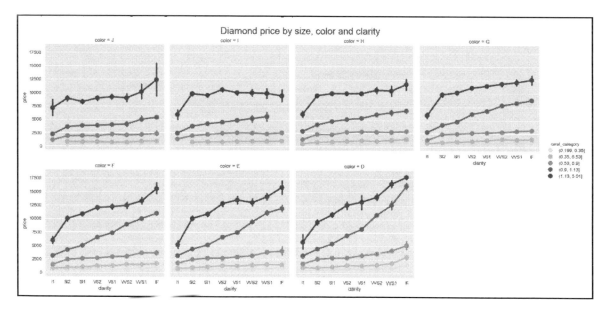

How it works...

In this recipe, it is very important to create categorical columns, as they are allowed to be ordered. Seaborn uses this ordering to place the labels on the plot. Steps 3 and 4 show what clearly appears to be a downward trend for increasing diamond quality. This is where Simpson's paradox takes center stage. This aggregated result of the whole is being confounded by other variables not yet examined.

The key to uncovering this paradox is to focus on carat size. Step 5 reveals to us that carat size is also decreasing with increasing quality. To account for this fact, we cut the diamond size into five equally-sized bins with the qcut function. By default, this function cuts the variable into discrete categories based on the given quantiles. By passing it an integer, as was done in this step, it creates equally-spaced quantiles. You also have the option of passing it a sequence of explicit non-regular quantiles.

With this new variable, we can make a plot of the mean price per diamond size per group, as done in step 6. The point plot in seaborn creates a line plot connecting the means of each category. The vertical bar at each point is the standard deviation for that group. This plot confirms that diamonds do indeed become more expensive as their quality increases, as long as we hold the carat size as the constant.

There's more...

The bar plots in steps 3 and 5 could have been created with the more advanced seaborn `PairGrid` constructor, which can plot a bivariate relationship. Using `PairGrid` is a two-step process. The first call to `PairGrid` prepares the grid by alerting it to which variables will be x and which will be y. The second step applies a plot to all of the combinations of x and y columns:

```
>>> g = sns.PairGrid(diamonds, size=5,
                     x_vars=["color", "cut", "clarity"],
                     y_vars=["price"])
>>> g.map(sns.barplot)
>>> g.fig.suptitle('Replication of Step 3 with PairGrid', y=1.02)
```

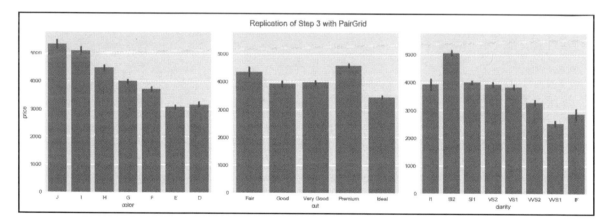

Index

27849302R00295